W9-ACJ-757

Vale, M   944.026
                                 V23
Charles VII   c.1

 CHARLES VII

by the same author
ENGLISH GASCONY 1399–1453

Adoration of the Magi, attributed to Jean Fouquet, from the
Hours of Etienne Chevalier, Musée Condé, Chantilly. This illumination,
painted between 1452 and 1461, shows Charles VII as the first of
the Three Kings.

CHARLES · VII

M. G. A. VALE

Lecturer in History
University of York

UNIVERSITY OF CALIFORNIA PRESS
Berkeley and Los Angeles, 1974

UNIVERSITY OF CALIFORNIA PRESS
Berkeley and Los Angeles, California

ISBN: 0–520–02787–6
Library of Congress Catalog Card Number: 74–79775

© 1974 M. G. A. Vale

Printed in Great Britain

Contents

Illustrations

Acknowledgements and thanks for permission to reproduce the plates are due to the Musée du Louvre for plate 1; to the Bibliothèque Nationale for plates 2, 5, 6a, 6b and 8; to Photographie Giraudon for the frontispiece and plates 3, 4, 7, 9, 10 and 12b; to D. A. Whiteley for plate 11; and to the Bodleian Library for plate 12a.

The map and chart were redrawn from the author's originals by Maureen Verity.

Preface

This book is not a conventional biography. Biographies of medieval kings often tend to reveal less about those kings than about the political, dynastic, military, constitutional and financial history of their reigns. This book attempts to study a peculiarly enigmatic medieval king by using the evidence in a rather more selective fashion. It takes a contemporary assessment of Charles VII as both a king and as a man for its starting-point. Within a broadly chronological framework this assessment is set against the surviving evidence. It is hoped that a picture, albeit an impressionistic one, will emerge in which Charles VII is the central foreground figure in what is often a group portrait. The king is, necessarily, surrounded – and sometimes hidden – by the figures of his servants and advisers. When the biographer lacks so many precious sources, he can easily transform dust into more dust, rather than dry bones into a recognisable human being. He is also thrown back on divining the character of his chosen subject from his actual behaviour. This means that certain stages of the reign will receive more attention than others. One can only interpret behaviour with any hope of veracity where one has the material to do so. A true biography is often a series of episodes.

Medieval biography has been declared impossible. The relative scarcity of its indispensable tools – journals, private correspondence, newspaper articles and so on – has led to the assumption that we can never know anything about medieval men as individuals. It is only through deduction and inference from recorded behaviour that we can assess motive, character and personality. Kings, because of the greater body of mendacious evidence which has accumulated around them, are perhaps even more impenetrably hidden than some of their subjects. This is, to say the least, unfortunate. In fifteenth-century France, the person, as well as the office, of the king was a vital part of the polity. The king supplied the driving force behind the governmental machine. The royal uncles must have been well aware of that fact during the reign of Charles VII's father, the deranged Charles VI. The writers of treatises on kingly rule were also aware of that fact. Why else would they have written in the first place?

The constantly growing fifteenth-century heap of sermons, petitions, exhortations, 'mirrors for princes', miscellanies of cautionary tales from ancient – and more recent – history, clerical harangues, memoranda and humanistic discourses, suggests that kings were considered open to persuasion by reason, emotion or rhetoric. The busybodies who produced some of these offerings were optimistic enough to believe that a king would take some notice of what they said. Many must have been sadly disappointed. But the fact remains that monarchy in fifteenth-century France was personal monarchy – and it existed long before Louis XI brought his distinctive personal style to the business of ruling.

It is possible to be too agnostic about historical biography, especially at a time when much academic history tends to be devoid of interest in living human beings. It has been said that 'while it is a part of the historian's business to analyse the great impersonal forces at work in society, he must take account of the human instruments, those who held power, through which those forces had in part to find expression'.[1] I therefore make no apologies for producing a book which attempts to use one who held power – who, with his servants, transmitted and even shaped those 'impersonal forces' – as its focus. Fifteenth-century men were at the mercy of many forces – plague, inclement weather, war and economic contraction. But they were also at the mercy of personal monarchies in which the will of a ruler, or of his officers, could directly affect their fate. Taxation, imposed by a ruler, could contribute enormously to social and economic problems, as could a decision to wage war. So much is obvious. But the reasons why rulers acted in the ways that they did are not always so obvious. Perhaps that is sufficient justification for studying the behaviour of a later medieval king.

In the course of doing so, I have incurred many debts. First of all, to the Department of History at the University of York, which gave me the sabbatical term without which this book would never have been written. I am also indebted to the University for a grant towards the research which I have undertaken in French archives. To Mr P. S. Lewis, of All Souls' College, Oxford, and to Professor Bernard Guenée, of the University of Paris, I am obliged for having given me the opportunity of airing some of the views of Charles VII expressed in this book. Both have also made helpful comments and given me suggestions to follow up. My students in tutorials and seminars at York have had ideas tried out upon them which they may recognise; and they have tried out ideas on me. I

[1] K. B. McFarlane, *Lancastrian Kings and Lollard Knights* (Oxford, 1972), 7.

have had fruitful conversations with Dr Michael Jones of the University of Nottingham. The staffs of the Bibliothèque Nationale, the Archives Nationales, the British Museum, the Brotherton Library at the University of Leeds, and the J. B. Morell Library at the University of York have all contributed to the appearance of this book. I am also indebted to Dr A. Mills for her comments on my diagnosis of Charles VII's illnesses. Last but by no means least, I must thank Miriam Hodgson of Eyre Methuen, and Dr Charles Ross, the latter for having first suggested the idea of a biography of Charles VII to me; the former for having been unfailingly helpful and for seeing it through the press.

University of York, May 1974   *M. G. A. V.*

Abbreviations

AB	*Annales de Bourgogne*
ABP	Archives Départementales des Basses-Pyrénées
ABSHF	*Annuaire-Bulletin de la Société de l'Histoire de France*
AHP	*Archives Historiques du Poitou*
AM	*Annales du Midi*
AMB	*Archives Municipales de Bordeaux*
A.N.	Archives Nationales, Paris
Basin	Thomas Basin, *Histoire de Charles VII*, ed. C. Samaran, 2 vols (Paris, 1933, 1944)
Beaucourt	G. du Fresne de Beaucourt, *Histoire de Charles VII*, 6 vols (Paris, 1881–91)
BEC	*Bibliothèque de l'Ecole des Chartes*
BIHR	*Bulletin of the Institute of Historical Research*
B.M.	British Museum, London
B.N.	Bibliothèque Nationale, Paris
BPH	*Bulletin Philologique et Historique*
CEH	*Cambridge Economic History*
Chartier	Jean Chartier, *Chronique de Charles VII*, ed. A. Vallet de Viriville, 3 vols (Paris, 1858)
Chastellain	Georges Chastellain, *Œuvres*, ed. Kervyn de Lettenhove, 7 vols (Brussels, 1863–5)
Cosneau, *Richemont*	E. Cosneau, *Le Connétable de Richemont* (Paris, 1886)
Dauvet	*Les Affaires de Jacques Cœur. Journal du Procureur Dauvet*, ed. M. Mollat, 2 vols (Paris, 1952–3)
Duclos	Duclos, *Recueil de pièces pour servir de suite à l'histoire de Louis XI*, in *Œuvres Complètes*, IV (Paris, 1806)
EETS	*Early English Text Society*
EHR	*English Historical Review*
Escouchy	Mathieu d'Escouchy, *Chronique*, ed. G. du Fresne de Beaucourt, 3 vols (*Société de l'Histoire de France*, Paris, 1863–4)
GBA	*Gazette des Beaux-Arts*
JWCI	*Journal of the Warburg and Courtauld Institutes*
Kendall and Ilardi	*Dispatches, with Related Documents, of Milanese Ambassadors in France and Burgundy, 1450–83*, 2 vols (Ohio, 1970, 1971)
La Marche	Olivier de La Marche, *Mémoires*, ed. H. Beaune and J. d'Arbaumont, 4 vols (*Société de l'Histoire de France*, Paris, 1883–8)

Leseur   Guillaume Leseur, *Histoire de Gaston IV, comte de Foix*, ed.
              H. Courteault, 2 vols (*Société de l'Histoire de France*, Paris, 1893,
              1896)
MA   *Le Moyen Age*
Martial d'Auvergne   Martial de Paris, dit d'Auvergne, *Les Vigilles de la Mort de
              Charles VII*, in *Poésies*, II (Paris, 1724)
OED   *Oxford English Dictionary*
Ord.   *Ordonnances des roys de France de la troisième race*, 22 vols (Paris,
              1723–1849)
Plancher   U. Plancher, *Histoire générale et particulière de la Bourgogne*, 4 vols
              (Dijon, 1739–81)
Recovery of France   *The Recovery of France in the Fifteenth Century*, ed. P. S.
              Lewis, tr. G. F. Martin (London, 1971)
RH   *Revue Historique*
RHDFE   *Revue Historique du droit français et étranger*
Rot. Parl.   *Rotuli Parliamentorum*, 6 vols (London, 1783–1832)
RQH   *Revue des Questions Historiques*
SHF   *Société de l'Histoire de France*
Stevenson   *Letters and Papers illustrative of the wars of the English in France
              during the reign of Henry VI*, 2 vols (Rolls Series, London,
              1861–4)
TRHS   *Transactions of the Royal Historical Society*
Vaesen, *Lettres*   *Lettres de Louis XI, roi de France*, ed. E. Charavay, J. Vaesen
              and B. de Mandrot, 11 vols (*Société de l'Histoire de France*,
              Paris, 1883–1909)

✣ CHARLES VII

Chapter 1 ✦ The King and his Reign

1 *Charles VII and the historians*

It is perhaps a revealing comment on historians and their prejudices that the most convincing character sketch of Charles VII of France is by a contemporary. Georges Chastellain, court chronicler to Philip the Good, duke of Burgundy, inserted an appraisal of the king into his *Chronique*.[1] It is all the more remarkable because of the distinctly unfriendly relations which existed between Charles and Chastellain's patron. It is from this account that all subsequent analyses must stem. Later historians have allowed nationalistic, moralistic and other prejudices to cloud the lens through which Charles VII has been viewed. It is thus refreshing to turn to the objectivity of a Burgundian – one to whom the king might have appeared more as an enemy than as an object of adulation. But Chastellain's verdict is not an unfavourable one. Criticism there certainly is – Charles possessed certain vices, wrote Chastellain, of which the chief were 'mutability, distrust, and more seriously . . . envy'. But 'from a very poor and miserable beginning, his reign achieved a glorious end'.[2] Dominated and manipulated by malevolent men during his early years, the king, thought Chastellain, began to prosper as a result of his reconciliation with Philip the Good at Arras in 1435. All subsequent historians have more or less accepted Chastellain's account of the chronology of Charles's success. Yet the picture of weakness and failure giving way to victory can be overdrawn. A more subtle gradation of tones is necessary. In his way of doing business as king, Charles VII displayed, if not consistency, at least certain recognisable traits which appeared as much in adversity as in prosperity.

Chastellain detected many of these during the period of relative and ostensible success. The king, he wrote, was not robust or warlike. But 'what he lacked in courage, which he did not have by nature, he gained in judgement [*sens*]'.[3] This quality was aided rather than hampered by the bitter experiences of his early years as dauphin and 'king of Bourges'.

[1] Chastellain, II, 177–88.   [3] Ibid., 181.
[2] Ibid., 178.

They made him timid and cautious, but flexible and astute as well. Surrounded by faction, he learnt to employ faction as a means to serve his own ends. His own mutability served him well. Changes of view created changes of courtiers and, inevitably, the formation of leagues and factions against the favourites in power. It was a dangerous game to play. But, observed Chastellain, Charles was ultimately able to make those factions compete for his own favour. By gaining control of the patronage system he could make both aspirants and those whom they sought to replace dependent on his own favour, whim or caprice. 'Those in power', wrote Chastellain with stunning obviousness, 'always try to hold on to it, while the rest hope to get their hands on it.'[1] It did not need the defection of the duke of Burgundy from the English in 1435 to teach Charles the techniques of this kind of management of men's acquisitive instincts. That ability was probably there from quite an early date. It was frustrated and impeded by a number of adverse circumstances, not least of which was the presence of the English within France. Yet even the English war, it could be argued, was not entirely incompatible with Charles's best interests as king.

The expulsion of the English from the whole of France except the town and marches of Calais in 1453 has coloured almost every subsequent interpretation of the reign. From the king's death in 1461, articulate Frenchmen could hardly speak of *Charles Septiesme de ce Nom* without adding the epithet *Le Trèsvictorieux*.[2] The eulogies and adulations have a fixity of form and a gushing tedium which tends to arouse immediate scepticism. Fervour can be a symptom of doubt and of insecurity. In the mid-fifteenth century many people needed to be convinced of Charles VII's victoriousness. They had little need to be convinced of his political skill. There was perhaps no need for them to look across the Alps for instruction in the art of political manipulation and the deceits of statecraft. One theme of this book will be the affinities which Charles VII seems to share with some of his Italian contemporaries and successors. His son, Louis XI, may have professed his admiration for Francesco Sforza, but it is sometimes forgotten that Charles VII had the blood of the Visconti of Milan in his veins. It is too easy to isolate Italy from the rest of Western Europe in the fifteenth century. To do so is to distort the perspective of that series of events which historians have miscalled the Renaissance. Because radical changes in thought and in the visual arts took place in fifteenth-century Italy, it is facile to seek the origins of

[1] Chastellain, 183.
[2] See M. G. A. Vale, 'Jean Fouquet's portrait of Charles VII', *GBA*, lxxi (April 1968), 243–8.

political innovations there. That other chimera of historians, the 'new' monarchies, might also be seen as the somewhat jejune concept which it really is if closer attention were paid to the medieval predecessors of Charles VIII or Francis I.[1]

'Are not Charles VII and Louis XI,' asks Professor Hay, 'more "modern" than Charles VIII or Francis I – in their attention to administrative detail, their domination of the Church, and their repression of franchises?'[2] It is a moot point, to which this book may, or may not, provide an answer. Chastellain could almost forestall Philippe de Commynes and Machiavelli when he wrote of Charles VII that he achieved his ends 'by ability [vertu] above all else, and by the close study of men'.[3] Those who wished to advance their own, as well as the king's interests, were 'practised' by him. Louis XI's skill in the devious management of men was perhaps not unprecedented. Nor was Pier Candido Decembrio's character sketch of his Milanese patron Filippo Maria Visconti (d. 1447) without parallel in Northern Europe.[4] Chastellain's analysis suggests that, like the duke of Milan, Charles feared and was feared. He was perhaps aware of Christine de Pisan's observations on Giangaleazzo Visconti (d. 1402), whom she compared to Charles V of France (1364–80). He was able to conquer large areas of territory 'without stirring from his palace'.[5] Bellicosity was not a *sine qua non* of the later medieval ruler. Such behaviour, whether the prince inhabited 'a sort of artistic Kremlin, with agents watching everybody'[6] or a more conventional dwelling, can be interpreted either as a sign of weakness or of strength. Charles VII's apparent withdrawal and neglect of what appeared to some as the duties of kingship led to the most severe accusations. Bernard de Girard, seigneur du Haillan, wrote in 1570 that Charles VII did nothing except 'amuse himself making love to his fair Agnès [Sorel] and creating *parterres* and gardens, while the English . . . marched through his kingdom'.[7] He was evidently another Nero, and du Haillan could have reinforced the image by referring to the king's apparent taste for music. The moralists had

1 For a useful discussion of 'absolutism' and 'centralisation' in later medieval France see B. Guenée, 'Espace et Etat en France médiévale', *Annales*, xxiii (1968), 744–58.
2 *New Cambridge Modern History*, i (Cambridge, 1957), 2.
3 Chastellain, II, 183.
4 L. Muratori, *Rerum Italicarum Scriptores*, xx (Milan, 1731), cols 983–1020 for

Decembrio's *Vita Philippi Mariae Vicecomitis Mediolensium Ducis Tertii*.
5 Christine de Pisan, *The Fayttes of Armes and of Chyvalrye*, ed. A. T. P. Byles (*EETS*, clxxxix, 1973), 20.
6 E. F. Jacob, *Italian Renaissance Studies*, ed. E. F. Jacob (London, 1960), 26.
7 Bernard de Girard, seigneur du Haillan, *De l'estat et succez des affaires de France* (Paris, 1570), fol. 68ᵛ.

THE HOUSE OF VALOIS

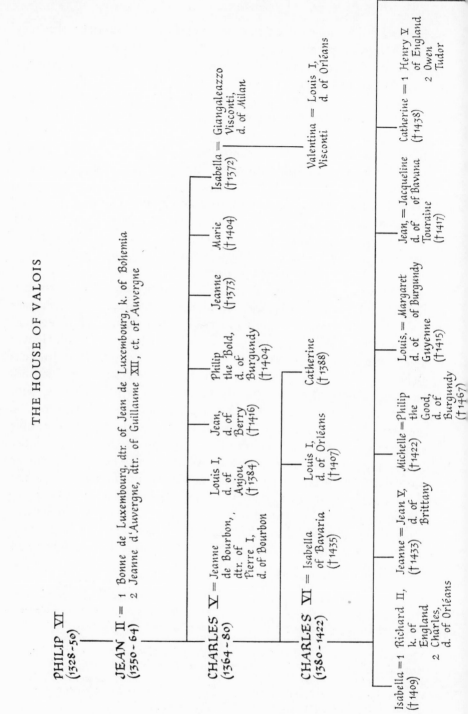

PHILIP VI
(1328-50)

JEAN II = 1 Bonne de Luxembourg, dtr. of Jean de Luxembourg, k. of Bohemia
(1350-64)   2 Jeanne d'Auvergne, dtr. of Guillaume XII, ct. of Auvergne

CHARLES V = Jeanne de Bourbon, dtr. of Pierre I, d. of Bourbon
(1364-80)

Louis I, d. of Anjou (†1384)

Jean, d. of Berry (†1416)

Philip the Bold, d. of Burgundy (†1404)

Jeanne (†1373)

Marie (†1404)

Isabella = Giangaleazzo Visconti, d. of Milan
(†1372)

CHARLES VI = Isabella of Bavaria (†1435)
(1380-1422)

Louis I, d. of Orléans (†1407)

Catherine (†1388)

Valentina = Louis I, Visconti   d. of Orléans

Isabella =1 Richard II, k. of England 2 Charles, d. of Orléans (†1409)

Jeanne = Jean V, d. of Brittany (†1433)

Michelle = Philip the Good, d. of Burgundy (†1422) (†1467)

Louis, = Margaret d. of of Burgundy Guyenne (†1415)

Jean, = Jacqueline d. of of Bavana Touraine (†1417)

Catherine = 1 Henry V of England 2 Owen (†1438) Tudor

Genealogical table

Marie of Anjou, = **CHARLES VII**
dtr. of Louis II, (1422–61)
d. of Anjou

LOUIS XI = 1 Margaret of Scotland, dtr. of James I, k. of Scotland (†1445)
(1461–83)   2 Charlotte of Savoy, dtr. of Louis II, d. of Savoy

Catherine = Charles, ct. of Charolais, son of Philip the Good, d. of Burgundy
(†1446)

Jeanne = Jean de Bourbon, ct. of Clermont

Yolande = Louis, pr. of Piedmont, later d. of Savoy

Madelaine = Gaston IV ct. of Foix

Charles of France, d. of Berry (†1472)

Marie = Olivier de Coëtivy, seneschal of Guyenne

Charlotte = Jacques de Brézé

Jeanne = Anthoine de Bueil

begun their assault. His contemporary critics, the ecclesiastics Thomas Basin and Jean Juvenal des Ursins, had some worthy successors.

Some, such as Etienne Pasquier in 1621, doubted Charles's sanity. Others, such as Mézéray in 1646, and Vallet de Viriville as late as the 1860s, saw the king enslaved by his mistresses, feeble, indolent, and indulging in 'immorality and remarkable sensuality'.[1] Evidently the Second Empire's scholars did not frequent *les bouffes parisiens*. If they did, they did not let it interfere with their historical judgements. It is to the later years of the nineteenth century that the most comprehensive continuous narrative of the reign belongs. In his massive life of Charles VII, Gaston du Fresne de Beaucourt, aristocrat and private scholar, attempted to explain Charles VII's behaviour by means of the notion that there are 'many men within one man'.[2] Consistency of behaviour, attitude and political technique was thus largely ruled out from the start. 'One could almost say,' he wrote, 'that there are in him [Charles VII] as many different men as there were periods in his reign.'[3] Beaucourt was borrowing his interpretative framework from the seventeenth-century Catholic writer Bossuet. Metamorphosis under the impact of changing political conditions is his *idée fixe*. His great book is organised into clearly defined chronological phases in which Chastellain's concept of a 'turning-point' is perpetuated. For Beaucourt, 'l'histoire n'est pour nous ni un plaidoyer, ni une apologie; c'est un jugement'.[4] His prose is as magisterial as his intentions. Yet some of his judgements are, necessarily, reached by pleading (sometimes special pleading) and by apology.

Beaucourt's scholarship, however, was meticulous. He published his *Histoire de Charles VII* between 1881 and 1891, having already edited texts. The fact that it appeared in six large volumes is some indication of the quantity of evidence which was sifted by Beaucourt. It is still a mine of information and my book relies heavily on the documented facts he presented, but his work lacks structure and general ideas. Such ideas as it contains are determined as much by Beaucourt's religious and political beliefs as by his undoubtedly genuine desire to discover 'what actually happened' in the reign of Charles VII. Gaston-Louis-Emmanuel du Fresne, marquis de Beaucourt, was born on 7 June 1833 and died on 12 August 1902 at the age of sixty-nine.[5] His interest in Charles VII resulted from

[1] For these see G. du Fresne de Beaucourt, *Histoire de Charles VII* (Paris, 6 vols, 1881–91), I, xiii–xvii and xlviii.
[2] Ibid., viii.
[3] Ibid., viii.
[4] Ibid., lxxxvi.

[5] For what follows I have used the following sources: *Dictionnaire de Biographie Française*, ed. M. Prévost and Roman d'Amat (Paris, 1951), VI, cols 1064–5; G. Monod in *RH*, lxxx (1902), 328–9; and Baron F. de Schickler in *ABSHF*

the publication in 1856 of Henri Martin's *Règne de Charles VII*, to which he took violent exception. His taste for polemic led him to attempt a rehabilitation of the king, attacking the works of Vallet de Viriville and Jules Quicherat. The six volumes on Charles VII were the result of thirty-five years of research. But he had also been engaged in other causes during that time. A Catholic aristocrat and member of the Royalist party, he founded the influential *Revue des Questions Historiques* in 1866. This journal was intended to disseminate erudite research, through a process of *haute vulgarisation*, to a larger audience. Gaston Monod, the writer of his obituary notice in the *Revue Historique* for 1902, remarked that the journal spread a taste for historical research among the clergy of France.

He went on to express doubts on some of Beaucourt's other educational projects. The greatest of these was the foundation of the *Société Biblio-graphique* in 1868. This was a militant Catholic body which pledged itself to 'propagate knowledge through faith and faith through knowledge'.[1] Its main function was to publish the *Polybiblion*, a bibliographical review of particular value to students of history and archaeology. But its literary section, according to Monod, 'bore rather too much resemblance to a branch of the general body of the Index and often concerned itself more with the orthodoxy of the books which it reviewed than with their literary and scientific value'.[2] During the Third Republic, Beaucourt produced a stream of didactic and polemical writings – his *Questions du jour* and his topical tracts on monarchism and republicanism. In 1890 he founded the *Société d'histoire contemporaine*, and, immediately after the publication of his *Histoire de Charles VII*, furthered the monarchist cause with an account of the captivity and death of Louis XVI (1892) and an edition of the letters of Marie-Antoinette (1895–6). The critical Monod considered that his work on Charles VII was his best, a work 'of serene impartiality'.[3] A reader of Beaucourt's concluding chapter might suspect that the obituary-writer had got the better of the critic in this instance. The president of the *Société de l'Histoire de France*, in his address of 5 May 1903, was a little less certain of Beaucourt's impartiality. One could reproach him with letting himself be 'dazzled by the radiance of the glorious and restorative side of the reign, to the extent of accepting too

(1903), 104–7. For the *milieu* in which Beaucourt wrote, see B. Guenée, 'L'Histoire de l'Etat en France à la fin du Moyen Age, vue par les historiens français depuis cent ans', *RH*, ccxxxii (1964), 331–60 (tr. in *The Recovery of France in the Fifteenth Century*, ed. P. S. Lewis [London, 1971], 324–52).

[1] *Dict. de Biogr. fr.*, VI, col. 1064.
[2] Monod, op. cit., 329.
[3] Ibid., 328.

easily the primary and supreme weaknesses'.[1] In other words, Beaucourt painted too favourable and too eulogistic a picture of Charles VII.

Beaucourt's conclusion reflected the moral preoccupation of his Church and his time. Although his work profited immensely from the institutional studies of that period, it did not always share their detachment. The reservations which he made about Charles VII's achievement were couched in terms of moral reproof. Beaucourt believed that, to be a good king, a king must be a good man. A good king must not show ingratitude, must not abandon his servants, must observe the moral injunctions of the Church. He did not apparently acknowledge that to be an effective fifteenth-century king one did not need to be a particularly good man. Indeed, a capacity to 'make or break' men might be considered highly advantageous, and a lack of moral scruple positively beneficial. Kings behaved in a Machiavellian way long before Machiavelli was born in 1469. 'In all things,' concluded Beaucourt, Charles VII 'never departed from a wise moderation which assured him the love of his subjects, the esteem of his allies and even of his enemies. These were truly royal qualities which can remove more than one stain.'[2] These were the words of one who believed monarchy to be the best form of government for France in an age of republicanism. Kings were to be loved and esteemed above all other rulers. The monarchist had emerged from the 'serene impartiality' of the scholar in order to advance his cause. Politics, to Beaucourt, was the province of lofty and noble ideals, not of sordid self-interest. The 'achievement of French unity by the king'[3] – the major preoccupation of the Second Empire's historians – was one such noble ideal. But the means whereby that end was achieved might not have been quite so noble.

Every historian is to some extent conditioned by the intellectual, moral and spiritual climate of his times. Beaucourt was no exception. From the mass of carefully assembled material in his *Charles VII* it is not entirely surprising that a rather moralistic general conclusion emerges. But this does nothing to reduce the value of his work as a source of information. Even if the interpretative gloss is totally discarded, for Beaucourt's careful presentation of the facts, and his editing of texts, every subsequent historian of fifteenth-century France is in his debt. But other kinds of historian have been attracted to Charles VII. He, as well as his much-studied son, Louis XI, has interested the historians of medicine. Some have sought the key to his behaviour in hereditary disorders of the nervous system. On his neuroses, Chastellain is perhaps still the most con-

[1] *ABSHF* (1903), 105.   [3] Guenée in *Recovery of France*, 328.
[2] Beaucourt, VI, 452.

vincing of witnesses.[1] The king was afraid of people, especially of the unknown individual in a familiar group. Yet his arrangements for his personal security were no more elaborate than those of his contemporaries Filippo Maria Visconti or Philip the Good.[2] Like the former, he feared assassination and violent death. To Chastellain, the 'cause and root of his distrust' was to be found in his witnessing the murder of John the Fearless, duke of Burgundy, on the bridge at Montereau early in September 1419. Charles was a youth of sixteen. His part in the events leading to that assassination was not entirely clear.[3] The shock may not have been a totally unexpected one. A further phobia identified by Chastellain was his distrust of floors and bridges. 'He did not dare to lodge on a floor, nor cross a wooden bridge on horseback, unless it was sound.'[4] Perhaps events at Montereau had something to do with this aversion to bridges. Or perhaps it was merely part of his agoraphobia. But his morbid dislike of public places was not without a certain *rationale*.

His fear of floors is more easily explicable. In October 1422 the floor of a room in which he was holding court at La Rochelle collapsed beneath him. In a letter of 28 July 1427 he referred to this alarming event. He endowed a Mass to be said at the Ste-Chapelle of Bourges on the anniversary of the 'day when God saved us from the danger that we were in at La Rochelle, when we fell from an upper to a lower room'.[5] Some of his entourage, including Pierre de Bourbon, lord of Preaulx, were killed. Charles escaped with bruises, but the shock must have been severe. His phobia about death in his lodgings may have been exacerbated by an event which took place twenty years later. One night in December 1442, when he was campaigning in Gascony, his lodgings in the town of La Réole were set on fire.[6] Once again, he escaped death, but only through the prompt action of his Scots archers, who made a breach in a wall by which he escaped. But his sword of state, St Louis's sword, was said to have perished in the fire. These were, however, dangers to which every prince might be exposed. We are perhaps on rather better tilled, though no less treacherous, ground when Charles's physical condition is considered. The chroniclers were agreed that he enjoyed good health

[1] Chastellain, II, 181, 185–6, and cf. A. Brachet, *Pathologie Mentale des Rois de France* (Paris, 1903), 64–6.

[2] See below, 33, 137–8, 218; Muratori, op. cit., xx, cols 1004–5; R. Vaughan, *Philip the Good* (London, 1970), 140. The number of archers in Philip's bodyguard rose from 12 in 1426 to 50 in 1438.

[3] See below, 28–31. Also Vaughan, *John the Fearless* (London, 1966), 263–86.

[4] Chastellain, II, 185.

[5] Beaucourt, I, 240.

[6] See *Official Correspondence of Thomas Bekynton*, ed. G. Williams (Rolls Series, London, 1872), II, 247.

until the last six or so years of his life. In September 1455 he was indisposed through a pain in his side.[1] By December 1457, a new complaint afflicted him. A chronic septic ulcer appeared on one of his legs. Late in 1458 he began to suffer from what appear to have been ulcers in the mouth, and, probably, trouble with his teeth. This condition worsened until early in July 1461 when he was unable to eat or drink. Fears of poisoning were adduced by the chroniclers to explain his 'refusal' to do so for eight days before his death. His condition could have made it impossible for him to do so. The precise nature of his illness will never be known. But there is a possibility that he was a victim of the 'new' disease which was to reach plague proportions in Renaissance Europe – *morbus gallicus*.

There are other, better documented areas in which Charles VII has been seen as a 'new' monarch. In 1788 the French historian Levesque could maintain that he was 'the author of the present constitution of our monarchy'.[2] Pierre Clément, in his book on Jacques Cœur, published in 1853, could go further and assert that the reign was the 'true starting-point of the new society'.[3] Reinforced by the institutional studies of Vallet de Viriville, Beaucourt, Thomas and Cosneau, the thesis is a superficially attractive one. But it ignores too much in the previous and subsequent history of French government and society. To attribute the creation of that form of government known subsequently as the *ancien régime* to the reign of Charles VII would give those forty years too great a burden to bear. The reign was undoubtedly crucial to French political and constitutional developments. But the reforms and innovations in justice, taxation and the army were not totally unprecedented. The means had often been extant in the past, but the power had not. Hence a study of the reign of Charles VII must essentially be a study of power – its justification, its delegation, and its direct, personal exercise. Only then can the novelty of the 'new monarchies' of Western Europe be assessed.

II *The reign and its context*

By way of introduction to the man, his reign can be briefly placed in its European context. Charles VII was born into a divided Christendom. The economic axis of Western Europe had shifted, after the plagues of the mid-fourteenth century, away from the East and towards the Atlantic

[1] See below, 172–3; also Beaucourt, VI, 471.

[2] Quoted in ibid., I, xxiv.

[3] Ibid., xli.

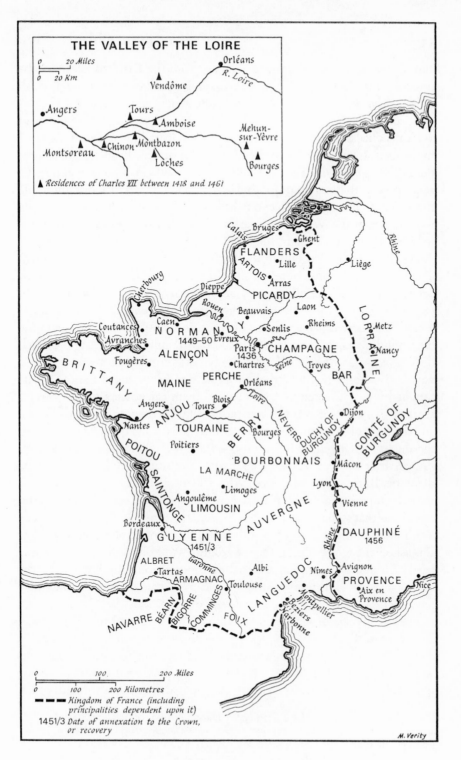

THE VALLEY OF THE LOIRE

0 _20 Miles_
0 _20 Km_

Orléans
R. Loire

Vendôme

Angers
Tours
Amboise
Mehun-
sur-Yèvre

Montsoreau
Chinon
Montbazon
Loches
Bourges

▲ _Residences of Charles VII between 1418 and 1461_

Calais
Bruges
Ghent
FLANDERS
ARTOIS
Lille
Liège
Rhine
Dieppe
Arras
PICARDY
Cherbourg
Rouen
Beauvais
Laon
Rheims
Metz
Coutances
Caen
NORMANDY
Senlis
LORRAINE
Avranches
1449-50 Evreux
Nancy
Fougères
ALENÇON
Paris
1436
CHAMPAGNE
BRITTANY
Chartres
Seine
Troyes
MAINE
PERCHE
Orléans
BAR
Angers
Blois
Loire
Nantes
ANJOU
Tours
Dijon
TOURAINE
BERRY
Bourges
Duchy of
Burgundy
COMTÉ OF
BURGUNDY
POITOU
Poitiers
NEVERS
BOURBONNAIS
Mâcon
SAINTONGE
LA MARCHE
Lyon
Angoulême
Limoges
LIMOUSIN
Vienne
Bordeaux
AUVERGNE
Rhône
DAUPHINÉ
1456
GUYENNE
1451/3
Garonne
Albi
Nîmes
Avignon
ALBRET
Tartas
ARMAGNAC
Toulouse
LANGUEDOC
PROVENCE
Aix en
Provence
Nice
NAVARRE
BÉARN
BIGORRE
COMMINGES
FOIX
Montpellier
Béziers
Narbonne

0 _100_ _200 Miles_
0 _100_ _200 Kilometres_

━ ━ ━ _Kingdom of France (including
principalities dependent upon it)_

1451/3 _Date of annexation to the Crown,
or recovery_

M. Verity

France during the reign of Charles VII

and the Western Mediterranean. Threats from the East had led to a contraction in trade and to a series of crusading ventures against the Turkish
infidel. The disaster at Nicopolis in 1396, when many French and Burgundian magnates had been routed and captured by the heathen, served
as a final check on the fervour of the West. Crusading was now directed
more against heretics, such as the Lithuanians or the Hussites, than against
the full weight of the Turks. Western Europe was now to concentrate its
acquisitive ambitions on objects nearer home. The fall of Constantinople
to the Sultan in 1453 was to evoke little in the way of retaliation from the
monarchies of the West. To Charles VII the fall of Bordeaux was infinitely more significant than the fall of Byzantium.

Europe was divided within itself when Charles VII was born in 1403.
The papacy had been contested since the outbreak of the great Western
Schism in 1378. The alignments of Western powers behind the rival
popes tended to reflect the alignments of another conflict – the Hundred
Years' War between England and France. In reality only one stage in the
four hundred years' war between the two countries, the Anglo-French
dispute was not merely a feudal or dynastic conflict between lord and
vassal. By the early fifteenth century it was becoming a national war,
fought by two sovereigns who claimed identical powers within certain
areas of France. Nor was the war purely one between the king of France
and the king of England, whether claiming the throne of France or merely
the duchy of Guyenne. It was also a French civil war. In 1521, a Carthusian friar showed Francis I of France the skull of John the Fearless,
duke of Burgundy. 'My lord,' the Carthusian was alleged to have
remarked, pointing to the place where the skull had been gashed by the
assassins, 'that's the hole through which the English entered France.'[1]
Without the support – or at least the neutrality – of certain French nobles,
English chances of realising their war aims would have been slim. It was
partly his ability to exploit internal divisions among the French princes
of the blood – Burgundy, Anjou, Orléans, Alençon, and so on – that
gave Henry V his considerable measure of success.

The early years of Charles VII's life saw the height of the Armagnac-
Burgundian feud. Two political assassinations – in 1407 and 1419 –
demonstrated the consequences of the feud and the climate in which he
was brought up. His father Charles VI was prevented from ruling by
sporadic attacks of insanity. The government was thus in the hands of his

[1] See Beaucourt, I, 177–8. Also C. Monget
and J. d'Arbaumont, 'Les restes des ducs et
princesses de Bourgogne à St-Bénigne de
Dijon', *Mémoires de la Commission des
antiquités du département de la Côte-d'Or*
(1901–5), XIV, 157–251.

brother, Louis I of Orléans, his uncles Jean, duke of Berry, and Philip the Bold, duke of Burgundy, and his nephew John the Fearless. As in England during the years immediately before the first battle of St Albans in May 1455, the struggle for power around the throne of an incapable king could lead to a paralysis of royal power in the country. Personal rule meant a great deal in the fifteenth century. When a king was unable or unwilling to rule – or was a child – the biblical texts 'The king and his throne are innocent' and 'Woe to the land when the king is a child' could ring true.[1] When that king was an absentee, an invalid or an imbecile, a heavy burden of political responsibility fell upon the shoulders of his 'natural counsellors' – the greater magnates. In France, between 1392 and 1422, it could be argued that they sometimes failed in their duties.

Charles VII thus lived through a period in which political slogans might provide a screen behind which self-interest could hide. In fifteenth-century France many men were in politics, as many of them were in the Church, largely for what they could get out of it. Pensions, grants, offices, liberties and immunities – such were the tangible gains sought by both individuals and groups, whether Armagnac, Burgundian, Dauphinist, or supporters of either side in the many private feuds which were being waged in provincial France. It was not surprising that Charles VII, in his later years, could attempt to 'obliterate the memory of discords born of civil war and foreign occupation from the minds of Frenchmen'.[2] The need to establish 'peace, concord and love' among all his subjects was a task which would have tried the patience and endurance of the most astute and magnanimous of kings. Legislation which decreed that anyone uttering the party catchwords of 'Armagnac' or 'Burgundian' was to have a hole bored through his tongue with a red-hot iron was perhaps hardly very effective in changing the mental attitudes of Frenchmen towards each other.[3] There were people in France (although they naturally became less numerous as they died off) to whom the terms 'Armagnac' and 'Burgundian' still corresponded with the realities of politics. After 1435 a certain artificiality was present in the continued employment of those words. A generation which had not been old enough to experience the feud at its most intense was coming of age and becoming politically influential by the 1440s and 1450s.[4] Many explanations can be offered for the evident changes which overcame French politics during those two

[1] See S. B. Chrimes, *English Constitutional Ideas in the Fifteenth Century* (Cambridge, 1936), 166; 2 Kings, xiv, 9; Eccl., x, 16.
[2] A. Bossuat, 'Le rétablissement de la paix sociale sous le règne de Charles VII', *MA*, lx (1954), 138 (tr. in *Recovery of France*, 60–81).
[3] Ibid., 365 n. 42.
[4] See below, 88–90.

decades. But a desire to heal the breach within France which had so often played into the hands of the English could arguably be more easily realised by that time.

It is possible to discern certain common patterns of government among the European monarchies and principalities of the early fifteenth century. Just as the courts of Europe – from Westminster to Prague – shared a common culture and language, so an accepted way of doing political and administrative business had developed, and was still developing, when Charles VII succeeded to a disputed throne of France. The exercise of power was becoming increasingly the prerogative of the prince. Whether that power was 'centralised' or 'de-centralised' depended greatly on the balance of forces within a given area and on the historical evolution of that area's government. Yet a class of agents who transmitted that power was common to the European monarchies of the period. Professor Jacob has observed that 'the courtier civil servant is the important man, and the growth of this class the key to the history of the later Middle Ages'.[1] It is this group consisting of laymen and to a lesser extent of ecclesiastics that must be examined when attempting to see Charles VII's government in action. Much needs to be written about these instruments of Charles VII's – and their own – schemes and ambitions. The king does not always emerge from the shadows which they cast. Behind the screen of courtiers and civil servants, whether they were styled 'counsellor and chamberlain of the king' or merely identified by their offices in the Chancery, the finances, the army, the artillery or the household, the king was certainly at work.[2] But it was often of the essence of personal rule that he should not always be seen at work.

The supremacy of the sovereign prince, whether king, duke or count, was a commonplace of fifteenth-century political thought. Yet the claims of a sovereign prince were often necessarily in conflict with the power of the Crown. By the later fourteenth century the attributes of sovereignty had been defined. Such rights as those of ennoblement, legitimisation, the hearing of judicial appeals, the creation of notaries and the granting of fairs and markets could be instanced as the tangible expressions of 'sovereignty'.[3] But the dukes of Brittany, Aquitaine and other peers of France also claimed to possess these rights. The Crown claimed that they could exercise them only by delegation from itself and that unlicensed exercise

[1] E. F. Jacob, *Essays in Later Medieval History* (Manchester, 1968), 150.
[2] See below, 134–51.
[3] For these see *Ord.*, v, 479–80 (8 May 1372); also P. Chaplais, 'La souveraineté du roi de France et le pouvoir législatif en Guyenne au début du xive siècle', *MA*, lxix (1963), 449–69.

would represent usurpation of the sovereignty of France. The notion of
lèse-majesté and of insult to supreme power was being more closely and
narrowly defined. Royal lawyers in France could argue that the king was
emperor in his kingdom.[1] As such, he possessed the powers of an emperor. No one but the king, it was argued under Charles VII, could
claim to rule 'by the grace of God'. No one but the king could impose
a tax on the whole kingdom of France at a time of national emergency or
evident necessity. But the transition from feudal to national taxation was
not yet complete by 1420 in France, while England had had a system of
national taxation since the late thirteenth century. No one but the king
possessed rights over the Church in the kingdom of France, unless those
rights were delegated by the king. The 'national' churches of the later
Middle Ages were in many ways reflections of the increasing power of
the prince. In England and France the Crown could act more or less inde-
pendently of the Papacy. In 1398 the 'Gallican' Church withdrew its
obedience from the rival popes until such time as a settlement of the Great
Schism was achieved. The legacy of this period in the history of the
French Church was to colour the reign of Charles VII.

A corollary of this evident and increasing growth of purely secular
power was the setting apart of princes from other forms of authority.
The collapse and fragmentation of the power of Empire and Papacy in
the later Middle Ages meant that, as in the Dark Ages, men began to turn
to sources of power, protection and prestige nearer home. The inter-
regnum in the Empire between 1250 and 1273, as well as the exile of the
Papacy at Avignon from 1305 to 1378, demonstrated that it was on the
'national' monarchies, and on the sovereign princes, that power would
devolve. But the ruling houses of fifteenth-century Europe inherited the
dangers as well as the advantages of this situation. Rivals to kingly power
were found among the princes, many of them related by blood or marriage to the monarch. In England, Poland, Hungary and Bohemia, ruling
dynasties had collapsed as a result of the weakness of kings and the power
of the greater magnates. Paradoxically, it was in France, with its comparatively weak monarchy and late 'centralisation', that the ruling house
of Valois rode the storm of magnate revolt for over 150 years. How was
this stability achieved? This is one of the questions to which an answer
will be given – but only for one Valois king – in this book.

A later medieval king such as Charles VII was faced with problems

---

[1] See A. Bossuat, 'La Formule "Le Roi est
empereur en son royaume". Son emploi au
xvᵉ siècle devant le Parlement de Paris',
RHDFE, 4th series, xxxix (1961), 371–81
(tr. in *Recovery of France*, 185-95).

which were not new and which were not to die with the 'new monarchies' of the Renaissance. First of all, he had to control and contain the
many actual and potential threats to his monarchy. These could be
foreign princes, such as the kings of England, or French princes of the
blood, such as Philip the Good of Burgundy. By what means could these
powerful and dangerous threats be eliminated, or at least minimised?
Under Charles VII, the position *vis-à-vis* the king of England was com-
plicated by the fact that, as duke of Aquitaine, he was also theoretically
a peer of France. National and feudal concepts merged and could not be
forced apart. Yet the problems which Charles VII inherited were not
products of the fifteenth century. Raymond Cazelles has shown how the
'crisis of the monarchy' in France must be dated back at least to the first
Valois, Philip VI (1328–50).[1] With the assumption of the title 'king of
France' by Edward III of England in 1340, Cazelles argues, the crisis
became 'first of all a dispute around a throne of two relatives whose
rivalry and possible legitimacy left to their subjects the problem and
need of choosing one or the other, giving the able and ambitious the
possibility of selling themselves to the highest bidder'.[2] But in certain
areas of France, such as Gascony or Normandy, the assumption of 1340
did not necessarily mean that the Gascons and Normans were obliged
to choose between two kings. They could choose between a king acting
as king, or a king acting merely as a duke. It is not surprising that many
of them chose the latter – the king of England, acting as duke of Aquitaine
or of Normandy. The collapse of English rule in Normandy was hardly
prevented by Henry V's resumption of Edward III's title and by the enforced recognition of it at Troyes in 1420. Similarly, the 'Burgundians',
whether in Burgundy itself or in the Netherlands, wanted to keep
their own duke. The Gascons, Normans and Bretons may have held a
similar view well into the fifteenth century.

Such attitudes could only cut across notions of the *rex-imperator* as they
were formulated by the lawyers of the Paris *Parlement*, the sovereign
court of the realm. Yet the conventional picture of France as a nation
destined for 'centralisation' under an absolute monarch is not a very
convincing one. There were too many impediments lying in the way to
make the process an easy or inevitable one. In 1453 the English war was
in effect brought to an end. But the French Crown was not totally freed
from the problems which had vexed both Charles VII and his predecessors. A second element in the 'crisis of the monarchy' has been detected

[1] R. Cazelles, *La Société Politique et la*   [2] Ibid., 430.
Crise de la Royauté (Paris, 1958), 8–9.

1 Portrait of Charles VII, attributed to Jean Fouquet. The frame bears the inscription *Le Trèsvictorieux Roi de France Charles Septiesme de ce Nom* (*Musée du Louvre, Paris*)

2 First surviving letter of Charles VII, as count of Ponthieu, signed in his own hand, 23 November 1415. The letter relates to his appointment to the captaincy of the castle of Vincennes by his father (*Bibliothèque Nationale, MS. fr. 20437, fol. 7*)

by Cazelles. Apart from the English claims, the crisis took the form of 'a series of protests against those able and ambitious men who had succeeded in getting hold of power and diverting the resources of the kingdom into their own pockets'.[1] The protests did not die with Philip VI. Among the targets of opposition chosen by the magnates of the Praguerie (1440) and the Public Weal (1465) were the pensioners and officers, who, it was claimed, did not deserve their pensions and offices. Nor were the French Wars of Religion after 1562 totally free from accusations and attacks against the court and its occupants. It is facile to see French political history in the fifteenth and sixteenth centuries as a struggle between those who were 'in' and 'out', with the court as the arena of conflict. There were other issues, such as local power and prestige, which could in-fluence the political behaviour of the ruling classes. But it was to the court that the locally powerful and prestigious came.[2]

To control the warring factions, each with their vassals, clients, sub-jects or *alliés* behind them, a king could employ a number of weapons. Firstly, there was military force. But without a standing army until 1445, Charles VII could not rely upon assured success against the magnates. Even after that date, as Louis XI discovered in 1465, a king could not always rely upon his own troops.[3] Secondly, he could manipulate the acquisitive instincts of the disgruntled and disaffected to his own advan-tage. Chastellain, as was quoted earlier, pointed to Charles VII's ability in this art. As Professor Jacob has observed, 'it does not take a learned political historian to know that in the later Middle Ages the art of govern-ment is the art of keeping the smaller seignorial units responsive to the prince's organization'.[4] There were many ways in which this could be done. Charles VII used his position as head of the patronage system to arrange marriages, offer positions at court, grant pensions and annuities, and promise rewards for past, present and future services. He bribed without shame and without scruple. One key to his ultimate success lies in his seemingly unlimited capacity for bribery. He bribed Jean I, count of Foix, in 1425. He bribed Philip the Good's most important servants in 1435. He bribed a number of smaller Gascon and Norman *seigneurs* from about 1442 onwards.[5] But to bribe effectively one needed money.

Lastly, a king could litigate against the over-mighty and the overtly rebellious. Many of the greatest magnates, including Burgundy, Foix,

[1] Loc. cit.
[2] See below, 217–28. For the court and its political significance see G. Zeller, *Les Institutions de la France au xvie siècle* (Paris, 1948), 94–6.

[3] See Philippe de Commynes, *Mémoires*, ed. J. Calmette and G. Durville (Paris, 1924), I, 18, 20.
[4] Jacob, op. cit., 150.
[5] See M. G. A. Vale, *English Gascony*,

Alençon and Armagnac, found themselves summoned before the *Parle-ment*. They were forbidden to rule 'by the grace of God'.[1] They were harassed by the personnel of royal courts in their own domains. The dukes of Brittany and Bourbon suffered from the activities of the royal *baillis* of the Cotentin and of Montferrand.[2] The traditional assaults of the monarchy against franchises, dating back as far as Philip IV, were merely perpetuated by the Valois. These kings were hampered by many obstacles. Not least among them was the need to delegate authority, to endow their younger sons with *apanages*, and to appoint lieutenants to govern the more remote provinces. The war with the English made delegation of power imperative, especially on the frontiers. Royal lieuten-ancies could be, and were, used by their holders to render themselves virtually independent of the Crown. Once more, the *conjoncture* of regional sentiment, English claims, and protest against the favoured merged to present a threat to the stability and permanence of royal power in France. Theoretically the monarchy was strong. Its pretensions and powers were set out and eulogised by its servants, lawyers and propagand-ists. But in practice it was very weak when Charles VII succeeded to the throne of which he had been disinherited by the English and by his father. How far, it may be asked, had this position changed by the king's death in 1461? To answer this question one must know far more about the instruments of royal power in France and the use to which they were put. How far can the king be seen behind the deceptive screen of his advisers and agents? What was his actual role in government and politics? How far is his known character confirmed or contradicted by his behaviour?

These are all important questions. Most biographies of medieval kings lack conviction, and the existing works on Charles VII are no exception.[3] The king emerges from them as, at worst, an icon, and, at best, a curi-ously enigmatic personality. There is too much that we do not know and can never know. But to accept the *président* Hénault's verdict on Charles VII is to admit defeat. 'He was,' Hénault wrote, 'the witness of the wonders of his reign.'[4]

1399-1453 (Oxford, 1970), 95-6, 206-13; Vaughan, *Philip the Good*, 112, and for Normandy, below, 123-4.
[1] See P. S. Lewis, *Later Medieval France. The Polity* (London, 1968), 233-6.
[2] For Brittany, see Dom Morice, *Mémoires pour servir de preuves à l'histoire ecclésiastique et civile de Bretagne* (1746), III, cols 46-7, and for Bourbon, see

A. Bossuat, *Le bailliage royal de Montferrand, 1425-1556* (Paris, 1957).
[3] Apart from Beaucourt's work, the only other scholarly biography remains Vallet de Viriville's *Histoire de Charles VII et de son époque* (Paris, 3 vols, 1862-5). See the critical comments in Beaucourt, I, xlvii-l.
[4] In his *Nouvel abrégé chronologique de l'histoire de France* (Paris, 1744), 177, quoted in Beaucourt, I, xx.

Chapter 2 ⚜ The Early Years 1403–1429

1 *Armagnacs and Burgundians (1403–1419)*

At two o'clock on the morning of 22 February 1403 a male child was born to Isabella of Bavaria, queen of France.[1] The boy was born in the royal *hôtel* of St-Pol in Paris, and was the eleventh in the long succession of Isabella's children. Whether or not the child, named Charles after her husband Charles VI, was in fact the king's son has been a matter of fruitless dispute. The extra-marital activities of Isabella were well known. Her *liaison* with Louis, duke of Orléans, led to scandalous gossip in Paris. There is absolutely no concrete evidence to suggest that Charles was not the king's son; even his own alleged doubts as to his legitimacy can be interpreted in the light of the cruel act of policy by which he was disinherited by Charles VI in January 1421.[2] There is little in his early years to arouse the suspicion which was allegedly to haunt him as dauphin. Yet the possibility of his illegitimacy can never be entirely ruled out, and his own son, the future Louis XI, was sufficiently uncertain of the fact to remark that Charles 'did not know whose child he was'.[3] Whatever the facts of his birth may have been, there was no doubt at that time that he stood third in the line of succession to the throne. His two elder brothers, Louis, duke of Guyenne (born in 1397), and Jean, duke of Touraine (born in 1398), both stood ahead of him. He was never really intended to be king. The death of Louis in December 1415 and of Jean in April 1417 left Charles as sole surviving son of the mad Charles VI.[4] His title of dauphin was accepted by some of his father's subjects. Others preferred to give their support to another claimant to the French throne – Henry V of England.

Hence the question of legitimacy does not necessarily provide a yardstick by which the future dauphin's political success or failure can be measured. It was only after he became dauphin that the question was raised by his enemies.[5] To see Charles as a victim of self-doubt throughout

---

[1] For this, and what follows, I have relied upon Beaucourt, I, 3–12.
[2] See below, 31–2.

[3] See Brachet, op. cit., 82–3.
[4] Beaucourt, I, 20.
[5] See below, 31–2.

his early career up to the appearance of Joan of Arc in 1429 would be to
ignore a great deal of evidence suggesting the contrary. It is too easy to
see the reign, as Chastellain perhaps first saw it, as a series of 'turning-
points'. Fortune, a concept much dwelt upon by his contemporaries, may
have been against him. But there is quite enough to explain that ill fortune
without introducing the highly speculative issue of Charles's bastardy.
His formative years were not spent in an environment which cast doubts
on his legitimacy. He was treated as any other royal child was treated in
the early fifteenth century. He was brought up in the luxury which was
the privilege of a young prince who might succeed to the throne. In
February 1404, just before his first birthday, he was given a harp, which
was to be played before him. His toys included a little brass pot (*chaudron*)
to divert him when he was 'ill disposed' – presumably a device, like the
harp, to quieten him.[1] In May 1408 he was presented with his first green
coat. The significance of this colour, which was to be incorporated into
his livery, will require further comment.[2] In April 1407 a 'robe royale'
had been made for him.[3] There was apparently no doubt at this time that
this infant was to be considered and treated as his father's son.

   A far more important influence during his early years was that exerted
by his future mother-in-law. On 18 December 1413, he was betrothed to
Marie of Anjou, daughter of Duke Louis II of Anjou, titular king of
Naples and Sicily, and Yolande of Aragon.[4] Unlike his two elder brothers,
who had been betrothed to children of the house of Burgundy, Charles
was to link the large and much-ramified Angevin house to the Crown.
Louis II had broken off an alliance with John the Fearless of Burgundy in
1413.[5] There was little doubt of his stance in the Armagnac-Burgundian
feud. The Armagnac victory over the Burgundians at Paris in the summer
of 1413 may have served to convince the house of Anjou that its fortunes
lay with the faction led by the families of Armagnac and Orléans. Burgundy and the English were forming an alliance on the other side. Louis
of Anjou's marriage agreement thus reflected the changing balance of
forces in French politics at this time. In the event, it was to prove more
significant for the future than other similar alliances. Between his betrothal, as a child of ten, in 1413, and his accession, as a youth of nineteen,
in 1422, a governing group had formed around Charles. It was to be the
source of many of his most able and most trusted servants. With the

---

[1] Beaucourt, I, 6–7. He was also given a
toy throne made of silver set into a 'petit
tableau de peinture'.
[2] Ibid., 11. This was for the Maying festivities at court. See below, 223–4.

[3] Ibid., 10.
[4] Ibid., 15–16.
[5] Vaughan, *John the Fearless*, 194, and
Beaucourt, I, 15.

future wife of the dauphin came her formidable mother and her servants. In 1415, Charles accompanied Yolande and her entourage to Provence, another Angevin possession.[1] He spent his time in the company of René of Anjou. Their close association was to be life-long.

Besides such personal connections, there were more formal attachments between the house of Valois and the house of Anjou. It has recently been observed that one of Charles VII's most 'intimate servants', the lawyer Jean Dauvet, 'began his career in the service of the Anjou family'.[2] He was one among many. Others can be found at an early date in his entour-age. Two reasons might be adduced for the prominence of the Angevin element in Charles's household at this time. First, it is known that he was very much under the influence of Yolande of Aragon. In a letter of 29 June 1418, addressed to the burgesses of Lyon, Charles announced a delay in his arrival at the town 'until we have had the advice of our mother the Queen of Sicily'.[3] Isabella of Bavaria was hardly a model matriarch and Beaucourt was probably right to accuse her of 'negligence'.[4] Charles looked to the Anjou family, perhaps, for other things beside capable and devoted servants. Secondly, the disaster at Agincourt in October 1415 had removed a group of powerful men from the court of Charles VI and of his sons. Bourbon, Alençon and Orléans had been captured and were in England. It is hardly surprising that the dauphin Charles should find his principal counsellors elsewhere, among men whom the Burgundians were to stigmatise with the inevitable smirch of being 'of humble extraction'.[5]

Who were these men, who were to play so important a part in the confused politics of the dauphin's court? First, there was the chancellor, Robert le Maçon, lord of Trèves in the *sénéchaussée* of Carcassonne.[6] He had been born in Anjou about 1365, the son of one of Duke Louis I's secretaries and counsellors. He himself entered the service of the king-duke, then became chancellor to Yolande and became a member of Charles's entourage in 1416. Then there was Jean Louvet, *président* of Provence. Born about 1370, he became *président* of the *chambre des comptes* at Aix in 1415 and a favourite of Isabella of Bavaria, with whom his name was associated as a lover. His connections with the court of France were further cemented by the betrothal of his daughter Marie to Jean, count

[1] Ibid., 16–17.
[2] Lewis, op. cit., 160.
[3] Printed in Beaucourt, I, 100–1.
[4] For an indictment of her, see ibid., I, 7–8. But she gave Charles a bay horse in June 1411 (ibid., 12). From the evidence of her household accounts it has recently been

argued that her children were brought up by 'affectionate parents and attentive servants'. But only three survived their mother. See Y. Grandeau, 'Les enfants de Charles VI', *BPH*, 1967, ii, 809–49.
[5] Beaucourt, I, 113.
[6] For this group, see ibid., I, 56–73, 411–15.

of Dunois, bastard of Orléans.[1] This took place a few days after Charles's betrothal to Marie of Anjou. Dunois was to grow up with Charles, and, with René of Anjou, was to be a loyal servant to him as king. Their Angevin marriages may have strengthened the personal bond. In at least one respect, Charles was perhaps less changeable than Chastellain and others have claimed. The *grand maître* of Charles's household was also a former servant of the house of Anjou. In 1412, Hardouin, lord of Maillé, had been married in the presence of the Anjou family. Like so many other intimate servants of Charles VII, he was styled *conseiller et chambellan* of the dauphin, and his signature is found on Charles's letters from 1417 onwards. Hardouin de Maillé was to outlive Charles himself, and died in 1468 after a lifetime in the service of the court.[2] Similarly, the two brothers Hervé and Jean du Mesnil served both the Crown and the Angevins.[3] Hervé, younger son of Charles's governess, became *bailli* of Montferrand in 1425 and stayed in that office for the greater part of the reign. His brother Jean was *conseiller et chambellan* to the king and also served him as a diplomatic envoy. Lastly, the Angevin connection in Charles's entourage as dauphin was also represented by Pierre, lord of Beauvau. Born in about 1380, he was a counsellor of Louis II of Anjou and entered the service of the Crown as *conseiller et chambellan*.[4] As seneschal of Anjou and governor of Provence he was a figure of great eminence in the administration of the Angevin lands. He served Louis in Italy and was more than literate, for he translated *Troilus and Cressida* from Italian into French.

Such were the servants who surrounded Charles as dauphin and during his early years as king. Such men, largely dependent on their standing at court, could be trusted as long as they were rewarded. They could also be played off against each other. None of them was entirely indispensable and there were plenty of candidates, rivals and suitors waiting for them to make a false step. As long as he could effectively control his entourage by dispensing his patronage, a prince was as secure as he could ever be. Instability was a political, and moral, commonplace of the age. Charles, with his limited resources, was to learn this aspect of the art of political management from an early stage in his career.

It is possible to attempt an analysis of the character and behaviour of Charles as dauphin and king up to the arrival at Chinon in February 1429

[1] Beaucourt, I, 236.
[2] Ibid., I, 62.

[3] See Lewis, op. cit., 161, and Beaucourt, I, 413.
[4] Ibid., I, 61–2.

of Joan of Arc.[1] Was Charles in a state of 'timid apathy' throughout this period? If so, what caused it and when did it manifest itself? Much has been made by historians of the impact of the murder of John the Fearless of Burgundy in September 1419 on Charles's personality. Less has been made of the act by which he was disinherited and dispossessed in January 1421. The military defeats which his forces suffered at Cravant (1423) and Verneuil (1424) have provoked historians into dismissing the dauphin's cause as a lost one. To do so is, perhaps, to ignore some of the more significant, if less obvious, features of this obscure period. The most striking of these concerns the objectives and ambitions which Charles must have held. Among these, 'national unity' or 'legitimate sovereignty' must have taken a second place to the problem of survival. On 29 May 1418, his servants Tanneguy du Chastel and Guillaume d'Avaugour took him by night from the palace of the Tournelles to the Bastille, and then to Melun.[2] He was not to see the city of Paris for nineteen years. The Burgundians made the city theirs. Charles was not the only member of the faction which had grown up in the houses of Armagnac and Orléans to leave Paris precipitately in May 1418. The Burgundian *coup* had created a 'dauphinist' group – men who had a vested interest in Charles's survival. Among them were, of course, some of his old servants and counsellors. Jean, bastard of Orléans, recollected in a receipt signed by him in his clear, bold hand in April 1421, that he had left Paris so hurriedly that his livery collar of the Bourbon Porcupine 'was lost . . . when the Burgundians entered' the city.[3] Charles thus inherited the feud of the house of Orléans against the house of Burgundy.

The composition of the court around the dauphin was to become more violently partisan as a result of the exile. Charles became the symbolic, as well as the tangible, alternative to the coalition which was forming between Burgundy and Henry V of England. The flight from Paris held further highly significant consequences. A separate administration was created for those parts of France which remained loyal to the dauphin. The power-centre from which Charles was to operate lay along the Loire and the Cher – at Bourges, Melun and Tours. It was a pattern of government which was to long outlive him. With its *Parlement* at

---

[1] For what follows I have drawn upon Beaucourt, I and II; Vaughan, *John the Fearless*; A. Mirot, 'Charles VII et ses conseillers assassins présumés de Jean Sans Peur', *AB*, xiv (1942), 197–210; Cosneau, *Richemont*; B. A. Pocquet, 'Le connétable de Richemont, seigneur bourguignon',

AB, vii (1935), 309–36, viii, 7–30 and 106–38; and G. Dodu, 'Le Roi de Bourges', *RH*, clix (1928), 38–78.

[2] Beaucourt, I, 87–8, and Vaughan, op. cit., 263–4.

[3] B.M., Add. Ch. 3168 (26 April 1421).

Poitiers, its *chambre des comptes* at Bourges, and its second sovereign court
(for the Languedoc) at Toulouse, the 'kingdom of Bourges' was to
become a viable instrument of government.[1] Around the fifteen-year-old
dauphin, a group whose own survival depended on his survival was
formed. Dispossessed by the Burgundians, then by the demented Charles
VI, these men knew that they could not afford to lose their uncrowned
king. As a result of the Burgundian *coup* and massacre, a complete administrative and judicial personnel found itself unemployed. From the *Parlement*, the *Châtelet* and the University, men such as Jean Juvenal des Ursins
left Paris for Poitiers or Bourges. Jean Juvenal lost rents, fine houses and
land to the value of 2,000 *livres*, and household goods worth 16,000 *écus*,
as a result.[2] Men who, as they alleged, had 'abandoned all' to serve a
young prince whom they considered to be the 'true heir of France' were
perhaps unlikely to be well received in the opposing camp should his
cause collapse.

On 29 June 1418, Charles assumed the title of lieutenant-general from
his incapable father to defend the kingdom against the Burgundians.[3]
The state of his affairs at this time is described in a letter written two weeks
earlier by one Jean Caille, *élu* of Lyon, to the councillors of his town.

Very dear and honoured lords, I recommend myself to you as strongly
as I can, and let it please you to know that my lord the dauphin is for
the present at Bourges, and, as people say, he has a great number of
men-at-arms, around Paris as well as in his company; he's got a good
four thousand men-at-arms from my lord's [Charles VI's] army. Be
pleased to know that when my said lord [the dauphin] was last on the
bridge at Charenton, my lord the cardinal of St-Marc came to him and
said that for God's sake he should work for the good of peace, notwithstanding the trouble in . . . Paris. And he replied to this that he
was all ready, and would never fail to work for it, notwithstanding
the fact that in guise of peace treason had been done, through which
he was very sad and angry. He spoke, moreover, in this fashion: 'I
know very well that they'll do to my lord [Charles VI] everything
they wish; but, with regard to the government, I'm content that my
lord provides as seems good to him. But those who get power should
be careful how they rule, because one day we'll come back against
them. . . .'[4]

[1] See G. Dodu, op. cit., especially pp. 50–
66 and Didier Neuville, 'Le Parlement
royal à Poitiers (1418–36)', *RH*, vi (1878),
1–28, 272–314.

[2] Ibid., 277.
[3] Beaucourt, I, 98 and 101.
[4] Printed in ibid., I, 439–41. The translation of this, and of subsequent

Jean Caille could tell the Lyonnais that Charles was 'very resolved' to prevent the internal conflicts which both the Burgundian and English threats had provoked. He was seeking the advice of Yolande and her children, the dukes of Brittany, Savoy and Alençon, the count of Foix and other lords 'to put an end to this painful conflict'. He had full confidence in the loyalty of Lyon, and, Jean Caille went on:

> I'll tell you the remark which my lord [the dauphin] made to my lord of Vertus at Gien-sur-Loire, speaking of the conflict within this realm in this way: 'My lord [Charles VI] and I shall now see the goodwill of our subjects and those truly obedient to us.' So I assure you that he's a lord of very great heart, and that once he's said something he sticks to it.[1]

These reported words of a youth of fifteen hardly suggest the 'timid apathy' of the conventional picture. Like that of Henry V of England, Charles's political maturity came early.[2] He was presiding over councils and meetings of the Estates from the age of fourteen onwards. From 15 August 1417 his signature appears beneath several important edicts of his father.[3] It is a well-formed, literary, practised hand, with a decorative flourish. There is no sign at this time of the hesitant mutability which is said to have characterised Charles's behaviour. Jean Caille may have been a devoted dauphinist – we do not know his exact political stance – but he was evidently impressed by the young prince's resolution and by his consistency of purpose. There is no evidence of mental instability or 'hereditary disorders of the nervous system' at this time. The dauphin was obviously convincing at least some of the members of the political nation that, in one sense, he was not his father's son.

From the surviving documents which chronicle the period from his flight to Bourges to the murder of John the Fearless on the bridge at Montereau on 10 September 1419, an impression of the dauphin's increasing frustration emerges. In a letter to the consuls, burgesses and inhabi-

---

documents, is my own, although, in order for the text to read more freely, I have translated them in a more modern idiom than the original French would seem to permit. For Lyon's position at this time, see L. Caillet, *Etude sur les relations de la commune de Lyon avec Charles VII et Louis XI (1417–83)* (Paris–Lyon, 1909), 90–105.

[1] Beaucourt, I, 440.
[2] See K. B. McFarlane, op. cit., 104–13.
[3] Beaucourt, I, 73–4. Charles's first surviving letter missive, bearing his signature, dates from 23 November 1415, when he was twelve. See Plate 2. Louis XI's first surviving signature dates from his fifteenth year (Vaesen, *Lettres*, I, 1–2).

tants of Lyon, written at Lusignan on 14 October 1418, Charles told them that he had heard that:

> One day this month, a messenger came to the town of Lyon, carrying a letter sealed with the great seal of my lord [Charles VI] tied with silk, and in green wax, making mention of a certain peace, which letter and messenger, obeying our previous orders – that is, that . . . you should send us all such letters, with their carriers, if they are not signed with our own hand – you have sent to the *bailli* of Mâcon and seneschal of Lyon, to return to us, so that we can deal with it according to our pleasure. . . .[1]

The 'peace' in question was the treaty of St-Maur-les-Fossés, which strengthened the hold of the Burgundians over Charles VI and the city of Paris. The dauphin could thus command the Lyonnais to ignore such letters, unless they bore his signature. The sequence of events which was to lead to the act of desperation and revenge on the bridge at Montereau had begun. In June 1418, Charles had told Jean Caille, who had given him a letter from the Lyonnais, that 'Here are loyal people; my lord [Charles VI] and I are much beholden to them'.[2] But there were many, including his father, who did not share the faith of the Lyonnais in the 'lawful heir of France'.

Historians have lingered long over the question of Charles's complicity in the assassination of John the Fearless.[3] The evidence inclines to the probability that the deed was done with his consent, if not his active encouragement, by the old servants of the murdered Louis of Orléans. The fatal blows were probably struck by Guillaume Bataille, Robert de Lairé and the *vicomte* of Narbonne.[4] As an act of revenge alone, the murder at Montereau seems quite explicable. But it also served to break the deadlock which had gripped both sides in the civil war. It was said of John the Fearless during a meeting held on 8 July near Pouilly that 'one might as well talk to a deaf ass as to him'.[5] Despite the affectionate words and the exchange of gifts which followed this setback, it was evident that the two factions were as far apart as they had ever been. One of Charles's servants, the Gascon Arnaud-Guillaume, lord of Barbazan, went so far as to refuse a gift of 500 *moutons d'or* from Burgundy, saying that he would 'never take money, except from the masters whom he served'.[6]

[1] Printed in Beaucourt, I, 445–6.
[2] Ibid., I, 444.
[3] For the most recent discussion of this question see Vaughan, *John the Fearless*, 263–86.

[4] Ibid., 278–80; Beaucourt, I, 171.
[5] Ibid., I, 144, quoting Jean Chartier, III, 219.
[6] B.N. MS. fr. 5061, fol. 116ᵛ.

Loyalty was still not, perhaps, entirely negotiable in terms of hard cash. Almost nothing is known, given the partisan and polemical nature of so much of the evidence, about Charles's own part in the planning and execution of the murder. That he was present in the enclosure on the bridge was of course inevitable. But it is doubtful whether he actually saw the murder committed. It was alleged that the faithful Tanneguy du Chastel again saved him from potential harm by pushing him out of the enclosure just before the first blows were exchanged.[1] He was spared the sight of the brutality with which Burgundy was hacked to the ground, as Louis of Orléans had been savagely cut down in the *rue du vieil Temple*. 'You cut off my master's hand,' Guillaume Bataille was alleged to have cried, 'and I'll cut off yours.'[2] It was becoming part of the ritual of political assassination to sever a hand – a hand which, the writers of propaganda literature claimed – had been guided by sorcery and the invocation of demons.[3] Witchcraft was added, almost *de rigueur*, to the alleged crimes of these victims of factional politics.

The only extant piece of evidence for the dauphin's behaviour immediately before the murder is a statement by Jean de Poitiers, bishop of Valence, in favour of Charles's chancellor, Robert le Maçon. It was made before a notary on 18 July 1426, almost seven years after the event.[4] Its trustworthiness is thus in doubt for two reasons: it overtly espouses a cause, and it post-dates the events which it purports to describe. But the bishop's testimony – amid a welter of conflicting, ambiguous and mendacious evidence – perhaps comes closest to that of an 'independent' witness. He did not see the murder. He was not a noted partisan of either Burgundy or the dauphinists. He had come to Montereau on family business, to see the dauphin about the grant of the *comté* of Valentinois to his brother, and to speak to his other brother, the bishop of Langres, who was 'in the company of my said lord of Burgundy'.[5] Jean de Poitiers, with close relatives on both sides, and no evident commitment to either, might be worthy of a hearing. On the day of the murder (Sunday, 10 September) both Jean de Poitiers and Robert le Maçon (who were friends) attended a

---

[1] Beaucourt, I, 171. All the sources are in conflict on this point.
[2] Ibid., I, 171 n. 6.
[3] For such notions in the works of Jean Petit (1408) and Pierre Salmon (1409), see C. C. Willard, 'The MSS of Jean Petit's Justification', *Studi Francesi*, xxxviii (1969), 273.
[4] Printed in Beaucourt, II, 651–8.

Arguments against the document's authenticity could be mounted on the fact that it bears no trace of a seal, and is found among the private archives of the La Trémoïlle family. These are not discussed by Vaughan, op. cit., 283–4, who accepts it as 'conclusive proof' of Charles's complicity in the murder.
[5] Beaucourt, I, 656.

council in which the Burgundian lords received the oaths of Charles's entourage. The statement goes on:

> . . . after the oaths had thus been taken, when the king – at that time regent [i.e. the dauphin] – wished to leave . . . he called the said lord of Trèves [Robert le Maçon] to him, told him that he should go with him, and spoke very little and briefly to him on one side. And we could see clearly, from the manner of the said lord of Trèves, that he wanted to hold the king back and speak with him at greater length, and, as it seemed to us, he disagreed with the king's remarks. And then the king left suddenly enough, and summoned the said lord of Trèves two or three times to go after him, but he didn't want to go, and stayed in the said room, with us and many others (whose names we don't remember). And we saw that as soon as the king . . . left, the said lord of Trèves fell down on to a bed; and we approached him and asked him what was wrong; and he replied . . . 'Please God, my lord of Valence, that I were at Jerusalem, without a penny or a stitch, and that I had never seen this lord here; for I'm very much afraid that he's badly advised, and that he'll do something today by which this kingdom and he himself will be lost. . . .'[1]

The dissident chancellor had his horses brought to him, and rode with his servants to the gate of Montereau, which, significantly, had been shut. As they rode out of the gate, which had 'with great trouble' been opened, they heard 'the hue and cry of the death of my said lord of Burgundy'.[2] All this, recorded the notary, was said by the bishop of Valence on his most solemn oath. Unless the bishop can be convicted of lying, then his testimony must stand. Beaucourt wrote his account of the Montereau murder without the benefit of this document. He could thus conclude that the dauphin 'had nothing with which to reproach himself in the catastrophe, accomplished in a fortuitous way, without his participation'.[3] His verdict has not been allowed to stand.

The dauphin's war with the Burgundians had become war to the death, a war waged, as the seneschal of Lyon wrote to the consuls of the town in June 1418, with 'fire and blood'.[4] He was, perhaps, unlikely to have had much sympathy for the dead Louis of Orléans. His mother's alleged behaviour with the duke was hardly advantageous to his cause.

[1] Beaucourt, I, 656–7.
[2] Ibid., I, 657, and Vaughan, op. cit., 283–4.
[3] Beaucourt, I, 179. The document in favour of Robert le Maçon came to light after Beaucourt had published his first volume (ibid., II, 651).
[4] Ibid., I, 442.

If there were doubts as to his paternity, the *liaison* between Isabella of Bavaria and Louis of Orléans provided the court with one source of speculation. It would be a far-fetched hypothesis which saw the murder at Montereau as an act by which an illegitimate son avenged his father's death. But if Charles had any suspicions about his legitimacy at this time, he did not show them. It would hardly have been politic to do so. It was perhaps more likely that he saw John the Fearless as the murderer of men whom he knew – the constable Bernard VII of Armagnac or the chancellor Henri de Marle, killed during the Burgundian *coup* of May 1418, and the 'other good and loyal servants of his father and himself'.[1]

ii *Disinheritance and its aftermath* (*1419-1429*)

The immediate consequences of the murder at Montereau were predictable. Charles's observation that 'they'll do to my lord everything they wish' held good for the events which followed the assassination as well as for those which preceded it.[2] By the treaty of Troyes (21 May 1420), Henry V of England pledged himself to recover all lands still in Charles's hands, and achieved two of his greatest ambitions, the disinheritance of the 'so-called dauphin', and a marriage with Catherine, daughter of Charles VI and Isabella of Bavaria. There was no question raised as to Catherine's legitimacy. The dauphin was deprived of his inheritance and banished from France. This, Charles VI's letter to the inhabitants of Paris (17 January 1421) observed, was to be a punishment for 'the evil deed he has done to the duke John of Burgundy'.[3] The issue of bastardy was not touched upon. Prompted by the Anglo-Burgundian group around him, Charles VI declared that 'one should not take account of the youth of the said Charles . . . because he is quite old enough to tell good from evil'.[4] His 'malice and wickedness' was thought to be ageless, and it was alleged that he himself had been most active, giving 'sweet words' of deceit whereby Burgundy had been done to death. The process of disinheritance was therefore a political act. A formal ceremony set the seal on that act. On 23 December 1420, in the very house in which Charles had been born, his father held a *lit-de-justice*.[5] Henry V, now styled 'heir and regent of France', sat beside him on the same bench. The Anglo-Burgundian alliance produced its case through the words of the *pro-*

[1] See *Chroniques de Perceval de Cagny*, ed. H. Moranvillé (*SHF*, Paris, 1902), 115.
[2] See above, 26.
[3] *Mémoires de Pierre de Fenin*, ed. L. Dupont (*SHF*, Paris, 1837), 119.
[4] Ibid., 117. For what follows, see Beaucourt, I, 179-216.
[5] Ibid., I, 217.

cureur-général, Nicholas Rolin. Speaking in the name of John the Fearless's widow, Rolin accused 'Charles, so-called dauphin of Vienne', of homicide, and requested that he and his accomplices be 'put in tumbrils and taken through all the crossroads of Paris, their heads bare, on three Saturdays or feast days, each one holding a burning taper in his hand, saying aloud that they had wickedly, treacherously and damnably murdered the duke of Burgundy through hatred, without any reasonable cause whatsoever'.[1] The citizens were not to see this moving penance enacted.

Could Charles VI legally disinherit and banish his own son? It was a point around which much legal discussion was to rage. The Anglo-Burgundian faction in January 1421 believed that he could. Having been summoned to appear, by sound of trumpet, before the Paris *Parlement* on 3 January, Charles's refusal to obey that summons led to the passing of sentence.[2] The firmness of conviction displayed by the counsellors of John the Fearless's son at that time was not strikingly evident in September 1435, when they sought advice on the case from the law school of Bologna university.[3] The doctors may have been time-servers, but they supplied enough legal argument to support non-observance of the treaty of Troyes and its implications. Charles VI, they argued, was not acting on his own authority. He was infirm of mind, and, above all, he 'could not deprive his son of the right to succeed him in the kingdom merely *on account of the death of that great prince*' (i.e. John the Fearless).[4] In any case, they said, a father could not have such jurisdiction over his heir at law in a land, like the Persian empire, where primogeniture was the rule. Lastly, the father could not be both judge and accuser. In a few strokes of the pen, the validity of the Anglo-Burgundian case of January 1421 was demolished.

Once given the Dauphiné, in 1417, the Bolognese lawyers observed, then Charles, the rightful heir, must succeed. Their views bore out the fact that, before the events of 1419–21, there had been no question of Charles's hereditary right to succeed as his father's eldest (and only) surviving son. The established customs of inheritance to the throne of France could not be broken in the interests of a private feud.

It was to those established customs that Charles appealed on his father's death on 21 October 1422.[5] He had already vowed to pursue what he

---

1 Beaucourt, I, 218.
2 Ibid., I, 218–19.
3 Printed in Plancher, IV, no. 122, cli–clvii.
4 Ibid., clvii.

5 Beaucourt, II, 55–6. The news of his father's death followed soon after his accident at La Rochelle. The latter made an indelible impression on his memory, if

considered his lawful cause against the Lancastrian double monarchy of England and France. That cause could be sustained in a number of ways. Firstly, there was military force. On 22 March 1421, his Scots troops were largely responsible for the victory at Baugé. The earls of Douglas and Buchan wrote from the field at midnight, sending him the banner of the dead Thomas, duke of Clarence, brother of Henry V.[1] Charles was safely at Poitiers. The victory gave rise to optimism in more than one heart. The captive Charles of Orléans, taken prisoner at Agincourt six years previously, sent his chancellor, Guillaume Cousinot, from Blois to Tours in the hope that 'one could have some of the English prisoners taken lately by the Scots lords at the battle of Baugé' in exchange for Orléans's liberty.[2] Support for the cause was thus determined by a multitude of motives. That some of that support came from abroad was significant. From the autumn of 1418 Charles had retained a company of archers under John Stewart of Darneley as a bodyguard. It was, as Beaucourt pointed out, the germ of the guard of Scots archers, a body which was to outlive Charles VII.[3] It was to this ancient ally of the Crown that he was to look for a wife for his eldest son.[4]

But the Scots could not sustain their successes against the combined forces of England and Burgundy. On 31 July 1423, Charles's army was cut to pieces outside the town of Cravant. In a letter of 2 August to the Lyonnais, Charles could beg them not to be too distressed by the setback, because there were 'almost none of the nobles of our kingdom there, but only Scots, Spaniards, and other foreign soldiers, accustomed to live off the country, so that the harm is not so great'.[5] Despite their failure, he considered it still worthwhile to retain his Scots. In November 1425, he gave John Stewart, constable of the Scots army in France, money with which to pay his ransom and 'to help him to release himself in order to serve us against our enemies'.[6] One great loss to his cause was James, earl of Buchan, killed at the battle of Verneuil (17 August 1424). His death left a vacuum to be filled in the military organisation of the kingdom of Bourges. The manner in which the office of constable was to be

Jean Juvenal des Ursins, writing almost twenty years later, is to be believed. He told Charles: 'I know that you well remember the danger that you were in at La Rochelle, when the floor gave way beneath you. . . .' (B.N., MS. fr. 2701, fol. 87). The effects of the incident on Charles's character are incalculable, but it cannot be dismissed entirely. See above, 11.

[1] Beaucourt, I, 220–1.
[2] B.M., Add. Ch. 3549.
[3] For its origins see Beaucourt, I, 428–30.
[4] See ibid., II, 396–9. The marriage treaty with James I of Scotland was made on 30 October 1428, and a Scots army was promised under its terms.
[5] Ibid., II, 14.
[6] B.M., Add. Ch. 3588.

given, and held, provides a test case for the nature of Charles's political skill.

Beaucourt could argue that the campaign which he led himself during the summer of 1421 formed 'a line of demarcation' in his life.[1] There is evidence that before this time the dauphin had appeared at the head of his troops, in full armour. His ceaseless journeying meant that he was often seen by the common people on the road, or at those royal ceremonies which attended his entries into loyalist towns.[2] The impressive entourage, decked out in his livery colours as dauphin – white, red and blue – served to convey an image of legitimate and prestigious authority to the spectator. His device of 'an armoured hand grasping a naked sword', with his banner of St Michael slaying a serpent, suggested that the dauphin was still prepared to conduct a war 'of fire and blood' against the 'enemies of the kingdom'.[3] But after his withdrawal in the face of Henry V in July 1421, his militant espousal of his cause was far less evident. 'Instead of throwing himself into affairs . . . putting himself at the head of his troops, showing himself to the people,' wrote Beaucourt, 'he went and shut himself up in places impenetrable to his subjects . . . and even more impenetrable to History.'[4] It is a revealing comment. There were, obviously, dangers in exposing Charles to the people, especially after the Montereau murder. His counsellors, recorded Pierre de Fenin, 'kept him always away from his enemies as much as they could'.[5] Charles was, for them, far too valuable to lose. It was only common sense that dictated their desire to prevent the young, uncrowned king from exposing himself to unnecessary dangers. An assessment of Charles's behaviour after this date can be determined more by preconceptions about what fifteenth-century princes should have been, rather than by what they were. At this time, Beaucourt wrote, 'we approach the moment . . . when the young prince, renouncing the initiative of which he had given more than one proof, resigned himself too easily to a passive role'.[6] This judgement appears to rest on the premise that the role of a fifteenth-century king or prince was a militarily active one. Yet Charles V of France had already demonstrated that a king could achieve a great deal by withdrawing from military leadership in battle and entrusting that function to the constable, Bertrand du Guesclin. His grandson was to act in a similar fashion, but with some important differences crucial to an understanding of his way of doing business as king.

1 Beaucourt, I, 230.   4 Ibid., I, 230.
2 Ibid., I, 198.   5 Pierre de Fenin, op. cit., 195.
3 Ibid., I, 199–200. For his livery colours   6 Beaucourt, I, 230.
as king, see below, 206, 224.

Both Chastellain and the *prévôt* of Arras, Pierre de Fenin, agreed that Charles was never bellicose by temperament. 'He didn't willingly arm himself, and he didn't love war at all, if he could avoid it,' wrote Pierre de Fenin in his *Mémoires* for 1422.[1] The knowledge that, after Cravant and Verneuil, he could not even hope for a speedy military victory, led him to adopt other means of survival. There could be no higher aims for his statecraft at this time. Contemporaries, on both sides of the dynastic fence, could allude (admiringly or disparagingly according to their political stance) to the acknowledged fact that he was 'a fine talker to all men'. His voice, 'very agreeable and subtle, not too high-pitched', made him appear well disposed, affable and clever (to his friends), devious, ingenuous and deceitful (to his enemies).[2] 'Willingly,' thought Chastellain rather later in his reign, 'would he surround himself with wise and bold men, and let himself be led by them. But, unbeknown to them, he would all the while be planning something new.'[3] He was, thought Chastellain, extraordinarily subtle and quite inscrutable: it was indeed to become extremely dangerous to be a member of his entourage. The first member of that entourage to experience Charles's manner of dealing with a 'loyal servant' was Jean Louvet. Like Louis XI, Charles was not a man to feel gratitude towards his servants. The fall of Louvet and the rise to power of the constable Arthur de Richemont may serve to illustrate this.

On 8 March 1425, the Breton captain Arthur de Richemont, disfigured by facial wounds received at Agincourt, entered the service of the uncrowned, unanointed Charles as his constable.[4] As such, the thirty-three-year-old brother of Jean V, duke of Brittany, was to assume command of the military resources (which were not derisory) of the kingdom of Bourges. It was, in its way, a spectacular success for the young king. Richemont had previously served the Anglo-Burgundian cause. On 10 October 1423 he had married Margaret of Burgundy, sister of Philip the Good.[5] His avowal of the Anglo-Burgundian alliance was broken by his assumption of the constable's sword. There can be little doubt that his agreeing to do so was a result of the mediation of Yolande of Aragon, who used her influence with Jean V of Brittany to win him over. On 21 October 1424, one year after Richemont's marriage to Margaret of Burgundy, Yolande engineered the marriage of her son, Louis III of

[1] Pierre de Fenin, op. cit., 196.
[2] See Chastellain, II, 178.
[3] Ibid., II, 181.
[4] For this, and what follows, see Cosneau,

Richemont, 88–92, and Beaucourt, II, 74–87
[5] See Pocquet, 'Le Connétable de Richemont, seigneur bourguignon', *AB*, vii (1935), 321–36.

Anjou, to Isabella, daughter of Jean V of Brittany.[1] The house of Anjou, as well as the house of Valois, profited from the winning of Richemont. Three days previously, Charles had met Richemont for the first time in the garden of the abbey of St-Aubin at Angers, in the very heart of Angevin power.[2] Charles received him, as was his wont, warmly and affably, and offered him the constable's sword. Richemont at first refused – citing his youth and lack of experience – and said that he would have to gain the prior agreement of the dukes of Burgundy, Brittany and Savoy. It was as if an Italian *condottiere* were signing a contract with an employer. Richemont had changed sides after Agincourt, his ransom was still unpaid, and, after his marriage, he had some grounds for claiming the duchy of Burgundy in the event of Philip the Good's death without male heirs.[3] But in November 1424 Philip married Bonne d'Artois – he had, perhaps, already heard of his enemy's offer of the constable's office to Richemont and was now resolved to beget a male heir.[4] Why, with the advantages conferred on him by his marriage, was Richemont wooed to the side of the disinherited and dispossessed Charles VII?

On 15 February 1425, Philip the Good, 'for certain reasons', seized all the Burgundian lands given in dower to his sister Margaret.[5] She was still permitted to draw an income from some of them, but her husband was no longer to be the beneficiary. By defecting to Charles VII, Richemont had lost lands worth about 6,300 *livres tournois* a year. What had Charles VII to offer, at this critical juncture, to the aggressive Breton adventurer? The lack of Burgundian attempts to prevent his acceptance of the constableship of France is perhaps surprising. It may reflect the beginnings of an estrangement, after the death of Henry V in August 1422, between Philip the Good and the English. But there was no hope of any kind of reconciliation between Burgundy and Charles until he had rid himself of those of his servants whom the Burgundians believed were responsible for the murder at Montereau. One of the more remarkable aspects of the agreement by which Richemont accepted Charles's offer was the oath which the new constable swore on the Gospels in March 1425. He pledged himself to 'love, sustain and support' Tanneguy du Chastel, Jean Louvet, Pierre de Giac, Guillaume d'Avaugour and Pierre Frotier.[6] He would not 'agree to anything which would be to the damage of their persons or their goods and estates'. Men thought to be

[1] Cosneau, *Richemont*, 85–6.
[2] Ibid., 85; Beaucourt, II, 76–7.
[3] Pocquet, op. cit., 333.
[4] Cosneau, *Richemont*, 87.
[5] Pocquet, op. cit., 28.
[6] Printed in Cosneau, *Richemont*, 503–4 (8 March 1425).

guilty of homicide were thus to be protected and sheltered by the former partisan of Burgundy. He was certainly well rewarded by Charles, with the constable's pension and the opportunities for personal profit which the position offered. But Richemont's biographer, Guillaume Gruel, told a rather different story.

Gruel was a partisan. His account is open to objection on grounds of partiality for his subject and master. But he often provides evidence not recorded elsewhere. When Richemont accepted the constableship, he wrote, the king 'promised him and swore to send out of the kingdom all those who had been the cause of my lord of Burgundy's death'.[1] Obviously, the statement could be an attempt to exonerate Richemont from the charge of having broken his oath by causing Charles's servants to be banished from his presence three months later. But the possibility of Charles having made such a promise cannot be completely disregarded. If Chastellain's assessment of his character was right, he would hardly have been likely to feel either gratitude or obligation towards any of his immediate entourage. He was bound to Louvet only by the tenuous thread of the cash nexus. To dispossess a principal creditor was to become one of the characteristic traits of his government.[2] It is known that Louvet's personal wealth, derived in part from his financial office in the *chambre des comptes* of the house of Anjou, was considerable. On 1 January 1423, for instance, he had lent 4,016 *écus d'or* from his own resources to Charles, so that certain merchants who had supplied him with cloth of gold, silks, furs, silver plate and jewels, both for his own use and for New Year's Day gifts, could be paid. Repayment was to be given on the security of 'our great diamond called the "Mirror" '.[3] The purchase of 'six *aulnes* of cloth of gold from which a robe has been made for us' hardly suggests that the court of Bourges was in a state of abject and shabby penury at this time.[4] That Louvet's financial dealings were somewhat irregular was only to be expected. A favourite had to keep himself in favour. He did so by all means in his power.

The impending *rapprochement* with Richemont and the Bretons could only serve to damage Louvet's position. Disliked by Jean V of Brittany as a supporter of the rival Penthièvre claim to the duchy, Louvet may have been the prime mover of the agreement to which Richemont swore

---

[1] Guillaume Gruel, *Chronique d'Arthur de Richemont*, ed. A. le Vavasseur (*SHF*, Paris, 1890), 36.

[2] See below, 127-34.

[3] B.M. Add. Ch. 3169. For Louvet's wealth, see Beaucourt, I, 237-8.

[4] B.M. Add. Ch. 3169. The robes, furs, plate and jewels were bought by Charles 'both to . . . clothe our person . . . [and] to give by ourself and on behalf of our . . . companion the queen, in *étrennes* on the said first day of the year. . . .'

in March 1425.[1] The insistence on the constable's being only *as* powerful as the king, not more so, suggests that Louvet and his friends thought that they had Charles in tutelage. Their repeated insistence that the constable should not 'suffer the sending away of the king's servants' from him seems almost paranoid. Charles was apparently quite prepared to let them do so. He had, perhaps, already begun to play Chastellain's game – setting a newly found servant against those already in power. The charges against Louvet, as they appeared in the letters announcing his dismissal, were entirely financial.[2] There was no mention of his complicity in the murder of John the Fearless. Among the members of the council at Poitiers who endorsed the document on 5 July 1425 was Tanneguy du Chastel, soon to be exiled as well. There was evidently no unity within the ranks of those allegedly responsible for the murder at Montereau. Charles was quite prepared to let them compete around him. He was quite prepared to allow letters to be issued in his name citing his own 'inadvertence' through which 'many great, excessive and unreasonable powers, both in the matter of our finances and otherwise', had been granted to Louvet.[3] A king was, after all, a man like other men – he was continually exposed to the 'importunity of unworthy suitors'.[4] It was an acknowledgement of the nature of kingship. The price of Richemont's military prowess and of an alliance with Jean V of Brittany, was Louvet's disgrace. It did not take very much time or trouble to allege charges of peculation. It was a technique which was to be used again, not only by Charles VII. His employment of the weapons of favour and disgrace was to be only one of the means whereby he outwitted his opponents and controlled his more importunate courtiers.

By August 1425, Richemont was exulting in his success. He had, he wrote to the burgesses of Lyon, persuaded the king to 'cast out all that bad seed from his household which the *président* [Louvet] had left there'.[5] Guillaume d'Avaugour, Pierre Frotier, the king's doctor Jean Cadart, and their accomplices, were sent into exile. It was in effect a total violation of the oath which Richemont had taken in March. But his success was

[1] Cosneau, *Richemont*, 83.
[2] Charles's letters of 5 July 1425 are printed ibid., 507–9.
[3] Ibid., 507. For a letter of Jean V, duke of Brittany, in which he claimed that Louvet and his supporters had prevented Richemont from getting money with which to pay his troops, see *Lettres et Mandements de Jean V, duc de Bretagne*, ed. R. Blanchard (Nantes, 1889), VIII, 72–3

(13 June 1425).
[4] *Ord.*, xiii, 117–19, for an ordinance of 26 June 1426 whereby Charles revoked grants from the finances, excepting the wages of officers and captains, for one year. See also, for the more general problems of requests for favour and office, Lewis, op. cit., 142–3.
[5] Printed in Cosneau, *Richemont*, 512–13 (3 August 1425).

not achieved without conflict. On 2 June, Richemont had claimed that Louvet had forced Charles to change his principal officers, Martin Gouge, bishop of Clermont, and Jean de Comborn, lord of Treignac.[1] They had been ejected from the household. Both were Richemont's men, although the chancellor Martin Gouge had been appointed during Louvet's hegemony in 1422.[2] The king had refused to see the constable – he must have been party to the act of provocation whereby they were dismissed. The constable then resorted to armed force in an attempt to win his way back into favour at court. In Charles's entourage, no success was ever complete. When Richemont was at the height of his success in September 1425 it was said that even the king's financial officers dared do nothing without Richemont's consent[3] – but Charles was raising new men to power. Two favourites of relatively low birth followed each other in rapid succession between the expulsion of Louvet and the rise of Georges, lord of La Trémoïlle. Pierre de Giac and Le Camus de Vernet, called de Beaulieu, were both sacrificed to the anger of the constable. Both were assassinated. Both were thought to be possessed by the Devil, and each had one hand severed by his murderers.[4]

In July 1427, Richemont, never politically astute, made his greatest mistake. In order to maintain a presence at court while he campaigned for the king on the 'frontier of war', the constable offered Charles the services of Georges de la Trémoïlle. La Trémoïlle had derived both status and wealth from his marriage to the widow of Jean, duke of Berry, in November 1416.[5] She had died in 1422, but her second husband gained the usufruct of her domains. On 2 July 1427 he married the widow of Pierre de Giac. His brother, Jean de la Trémoïlle, was in the Burgundian camp. He was, thought Richemont and Yolande of Aragon, potentially a valuable instrument of reconciliation between Charles and Philip the Good. He would not, they thought, act as the two previous creatures of the king's favour had acted. They had contrived to prevent anyone except a very few from 'approaching' the king. But Richemont was wrong. Even his biographer Guillaume Gruel was candid enough to admit as much. Charles, he recorded, had said to the constable: 'dear cousin, you give him [La Trémoïlle] to me, but you'll repent of it, because I know

[1] Ibid., 99–100; Beaucourt, II, 90–3.
[2] Ibid., I, 348.
[3] The financial officers had told Roulin de Mâcon that 'it was necessary to speak about the matter to my lord the constable, without whom they did not dare to do anything'. He was at Poitiers on behalf of the councillors of Lyon, haggling over a tax imposed on them for the payment of Richemont's troops. See Beaucourt, III, 503, and Caillet, op. cit., 95–8.
[4] Cosneau, *Richemont*, 129–32, 140.
[5] Ibid., 141–2; Beaucourt, II, 144–6.

him better than you do'.[1] Discord between the two men was sown –
perhaps intentionally – by Charles's grant to La Trémoïlle of the duchy
of Berry.[2] Richemont's place was jeopardised by the behaviour of his
brother, Jean V of Brittany. On 8 September 1427, the duke signed a
treaty with Henry VI of England.[3] It was a gift to La Trémoïlle, who
now worked for the exile of Richemont and his allies. Deprived of his
pension, Richemont was banished from court. He retired in dudgeon to
his lordship of Parthenay. He had not served his purpose. The defection
of his brother had sealed his fate, and he had conspicuously failed to
reconcile France and Burgundy.

Was Charles 'complacent about the abuses of royal favour, and about
the self-interest of his servants'?[4] Beaucourt thought that he was, and so,
of course, did the Burgundians. But this view, it can be argued, may mis-
interpret the nature of his political technique. Could a king afford to be
anything else but complacent? Although he was writing at a later date,
Chastellain's observations might hold good for the early years of the
reign – the dark days before the dawn of victory. It was, wrote Chastellain, evident that Charles was changeable. As a result of his mutability

all sorts of changes frequently took place around him, and leagues and
factions formed between the courtiers so that, setting one against the
other, they could get into power; in this way of doing things, each
party always took care to achieve something great – the ruling party
in order to remain in favour, the others in the hope of succeeding.
And so, from two opposing wills both straining towards a virtuous
end, there always was born something fruitful to the nourisher; that's
to say, the master, who, by a subtle appreciation of what he had to do
with them, let them both clash and reaped the profit from it. For he
had a disposition such that after a time, when someone had been raised
up on high beside him, to the very top of the wheel, he began to tire
of him; then, at the first opportunity he could find, he deliberately
knocked them down from high to low, always in confusion. Through
this, others, having struggled in competition for a long time outside
the door, achieved new favour, and arrived at a newly exalted position,
which they'd long coveted, where – by reason of the hope they'd had
of staying longer than their predecessors – they worked to deserve
their position more fully . . . and to base their long tenure of power

[1] Cosneau, *Richemont*, 142, and Gruel,
op. cit., 194.
[2] Cosneau, *Richemont*, 143.
[3] Ibid., 148, and G. A. Knowlson, *Jean V,
duc de Bretagne et l'Angleterre (1399–1442)*
(Cambridge–Rennes, 1964), 137–8.
[4] Beaucourt, II, 259–63.

on a multitude of useful services rendered; but they – having ruled for a time as well, when he had drained from them what was there – suddenly found themselves thrown out like the others and paid the same wages. . . .[1]

It is an analysis which is by no means unconvincing. The ability to turn what might be considered a defect to a profitable end could serve a prince in Charles's position well. He was, as his dealings with Louvet, Giac, Le Camus, Richemont, and La Trémoïlle demonstrated, permanently bound to no man. The greatest danger in such a mode of behaviour lay in the possibility that the basis of support for his régime might narrow so drastically that the régime collapsed. But he was playing only for survival. The composition of his entourage was constantly changing. One grouping might replace another, but both had their bases of support among the households of the greater magnates. Political alignments were not always determined, in any case, by the situation at Charles's court. In January 1427, Richemont made an alliance with Jean I, count of Foix, in which he agreed 'not to serve nor aid our brother and nephew of Armagnac and of Pardiac against our said cousin of Foix, except by the counsel of the queen of Sicily [Yolande of Aragon] and our brother, Charles de Bourbon, count of Clermont, and by their common assent, if they were not allied together'.[2] Local feuds – in this instance that of the houses of Foix and Armagnac – could thus determine the stance of members of the factions at court. By 1427, the court consisted of three factions: the Angevins, the Bretons under Richemont, and the Gascons under Jean I, count of Foix.[3] Membership of one group did not preclude association with the others. There was no conflict of ideologies. The 'implacable hatreds' among the courtiers did not stem from their convictions, but from pragmatic considerations. Charles exploited those hatreds. Hedged around with his Scots archers, his personal loneliness must have been great, but his security was more or less assured. No faction could afford to eliminate the fount of patronage. His near-contemporary, Filippo Maria Visconti, duke of Milan (1412–47), was similarly adept. 'He continually sowed dissension among his counsellors,' wrote his biographer, Pier Candido Decembrio.[4] He too coupled good men with bad, made them spy upon each other, and used the weapons of favour and disgrace to achieve his ends. After his return, victorious, to Milan, he too never led his troops to battle in person. He too shut himself up in impenetrable

---

[1] Chastellain, II, 182–3.
[2] ABP, E.434 printed in Cosneau, *Richemont*, 525–6 (6 January 1427).

[3] See Beaucourt, II, 127, 116–19.
[4] See Muratori, op. cit., cols 994–5, 997.

retreats. Yet he was quite effective as a prince – a model of 'Renaissance tyranny' for Burckhardt.[1] Political techniques south of the Alps were not, perhaps, so very different from those to the north – even in the kingdom of Bourges.

It is just possible, given the limitations of the sources, to form some impression of what Charles's character was like at this early stage of his career. If, as has been argued, these years saw the emergence of certain characteristic traits in his personality, then it is worth inquiring about their origins. That he was distrustful needs little explanation, given the political climate of feuding and violence in which he was brought up. He could be resolute when he wished, and some of his recorded remarks convey a cynicism and a realism unusual in one so young. He could be inclement and cruel. Late in July 1418, he was stung into fury by the taunts of the Burgundian garrison at the castle of Azay-le-Rideau, between Tours and Chinon.[2] His troops took the place by assault, the captain was beheaded, and the two or three hundred men of the garrison hanged. It was not the last time that he was to react savagely to this kind of mockery of his person.[3] He could be affable and gracious in manner. In June 1429, the brothers Guy and André de Laval were particularly impressed by the way in which he greeted them, talked to others, and then came back to speak to them again.[4] There was evidently an informality in his manner, at least when dealing with men whom he knew, and with men on their own. He had charm, and knew how to exploit it. He was also well read, a good latinist, and highly literate – *literatus* in the fullest sense.[5]

We know a little about his early education. When he was eight or nine years old, his tutor, Jean de Bony, received from the royal library a small Latin Bible and a Latin treatise called *De dirivationibus nominum et*

[1] Jakob Burckhardt, *The Civilisation of the Renaissance in Italy* (New York, 2 vols, 1958), I, 53-4, where Burckhardt, using Decembrio, writes: 'his safety lay in the fact that none of his servants trusted the others, that his *condottieri* were watched and misled by spies, and that his ambassadors and higher officials were baffled and kept apart by artificially nourished jealousies, and in particular, by coupling an honest man with a knave'.
[2] Beaucourt, I, 101-2.
[3] See below, 140, for a somewhat similar, though less vindictive, instance in 1453.

[4] Letter of 8 June 1429 printed in Beaucourt, II, 218-19.
[5] Chastellain, II, 184, speaks of his vivid and fresh memory and goes on: 'he was a good *historien*, a fine story-teller, a good latinist, and very wise in council'. For Charles as a reader see below, 184, 198; also the dedication of Jean Le Bègue's translation of Leonardo Bruni's history of the First Punic War, dated 9 June 1454, where the translator writes: 'I am not ignorant that from your youth, you have been, and are, perfectly trained in Latin and rhetorical letters.' See Plate 6a, and B.N. MS. fr. 23085, fol. 1ᵛ.

verborum, covered in white leather.[1] It was presumably from these that Charles learnt his Latin and received his first lessons in grammar. By November 1416 he had in his possession his grandfather Charles V's great illuminated Breviary, which he declined to return to the executors of Jean, duke of Berry, to whom it had been given by Charles VI.[2] It was the first of the many illuminated books which we know to have come into his possession.[3] His piety was noted from an early date. As early as 1405 he had his own chapel, that is, a chaplain, vestments and a portable altar.[4] His pious gifts and religious observances were lavish and unstinting. He was received as a canon, attired in the appropriate vestments, at Loches, Tours, Notre-Dame-du-Puy and the Sainte-Chapelle of Bourges. Two days before the victory at Baugé, dressed in sackcloth, he washed the feet of twelve paupers.[5] As dauphin, he had his confessor – Gérard Machet, who remained in his service until 1417 – his almoner, and a number of chaplains. He heard two or three Masses a day.[6] At Saumur, in October 1425, we can gain some impression of the king at work. On Friday 5 October, he heard his two Masses at ten o'clock in the morning, together with the duke of Brittany, who brought him the offering and the pax. They then went into the council together, and, for the next three days, attended two sessions per day.[7] Affairs of state were never permitted to interrupt Charles's devotions.

But there was another aspect to the king's dealings with the supernatural world. He put his trust not only in God, but in astrologers. He always had around him, observed Symon des Phares in his *Recueil des plus célèbres astrologues,* 'the most expert astrologers that he could find'.[8] Chastellain agreed that the king 'strongly believed in them'.[9] By doing so, he was not only following the example of his grandfather Charles V, but was indulging in a habit shared by most of the greater men of his time. In both medicine and political prognostication, the astrologers held

---

[1] See L. Delisle, *Recherches sur la Librairie de Charles V* (Paris, 1907), II, 4, art. 8; 173, art. 1047. Henry V of England was also learning Latin at the age of eight. See K. B. McFarlane, op. cit., 115 n. 4.

[2] Delisle, op. cit., I, 187–9. The Breviary is now B.N. MS. lat. 1052.

[3] He lost at least 843 books from the royal library amassed by Charles V and Charles VI as a result of the English occupation of Paris after 1420. See Beaucourt, VI, 400–1. For later acquisitions by him see ibid., VI, 401–8.

[4] See ibid., I, 10. All the royal children had such investments made for them. At Christmas 1403 – in his first year – Charles's offering at the midnight mass was the largest. See Grandeau, op. cit., 835.

[5] See Beaucourt, I, 69, 243–4.

[6] Ibid., I, 244–5.

[7] Letter of Roulin de Mâcon to the councillors of Lyon, 12 October 1425, printed in ibid., III, 505.

[8] *Recueil des plus célèbres astrologues . . . par Symon des Phares,* ed. E. Wickersheimer (Paris, 1929), 4.

[9] Chastellain, III, 446.

sway.[1] When set beside a devotional religion which was more than normally conventional, Charles's faith in the predictions and cures of astrologers may seem bizarre, or even contradictory. Yet this was a part of
'the later medieval psychomachy, the conflict of the soul'.[2] His predilection for this area of the occult did not go unnoticed by his spiritual
advisers. From 1419 onwards it was deep enough to cause them concern.
Both Pierre d'Ailly and Jean Gerson, foremost among the theologians
and scholars of their day, warned him against this cult which, wrote
Gerson, was 'pestilential and noxious to the Christian religion'.[3] D'Ailly
told Gerson that 'I intend to write to the lord regent [Charles] that he
should beware of such superstitions'.[4] Gerson took up his pen and wrote
his *Astrologia theologizata*, attacking the prognosticators, but the previously slandered Symon des Phares considered it to be a work motivated
by envy.[5] It did not prevent Charles from giving Germain de Thibouville, doctor of medicine, one of his best astrologers, to James Stewart,
earl of Buchan, as a reward after the victory at Baugé. Thibouville went
on to serve Charles's cause by predicting the deaths of Charles VI and
Henry V correctly.[6] But Gerson returned to the assault in December
1428, when he wrote a refutation of the theories of a practitioner of
astrological medicine at Montpellier.[7] He was still concerned to discredit
the casters of horoscopes, the givers of 'elections', and those who predicted political and military events. In one of his works, he warned
Charles, as dauphin and true heir to the kingdom of France, against
spiritual seduction by 'a strange woman' who might claim to know the
future and to perform wonders.[8] It was a warning which was, once
again, to pass unheeded by the king.

[1] See Lewis, op. cit., 24–7.
[2] Ibid., 18.
[3] Beaucourt, VI, 399 n. 5.
[4] Ibid., VI, 399 n. 4.
[5] See Symon des Phares, op. cit., 249.
Gerson also sent Charles a diagram of a
game of chess in which the virtues were
set against the vices and the spirit defeated

the flesh. See A. Thomas, *Jean de Gerson et
l'éducation des dauphins de France* (Paris,
1930), 193.
[6] Symon des Phares, op. cit., 250–1.
[7] See L. Thorndike, *A History of Magic and
Experimental Science* (Columbia, 1934),
IV, 122–5.
[8] Beaucourt, VI, 399 n. 5.

Chapter 3 ✤ The King and Joan of Arc 1429–1456

> The dauphin is at Chinon, like a rat in a corner, except that he won't fight. We don't even know that he is the dauphin: his mother says he isn't; and she ought to know. . . .
>
> George Bernard Shaw, *St Joan*, Scene I.

By putting these words into the mouth of Bertrand de Poulengy, Joan of Arc's companion in arms, Shaw prepares his audience for a conventional view of the character of Charles VII. The comically pathetic figure of Shaw's imagination bears only a slight resemblance to the historical Charles VII. Aversion to warfare provides virtually the only common ground between them. Charles emerges from the play as a petulant, ineffective creature, tortured with doubts about his own legitimacy and, consequently, his right to the Crown. It is a characterisation, however, which had some basis in the historical sources for the reign. From an early date, the literature concerning Joan of Arc cast her, primarily, in the role of a psychotherapist.[1] She allegedly performed two outstanding and essential services for the king – she resolved his alleged doubts that he was 'true heir of France', and she assured him that he was indeed 'son of the king'. So that there should be no doubt of these two facts, she had him crowned and anointed at Rheims. The issue of Charles's bastardy, and hence his hereditary claim to the Crown, was not touched upon in the act by which he was disinherited by his father. Chastellain's comment that he had been 'disowned like a bastard' did not mean that he *was* a bastard.[2] He was well aware that his disinheritance had been an act of policy. But it will become apparent that this awareness could hardly profit Joan's cause, or that of her partisans.

Joan of Arc was born about 1412, at the village of Domrémy, on the

[1] The most comprehensive collection of texts relating to her 'mission' remains Jules Quicherat's *Procès de Condamnation et de Réhabilitation de Jeanne d'Arc*, 5 vols (Paris, 1849). For a recent and easily accessible survey of the literature, see R. Pernoud, *Joan of Arc, by herself and her witnesses* (English edition, tr. E. Hyams, London, 1964).

[2] See A. Thomas, 'Le "Signe Royal" et le secret de Jeanne d'Arc', *RH*, ciii (1910), 279.

borders of the duchies of Bar and Lorraine. She was the daughter, not of a peasant, but of a fairly substantial tenant farmer. There is no subsequent surviving record of her existence from the time of her childhood until May 1428, when she arrived at the castle of Vaucouleurs, where Robert de Baudricourt was captain. He held the castle in the name of the uncrowned Charles VII. Baudricourt, initially sceptical, was eventually won over and dispatched Joan with an escort to see Charles at Chinon. She claimed that she would raise the siege of Orléans which the English, under the earl of Salisbury, had begun on 12 October 1428. She arrived at Chinon pro- bably on 23 February 1429, saw Charles two days later, and evidently impressed him deeply. A month later, after an examination at Poitiers, she began her campaign against the English and their Burgundian allies by sending them a letter, calling upon them to surrender outside Orléans in God's name. On 29 April she arrived with an army to raise the siege, and on 8 May she entered the town in triumph. The following two months saw a series of French military successes, ending with a thrust to Rheims – then in Anglo-Burgundian hands – where, on 17 July 1429, Charles was crowned and anointed.

There Joan's successes ended. On 23 May 1430 she was captured by Burgundian troops at the siege of Compiègne, and two days later the University of Paris, acting in Henry VI of England's name, demanded that she be tried as a heretic. She was sold by her Burgundian captors to the English administration, and was delivered into the hands of the Inquisition. As she had been captured within the diocese of Beauvais, a com- mon Inquisitorial practice was followed and Pierre Cauchon, bishop of Beauvais – although exiled from his see because it was in territory then occupied by Charles – was appointed to judge the case by Jean Graverent, Inquisitor of France. With Cauchon sat Jean Lemaître, a preaching friar, vicar of the Inquisition in the diocese of Rouen, where the trial was held. It began with preliminary investigations and interrogation of witnesses lasting from 9 January until 26 March 1431. This was followed by the trial itself, which ended with Joan's abjuration on 24 May. On Sunday 27 May she relapsed into heresy, and the swift series of interrogations which followed this relapse ended with her being delivered to the secular power for execution. Three days later she was burnt at the stake in the Old Market Place of Rouen.

Joan of Arc has received more attention than any other female visionary of the later Middle Ages. Despite (or perhaps because of) this, the Saint has tended to oust the girl from Domrémy from serious historical investig- ation. It is appropriate that her canonisation in 1920 should have been in part a result of pressure from France upon the Holy See. She was one of the most valuable of Saints politically. Her arrival at Chinon in February 1429 was, arguably, a political act. Her execution as a heretic at Rouen in May 1431 was also, allegedly, a political act. John, duke of Bedford, could announce that she was 'a disciple and lyme of the feende called the Pucelle, that used fals enchauntments and sorcerie'.[1] Her beliefs were not strictly orthodox, at least in fifteenth-century terms. She was no friend of the earthly Church Militant. Like other mystics and visionaries, she posed a threat to the hierarchy of the Church. If men were able to communicate so directly with God – through visions or 'voices' – what need was there for the clergy? Mediation between God and Man, except through the Saints, was therefore redundant. Shaw could point to this aspect of her 'Voices' when he made Pierre Cauchon, bishop of Beauvais, exclaim:

A faithful daughter of the Church! The Pope himself at his proudest dare not presume as this woman presumes. She acts as if she herself were The Church.[2]

The fictitious Cauchon was merely being made to voice an objection which had already been made in fact – but by the other side. After her capture, Charles's adviser, Regnault de Chartres, archbishop of Rheims, told the inhabitants of the town that 'she raised herself in pride'.[3] Her pride and presumption – that *superbia* which was noted by her interrogators[4] – was her downfall. Her answers to the tribunal which tried her at Rouen served to indict her. Similarly, her avowed ability to predict and prognosticate the future course of events placed her in a very dangerous position. The line dividing permissible astrology from sorcery was thin and was becoming thinner.[5] Her trial may have been in some respects irregular, but there were many fifteenth-century men – even among those who were on the side of Charles VII – who were not unduly disturbed by her fate. It was dangerous to have so unorthodox a *fille du régiment* in your camp. Her interrogator, Guillaume Erard, could voice the views of many when he said to her on 24 May 1431: 'I'm talking to you, Joan, and I tell you that your king is a heretic and schismatic.'[6] The trial at Rouen was in part

---

[1] B.M., Cotton MS. Titus, E.V., fol. 372ᵛ (18 December 1434).
[2] Bernard Shaw, *St Joan*, ed. A. C. Ward (London, 1964), 102.
[3] See Quicherat, *Procès*, v, 168–9, and Beaucourt, II, 250.
[4] See the marginal note 'Responsio superba Johanne' in the facsimile of MS.

[1] 119 of the Bibliothèque de l'Assemblée Nationale, ed. by J. Marchand (Paris, 1955).
[5] See Thorndike, op. cit., IV, 122–3, 299–301.
[6] Deposition of Jean Massieu, in Quicherat, *Procès*, II, 17.

a device to discredit Charles VII as a heretic by association. It was conducted largely by Frenchmen, born in France. Of the 131 judges, assessors and other clergy concerned with her trial and condemnation, only eight were Englishmen. Of those eight, only two attended more than three sessions of the trial.[1] One of France's patron Saints was thus condemned by Frenchmen. She was a victim as much of a civil war within France as of a war with the English. But the role of the *collaborateurs* will be discussed later, when her second, posthumous trial is examined.[2] This, which was conducted in Charles VII's name between 1450 and 1456, was not, however, prompted by a conviction that she was a martyr, worthy of a place among the Saints. It was a procedural inquiry which resulted not in an affirmation that Joan 'had remained faithful and Catholic up to and including her death', but merely in the statement that her judges had acted improperly.[3]

Joan's career still poses many unanswered (and perhaps unanswerable) questions. What was the 'sign' given by her to Charles which, it was alleged, so effectively convinced him of his legitimacy? How was Joan able to win his confidence so quickly, and so easily? What was the king's 'secret'? Why was the trial of rehabilitation so long delayed? Many answers have been given to these questions. Some are ludicrous and many are unconvincing. Among the latter stands a recent contribution to the literature on Joan of Arc, entitled *Histoire Véridique et Merveilleuse de la Pucelle d'Orléans*.[4] Its author, M. David-Darnac, attempts to argue that she was not the daughter of a substantial tenant farmer at Domrémy, but the illegitimate child of Louis, duke of Orléans, and Isabella of Bavaria. She was born, not at Domrémy in about 1412, but in Paris on the eve of Orléans's murder in 1407. She was then (for reasons which are by no means clear) transported to Lorraine and left there in the care of the d'Arc family. David-Darnac's account of the story is fairly orthodox from this stage until her capture and trial in 1430-1. But he sees Cauchon as being concerned throughout the trial to have her released. At the very last moment, Cauchon, it is asserted, allowed her to escape by way of a secret tunnel under the walls of the castle at Rouen. To introduce such Gothic

[1] See the new edition of the *Procès de Condamnation de Jeanne d'Arc*, ed. P. Tisset and Y. Lanhers (*SHF*, Paris, 1970-2), II, 383-425, for biographies of Joan's judges and assessors. The eight Englishmen are listed on pp. 384, 385, 387, 392, 402, 404, and 421.
[2] See below, 60-1, 64, 67-9.
[3] See *La Rédaction Episcopale du Procès de*

1455-56, ed. P. Doncœur and Y. Lanhers (Paris, 1961), 19.
[4] M. David-Darnac, *Histoire Véridique et Merveilleuse de la Pucelle d'Orléans* (Paris, 1965). The main theses of this book were set out by P. Caze in 1805, by Gaston Save in 1893 and by Grillot de Givry in 1914. See C. Samaran, 'Pour la défense de Jeanne d'Arc', *ABSHF* (1952-3), 50-63.

novelist's nonsense into a work which purports to be history, albeit popular history, seems inexcusable. Joan is then said to have gone into hiding and reappears (for reasons which are again unclear) as the wife of one Robert des Armoises, a minor noble of Lorraine. A substitute has therefore to be conjured up and burned at Rouen in her stead. Undeterred by the sheer improbability of all this, David–Darnac concludes his book with an account of the activities of Joan, identified as 'la Pucelle de France', between 1436 and her supposed death in 1449.

The grounds for objection to this version of events are basically two-fold. First, Joan's date of birth has to be put back by at least four years if David–Darnac's assertions are to be entertained. A child was born to Isabella of Bavaria in 1407, but it was male and died soon after birth.[1] Joan herself said in 1431 that she was about eighteen or nineteen years old.[2] This would put her date of birth at about 1412 or 1413, at least five years after the death of her pretended father Louis of Orléans. David–Darnac also demands that the evidence of the rehabilitation process of 1455–6 is ignored. On this argument, about 150 witnesses must have perjured themselves to a man in giving evidence on Joan's early life and subsequent career. Secondly, both the thesis of Joan's bastardy and her escape from burning have been long discredited. In 1805 the thesis of bastardy was first put forward.[3] David–Darnac adduces no new documentary evidence to support that contention. Nor has the 'survival' of Joan received further documentation. A woman calling herself 'la Pucelle de France' certainly appeared in Lorraine, at Orléans and in the South-West between 1436 and 1449. A document referring to her was published by Dom Calmet, in his *History of Lorraine*, in the early eighteenth century.[4] The 'false' Joan of Arc, moreover, confessed before Charles VII and the Paris *Parlement* to being an impostor, a piece of evidence which David–Darnac chooses to ignore. There seems no reason to suppose either that Joan was not burnt by the English administration at Rouen in 1431 (as every witness at the inquiries of 1450, 1452 and 1455–6 deposed), or that she was not a girl from the borders of the duchies of Bar and Lorraine.

Her place of birth perhaps reveals something. Shortly before Joan's birth, Isabella, daughter of Charles, duke of Lorraine, had married René of Anjou, second son of Louis II of Anjou and Yolande of Aragon. The

---

[1] See Beaucourt, I, 3 n. 2, for the birth of a son, Philippe, to Isabella of Bavaria on 10 November 1407. He died on the same day.
[2] See Quicherat, *Procès*, I, 52, 65, 73, 128, 215, 216, 218.

[3] By P. Caze, on whom see Samaran, op. cit., 50, and Pernoud, op. cit., 24–5.
[4] See Calmet, *Histoire de Lorraine* (1728), III, cxcv–cxcvii. Also, for documents on the 'false' Joan of Arc, see Quicherat, *Procès*, V, 321–36.

duchy of Bar, in which Domrémy was, had become one of René's fiefs. One of Joan's first public actions was thus a visit to Charles of Lorraine at Nancy in February 1429.[1] Although she was unable to perform an act of therapeutic healing on the duke, he gave her money to go away. She had asked him to 'lend her his son-in-law [René] and some men to lead her into France'.[2] It would be impossible to prove any involvement of Yolande and the Anjou family (or its servants) in the affair. But one can certainly speculate about the means whereby Joan came to Charles at Chinon in February 1429. It is known that Yolande was one of the ladies of the court who, at Tours, examined Joan for virginity.[3] There is no evidence of opposition to Joan's 'mission' from any member of the house of Anjou. It might not be too rash a speculation to see Charles, with his known interest in astrology and the arts of prognostication, being influenced by a scheme devised by one of the political groupings at his court. He probably knew of the prophecies of Marie of Avignon, who, it was alleged, had foretold the salvation of France by means of a virgin.[4] Joan, during her short career as a military leader, was virtually inseparable from that strange patron of astrologers, Jean II, duke of Alençon.[5] To introduce a prophetess to the impressionable Charles could have been a stroke of something approaching political genius.

Who could have considered such a step both necessary and desirable? It is known that Arthur de Richemont, supported by Yolande, was reconciled with Charles VII, for the first time since late 1427, through Joan's agency.[6] (He had served in her army at the victory of Patay on 19 June 1427.) La Trémoïlle, supported by the archbishop of Rheims and Raoul de Gaucourt, *grand maître d'hôtel*, opposed this reconciliation and tried to keep Joan and the duke of Alençon apart.[7] They obviously feared displacement from power if Richemont came back to court, allied to a

[1] For a good account of these events in English, see A. Lang, *The Maid of France* (London, 1908), 77. Also Quicherat, *Procès*, I, 54; II, 391, 444; and III, 87.

[2] Lang, op. cit., 77.

[3] See P. Boissonade, 'Une étape capitale de la mission de Jeanne d'Arc', *RQH*, 3rd series, xvii (1930), 49–50. This was intended to withdraw any suspicion of sorcery.

[4] See N. Valois, 'Jeanne d'Arc et la prophétie de Marie Robine', *Mélanges Paul Fabre* (Paris, 1902), 452–67. Her book of revelations does not include this prophecy. They took place in 1398 and 1399 (ibid.,

461–2). But the book did not, apparently, contain all her visions. For an allusion to her prophecy that 'a virgin shall come after me and . . . save the kingdom' in 1456, see Quicherat, *Procès*, III, 83.

[5] See his deposition in her favour in Doncœur and Lanhers, *Rédaction*, 210–16 (3 May 1456). Also Perceval de Cagny's testimony printed in Quicherat, *Procès*, IV, ii.

[6] Beaucourt, II, 221–2.

[7] Ibid., I, 222–3; Doncœur and Lanhers, *Rédaction*, 167–8, 316 n. 85; and Perceval de Cagny in Quicherat, *Procès*, IV, 30.

3 The ruins of the castle of Chinon, at which Charles VII received Joan of Arc in February 1429

4 Portrait of Agnès Sorel by an anonymous sixteenth-century artist. It is obviously derived from the Antwerp portrait of the Virgin and Child surrounded by Angels, attributed to Jean Fouquet, *c.* 1450–60, thought to have formed the right wing of the so-called 'Melun Diptych', and it shows that the tradition of identifying the Virgin as Agnès Sorel had been established by this date (*Château de Mouchy, Paris*)

warlord such as Alençon. The archbishop, Regnault de Chartres, did not disguise his antagonism towards Joan after her capture. She 'would not take advice and did everything of her own will', he wrote.[1] To him, she deserved to be taken prisoner by the Burgundians. Others thought differently. A letter from three servants of the house of Anjou to Marie of Anjou, Charles's wife, who was pregnant at this time, and Yolande, written at Rheims on 17 July 1429, was more than enthusiastic about Joan's mission.[2] They described the coronation ceremony as 'le beau mystère', as if it were some piece of court drama. 'During the said "mystery",' they continued, 'the Maid was always close to the king, holding her standard in her hand. And it was a very fine thing to see the splendid way in which the king and the Maid behaved. God knew how much you were wished for there.'[3] It is perhaps surprising that they were not there. If Joan had been employed by any group at the court to attain some political end, then its grandest members may have thought their absence desirable. It was essential for Joan to seem as if she had come to Charles unaided by anything except the will of God and a letter of recommendation from Robert de Baudricourt, the loyal captain of Vaucouleurs. If she had come from one of Yolande's son's fiefs, a display of patronage was not politic.

What then was the sign which Joan gave to Charles in order to convince him of her good faith and the validity of her mission? She maintained that her Voices had told her that Charles 'would have a good sign so as to receive you and believe in you'.[4] Witnesses, such as the admittedly lukewarm, if not hostile, Raoul de Gaucourt, claimed in 1456 that the sign was the raising of the siege of Orléans. At her preliminary examination by the clergy at Poitiers in the spring of 1429, he claimed, she was asked the question 'What sign would she show so that her sayings would be believed?' She replied that the sign 'would be the raising of the siege of Orléans'.[5] Yet she consistently refused to tell her judges at Rouen what the sign had been which she had given to Charles at Chinon in February 1429 to convince him of his title to the Crown. Evidently, to her judges, there were two signs: one which would prove her good faith and her credibility; and another which would serve, they claimed, to banish Charles's doubts about his birth. It would be fanciful to argue that an aged drunk called Jean Batiffol of Bialon in the Auvergne underwent a revelation in June 1457 which told him that Charles did not have the

[1] Beaucourt, II, 250.
[2] Printed in Quicherat, Procès, v, 127–31.
[3] Ibid., v, 129.
[4] See Tisset and Lanhers, Procès, III,

261–2, 292–3; I, 133–4; Thomas, op. cit., 278–9.
[5] Doncœur and Lanhers, Rédaction, 167–8 (25 February 1456).

C—C

royal birthmark of the *fleur-de-lys*.[1] It hardly needed the arrival of Joan of Arc to point out the existence of that 'enseigne de roy' to Charles. Nothing is known of the obstetric peculiarities of the house of Valois.

By 22 April 1429 it was generally known at Chinon that Joan had promised to raise the siege of Orléans, to have the king crowned at Rheims (then in Anglo-Burgundian hands), and to have referred to other things 'which the king keeps strictly secret'.[2] There was as yet no reference to a 'sign' which would convince Charles of his legitimacy. It is difficult to believe that any such sign would carry conviction. To say, as her confessor Jean Pasquerel said in 1456, that she told Charles, 'I tell you, on behalf of God, that you are the true heir of France and son of the king' does not necessarily imply that any sign accompanied her words.[3] The notion of a sign which would demonstrate beyond any possible doubt that Charles was legitimate seems to have been introduced into the affair at a much later stage. Perhaps Joan was confused by her interrogators at Rouen and, as Quicherat argued, based her story on the questions put to her.[4] By introducing such things as symbolic crowns and angels into their questions, the interrogators produced a confusion between the sign of Joan's credibility and the token by which Charles would know his legitimacy. Yet a further alleged sign which she gave may have been what must have appeared to Charles as the product of divination and, to us, of telepathy. According to the writer Pierre Sala, whose *Hardiesses des grands Rois* appeared in 1516, Guillaume Gouffier, lord of Boissy, one of Charles's *chambellans*, had told him, long after the event, what the king's 'secret' was. In 1428, Sala reported, Charles had silently prayed in his oratory,

> saying nothing, but begging God in his heart that if he were indeed the true heir, of the blood and noble house of France, and the kingdom lawfully his, God would protect and defend him; or at least grant him grace to be spared death or captivity, and escape to Spain or Scotland, whose kings had long been brothers in arms and allies of the kings of France; hence he had chosen them as his last refuge.[5]

When Gouffier became aware of this secret prayer, Sala does not reveal. He could not have heard of it much before 1444, when, for the first time, he entered the king's household.[6] A telepathic chamberlain as

[1] Thomas, op. cit., pp. 279–80.

[2] Quicherat, *Procès*, IV, 426.

[3] Ibid., III, 103.

[4] See Quicherat, *Aperçus nouveaux sur l'histoire de Jeanne d'Arc* (Paris, 1850), 64–6.

[5] Extract printed in Quicherat, *Procès*, IV, 280; Beaucourt, II, 208, 253.

[6] Ibid., IV, 178. He had previously been in the household of Charles of Anjou, count of Maine. He was to be arrested on

well as a telepathic virgin impose certain strains upon one's credulity. Yet the plausibility of the sentiments ascribed to Charles depends very much on one's view of the nature of the circumstances in which he found himself. The king may have confided in some of his entourage in order to convince them of Joan's credibility some time after the first interview at Chinon in February 1429. Or the story may have been devised at a very much later date. Whatever the truth really was, Joan could not have given any token that she could prove Charles's legitimacy. No one could do that. It is, in any case, not clear that he wished for any such proof. But he was evidently prepared to put the girl to the test. If she could raise the siege of Orléans, she would serve her purpose. If she could get him crowned at Rheims, so much the better. After all, his astrologer, Master Pierre de St-Valerin, was in favour of her.[1]

The rapid sequence of events which was the career of Joan of Arc has often been related and it is not intended to repeat that account here.[2] It is Charles's attitude and behaviour towards the Maid which must be evaluated. First, what did he hope to gain from her? Second, why was no attempt made by him to have her released from captivity after she had been taken outside Compiègne on 23 May 1430? Third, why was the process of rehabilitation so long delayed?

In order to assess what Charles hoped to gain from Joan, it is necessary to consider the circumstances in which he found himself in February 1429. The previous two years had been turbulent. With the rise to favour of La Trémoïlle, the constable Richemont had gone into open rebellion against the court.[3] Allied to the counts of Clermont, Pardiac and Armagnac, Richemont had taken the castle of Bourges itself. But Charles recovered the place in person, and, on 17 July 1428, granted letters of pardon to the rebel magnates. It was a victory for him, supported by the houses of Albret, Foix, Anjou, Alençon, and Jean de Blois, the Penthièvre claimant to the duchy of Brittany. It could be argued that Richemont's rebellion was more a product of the dispute which had raged between the families of Montfort and Penthièvre over their claims to Brittany than a result of

charges of necromancy and conspiracy against the king in January 1457 (ibid., VI, 119–20 and 453–4). Sala claimed that he told him that the 'secret' had been divulged by Charles when Gouffier slept, as a *mignon*, in the king's bed.
[1] Ibid., II, 210 n. 1; VI, 399. Also Symon des Phares, op. cit., 253.

[2] Among a voluminous literature, the works of Andrew Lang and Régine Pernoud (above, p. 50 n. 1 and p. 45 n. 1) provide reasonably satisfactory narratives for the English reader. Both seem to me over-indulgent towards Joan.
[3] For what follows, see Beaucourt, II, 154–65; Cosneau, *Richemont*, 141–64.

Charles's 'mismanagement' of the affairs of the kingdom.[1] It was yet another instance of the constable's pursuit of self-interest under the cloak of the 'public weal'. By the early months of 1429, it is normally held, Charles's situation was 'desperate'. How far is this a just appraisal of the position at that time?

The passage already quoted from Pierre Sala's much later work of 1516 retells a story which was common by that date. That it was common in 1429 is not so certain. The evidence for the king's desire to flee to Spain or Scotland is reported by foreign, and posterior, witnesses.[2] His alleged plan to seek refuge in Scotland was, naturally, reported by a Scots chronicler, known as the Religious of Dumfermline. Thomas Basin, writing at least forty years after the event, thought that he was planning to flee to Spain. Other sources give the perhaps more plausible information that Charles intended to withdraw to the Dauphiné if Orléans was taken by the Anglo-Burgundians. Matthieu Thomassin, in his *Registre Delphinal*, commissioned by the dauphin Louis (later Louis XI) in May 1456, reported the view of some of Charles's advisers that 'if it [Orléans] were taken, it was unnecessary to take account of the rest of the kingdom, given the state it was in, and there was no remedy except to withdraw my lord the dauphin [Charles] into this land of the Dauphiné, and to keep him there while awaiting God's grace'.[3] The local origins of a fifteenth-century chronicler could thus have some effect on his reporting of events. But, even if Charles was advised to retire to the Dauphiné, the extent of his kingdom was still not derisory. With the exception of English Gascony, the greater part of Southern France was in his hands, and the *sénéchaussées* of Lyon, Toulouse, Carcassonne and Beaucaire-Nîmes accounted for the loyalty of the Languedoc. It was from these areas that recurrent grants of taxation came throughout this period of the reign.[4] It is not obvious that, to quote a recent writer on Joan of Arc, 'the case was, indeed, desperate' and that this 'is attested by all the writings of the times'.[5] Orléans was undoubtedly a strongpoint of great strategic significance, for it opened the way to the south of the Loire and the very centre of Charles's power. But, benefiting from La Trémoïlle's loans to Charles, the besieged inhabitants and garrison within the town showed every sign of holding out for a long time.[6] On 24 October 1428, moreover, the earl of Salisbury, commanding the besieging Anglo-Burgundian army, was killed by a cannon

[1] See Cosneau, *Richemont*, 153–6.
[2] Beaucourt, II, 175–6; Basin, I, 6–8; Quicherat, *Procès*, v, 339–40.
[3] Printed in ibid., IV, 308–9.

[4] Beaucourt, II, 630–2; Dodu, op. cit., 65–6.
[5] Pernoud, op. cit., 56.
[6] Beaucourt, II, 172–4, 175.

shot in the fort of the Tourelles. Burgundian participation at the siege was at best half-hearted, and a dispute between Philip the Good and John, duke of Bedford, in February 1429 led to the withdrawal of Burgundian troops.

The situation was perhaps not quite as desperate as the partisans of St Joan and her 'mission' have been concerned to show. The English themselves, indeed, were apparently not happy with the decision which led to the march on Orléans. The council of England and the regency council in France debated hotly the question as to whether a consolidation of the position in Normandy, Maine and on the frontiers of Anjou and Brittany was not to be preferred to the sally which Salisbury made to Orléans. Bedford himself, admittedly in a document of December 1434, told the twelve-year-old Henry VI that in France 'alle thing there prospered for you til the tyme of the Siege of Orléans, taken in hande God knoweth by what advis'.[1] In the event, the siege was raised. It was, a modern commentator observes, 'the essential feat of arms, the very sign of her [Joan's] mission'.[2] It was a feat of arms partly achieved by unorthodox means. Joan sent three letters of summons to the English at Orléans, calling upon them to surrender in the name of the 'King of Heaven'. Her letters were headed 'Jhesu Maria', and this might breed suspicion of her devotion to the novel (and suspect) cult of the name of Jesus. One of its exponents, a Franciscan known as Brother Richard, active in producing a wave of religious mania at Orléans in 1430, was to be forbidden by the pro-French archbishop to preach at Poitiers in March 1431. The cult did not have the sanction of Pope Martin V, but it did have the sanction of his rival, the anti-pope Calixtus.[3] To employ such means in the reconquest of one's kingdom could be, to say the least, embarrassing for a king.

By converting the Anglo-French conflict into a religious war, Joan performed a great service for Charles VII. But it was in another sense a disservice. The fears felt by his advisers on the vexed question of Joan's orthodoxy were to rise to the surface again later in the reign. Unless it could be proved that Joan was neither a heretic, a schismatic, nor a sorceress, the claim could always be made by the king's enemies that he owed his kingdom to the work of the Devil. The commission of inquiry at Poitiers which declared her to be of irreproachable life, a good Christian, possessed of the virtues of humility, virginity, honesty and simplicity, in

---

[1] B.M., Cotton MS. Titus, E.V., fol. 372ʳ.
[2] Pernoud, op. cit., 72.
[3] See J. de la Martinière, 'Frère Richard et Jeanne d'Arc à Orléans, mars–juillet 1430', *MA*, xliv (1934), 189–98. For Joan's views on Anti-Christ and Christ-the-King, which bear similarities to those held by San Bernardino of Siena and St Vincent Ferrier, see E. Delaruelle, in *Atti del 3º Convegno Storico Internazionali, Ottobre 1960* (Todi, 1962).

April 1429, could have appeared to the king's enemies as a partisan tribunal.[1] The theologians at Poitiers did not pronounce on her divine inspiration. They merely told Charles that there was a 'favourable presumption' to be made for the divine nature of her mission. It could, moreover, be argued that a treatise favourable to her, attributed to the hand of Jean Gerson, allegedly written between March 1429 and the great theologian's death on 12 July, may not be his work at all.[2] Given his warnings to Charles in 1419 on the errors of 'strange women' claiming to predict the future and perform wonders, the treatise *De Quadam Puella* sits rather uneasily on his shoulders.[3] The propagandists of the 'Dauphinist' cause could act in as partisan a fashion as the propagandists of the Anglo-Burgundian alliance when they so wished. To attribute to Gerson a work justifying Joan added weight to the cause. Whatever the truth of the matter, the judges at Poitiers in April 1429 told the king what he, perhaps, wanted to know. To put Joan to the test, they said, was an obligation upon him. 'To doubt or abandon her without suspicion of evil,' they wrote, 'would be to repudiate the Holy Spirit and to become unworthy of God's aid.'[4] The test would be the raising of the siege of Orléans. It was a very convenient test for God to have proposed.

Once Orléans had been relieved in May, the second part of Joan's divinely inspired mission was undertaken by Charles – his consecration and coronation at Rheims. It has recently been observed that 'strictly speaking a king's coronation was simply a blessing upon a king already created; but popular feeling seems to have been that a king was hardly a proper king without coronation and unction'.[5] But, as befits popular feeling, the notion was a little archaic in 1429. When the practice of election to kingship disappeared in favour of hereditary right, as it had long disappeared in France, the coronation ceremony no longer 'made' the king.[6] The regnal years by which the formal documents of his chancery were dated did not begin at Charles VII's coronation at Rheims on 17 July 1429. By that time he was already in the seventh year of his reign as king. No change was introduced into the practice of his chancery. On 30 October 1422 Charles had been acclaimed king by the lords loyal to his

---

[1] See Boissonade, op. cit., 28–32.

[2] It was first published in the Cologne edition of Gerson's works in 1483–4. For an attempt to attribute it to Gerson, see D. G. Wayman, 'The Chancellor and Jeanne d'Arc, February–July 1429', *Franciscan Studies*, xvii (1957), 273–305. In the Strasbourg edition of 1514, the

ascription to Gerson is doubted (ibid., 284).

[3] See above, 44.

[4] See Quicherat, *Procès*, III, 391–2; Boissonade, op. cit., 59.

[5] Lewis, op. cit., 82.

[6] See B. Guenée, *L'Occident aux xive et xve siècles. Les Etats* (Paris, 1971), 136. Also below, 215.

cause, by virtue of his hereditary right to the Crown. The coronation at Rheims was thus, in some respects, otiose. On 22 February 1456, Jean, count of Dunois, justified Joan's insistence on consecration at Rheims by quoting what he recalled as her words. She said, 'when the king shall be crowned and consecrated, the power of [his] enemies will always be lessened, nor will they ultimately be able to harm him or the kingdom'.[1] The events of the following twenty-four years did not all bear out her prediction. It was made in reply to the members of a council which Charles was consulting after the victory at Orléans. Joan, Dunois reported, burst in to the king's secret chamber at Loches, fell to her knees, kissed his feet, and exclaimed 'Noble Dauphin, do not hold any more such long-winded councils; but come as soon as possible to the crown of which you are worthy at Rheims'.[2]

Regnault de Chartres's later observation that Joan 'would not take advice and did everything of her own will'[3] was not entirely inapposite. Relying solely on her 'Voices', she had no need of earthly counsels, and the protracted debates of the council chamber irked her sorely. But, as Dunois deposed in 1456, after the relief of Orléans 'the lords of the blood royal and the captains wished that the king would go to Normandy and not to Rheims'.[4] It was a perfectly sensible idea. A blow struck at Normandy – the stronghold of Bedford's régime – with the retreating English forces reeling from the shock delivered by the 'miraculous' victory of the Maid, might serve to break the deadlock. But, Dunois went on, even the hardened soldiers in the council were won over, and all, he alleged, agreed to put their faith in Joan's Voices. An advance on Paris, which might have been made possible if Normandy and Beauce had been attacked, was now to be delayed until the following year.[5] Volunteers came to serve the Maid – it was as though a popular preacher had roused the hearts of the soldiery. Her army, with her banner bearing the name of Jesus, her standard bearing the image of Christ in Judgement, her banner showing Christ Crucified, with the mendicant friars marching in front of the troops, singing hymns and anthems, was like a revivalist meeting in motion. The astonished inhabitants of Troyes could go as far as to send Brother Richard himself out to meet her. On her own testimony, he came towards her, crossing himself and sprinkling holy water, lest she be possessed by the Devil.[6] To the more ribald among the Anglo-Burgundian soldiery, she

[1] Doncœur and Lanhers, *Rédaction*, 165.
[2] Ibid., 165.
[3] Quicherat, *Procès*, IV, 168-9.

[4] Doncœur and Lanhers, *Redaction*, 165; Beaucourt, II, 215-16, 224, 239.
[5] Ibid., II, 237-8.
[6] Quicherat, *Procès*, I, 100.

was 'the Armagnac's whore'. But to the God-fearing among her enemies, she was a heretic and sorceress, using the black arts to conjure them out of France.

On 23 May 1430, outside Compiègne, Joan was captured by the Burgundians. Much has been made of the 'betrayal' of the Maid by Charles VII. Some historians, such as Quicherat, saw Charles playing a double game from an earlier date.[1] On 28 August 1429, one month after the coronation at Rheims, a truce was made, excepting Paris, with Philip the Good of Burgundy, until Christmas Day of that year. On 18 September the city of Paris and its neighbourhood were included in the truce.[2] There was no possibility of recovering the capital without breaking the truce. Was the coincidence of this diplomatic activity with Joan's mission evidence that Charles had already decided to betray her? It was not the first time that truces had been made with Burgundy. Since the beginning of the reign, through the mediation of the duke of Savoy, discussions had been in progress. Joan herself, moreover, could write to Philip the Good on 17 July 1429 calling on him to make 'a good firm peace, which will last a long time'.[3] Reconciliation between France and Burgundy was not anathema to her. With the ceremony at Rheims, Joan confessed, her mission was at an end. Her Voices, she claimed, ceased.[4] From 17 July onwards she was in the hands not of God, but of men. The subsequent course of her career was determined by the war party in Charles's council – Dunois, Alençon and their friends. On 8 September their attack on Paris failed. Regnault de Chartres and Raoul de Gaucourt, who negotiated the truce of 18 September, saw that the Maid had begun to outlive her usefulness. Alençon was urging for her to be sent to Normandy, but the council was divided.[5] Joan was kept in a state of inaction until she escaped, without Charles's permission, to fight again at Lagny. Two months later she was taken at Compiègne.

Why did Charles VII make no attempt to have her released from captivity? Beaucourt could argue that he was at the mercy of evil advisers and could not help her.[6] By April 1430 he had already begun the diplomatic exchanges which were to result in an important treaty of alliance drawn up between him and Jean V, duke of Brittany, on 5 December 1430.[7] The 'way of peace' might lead to more tangible gains than the

---

[1] See Beaucourt, 'Jeanne d'Arc trahie par Charles VII', *RQH* (1867), 1–2.
[2] Ibid., 3–6.
[3] Ibid., 3.

[4] Ibid., 6; Beaucourt, II, 230–1.
[5] Ibid., II, 238–9.
[6] Ibid., II, 251–2.
[7] Ibid., II, 271–2.

prosecution of open war. There is no evidence for any attempt by Charles to retrieve Joan from the hands of the English, to whom she had been sold on 21 November 1430. But there is a receipt from Dunois, dated 14 March 1431, which acknowledged the payment to him by the king of 2,000 *livres tournois* for the cost of an expedition which he was to lead 'into the lands beyond the river Seine', that is, into Normandy.[1] Beaucourt, anxious to defend Charles, associated this expedition with an attempt to recover Joan. There is no further evidence. The king's attitude towards her fate is given only in sources which post-date the event by many decades. Pierre Sala, Pope Pius II, and the poet Valeran Varanius asserted that Charles was much saddened by the news of her death at Rouen.[2] But their testimony is worth little. From her capture in May 1430 until the opening of the first inquiry into her case by Guillaume Bouillé, canon of Noyon, in February 1450, the king observed an unbroken silence on the affair.

His silence prompts a third, and final, question. Why was there so long a delay before a second trial – the process of rehabilitation – took place? There were three obstacles in the way until 1449.[3] First Charles needed to hold Paris, because the University had provided assessors for the trial of condemnation at Rouen which began on 9 January and ended with her execution on 30 May 1431. In May 1430, the doctors and masters of the University of Paris, then in Anglo-Burgundian hands, wrote to Philip the Good of Burgundy requesting that Joan should be 'put into the hands of the Church's justice, to be duly tried for her idolatries and other things touching our holy Faith'.[4] From the very beginning of the proceedings against her, the University played an active part. It was only to be expected that it should be permitted to hear, and answer, the case against it. It was not until April 1436 that Paris was recovered for Charles VII by the constable Richemont. Similarly, Rouen had to be in Charles's hands before any form of inquiry could be begun. The documents relating to the trial of condemnation were kept at Rouen, and the town did not fall to Charles until November 1449. Thirdly, the consent of the Papacy was essential if the inquiry was to be a valid one. Relations between the popes and the Crown of France during the reign of Charles VII were nothing if not stormy. It was, regrettably, essential that an inquiry should proceed with the blessing of the Holy See. The tribunal which tried Joan had, after all, been established by the Inquisitor of France.

[1] Ibid., II, 254-5.
[2] See Quicherat, *Procès*, IV, 281-2, 518; V, 84-5.

[3] For what follows, see Beaucourt, II, 256-8.
[4] Quicherat, *Procès*, I, 9 (16 May 1430).

Thus it was not until 15 February 1450 that the theologian Guillaume Bouillé, doctor of the University of Paris, dean of Noyon, was ordered by Charles VII to inquire into the 'faults and abuses' committed by her judges and assessors at Rouen almost twenty years previously.[1] It was an embarrassing situation. A member of the University of Paris was being required to re-examine a verdict reached on the advice of other members of the same University. What made it even more embarrassing was that some of them were still alive, some holding eminent positions within Church and State. The wording of the king's order to Bouillé suggests two motives: first, a desire to ascertain the facts about the trial; secondly, to use those facts, if possible, against the English, who were still holding part of Normandy, as well as Gascony, in February 1450. There was as yet no question of Joan's rehabilitation, let alone her sanctity. 'We wish,' wrote Charles, 'to know the truth about the said process and in what manner it was conducted.'[2] That was all. There was a suspicion of unjust condemnation, prompted by 'the great hatred which our said enemies had against her'.[3] But there was no question, at this stage, of Charles's honour being impugned, and no question of this inquiry leading to a revocation by the Inquisition of its own sentence. The conscience which prompted the inquiry may have been Bouillé's, not the king's – he was evidently a man fervent in Joan's cause and ashamed of the allegedly partisan behaviour of his own University. He was in fact prepared to act in favour of a girl whom his own bishop, Jean de Mailly, at Noyon, had sent to the scaffold in May 1431. Now Jean de Mailly was aged about fifty-four in 1450, but his memories were – probably intentionally – very vague when he was called upon to depose at a later inquiry. On 12 June 1431 he had signed the letters, issued in Henry VI's name, whereby protection was guaranteed to all concerned in the case against Joan.[4] Since then, Jean de Mailly had changed his tune. He received Charles VII at the gates of Noyon in 1443, and was to live on, as a loyal Frenchman, until 1472.[5] He had been compromised beyond redemption in 1431. It was hardly surprising if some members of the ecclesiastical hierarchy of France in the 1450s were not enthusiastic about plans to rehabilitate a victim of their own previous disloyalty.

---

[1] See Doncœur and Lanhers, *La Réhabilitation de Jeanne la Pucelle: l'Enquête ordonnée par Charles VII en 1450 et le Codicile de Guillaume Bouillé* (Paris, 1956), 33–5 endorsed 'by the king, at the relation of his *grand conseil*'.

[2] Ibid., 33.

[3] Loc. cit.

[4] Doncœur and Lanhers, *Bouillé*, 7–8; for Henry VI's letters see Doncœur and Lanhers, *La Minute française des Interrogatoires de Jeanne la Pucelle* (Melun, 1956), 14–15.

[5] See Tisset and Lanhers, *Procès*, II, 414–15.

The unlocking of a cupboard which contained a skeleton which twenty-eight members of the French clergy would have preferred to forget was not without its dangers. Guillaume Bouillé's inquiry was suddenly broken off in March 1450, before the dossiers and minutes of the trial of condemnation had even been examined.[1] The war was still in full cry in Normandy against the retreating English, and there was trouble with the Papacy over the vexed question of the Pragmatic Sanction of Bourges.[2] Perhaps the time was not opportune for a large-scale inquiry. But there was another prominent ecclesiastic to whom its pursuit could hardly have been desirable. Raoul Roussel, archbishop of Rouen, had been a canon of the cathedral there in 1429.[3] On 7 November of that year he had replaced the exiled Gerson as a canon of Notre Dame in Anglo-Burgundian Paris. Roussel had been a counsellor and *maître des requêtes* of the English administration at Rouen, and received the archbishopric in 1444. He had been a loyal supporter of the English cause in Normandy until he too took the oath to Charles VII in 1450. He too was compromised, but his death on 3 December 1452 removed a substantial obstacle to the rehabilitation proceedings. He was not summoned to the inquiry of February–March 1450. But one of his colleagues at the trial of 1431 did come to testify before Bouillé's commission. He was the unwholesome Jean Beaupère, canon of Rouen, who was to live on until 1462.[4] As a result of the letters of pardon which Charles VII had issued to all holding benefices in Rouen after its recovery in November 1449, Beaupère had kept his canonry.[5] He had received it from Henry VI in April 1431 while Joan's trial was in progress. Of the seven witnesses summoned in 1450, Beaupère was the only hostile one.

He refused to answer questions relating to the procedure at the trial of condemnation. Joan, he said, was a fraud. She was 'subtle, of the subtlety belonging to women' but, to his mind, 'if the said Joan had had wise and frank teachers, she would have said many things serving to justify her, and withheld many which led to her condemnation'.[6] It was not surprising that his evidence was discounted in the codicil which Bouillé drew up for

---

[1] Doncœur and Lanhers, *Bouillé*, 10.
[2] See Doncœur and Lanhers, *L'Enquête du Cardinal d'Estouteville en 1452* (Paris, 1958), 7–9. The Pragmatic allowed the king very great freedom in provision to benefices and gave the concept of a 'Gallican' Church some reality in fact. See, for its operation, N. Valois, *La Pragmatique Sanction de Bourges sous Charles VII* (Paris, 1906). Also Beaucourt, III, 332–61, for the context in which it was issued in 1438.
[3] See Doncœur and Lanhers, *Bouillé*, 11; *Estouteville*, 20–1; Tisset and Lanhers, *Procès*, ii, 422.
[4] Doncœur and Lanhers, *Bouillé*, 15; Tisset and Lanhers, *Procès*, II, 385–6.
[5] Ibid., 386; *Ord.*, xiv, 76, art. 3.
[6] Doncœur and Lanhers, *Bouillé*, 15.

the king's information. Bouillé did not say whether or not the king had initiated the inquiry. But he declared that it was in the king's interest to pursue the matter further. The very important notion that it was essential to clear Joan of the charges of heresy and sorcery made against her in order to defend the king's own honour appears in Bouillé's *Mémoire*, probably written late in 1450 or early in 1451. The king was not bound to keep silence, he wrote, on an 'iniquitous, scandalous sentence which threatens his crown'.[1] It was an argument which was taken up two years later by another ecclesiastic anxious to ingratiate himself with the king, the cardinal Guillaume d'Estouteville.[2] By that time it seemed, and had to seem, beyond doubt that Joan's judges had acted contrary to justice. Many of them, said the compromised Martin Ladvenu, acted 'more through love of the English and the favour they had from them . . . than through zeal for justice or the Faith'.[3] The majority of the witnesses at Bouillé's inquiry denounced the English for their sentiments of revenge against Joan, and above all for their attempt to dishonour Charles VII's title by making him guilty of heresy by association. But the king did not take the initiative. It was left to the papal legate in France to take the unfortunate affair further.

The legate, Cardinal Guillaume d'Estouteville, had been appointed by Pope Nicholas V to negotiate an Anglo-French peace so that the Turkish threat to the West might be contained.[4] The previous papal legate had been commissioned to convoke an assembly of the French clergy at Rouen in December 1449. The assembly was to discuss the abrogation by the pope of the Pragmatic Sanction of Bourges.[5] This, the bastion of the liberties of the Gallican Church, was again under attack in 1450. On 9 March, Charles VII wrote to Nicholas V informing him that the assembly at Rouen had proved inconclusive.[6] The arrival of Estouteville in France was not greeted with enthusiasm by the king. He had already been kept at Rome, waiting until 'he knew the good will of the king on this matter'.[7] Why was the cardinal concerned to have Joan of Arc rehabilitated?

[1] Donceur and Lanhers, *Bouillé*, 9, 20.

[2] See P. Ourliac, 'La Pragmatique Sanction et la légation en France du Cardinal d'Estouteville (1451–3)', *Mélanges d'archéologie et d'histoire de l'Ecole française de Rome* (1938), 403–32.

[3] Donceur and Lanhers, *Bouillé*, 43.

[4] See Ourliac, op. cit., 403–5; Donceur and Lanhers, *Estouteville*, 8–11.

[5] Ibid., 7–8; Beaucourt, v, 203–4.

[6] B.N., MS. lat. 5414ᵃ, fol. 94ʳ.

[7] Donceur and Lanhers, *Estouteville*, 11, 12. For Charles's reply to Estouteville's envoy on 28 September 1451, see B.N., MS. fr. nouv. acq. 1001, fol. 42ʳ. The king was present at Taillebourg when the reply was given to Master Guillaume Seguin. Estouteville was to be kept at Rome until he told the king the reason for his coming to France. Charles cited the Pragmatic against permitting the legate to enter the kingdom.

First, his family had been devoted partisans of Charles VII's cause in Normandy. They had lost lands and goods during the English occupation of 1417–49. Secondly, he desired to clear the king of any suspicion of guilt through association with a condemned heretic. Thirdly, and perhaps most importantly, Estouteville was anxious to demonstrate his loyalty to the land of his birth. As the representative of Nicholas V in France, and therefore a defender of the pope's rights against those of the king, he was concerned to stress his interest in upholding Charles's honour. But, although Estouteville could inform the king in May 1452 that 'I know that the matter greatly concerns your honour and estate [and] I am working on it with all my power . . . just as a good and loyal servant should do for his lord', it is unlikely that the king received this pledge with much pleasure.[1] After all, he was not anxious to receive a legate who was about to undertake the summons of the next assembly of the clergy at Bourges in order to discuss the Pragmatic yet again.

It was not until early in July 1452 that Charles consented even to see Estouteville.[2] Guillaume Bouillé had already introduced the notion that the king's 'honour and estate' had been damaged by Joan's trial and condemnation. The idea was to be taken up and exploited by Estouteville. Although he handed over the inquiry to the Inquisitor of France, Jean Bréhal, it was he with whom the responsibility for pressing the case lay. Estouteville served two masters – the pope and the king. In the state of Franco–papal relations as they existed in 1452, the insistence with which Estouteville argued that it was Charles's honour, as well as Joan's, which was at stake could have been a device to put pressure on the king. A rehabilitation which, Estouteville alleged, was much desired by the king himself, was perhaps to be granted by Rome only at the price of revoking the Pragmatic Sanction. If Charles's silence is indicative of anything, it seems that the cardinal may have been wrong in his reading of the king's sentiments. Charles merely wished to know the facts about the case, not to institute proceedings which might lead to a demonstration of papal sovereignty, through the operation of the Inquisition, within Gallican France. The king was as concerned as Henry VI had been in 1431 to prevent an appeal to Rome.[3] But, by December 1452, after Estouteville's unwanted intervention, the affair would not rest. In a letter of 31 December, Bréhal observed to Brother Leonard of Vienne, an eminent theologian whose advice he was seeking, that the matter was one 'which concerns

[1] Doncœur and Lanhers, *Estouteville*, 11–12, 13, 28–9.
[2] Ibid., 30; Beaucourt, v, 209–10.

[3] See Doncœur and Lanhers, *Minute française*, 14; *Rédaction*, 291–4 (12 June 1431).

the honour of the very Christian king [Charles VII] and which he has very much at heart'.[1] There is no evidence that the king shared the ardour imputed to him.

The problem of the *collaborateurs* became an acutely embarrassing one. If Estouteville, Bouillé and Bréhal were to have their way, the process of rehabilitating Joan of Arc could become a trial of her surviving judges and assessors. Letters of remission, abolition and pardon could be – and were – issued to them, but such letters could be contested. Charles was anxious to have the learned opinions of canonists and theologians, Bréhal wrote, 'especially foreigners, so that it should appear that all partisan spirit is excluded from this affair'.[2] But if Bréhal and his zealous associates proceeded much further they might easily revive 'partisan spirit' within a recently pacified France. Old wounds and old party slogans – 'Armagnac' and 'Burgundian' – could be re-opened and re-adopted if proceedings were initiated against any of the judges and assessors from the trial of 1431.[3] They now lived under the sovereignty, and in the favour, of Joan's 'Dauphin'. It has already been shown how Jean de Mailly, Jean Beaupère and Raoul Roussel were incriminated beyond salvation in the condemnation of 1431.[4] At Estouteville's inquiry of May 1452, two more *collaborateurs* appeared to give evidence, both canons of Rouen cathedral. Nicholas Caval and André Marguerie were both regular attenders at Joan's trial but neither remembered very much about it in May 1452.[5] Both lived on – Caval until 1457, Marguerie until 1465. Guillaume du Desert, also canon of Rouen, was one of the men responsible for drawing up the articles of Estouteville's inquiry. On 29 May 1431 he had signed the declaration of Joan's relapse into heresy.[6] Two vital witnesses – Raoul Roussel, archbishop of Rouen, and Jean le Maître, vicar of the Inquisitor in 1431 – were not summoned before the inquiry. The spectacle of an archbishop being cross-examined about his previous improper behaviour in his own see was not desirable. It might lead to mockery of the Church.

By 3 January 1453, Estouteville had returned to Rome.[7] His mission had not been successful. But he was determined to pursue the affair of Joan of Arc further. Bréhal was diligently collecting information and learned opinion on the case. Almost two years were to elapse before the next, and final, stage was begun. It was again not initiated by the king. In the spring of 1455, the mother and brothers of Joan suddenly addressed a

---

[1] Doncœur and Lanhers, *Estouteville*, 31–2.
[2] Ibid., 32.
[3] Cf. A. Bossuat in *Recovery of France*, 78–9.
[4] See above, 60–1.

[5] Doncœur and Lanhers, *Estouteville*, 19–20; Tisset and Lanhers, *Procès*, II, 392, 416.
[6] Ibid., II, 397; Doncœur and Lanhers, *Estouteville*, 14. He died in 1471.
[7] Ibid., 32.

petition to the new pope, Calixtus III.[1] They demanded the reparation of Joan's honour, a redress of the injustice which she had suffered, and, most riskily of all, the citation of her judges of 1431, or their heirs and successors, before a tribunal of rehabilitation. It was political dynamite. On 11 June 1455, Calixtus and Estouteville replied to the petition of the d'Arc family.[2] In the papal rescript, pope and cardinal were now concerned to stress not the honour of Charles VII, but that of the d'Arc family. The petition was probably Estouteville's work, for he was the family's 'representative' at Rome. His motives can only be guessed at. In reply to the piteous complaint, Calixtus appointed three of the most eminent men among the higher clergy of France to cite the Inquisitor and promoter of criminal cases in the diocese of Beauvais to appear before them.[3] They were to act in conjunction with the Inquisitor of France, Jean Bréhal. Joan had been tried by the bishop of Beauvais, in whose diocese she was captured.[4] It was incumbent upon the diocesan authorities to repudiate the sentence of its own tribunal. One of the more remarkable features of the rehabilitation proceedings of 1455-6 was that they never did so.

Of the three delegates appointed by the pope, the most distinguished was Jean Juvenal des Ursins, archbishop of Rheims, first in precedence among the spiritual peers of France. His attitude towards his task has often been commented upon. It has been observed that he was 'hostile' to Joan.[5] This is to read too much into his evident reticence towards the affair. But this reticence is explicable. First, he himself was Cauchon's successor in the diocese of Beauvais, where he had held the see from 1432 until his translation to Laon in 1444.[6] It was a pedigree which hardly assisted the doctrine of apostolic succession. As a staunch defender of the Pragmatic Sanction, Jean Juvenal could hardly look with indulgence upon the efforts of both Calixtus III and Estouteville to interfere in the internal affairs of the French Church and, indeed, the kingdom of France. A supporter of Charles VII's cause from an early date, it might be expected that he would embrace Joan's cause with vigour. But, in a letter of 7 November 1455, he cautioned Joan's mother against proceeding with her

---

[1] Doncœur and Lanhers, *Rédaction*, 8-9.
[2] Ibid., 9.
[3] They were Jean Juvenal des Ursins, archbishop of Rheims, Richard Olivier de Longueil, bishop of Coutances, and Guillaume Chartier, bishop of Paris (ibid., 9; Quicherat, *Procès*, II, 95-8).
[4] It was common Inquisitorial procedure to appoint the bishop in whose see a suspected heretic was found to assist in trying the

case. Cauchon was exiled from his see because it was in Charles VII's hands in 1430. There was thus nothing particularly 'irregular' in Cauchon's participation in Joan's trial. See H. C. Lea, *History of the Inquisition of the Middle Ages* (London, 1888), III, 388-91.
[5] See Doncœur and Lanhers, *Rédaction*, 13.
[6] Ibid., 11-12. He became archbishop of Rheims in 1449.

family's claim.[1] She should, he wrote, reflect well before embarking on a course of action of which the issue was uncertain. The proceedings should be inspired only by 'the purest concern for the Faith'. What other motives did he fear? Perhaps a spirit of revenge animated the d'Arc family, especially the desire to revenge themselves on Joan's judges and assessors. Or Jean Juvenal may have been concerned for the cause of Gallicanism – the Pragmatic could not be revoked at any price. His view of the *rationale* behind the rehabilitation is noteworthy. He wrote to Jean d'Aulon, seneschal of Beaucaire, on 20 April 1456, that it was the English who wished to maintain that Joan was a 'sorceress and heretic and invoker of devils; and that, by this means, the king had recovered his kingdom; and so they held the king and those who have served him [to be] heretics. . . .'[2] Bouillé and Estouteville had evidently had some degree of success in providing the more reluctant of the king's servants with a pretext on which to justify an inquiry.

One of the notable features of this species of justification was that, in 1456, it hardly held water. Charles VII had not recovered very much of his kingdom by means of Joan of Arc's alleged heresy and sorcery. The English, in the 1450s, were not apparently alleging that he had done so. In 1444, Henry VI had married Charles's niece, Margaret of Anjou.[3] There was no question of the Lancastrians resurrecting the affair, which had become a matter of past history. The attitude of the house of York to Charles's heresy by association is not clear. It could be that the partisans of Richard, duke of York, were making such allegations against him at a time when the fate of Henry VI's government was uncertain. But York had not claimed the crown in 1456, and it was unlikely that an attempt would be made by him to recover the 'ancient inheritance' of Normandy and Gascony.[4] The concern displayed by Jean Juvenal for Charles VII's 'honour and estate' was thus, perhaps, not entirely spontaneous. It may have been provoked by skilful exploitation of the case by Estouteville and the supporters of papal intervention in the affairs of the Gallican Church. Military victories, if nothing else, had convinced many that God was on the side of the Valois. But caution was still necessary. If the quashing of the sentence against Joan would serve to clear away even the slightest remaining objection to Charles's claim to sovereignty over his kingdom, then the sentence must be quashed. There was no need for any positive pronunciation on the question of Joan's orthodoxy. As long as the negative verdict that she was unjustly condemned could be returned, then the

---

[1] Doncœur and Lanhers, *Rédaction*, 14.
[2] Ibid., 297.
[3] See below, 137.
[4] See below, 156–8.

inquiry need not go further than a denunciation of Cauchon's procedure at the trial of 1431. This would lead inexorably to the annulment of the sentence, on the grounds that her judges and assessors had proceeded improperly, through fear, malice, or merely error.

On 7 July 1456, the process of rehabilitation ended with the annulment of their sentence. The victim was said to have been tried as a result of 'false articles of accusation'.[1] Those articles, and Cauchon's sentence, were to be torn out of one copy of the proceedings of 1431 and burnt by the public executioner at Rouen. But the d'Arc family's demands were not met. At the beginning of the rehabilitation process, their proctor Guillaume Prevosteau had requested that the three delegates – the archbishop of Rheims and the bishops of Paris and Coutances – 'should take good care to declare that Joan had remained faithful and Catholic up to, and including, her death; setting out in the most explicit fashion that she had not merited any imputation of heresy, perverse credulity, error in the Faith, nor breach with the Church'.[2] They did not do this in July 1456. The definitive sentence did not pronounce on her orthodoxy or her sanctity. Although 150 witnesses had more or less unanimously testified to her purity of life, her integrity, her extraordinary physical and mental courage, none of these qualities was even mentioned in the delegates' conclusions. Although the prosecuting advocate for the d'Arc family had declared that they had no wish to 'disturb those who had been present at Joan's trial, or had expressed their opinions'[3] – with the exception of the dead Cauchon and his immediate assistants – there was no guarantee that they might not carry their private lawsuit further. They received no damages as a result of the rehabilitation process, and it was expressly forbidden that 'images and epitaphs' should be set up at Rouen or elsewhere. The authorities were evidently determined to prevent a cult of Joan of Arc growing up.[4]

Above all, there was no penalty exacted from her judges and assessors of 1431. One of them, indeed, could hardly condemn himself. Jean Le Fèvre, suffragan to the archbishop of Rouen, and a noted preacher, had attended Joan's trial between 21 February and 29 May 1431. Exactly twenty-five years later, on 30 May 1456, he was appointed sub-delegated judge at the process of rehabilitation.[5] He was an old man, and old men, allegedly, forget. But he remembered his 'emotion' at the death of one

[1] Doncœur and Lanhers, Rédaction, 19–20.
[2] Ibid., 19.
[3] Ibid., 15, 85; Quicherat, Procès, II, 166.
[4] Doncœur and Lanhers, Rédaction, 19–20.
[5] Doncœur and Lanhers, Bouillé, 8; Tisset

and Lanhers, Procès, II, 409. He was appointed bishop of Demetriade, acting as suffragan to the archbishop of Rouen, in 1441. He died, aged 77, in 1463.

whom he had considered to be 'pertinacious, contumacious and disobedient' in 1431.[1] To hypocrisy, overt lying – and thus perjury – was added in the case of Master Thomas de Courcelles, distinguished theologian and preacher, and dean of Notre Dame of Paris. On 15 January 1456, Courcelles gave evidence at Paris to the inquiry. Questioned as to his behaviour in 1431, 'he said that he had never decided that any physical pain [pena] should be inflicted upon the said Joan'.[2] But on 12 May 1431, at the hour of Vespers, he had been at a meeting in Cauchon's house which discussed the issue of putting Joan to the torture.[3] Courcelles was one of the two assessors who advised that she should be tortured, and interrogated, to see if she would submit herself to the judgement of the Church.[4] Questioned further, he claimed to be unable to remember anything about the affair. The notes, 'he knows no more', or 'he cannot depose further' recur throughout the record of his depositions.[5] He was to live on until 1469, and was to preach a funeral sermon for Charles VII in St-Denis which moved the listening multitude to tears.[6] *Collaborateurs*, like converts, can be among the more fervent advocates of the cause of their new masters.

The rehabilitation process of 1455–6 thus condemned no one, because it could not afford to condemn anyone. Cauchon, Estivet and Le Maître – the architects of Joan's condemnation and death – were not mentioned by name in the definitive sentence. It condemned documents, and by the implication, the procedure which they recorded. It was documents, not human beings, that were burnt by the public executioner at Rouen in July 1456. That was as far as the symbolic act of reparation in favour of the d'Arc family went. Their desire that the sentence of rehabilitation should be inserted into the *Chroniques de France* was not fulfilled.[7] Nor was their demand met that the bishop, promoter of criminal cases, and sub-inquisitor of the diocese of Beauvais be summoned before the inquiry. Not a word came out of Beauvais during the course of the proceedings. Cauchon's nephews refused to appear to defend their uncle, and cited Charles VII's letters of pardon in their favour.[8] The raking over of ashes which many preferred to leave undisturbed could only lead to that discord and lack of goodwill which, in the 1450s, the king and his counsellors were trying to prevent. The 're-establishment of social peace' in

---

[1] Doncœur and Lanhers, *Procès*, II, 409.

[2] Doncœur and Lanhers, *Rédaction*, 192. For his career, see Tisset and Lanhers, *Procès*, II, 394–5.

[3] Doncœur and Lanhers, *Minute française*, 246–7.

[4] Ibid., 249. The other assessor was Master Nicholas Loiseleur.

[5] Doncœur and Lanhers, *Rédaction*, 192–4.

[6] See below, 214.

[7] Doncœur and Lanhers, *Rédaction*, 20.

[8] Ibid., 15. My debt to these excellent volumes must be obvious.

fifteenth-century France would not be assisted by the prosecution of old grievances.[1] Nor was the cause of Gallicanism furthered by the setting up of inquiries, under papal aegis, into the murkier aspects of the careers of some important members of the French clergy. 'The past' wrote Jean Juvenal des Ursins in 1445, 'has been pretty amazing and there have been people with different views.'[2] To the king, and to many of the higher clergy, the less said about that past, and those views, the better the future might be.

[1] See below, 151–4.   [2] Quoted in Lewis, op. cit., 68–9.

Chapter 4 ✤ The King, the Dauphin and the Nobility 1431–1449

1 *The Praguerie and its sequel*

The conventional picture of the 'middle years' of the reign of Charles VII is one of the king's feeble complacency giving way to a more decisive and less apathetic role. Once again, Chastellain's analysis, which saw the king emerging as politically adept only after the defection of Philip the Good from the English in 1435, has been perpetuated by historians. The rise and fall of 'favourites' has been interpreted as an index of the king's weakness. Less attention has been paid to the curious ability with which the king put down rebellions and dealt with the conspiracies which it is the purpose of the second part of this chapter to unravel. It was this period which saw the magnate rebellion known as the Praguerie (1440), and the subsequent movement leading to the great assembly at Nevers in 1442. These were followed by a series of plots, judicial interrogations and treason trials. Soon after his accession in July 1461, Louis XI's secretary Jean Bourré drew up a list of these. Under the heading 'Notice of what has been done' since 1445, Bourré provided an account of Charles VII's judicial *procès* up to 1458.[1] There was at least one treason trial per year during this period. In 1445 a *procès* was brought against Jamet du Tillay, a servant of the dauphin Louis; in 1447–8 it was the turn of another of Louis's officers, Guillaume Mariette; in 1449, the financier Jean Xaincoins was put on trial; in 1451 Jacques Coeur, the king's *argentier*, was deposed. A series of 'petty *procès*' then led up to the *lit-de-justice* of October 1458, in which Jean II, duke of Alençon, was convicted of treason.

That Louis XI's trusted *confidant* should have the records of some of these proceedings is noteworthy. The newly crowned dauphin was anxious to discover what had been happening at his father's court, while he had plotted from the safety of the Dauphiné. A further document among Bourré's papers testifies to this concern. It is an 'inventory of the letters and acts which Master Pierre Puy has delivered by the king's [Louis's]

[1] B.N. MS. fr. 20491, fols 31ʳ–31ᵛ
(? August–September 1461).

command to Master Jean Bourré'.[1] This was drawn up very soon after Louis's accession in 1461. It lists the surviving records of the interrogation and trial of Guillaume Mariette in 1447-8, a letter of pardon granted to Pierre de Brézé, and a number of confessions and spies' reports. These documents – as far as they still survive – are an indispensable source for the political behaviour of Charles VII. The themes of the 'middle years' are largely moulded by the king's relations with his son, the changing composition of the court, and the pressure of external powers – especially Burgundy and England – on the king. In these documents there is information concerning all these subjects. The king occasionally emerges from them as something more than the stereotype which has often been presented. It is thus possible to construct a picture of Charles VII as a rather different kind of monarch than his critics, and his historians, were prepared to acknowledge.

With the fall of La Trémoïlle, engineered by a coalition between the Angevins and the Bretons at court, in June 1433, Charles was left without a clearly marked 'favourite'. The charges brought against La Trémoïlle, through the intervention of Richemont, were entirely financial, and bear comparison with those which led to the fall of Louvet.[2] On 5 March 1432 an agreement at Rennes had reconciled Richemont to the king, and La Trémoïlle's days were numbered.[3] Richemont recruited a group of courtiers to his affinity, who were to enter the king's council in the wake of La Trémoïlle's departure. Among them were four of the most significant of the politically influential during the later part of the reign. Pierre d'Amboise, lord of Chaumont, Prégent de Coëtivy, Jean de Bueil, and Pierre de Brézé were servants of the houses of Anjou and Brittany.[4] The alliance of the two houses, endorsed by the king on 22 February 1431, ended the conflict of Yolande of Aragon and Jean V of Brittany with a marriage treaty.[5] A united Angevin and Breton group at court, formed during the winter of 1430-1 at Chinon, brought Richemont back into favour. It also prepared the way for the elevation of Charles of Anjou, count of Maine, third son of Yolande, to the position formerly held by La Trémoïlle. On 22 December 1432 he was given a gift of 1,000 *moutons d'or* by the king.[6] This was unusual, in that he was the first object of Charles's favour who was a prince of the blood, related intimately to the royal line. The king, it could be argued, was merely ensuring the services of one of his natural counsellors. This was perhaps the view taken by the exiled Jean Louvet

[1] B.N. MS. fr. 20487, fol. 44ʳ.
[2] See Beaucourt, II, 259-68, 274-5, 293.
[3] Ibid., 282.
[4] Ibid., 296-9.

[5] Knowlson, op. cit., 149; Beaucourt, II, 279.
[6] Ibid., 298 and n. 2.

when, in November 1435, he composed a *mémoire* for the duke of Savoy on the subject of alignments at the king's court.[1]

The court which the king held at Vienne in the winter of 1434–5 celebrated the Angevin ascendancy, and led Beaucourt to claim that it formed 'a new spectacle: the monarchy appeared surrounded with great pomp, and Charles VII held a sort of plenary court'.[2] In his *mémoire*, Louvet announced his intention that 'the state of affairs at the court of France should be well understood'.[3] Louvet began by observing that 'to-day the king has no particular servant' – not even Charles of Anjou – 'who has more influence with him than the others'. Yolande, Charles of Anjou, and Dunois, however, enjoyed an undisputed hegemony. Richemont's role was an entirely military one, while Charles, duke of Bourbon, bided his time, hoping for a return of Burgundy to court. 'The principal aim of Bourbon,' wrote Louvet, 'is that my lord of Burgundy should come back to the king, and that then they could both do everything and gather up all the others.'[4] Closest in the king's affections, Louvet claimed, was Dunois. But he was interested only in the war, and stayed away from the intrigues of the court, which he found loathsome. Bourbon hoped to woo him to his side, so that Charles of Anjou might be deposed. But it was a hopeless device, which was to fail once more in 1440.[5] Charles of Anjou and Dunois were bound, Louvet observed, in an indissoluble alliance. In the total lack of evidence for the composition and activities of the king's council at this time, Louvet's *mémoire* provides useful information. The king himself, he noted, could rely on a number of counsellors who were devoted to him, and to no other interest. Among them were the archbishop of Toulouse, the bishop of Maguelonne, and Gérard Machet, bishop of Castres, the king's confessor. Despite their connections with the duke of Bourbon, these political bishops would no longer support him once any move hostile to the Crown was made. Bourbon could therefore rely only on the chancellor, Regnault de Chartres, Christophe d'Harcourt, and the archbishop of Vienne. Against them there were the partisans of the house of Anjou – the aged Robert le Maçon (who, in the event, retired from the council after 16 August 1436),[6] the bishops of Poitiers and Maillezais, and 'new' men, such as Bertrand de Beauvau, lord of Précigny.

On 28 July 1436 Louvet sent a second letter to the duke of Savoy, which referred to 'certain novelties in the king's court, as a result of which my lord the bastard [Dunois] has been suddenly summoned to the king's

[1] Beaucourt, III, 41–2.
[2] Ibid., II, p. 304.
[3] Ibid., III, 41 n. 1.
[4] Ibid., 41 n. 3.
[5] See below, 77.
[6] Beaucourt, III, 42.

presence'.[1] Beaucourt considered that the 'novelties' were the introduction of a stronger Angevin group into the council, and the dismissal of Jean de Norry, archbishop of Vienne. Regnault de Chartres, formerly a client of Bourbon, was induced by the king to support Charles of Anjou. On 16 August the result of Louvet's work became apparent. The marriage contract of Yolande, the king's third daughter, a child of under two years of age, was signed at Tours. She was betrothed to Louis of Savoy, prince of Piedmont.[2] Immediately afterwards, the king and his council left the Loire valley for Languedoc, where there was an investigation to be conducted into the depredations of the *routiers* (companies of freelances) in areas loyal to the Valois. The pattern of court life remained unchanged. In the winter, the court resided at one of the king's *châteaux* in the Touraine – usually Chinon, Amboise or Tours – while the rest of the year was spent moving from place to place. There is no evidence at this time of the illness which was to restrict the king's itinerary in his later years.[3]

It is from July 1432 that the first evidence for a plot to gain possession of the king's person is drawn. An admittedly ambiguous document refers to an undertaking by the captain La Hire to deliver 'the king' into the hands of Jean I, count of Foix.[4] This was to be done at the instigation of Foix, the count of Comminges, and the bishop of Laon. According to the agreement, La Hire was not to put any man near to the 'king' who could not be immediately removed. It was an attempt by a third party at court – the Gascons surrounding the house of Foix – to gain power. They had failed, and La Trémoïlle had been disposed of by other means. But Jean I of Foix had been gathering his *alliés* around him at court, just as the other magnates had done, and were to do in the Praguerie. For those who came to court in the following of a great lord, as did Jean I's *alliés* in 1425, a pension from the Crown invariably followed.[5] Others might be retained in a magnate's service by the payment of a fee – the contracts of *alliance* made between Jean I and two of the courtiers, Amaury, lord of Estissac and Jean de Daillon, in 1425 and 1444, meant that the house of Foix had its agents at the courts of king and dauphin.[6] Men bound by no local ties

[1] Ibid., 43-4.
[2] Ibid., 44.
[3] See below, 172-7.
[4] Beaucourt, II, 285-91. Vallet de Viriville considered that the 'king' in question was not Charles VII but Jacques de Bourbon, king of Jerusalem and Hungary. This is refuted in Beaucourt, II, 288.
[5] See P. S. Lewis, 'Decayed and Non-

Feudalism in Later Medieval France', *BIHR*, xxxvii (1964), 165 nn. 11 and 12. For Charles's grant to Jean I of the lieutenancy of Languedoc and Guyenne, and the *comté* of Bigorre in 1425, see Vale, op. cit., 95-6.
[6] ABP, E.432 and 439 (12 September 1425 and 22 April 1444). For these two men see below, 75, 103.

to a great magnate could thus serve their interests – paid clients, in no way the equal of those who paid them, keeping the latter 'in the good grace and love of my sovereign lord the king and of my said lord the dauphin'. During periods in which a great lord was absent from court, their presence was vital. As an intelligence service alone, the courtier *alliés* were, perhaps, worth their pensions and annuities.

It is in this light that the political manœuvrings which preceded the outbreak of the Praguerie must be viewed. Some of the nobility of France followed the example of the Hussite nobility of Bohemia, and rose against their sovereign lord. The possibility of an armed insurrection, led by the duke of Bourbon, had been apparent since the spring of 1437.[1] Employing the notorious *routier* captain Rodrigo de Villandrando, Bourbon raised an army against the king. He had married Villandrando to his bastard daughter – a practice emulated in Italy by the Visconti of Milan.[2] It was one means of gaining military power in a period of increasing royal pressure on the freedom of a great lord to raise troops. The attempt, supported by the dukes of Alençon and Brittany, and by René of Anjou, probably swayed by the recent marriage of his son to Marie de Bourbon, proved abortive.

During the campaign in which the revolt was suppressed, the king played an active part. The writer of the *Chronique d'Alençon* described how at the siege of Montereau, on 10 October 1437, Charles himself led the assault. 'He was there in person,' claimed the chronicler, 'as far in front as any knight or esquire of his company; and so much so that he was in the moat of the place, in the water to well above the belt.'[3] This act of considerable courage was preceded by a solicitude for the placing of his artillery before Montereau, which was considered unusual by the chronicler. The count of Pardiac and the lord of Albret were anxious lest his safety should be endangered, but the king replied that 'the war was his and none other's, and that he ought to play his part in the preparations'.[4] It was ironic that he should so expose himself at the very place in which John the Fearless had been assassinated in 1419. That event had led his advisers to keep him as far away from the war as possible. This reversal of previous policy is perhaps explicable less by the king's alleged emergence from 'timid apathy' than by the changed political conditions of the time. Since the reconciliation – however partial – with Philip the Good in 1435, the vendetta of the house of Burgundy against him was at an end. In

---

[1] See Beaucourt, III, 44–8.

[2] Ibid., 46; Quicherat, *Rodrigue de Villandrando . . .* (Paris, 1879), 290–1.

[3] Beaucourt, III, 49–50.

[4] Ibid., 50.

October 1437 Charles could exult in the fact that, even at Montereau, the risks to his personal security were now no greater than those encountered by other princes. But there were other areas besides Burgundy from which such threats might come.

At Montereau, the dauphin Louis, aged fourteen, had been present with his father. The birth of a son to Charles VII and Marie of Anjou on 3 July 1423 had been greeted with a letter of congratulation from Pope Martin V, if nothing else.[1] The Papacy was on the side of the house of Valois, and the pope urged prayers for the survival of the royal child 'for the conservation of the house of France and the consolation of the peoples subjected to its authority'.[2] The prayers were evidently efficacious. Louis survived. When he was ten years of age he was placed under the governorship of Guillaume d'Avaugour, the old Orléanist and ex-counsellor of his father.[3] His confessor and tutor was Jean Majoris, canon of Rheims, and his father was anxious that he should learn from 'well-written manuscripts, on good parchment, and richly illuminated'.[4] In 1436, Bernard d'Armagnac, count of La Marche, Pardiac and Castres, was appointed his governor. He was a severe, almost puritanical, guardian, and kept the boy on a tight rein. The dauphin's household, over which he presided, was as proper, wrote Chastellain, as a Carthusian refectory.[5] Among his servants there were men whose names were to become distinguished in the future. Joachim Rouault served him as first esquire, and his assistant governor was Amaury, lord of Estissac, retained as an *allié* by Jean I of Foix in 1425, and by Gaston IV in 1439.[6] The great Southern house thus had its agent at the side of the dauphin, and of Bernard d'Armagnac, a member of the house with which the counts of Foix had been locked in a feud of very long standing. The dauphin's household, like the king's, was the scenario against which many essentially private feuds were acted out.

It was soon apparent that the person of the dauphin Louis might provide a rallying point for the disaffected. Knowledge of the origins of the estrangement between him and his father is scanty. There is little evidence before February 1440 for any kind of worsening of relations between them. Charles was evidently ready to entrust his sixteen-year-old son with the responsibilities of government and administration. In the spring of 1439 he was left as his father's lieutenant in Languedoc, while Charles

[1] See M. Thibault, *La Jeunesse de Louis XI* (Paris, 1907), 69–70, 75.
[2] Ibid., 75.
[3] Ibid., 121–2.
[4] Ibid., 117.

[5] Ibid., 148; Chastellain, I, 169.
[6] ABP, E.438 (7 July 1439), printed in Lewis, op. cit., 183–4. He excepted the king, the dauphin and Charles of Orléans from the terms of the alliance.

returned north to prepare for the meeting of the States-General at Orléans in September.[1] In October, Louis was recalled. His father was evidently not displeased with his son's services in Languedoc, for, in November, he sent him on a second mission.[2] This followed the military *ordonnance* of 2 November, in which no one but the king was permitted to raise troops. Louis was to tackle the problem of military reform – especially the behaviour of anarchic freelances – in Poitou.[3] There is no evidence whatsoever at this time that 'his father meant, consciously or unconsciously, to revenge himself for his weakness by thwarting a son who was anything but weak'.[4] There is also no evidence that Louis felt within himself 'the stirring of uncommon powers'[5] at this period of his life. Both his biographers – Thibault and, more recently, Kendall – assume that Louis's initiative lay behind the plots and insurrections of these years.[6] It could be argued that this falsifies reality by arguing from hindsight. The adolescent dauphin was an easy target for a disaffected magnate such as Bourbon or Alençon. It was, for instance, only after a meeting with Jean, duke of Alençon, at Niort in February 1440, that Louis made what might be interpreted as his first gesture of defiance towards his father.[7] He purged his household. Bernard d'Armagnac was accused of being his father's spy, and those of his officers suspected of aiding him were dismissed.[8]

It was all too easy for a youth, however politically mature, to be persuaded, if not suborned, by the magnates. It must not be assumed that the latter were unanimous in their grievances against Charles VII's government. Their protestations that they were acting for the 'public weal' have to be viewed with the scepticism, if not contempt, which they deserve. The malcontents of 1440, like those of 1465, pursued private interests under the cloak of the public good. At their head were the dukes of Bourbon and Alençon, supported by Dunois, and by the count of Vendôme, the marshal Lafayette, the two bastards of Bourbon, and Jacques de Chabannes, seneschal of Bourbonnais.[9] There can be little doubt, as

---

[1] Beaucourt, III, 19–20; Thibault, *Louis XI*, 191–6.

[2] Ibid., 214–17. For the military reform of 1439 see Cosneau, *Richemont*, 297–9; Beaucourt, III, 384–416.

[3] Thibault, *Louis XI*, 217. For military disorder at this time see P. Contamine, *Guerre, Etat et Société à la fin du Moyen Age* (Paris–The Hague, 1972), 234–73.

[4] See P. M. Kendall, *Louis XI* (London, 1971), 47. It will be obvious that I disagree

with Professor Kendall's assessment of Louis's behaviour as dauphin from this time onwards.

[5] Ibid., 47.

[6] Thibault, *Louis XI*, 197, 217; Kendall, *Louis XI*, 42–4.

[7] See Thibault, *Louis XI*, 221–2; Beaucourt, III, 120–1.

[8] Thibault, *Louis XI*, 222.

[9] Ibid., 229.

the writers of a *mémoire* of June 1440 implied,[1] that Bourbon was the ringleader of the rebels. He objected to the terms of the peace negotiations with the English, which seemed, in the spring of 1439, to be moving towards a settlement. He objected to the withdrawal of companies under his command from Lorraine and Alsace in order to besiege Meaux for the king. Whether by accident or design, Bourbon's troops, on their passage towards the Ile-de-France, marched through the lands of the duke of Burgundy. This was in flagrant violation of the king's orders, and likely to alienate Philip the Good. The king, 'as much by sweetness [*douceur*] as by the use of money',[2] gained the oath from Bourbon's captains to go to Meaux. But they delayed, and spent two months ransoming the inhabitants of Auvergne, Rouergue and Berry.[3] Behind the problem of the disaffected magnate, therefore, lay the question of military reform. Until the hold of the magnates on certain companies of the king's army could be broken, there was little hope of a solution to the problem of disorder. It was, again, all too easy for a great lord such as Bourbon to recruit military support for his treasonable designs. Military reform had become essential by 1439, not only to end the war with the English, but to deprive the potentially rebellious magnate of the means of revolt.

The presence of the notorious *écorcheurs*, the two bastards of Bourbon, in the ranks of the disaffected is easily explicable. Their bond of blood linked them to the house, and they provided military support for the rebels.[4] Less explicable is the presence of Dunois among the rebels. It was alleged that he had been persuaded by Bourbon that, at the peace negotiations of the summer of 1439, the king had signified that he did not wish the captive Charles of Orléans to be released.[5] Orléans had been held in England since his capture at Agincourt, and Dunois, as a representative of the house of Orléans, could hardly agree to that. The *mémoire* of June 1440 continued:

> and from that moment he [Bourbon] began to plot, with my said lord the bastard [Dunois] and others, by the advice of the marshal of Lafayette and my lord Jacques de Chabannes, the enterprise since undertaken by him, that is to say, to seduce my said lord the dauphin . . . into complete disobedience against him [the king] and the greatest members of the kingdom, under the pretext of reducing the *aides*. . . .[6]

[1] See Escouchy, III, 4–16; Beaucourt, III, 115–17, 122–3.
[2] Escouchy, III, 6.
[3] Ibid., 6; Contamine, op. cit., 267–8.
[4] Escouchy, III, 9.

[5] Beaucourt, III, 116–17. For these negotiations see C. T. Allmand, 'The Anglo-French Negotiations, 1439', *BIHR*, xl (1967), 1–33.
[6] Escouchy, III, 7.

It was an effective seduction. To urge a mitigation of taxation, especially of the *aides* taken for the conduct of war, would also serve to recruit popular support. This Bourbon attempted to do in the letters which he made Louis sign, addressed to the hard-pressed inhabitants of Champagne, Languedoc and the Dauphiné.[1] In an obscure alliance with Pierre d'Amboise, lord of Chaumont, and his wife, Bourbon sowed dissension between Louis and his father.[2] Exactly who was persuaded by whom is not known. But by the time that the court had moved to Angers for the Christmas of 1439, Bourbon was apparently assured of the support of Louis, Alençon, Vendôme and Dunois.

But Dunois was only temporarily taken in. He allowed Bourbon's troops to march against the king's army on the frontiers, but suddenly abandoned them and went back to the king.[3] Again, the means by which this reconciliation was achieved is not known, but news of the impending release of Charles of Orléans must have played its part. Bourbon, however, retained his hold over the companies. Although their captains had been paid pensions by the king – Guy, bastard of Bourbon, receiving 2,000 francs per year[4] – their loyalty, cemented by their oaths to keep the *ordonnance* of 1439, was still extremely doubtful. Unable to replace the king with his son, and kill his principal servants, Bourbon showed signs of coming to terms at Angers early in 1440.[5] Mutual promises were exchanged, and the meeting ended with Bourbon's remark:

'My lord, I shall certainly do nothing against what I've promised you, but I'll meet a lot of people who aren't too pleased with the court; by your leave, you must give me licence to join them in saying the worst about it that we can.' And the king answered him: 'Fair cousin, you can speak as badly about me as you like, but, for myself, I won't speak so about you.'[6]

Bourbon was as good as his word. The king's affable answer had no impact on him. The rebels met at Blois, determined to render the military *ordonnance* a dead letter. They refused to 'clean out' their companies of undesirables, and refused to muster their men before Raoul de Gaucourt and Poton de Xaintrailles, deputies of the constable Richemont.[7] The attempt at military reform had failed. It was not until 1445 that some semblance of order was brought to the companies. Their captains, until that date, relied not only upon the disturbed conditions which the war

[1] Escouchy, III, 7.
[2] Loc. cit.; Beaucourt, III, 119, 122, 127.
[3] Escouchy, III, 8–9; Beaucourt, III, 126.
[4] Escouchy, III, 9.
[5] Ibid., 8; Beaucourt, III, 118–19.
[6] Escouchy, III, 10.
[7] Ibid., 11; Contamine, op. cit., 267.

had created, but upon the patronage of the greater magnates. 'These captains,' wrote the chronicler Jean Chartier, 'always avowed some promise from one of the lords of France, which was the cause of the evil that they did.'[1] Without such men there would have been no Praguerie.

The defection of a substantial part of the military resources of the kingdom to the rebels was a cause for serious concern to the king. The *mémoire* of June 1440 stated that Charles, 'not wishing that my said lord of Bourbon and his supporters did with him as the English did with king Richard', had six of the *écorcheur* captains arrested.[2] Jean de Blanchefort and his brothers, the captain Archambaud, Alain Ferlin, Jean d'Apchier, and Anthoine de Chabannes, younger brother of Jacques de Chabannes, seneschal of Bourbonnais, were seized. The king arrived at Loches on the same day, hoping to besiege Bourbon there. But, despite a summons to surrender, Bourbon left the place at dawn on the morrow.[3] Hearing that Alençon had gained hold of the dauphin at Niort, Charles decided immediately to leave a garrison in the *faubourg* of Loches, and hastened towards Poitou. Alençon had already taken the town and castle of Melle, and was about to besiege St-Maixent. There was no time to be lost. In less than five days the king had recovered Melle, St-Neomaye and L'Isle, and negotiated through Richemont and La Marche with Alençon, who was unaware of events at Loches.[4] When news reached him of the flight of Bourbon and the arrest of his captains, Alençon took the desperate course of seeking aid from John Holland, earl of Huntingdon, lieutenant of Henry VI of England in Guyenne. It was the first act in a series of treasons which was to end only at Vendôme in 1458. Huntingdon refused to aid Alençon unless he was given places in Poitou which were not in the duke's hands.[5]

The king's capacity for decisive action cannot be doubted from the evidence of this time. At Poitiers, just as he came from Mass, he heard that St-Maixent had been taken by Alençon.[6] He ate hurriedly, and left with a small force of troops to relieve the loyal inhabitants who had taken refuge in one of the gates of the town. The place was relieved on the same day, and Alençon took advantage of nightfall to make his escape. The castle, however, was a different proposition. For over a week the king besieged it, bombarding it with cannon and siege engines. The garrison surrendered, and about twenty-five of them were decapitated. The fate of the defenders

---

[1] Quoted ibid., 272.
[2] Escouchy, III, 11.
[3] Ibid., 12; Beaucourt, III, 122.
[4] Beaucourt, III, 123–4; Escouchy, III, 12–13.

[5] Escouchy, III, 13; Beaucourt, III, 123; Thibault, *Louis XI*, 234, 237.
[6] Beaucourt, III, 123–4; Escouchy, III, 13.

of Azay-le-Rideau in 1418 was re-enacted – but sixty of the troops inside St-Maixent were spared.[1] They had served well on the frontiers and were too valuable to lose. From this point onwards, the events of the Praguerie revolved around the person of the dauphin Louis.

The scene now changed from Poitou to the Bourbon stronghold of Auvergne. Taking the dauphin with him, Alençon joined forces with Bourbon, and laid siege to the royal town of Montferrand.[2] Charles resolved to march into Auvergne, postponing the meeting of the Three Estates of Languedoïl, who had been waiting at Bourges.[3] An unexpected move then took place. Just before his departure from Poitiers, an envoy from Philip the Good of Burgundy came, bringing letters from the duke.[4] He was also empowered to attempt a reconciliation between the rebels and the king. Meanwhile the king took Bourbon-l'Archambault and Buxière-la-Grue from rebel hands, and received proposals from Bourbon and Alençon. After three more places had fallen, Charles replied to the proposals, saying that he would not entertain any terms until Raoul de Gaucourt, who had been captured by the rebels, was released. While the king's army – of 800 mounted men-at-arms and 2,000 archers – recovered more than twenty-five fortresses in Bourbonnais and Auvergne, the rebels resolved to come to terms. They sent Gaucourt back to the king. It was the beginning of the last stage of the revolt.[5]

The peace-talks took place in May 1440 in the houses of the Franciscans and Jacobins just outside the town of Montferrand.[6] The king's terms were an assertion of his sovereign rights. Bourbon and Alençon were to acknowledge those rights in their lordships. Above all, they were to disband the troops whom they had raised, for 'all the war of the said kingdom belongs to the king and his officers, and to none other, and there is no one so great in the said kingdom that he can levy war nor retain troops, without the authority, commission and command of the king'.[7] It was a restatement of the notions which had produced the military *ordonnance* of 1439. The rebels were to deliver the dauphin to his father, handing over certain of the disaffected – especially the captains who took the oath to the king at Angers – at the same time. If Bourbon and Alençon claimed that this was not within their power, they were at least to purge them from their companies.[8] The lords replied that they acknowledged the

---

[1] Escouchy, III, 13; Beaucourt, III, 124; cf. above, 42.
[2] Beaucourt, III, 124-6; Escouchy, III, 13-14.
[3] Escouchy, III, 14; Beaucourt, III, 124-5.
[4] Escouchy, III, 14-15; Beaucourt, III, 125-6.
[5] Beaucourt, III, 126-7; Escouchy, III, 15-16.
[6] Escouchy, III, 16; Beaucourt, III, 127.
[7] Escouchy, III, 18; Contamine, op. cit., 271-2.
[8] Escouchy, III, 18-20.

king's sovereignty, but, somewhat hypocritically, claimed that it was the king's responsibility to establish better order among the troops, and to relieve the 'poor people' from their pillaging. They agreed to return the dauphin to his father.[1] Perhaps the lack of any broader basis of support for the rebellion, together with the propagandist activity of loyalists such as Bernard du Rozier on the king's behalf, had convinced them that the cause was now lost.[2] They claimed that the dauphin, far from being the blind instrument of their designs, was 'chief of them and all their company'.[3] It is not necessary to take them at their word, as Louis's biographers have done. To suborn the adolescent dauphin, and then claim that the rebellion was his responsibility, not theirs, was a transparent device.

The humility of Louis's petition to his father perhaps endorses this view. He begged for a full pardon, and for mercy towards the rebels. Although he referred to them as having 'served, advised, comforted and supported' *him*,[4] the fact that his last reply to his father's final terms at Montferrand largely reiterates those of the rebel magnates suggests that Louis's hand was evidently not the only one behind the propositions.[5] His major grievance – if it was really his – was that he had not yet been given the Dauphiné. His father was endowed with it at the age of fourteen.[6] Louis was seventeen in July 1440. He also requested the lieutenancy of Languedoc and Guyenne, or of France', from his father. The latter's reply was politic and related only to the requests put forward by Louis himself, about his situation and that of his wife, Margaret of Scotland. Charles replied:

> That when my lord the dauphin shall come back to the king in the humility that he owes him, the king will treat him as his only son, and provide for his estate, and for that of my lady the dauphine, in such a way that he will be satisfied; and as to the other requests . . . which concern others than . . . the dauphin, when he shall come back to the king, as much shall be done as shall satisfy him. . . .[7]

On 28 July Louis was granted the Dauphiné and a pension of 800 *livres* per month.[8] Bourbon and Alençon accepted the king's terms, with one exception. That was the demand that certain individuals should be handed over. The lords of Chaumont, Montjean and Prie, Jacques de Chabannes,

---

[1] Ibid., 20–1.

[2] B.N., MS. lat. 6020, fols 89ᵛ–91ᵛ; cf. fols 67ʳ–67ᵛ and Plate 5.

[3] Escouchy, III, 21.

[4] Ibid., 22–4; Beaucourt, III, 128–9.

[5] Escouchy, III, 24–6 and cf. 28–9.

[6] See above, 21.

[7] Escouchy, III, 24.

[8] Beaucourt, III, 134; Thibault, *Louis XI*, 259.

the disgraced La Trémoïlle, and certain captains, were thought to be responsible for seducing Louis to the side of the rebels. Despite Bourbon's and Alençon's pleas for mercy, Charles refused to pardon La Trémoïlle, Chaumont and Prie.[1] They were banished from court. Bourbon and Alençon retired to their lordships. The king's promptitude and intransigence towards the rebels hardly lent credibility to the idea that he was a cypher in the hands of his courtiers. It was, perhaps, his son who might more convincingly be cast in that role.

Given the strenuous activity in which Charles had indulged during the Praguerie, it is a little surprising that one of his most prominent counsellors should accuse him of negligence, lassitude and somnolence. Jean Juvenal des Ursins, bishop of Beauvais, composed his harangue *Quare obdormis, Domine?* during the rebellion.[2] His work tells more, perhaps, about the political views of Jean Juvenal than about Charles VII's actual behaviour. He accused the king of ignoring the Estates of his kingdom. They had been kept waiting at Orléans in 1439. They had seen the king but rarely during the sessions. They had been excluded from the king's chamber and could not have their petitions heard.[3] Whose petitions were not heard, Jean Juvenal does not make clear. Perhaps his own, allegedly as representative of his flock at Beauvais, bearing the brunt of the war on the frontiers? But Jean Juvenal was assuming that the king shared his views on the utility of the Estates. There is evidence from this period of a desire on the king's part to dispense with them. If he could raise taxation without their mediation, why should he pay so much attention to their meetings? In 1442 he told the Estates of Languedoc that he 'did not wish such assemblies to meet in future'.[4] They were expensive, they burdened the people, and the *tailles* and *aides* for the war were granted without their convocation. Many of the king's subjects were prepared to pay the price of peace without the sham 'representation' of their 'interests' by an assembly.

Sometimes, as has been seen, the sessions of the Estates were overtaken by more pressing events.[5] The allegation that the king 'slept' at this time seems to make nonsense of the evidence. There was more than a subtle

---

[1] Beaucourt, III, 132–3, for Charles's reply to Louis.

[2] Ibid., 136–7, quoting MS. fr. 5022, fols 5–6ᵛ. This was probably written soon after 24 February 1440, not, as Beaucourt claimed, 'a little after the Praguerie' (ibid., 136). An edition of this, and other works of Jean Juvenal, by P. S. Lewis is soon to be published by the Société de l'Histoire de France.

[3] Beaucourt, III, 136: 'if they enter your chamber to make any *requêtes* . . . you shut yourself up in a little retreat, and the door is locked so that no one can speak to you.' Cf. Charles's hearing of *requêtes* at a later period, below, 146–50.

[4] Lewis, op. cit., 372–3; H. Gilles, *Les Etats de Languedoc au xvᵉ siècle* (Toulouse, 1965), 55.

[5] Escouchy, III, 14, and above, 124.

difference between a dormant and a circumspect ruler. Jean Juvenal had evidently little idea of what the king actually did in his 'castles, evil places, and kinds of little chambers' in which he shut himself up. The embattled bishop of Beauvais thought that Charles read and prayed, far from the frontiers of war.[1] But the endorsement 'by the king in his council' on many of the documents issued in Charles's name at this time suggests that he was not merely cultivating his mind and his soul.[2] Jean Juvenal went on to preach the doctrine of vicarious suffering at the king. His people suffered – he should also suffer.[3] The force of his argument was somewhat blunted, however, by his reference to the events of the Praguerie. Whether, like his fellow-bishop Thomas Basin in 1465, Jean Juvenal was in the pay or patronage of any of the rebels, will probably never be known. There is evidence, from a rather later period, that both he and his brother – the chancellor Guillaume Jouvenel des Ursins – were not impervious to bribery.[4] In 1440 he told the king that the letter of 24 February which he had sent to his subjects during the revolt was useless. 'What little comfort,' he wrote, 'has there been to us, your poor sheep, who are here on the frontier [at Beauvais], in a letter which you have been pleased to send, mentioning an assembly which *is said to have been made* by my very redoubtable lord . . . the dauphin, your one and only son, and others your relatives, with which you have been displeased.'[5] The disbelief implied in this statement gives rise to suspicion.

To chastise the king for failing to remedy the problem of military disorder, while declining to condemn the Praguerie, appears somewhat hypocritical. The rebels themselves had contributed greatly to a worsening of that problem. To appear on the frontiers, showing himself to the people, would not automatically bring a solution to the king's predicament. Until a system of regular pay, muster and review of troops was established, the problem would remain. His good intentions had been thwarted by the behaviour of members of the nobility. Jean Juvenal's proposal for the ending of the envies and jealousies which, he alleged, divided the king's court, was unlikely to help in the circumstances. The princes of the blood, he wrote, should be sent away from the court, and employed in the war against the English.[6] The dukes of Burgundy and Bourbon,

[1] Beaucourt, III, 137. Jean Juvenal compared Charles (unfavourably) with both Charles V and Henry V of England (ibid., 137).
[2] See *Ord.*, XIII, 305, 319, 321.
[3] Beaucourt, III, 137.
[4] See below, 110.

[5] Beaucourt, III, 138, 121, 529-31. The letter ended with the postscript: 'Since the writing of these letters, we have heard that our said son the dauphin has, by seduction, joined . . . the abovesaid' (rebels) (ibid., 530).
[6] Beaucourt, III, 138 and n. 2.

the counts of La Marche, Armagnac and Foix should be used in a military capacity against them. Charles V, he claimed, sent his brothers away from court, 'and when they came to see him, he gave them a few thousand *écus* to go away again'.[1] As long as the princes could be relied upon to use their military forces on the king's behalf, then the proposal might work. But if, as the events of the Praguerie clearly demonstrated, those forces were merely directed towards private ends, then it was doomed from the outset. It was more realistic for a king to keep his relatives at court, play them off against each other by using the old weapons of favour and disgrace, and prevent the accumulation of local power in the hands of a great house. Jean Juvenal misread the king's mind. It was hardly surprising that Charles did nothing as a result of his advice – that is, if he ever received it.

The princes themselves, however, may not have shared Jean Juvenal's views. The demands which they put forward at Nevers in March 1442 at some points suggest the contrary. They believed that the princes and lords of the blood should serve at court, as the king's best counsellors.[2] The pretext on which the princes had come together at Nevers was the discussion of the proposed marriage between Charles of Anjou and Mary of Guelders, niece of Philip the Good of Burgundy.[3] Since the peace of Arras, Franco-Burgundian marriages could be used to cement the alliance. But they could also serve other purposes. It has been observed that such schemes 'inaugurated a new phase of the policy of Philip the Good towards the other princes of the *fleurs-de-lys*. Its essence was to forget old rancours in order to facilitate the creation of a feudal league which the duke of Burgundy would lead.'[4] It was not a successful policy. The initiative behind the Anjou–Guelders proposal seems to have come from Charles VII. A marriage between Charles's daughter, Catherine, and Philip's eldest and only son, Charles, count of Charolais, had been celebrated at St-Omer on 11 June 1439.[5] There was a dispute about the terms under which Catherine received her dower. She had been assigned 120,000 *écus* on five lordships. As these lordships lay within the area ceded by Charles to Philip at Arras, and which he could redeem for 400,000 *écus*, the king now stood to pay 520,000 *écus* for the recovery of these 'Somme towns'. The marriage contract stipulated that neither Charles nor his successors could buy back the land without having previously paid the entire

---

[1] Loc. cit.

[2] Escouchy, III, 76–7.

[3] Ibid., 53; for the assembly, see Beaucourt, III, 211–31.

[4] C. A. J. Armstrong, 'La Politique Matrimoniale des ducs de Bourgogne de la Maison de Valois', *AB*, xl (1968), 20–1.

[5] Armstrong, op. cit., 39; for what follows see ibid., 40 n. 3.

dower of Catherine in cash to Philip. It was therefore desirable for the king to find ways of evading what was likely to be a crippling financial burden. His ambassador to the princes assembled at Nevers in March 1442 told them that he wished to reduce Catherine's dower to 20,000 écus. If Philip would agree to the marriage of Mary of Guelders to Charles of Anjou, the remaining 100,000 écus of Catherine's dower need not be paid by the king. Philip had merely to endow Mary with them. It was a clever move, but it came to nothing.

The house of Anjou was thus not allied to the house of Burgundy through marriage. But the house of Orléans was so linked. Old enmities were forgotten, and Charles of Orléans married Mary, princess of Cleves, niece of Philip the Good, at St-Omer on 26 November 1440.[1] It was a point of conflict between Orléans and the king. Charles knew that Burgundy had been pressing for Orléans's release from captivity since 1438, and was seeking to make him dependent on Burgundian aid. This was perhaps why Charles refused to meet Orléans when he arrived on French soil after his release.[2] At Nevers, it was evident that Orléans and Burgundy were in league together. Charles's distrust of their intentions is evident from his insistence that Orléans and the duchess Isabella of Burgundy might resume peace negotiations with the English, but only at a time when 'the king could be near enough to the place where the meeting shall be, so that his men can easily and quickly come and go to and from him, and from one place to another'.[3] The king's concern was voiced for the very good reason that a more pressing matter had to be resolved. The date for the resumption of peace talks with the English between Calais and Gravelines had been fixed. It was 1 May. But another deadline had been imposed upon him. In the south-west, the English were besieging the Gascon town of Tartas. The defender of the town, Charles II, lord of Albret, had agreed with the English that the place would be surrendered if aid had not arrived from Charles VII by the end of June 1442.[4] It might be thought that the surrender of a small Gascon town was not a pressing enough concern for a king. But the agreement which Charles II of Albret drew up with Thomas Rampston, the English seneschal of Guyenne, was potentially disastrous for the survival of Charles's régime in the south-west. If Tartas was not relieved, the cadet line of the house of Albret would swear allegiance to the English, taking their lands with them.[5] One of the

[1] Ibid., 19-20.
[2] Beaucourt, III, 163-4. He arrived in Paris on 14 January 1441.
[3] Escouchy, III, 65.
[4] See Vale, op. cit., 161-3; Beaucourt, III, 232-4.
[5] ABP, E.229, no. 12; Vale, op. cit., 161-3.

props of the Valois would be knocked away. Tartas was Charles VII's Mafeking.

The princes assembled at Nevers thus received short shrift. The king was determined not to delay the expedition to relieve Tartas on any account. Their demands went unheeded. He would go into Gascony in person, with the dauphin Louis. He would raise the forces of Albret, Armagnac and Foix under his banner. A show of strength was essential if the English war effort in the south-west was to be checked.[1] An alliance between Henry VI and Jean IV, count of Armagnac, was mooted. Henry was to marry Armagnac's daughter.[2] It was obvious that no time could be lost. Accompanied by his son, Charles reached Toulouse on 8 June.[3] The date for the relief of Tartas had been fixed as 24 June, and the king reached the place between ten and eleven o'clock on the morning of that day.[4] No English force arrived. Tartas was entered and the *fleurs-de-lys* flew over its gates. The Gascon campaign had served its purpose.

11 Court, council and conspiracies (1442-1449)

The preoccupation of the princes and lords of the Praguerie with the composition of the king's court and, especially, of his council, was reflected in one of their demands made at Nevers in March 1442. They begged the king

> that he be pleased to choose and elect to his council . . . worthy men, fearing God, and well known for integrity, wise and very expert, and not extreme or partisan in the conflicts which have taken place in this kingdom; and to have them in sufficient number, without committing power in the conduct of the high and important affairs of this kingdom to one, two or three only, as has been done sometimes before, but to communicate those great matters principally to the princes and lords of his blood, and, after having taken their advice and that of the others of his *grand conseil* in sufficient number . . . to ordain and decide matters for the good of himself and his lordship.[5]

This petition for conciliar government is interesting. The king's right to 'choose and elect' his counsellors was admitted, but their identity, nature and number was thought to be within the competence of the mag-

[1] Escouchy, III, 45-6; Beaucourt, III, 233-4.
[2] For the negotiations see Bekynton, *Correspondence*, II, 177-243.
[3] Beaucourt, III, 240; see below, 202.
[4] Ibid., III, 238, 241.
[5] Escouchy, III, 77.

nates to suggest. A large council was what they wanted, in which they themselves should play a leading part. The surviving lists of counsellors present at the issue of the king's ordinances at this time are occasionally revealing. The number of counsellors seems to be determined by the nature of the business in hand. An ordinance reducing the number of mounted serjeants in the kingdom was issued at Orléans on 24 August 1439. It was endorsed 'by the king', in the presence of Charles of Anjou, Dunois, the archbishop of Vienne, the lord of Chaumont, and Master Jean Rabateau, president of the *Parlement* of Paris.[1] A small, working council is obviously in action here. On 21 November 1440, however, a much larger body attested the issue of letters patent concerning the levy of a tax on all the clergy of France and the Dauphiné. The document was endorsed 'by the king in his council, at which my lord the Dauphin of Vienne [Louis], my lord Charles of Anjou, count of Maine, the constable, the count of La Marche, the bishops of Clermont and Maguelonne, the admiral, Master Jean d'Etampes, and others, were'.[2] This was evidently the *grand conseil*, summoned for such business as could not be transacted by the small, workaday group. But it was, perhaps, that group which made the decisions. The 'one, two or three only', complained of by the magnates in March 1442, were perhaps – and inevitably so – the normal accomplices of kingship.

Until the appearance of the sole surviving register of council proceedings for the reign – dating from 1455[3] – the study of Charles VII's council and counsellors is crippled by lack of evidence. The *ordonnances* are not always helpful, often merely carrying the endorsement 'Par le roy en son conseil', or, when names are included, ending with a tantalizing 'and many others'.[4] There is no reason to suppose that the king changed his ways as a result of the demands at Nevers. In one respect, however, the requests of the magnates were answered, though not entirely to their advantage. They had asked that men who were not 'extreme or partisan' be chosen by the king. Few of their number, or any others for that matter, had been exempt from the partisan strife of the early part of the reign. Armagnac and Burgundian stances were all too easy to adopt, even after the reconciliation of 1435.[5] So were *liaisons* with the English. Jean II, duke of Alençon, was virtually exiled from the king's presence, his pension

[1] *Ord.*, XIII, 303.
[2] Ibid., 327.
[3] See N. Valois, *Le Conseil du roi aux xive, xve et xvie siècles* (Paris, 1888), 231–323. Also below, 143–6.
[4] See *Ord.*, XIII, 305, 319, 321, 325, 327.

[5] See Bossuat in *Recovery of France*, 78–9, 365. For attempts to smooth the path of transition from English to Valois jurisdiction at Paris see *Ord.*, XIII, 216–17, 218–19 (March and May 1436).

was reduced, and his lordship of Niort seized.[1] Here then was a great magnate – one of the king's 'natural' counsellors – behaving in a partisan fashion. The other magnates might plead for him, as they did in March 1442, but the king remained adamant. Alençon would not be received back into favour, let alone be summoned to the council, 'until he conducts himself as he ought to do'. Alençon had been negotiating with the English, and it was alleged that Henry VI treated him 'as a prince of his own house'.[2] Such men were hardly to be welcomed as counsellors by Charles VII.

Yet the king could find men who were not 'extreme or partisan' in other quarters. From this time onwards there is evidence for the appearance of younger men at court and in his council. It was the period which saw the rise of the *mignons*.[3] If the 1440s produced anything new, then the formation of a *clientèle* of young courtiers around Charles needs to be taken into account. Men who had not experienced those 'divisions' within France to which the magnates referred, now attained political power. The forty-year-old king took advice from men who were, politically, comparatively inexperienced. To the civil servants in the council, a group of courtiers, all in their twenties and thirties, was added. How far they were there entirely as a result of the king's volition is uncertain. Jean Juvenal des Ursins, writing in 1445, claimed that

> truly, I've seen that, at the request of particular lords, young ignorant men are made *maîtres des requêtes* of the king's household . . . and of the king's *grand conseil*, to whom all that matters is pleasing those people who put them there, without wisdom, prudence, justice, reason nor experience; and they often speak their opinion in a hasty, impulsive, angry and cruel manner, when they ought to advise mercy. . . .[4]

Others, he told his brother, merely 'chattered and gossiped, and didn't attend to the business in hand'.[5] Jean Juvenal observed that 'aged, wise and experienced men' should only be chosen as counsellors.[6] He was, perhaps, reacting unfavourably to the introduction of the *mignons* into the council in the 1440s. Who were these men, and who put them there? Jean Juvenal may well have been indulging in classically inspired rhetoric when he celebrated the virtues of the *senex* as a king's counsellor. But the fact remains that a group of *juvenes* was forming around the king. The

---

[1] Escouchy, III, 59–60, 68–70, 79–81. See below, 156–9.
[2] Beaucourt, III, 228.
[3] Ibid., IV, 177–9.

[4] B.N., MS. fr. 2701, fol. 43ʳ. For the work of the *maîtres des requêtes* of the household, see below, 147–8.
[5] Ibid., fol. 43ʳ.
[6] Ibid., fol. 45ʳ.

first of these young men to attract attention was Pierre de Brézé.[1] Born in about 1410, he was in his late twenties when he became a member of the king's council in 1437. By 1441, having served the Anjou family loyally, he became seneschal of Poitou, and his political ascendancy was at its height from 1443 to 1449. He was the first of the *mignons*, and perhaps the most successful. Gifts, pensions and bribes were at his command during these years. But there were others who moved into the king's intimacy at this time. Above all, there was André de Villequier, described by Chastellain as 'a Norman, who was the king's *mignon*, and, so young, rose so high on the wheel of fortune that no one was his equal in his time'.[2] With his sisters, Marguerite and Antoinette, he did more than cut a dash at court. By 1444 he was in receipt of royal gifts – money for 'the upkeep of his estate', for horses and armour. In July 1445 he was styled king's chamberlain. In the following year he was continually in the king's company, and Marguerite was married another *mignon*, Antoine d'Aubusson, lord of Monteil.[3] Born in about 1413, Antoine d'Aubusson rose in the service of the duke of Bourbon, and became king's chamberlain soon after 1441. He was, perhaps, an example of Jean Juvenal's *protégé* of a 'particular lord'. With him served Guillaume Gouffier, formerly in the household of Charles of Anjou, count of Maine, which he left in 1444.[4] He was receiving royal gifts from that date onwards, and often slept in the king's chamber. With his fellow-esquire from the household of Charles of Anjou, Guillaume Gazeau, he was well rewarded for his services, receiving from the king 96 *livres* 5*s* for expenses at a joust at Razilly.[5] Lastly, there was François de Clermont, lord of Dampierre, from the Dauphiné. In March 1446 he married Jeanne de Montbéron, one of Marie of Anjou's *damoiselles*, and was lavishly endowed by both the king and the queen.[6]

From these instances it may be deduced that the nature of the court – that is, the royal household in its most extended form – was changing in the 1440s. It would be too extreme to claim, with Beaucourt, that in September 1444, at Nancy, there appeared a court which was 'new' in some fundamental way.[7] The household accounts of the early part of the

[1] For his career see P. Bernus, 'Louis XI et Pierre de Brézé (1440–65)', *Revue de l'Anjou*, new series, lxiii (1911), 241–89, 355–71; Bernus, 'Essai sur la vie de Pierre de Brézé (vers 1410–65)', *Positions des thèses de l'Ecole des Chartes* (1906), 7–17.
[2] Beaucourt, IV, 177–8.
[3] Ibid., 179.
[4] Ibid., 178, and above, 52–3.
[5] Ibid., 178 n. 4.

[6] Ibid., 178–9, and below, 133.
[7] See Beaucourt, IV, 77–8, 184–5. Some chroniclers recorded that Charles made a rare appearance as a jouster at Nancy in 1445, wearing green and breaking two lances with Brézé and one with René of Anjou. See Beaucourt, IV, 93; F. Piponnier, *Costume et Vie Sociale. La Cour d'Anjou, xive–xve siècles* (Paris–The Hague, 1970), 55–6.

reign suggest that the pomp and extravagance which Beaucourt traced to the 1440s was not unknown before that time.[1] Whether the return of René of Anjou to his duchy of Lorraine provided the occasion for a more lavish style of courtly life at Nancy is debatable. After all, the English embassy which was to negotiate the marriage of Henry VI to René's daughter, Margaret of Anjou, had to be impressed by the wealth and splendour of the Angevin household.[2] Whatever the significance of the autumn of 1444 as a 'turning-point' in the external attributes of the court of France, it seems arguable that subtler changes were taking place. First, as has been argued, a group of courtiers marked off by their comparative youth had formed around the king. But there were other common factors which bound them together. They tended to marry into the household of the queen, Marie of Anjou. They might have female relatives among the queen's *damoiselles*. As chamberlains of the king, they might have access to the king's ear. It was through them that influence might be exerted and favours obtained.[3] The manner in which this was achieved is obscure. But there are clues in a number of sources, not least of which is the scanty evidence for that most personal aspect of private life – the marital and sexual activities of Charles VII.

Chastellain, writing of Charles the Rash of Burgundy, thought that his sexual life was worthy of special note. 'He lived more chastely,' he wrote, 'than princes normally do, who are full of sensuality.'[4] Unlike his father, Philip the Good, he was not an 'homme lubrique'.[5] It was thus a common fifteenth-century assumption that princes were not chaste. The tolerance of bastards at the courts of France and Burgundy at this time may tell more about attitudes towards marriage than towards morals. At a period in which marriages at this social level were often arranged, bought and sold without the consent or even knowledge of their victims, it was hardly surprising that sexual satisfaction would be sought outside wedlock. Prostitution at all social levels was tolerated to a high degree, and public ownership of brothels an unquestioned assumption. In February 1425 Charles VII took into his protection the public whorehouse at Toulouse.[6] A gang of ribalds, pimps and evil-doers were terrorising its inmates, and, in order to protect them, and ensure that the consuls and syndics of the town did not lose a valuable source of municipal income, the place was

[1] See above, 37; L. Douët d'Arcq, *Comptes de l'hôtel des rois de France* . . . (*SHF*, Paris, 1865), xxxiii. These accounts for 1421 and 1422 all show a deficit.

[2] Beaucourt, IV, 90–4.

[3] See Lewis, *Later Medieval France*, 123, and below, 218, 221.

[4] Chastellain, VII, 231.

[5] See Vaughan, *Philip the Good*, 132–3.

[6] *Ord.*, XIII, 75–6 (13 February 1425).

put under royal safeguard. It was the ribalds, not the women and their clients, who were not 'reverencing God, nor Justice'.[1] Such solicitude for *las fillas communes* was indeed becoming in a king. The fact that many of the inhabitants of his *bonnes villes* were quite openly using the earnings of prostitutes to swell the civic coffers could hardly have passed unnoticed by the king. Yet there is no evidence for any kind of latitude in his own sexual behaviour before the early 1440s. He had fourteen legitimate children by Marie of Anjou, the last of which was Charles of France, born in December 1446.[2] The queen's life was thus devoted to child-bearing. She played no evident political role. Residing at Tours or Amboise she remained a stranger to the itinerant life of the king. She lost four children in three years, between 1436 and 1439. Habitually dressed in black, she kept her household outside politics, retreating into family and devotional life.[3]

In November 1442 her mother, Yolande of Aragon, died. It was the last of a series of bereavements which had begun in 1434.[4] Although Yolande had played little part in politics during her last years, her influence over both Charles and his queen had never been less than strong. It might not be too fanciful to see her death as the passing of a régime which was essentially partisan, born and nurtured amid the feuds of Armagnac and Burgundian. Political groupings around the great houses were constantly changing. But the structure and climate of politics in the 1440s were, perhaps, peculiar, and, in some respects, unprecedented. The king was now subject to new influences. Above all, the role of Agnès Sorel in this process needs to be investigated.[5] It is all too easy to dismiss the study of the career of a royal mistress as *histoire pittoresque*, unworthy of the 'scientific' historian's attention. But it is dangerous to do so. Men's public and private lives can be closely interwoven. To divorce 'life' from 'work' is possible only in a modern, industrial society. That kings in a remote era should not act like modern men is hardly worth arguing over. To claim that because so little is known about the 'private' lives of fifteenth-century men it is impossible to study them is perhaps too defeatist an attitude. When public and private concerns were intermingled, it is less easy to distinguish the one from the other. The court of Charles VII was not only a domestic household, it was a centre of political power. Access to, and acquisition of, that power might depend on many things. Not least of these was the company which the king kept. The men in furred doublets and gowns,

[1] *Ord.*, XIII, 76.
[2] See Beaucourt, III, 289.
[3] Ibid., 279–80.

[4] Ibid., 279.
[5] For what follows, see Beaucourt, III, 279–93.

moving through rooms hung with tapestries, off which smaller rooms opened, talking in low voices, catching the eye of a victim or potential patron – this is the scenario in which the historical imagination must be brought into play. The atmosphere of *Le Roi s'Amuse* or *Rigoletto* is not to be scorned.

The first authentic evidence for the existence of Agnès Sorel is found in an account of the household of Isabella of Lorraine, queen of Sicily, wife of René of Anjou. Between 1 January and 31 July 1444, a certain 'Agnès Sorelle' was paid ten *livres*.[1] She was then in a low place in the hierarchy of the household, below most of the ladies and *damoiselles* who served Isabella. The king could not have seen her before March 1443, when she was probably with Isabella at Toulouse, following her to Saumur in April.[2] Charles was at Saumur from September 1443 until mid-February 1444.[3] Marie of Anjou gave birth to a daughter on 1 December. An illegitimate daughter – Marie – may have been born to the king and Agnès Sorel in the summer of 1444.[4] By the end of that year she was a *damoiselle* of the unfortunate queen's household. The house of Anjou-Sicily evidently looked after its own. An inscription recorded as being in the collegiate church at Loches in 1749 confirmed that Sorel was at court by 1444. A silver-gilt statue there bore the following legend:

> In honour and reverence of St Mary Magdalene, the noble *damoiselle* my *damoiselle* of Beauté has given this image to this church of the castle of Loches, in which image there is enclosed a rib and some hair of the said saint, and it was in the year 1444.[5]

This offering of a reliquary might be interpreted in many ways. The dedication to the Magdalene is suggestive. The patroness of *las fillas communes* was, perhaps, an apt recipient of Agnès's libation. Could the gift have been some kind of penance for the birth of an illegitimate child? We will never know, and it would be vain to speculate. That she was already styled 'lady of Beauté' indicates the extent to which she had gained the king's favour. She had, appropriately, been given the *château* of Beauté, near the Bois de Vincennes, by the king.[6] Contemporaries were unanimous in their opinion of her beauty. She was about twenty-two years old when she became a member of the queen's household. She was the daughter of

[1] See Vallet de Viriville, 'Recherches historiques sur Agnès Sorel', *BEC*, xi (1849), 304.
[2] Beaucourt, III, 290.
[3] Ibid., 285, 291.

[4] Ibid., 288–9; VI, 432–4. Charles had three illegitimate daughters by Agnès Sorel – Marie, Charlotte and Jeanne.
[5] Vallet de Viriville, op. cit., 319; Beaucourt, III, 284.
[6] Beaucourt, III, 285; IV, 173–4.

Jean Soreau, lord of Coudun, and Catherine de Maignelais. Born perhaps in Picardy, her early life is completely obscure. From an early date after her appearance at court, however, her name was coupled with that of the 'finest talker of his time', the volatile Pierre de Brézé.[1] His Angevin connections might have brought him into contact with *la belle Agnès* before her entry into the queen's household. Beaucourt believed that 'he had wished to make use of her in order better to ensure his ascent'.[2] Was he responsible for introducing her into the king's presence? Certainly allegations were made that he was using her as an instrument of his own aggrandisement. On 27 October 1446 it was alleged that he 'kept the king in subjection by means of this Agnès who is attendant upon the queen'.[3] Thomas Basin could claim, many years later, that those who spoke ill of her lost the king's favour – the possibilities of informing on them were unlimited.[4] The likely effects of an 'Agnès up to the hilt' were well enough known to Brézé in March 1447.[5] A secret memorandum to Philip the Good, of about the same date, stated that 'the said seneschal [Brézé] keeps himself marvellously well in with the king, partly by means of Agnès, from whom he has what he wants'.[6] Such devices could work in more than one direction, as Brézé was later to discover. But there can be no doubt that Charles was 'heavily besotted' with Agnès Sorel from the winter of 1443–4 onwards.[7] If Brézé *was* a procurer, his services were not freely given. His price was political power.

There were perhaps others besides Brézé who were advanced in the king's favour by Agnès Sorel. Her relatives benefited from her ascent. Her brothers Charles and Jean were members of the king's household in 1446, and two other brothers, Louis and André, were in the royal bodyguard.[8] Her uncle, Geoffroy Soreau, did even better, and became bishop of Nîmes in 1450.[9] Olivier de la Marche claimed that she also 'did . . . much good to the kingdom of France, because she introduced to the king young men-at-arms and noble companions by whom he was subsequently well served'.[10] Her influence on the life of the court gave rise to unfavourable comment as well. Chastellain – conveniently forgetting the proclivities of his patron, Philip the Good – wrote that 'of all that can

[1] See ibid., III, 292–3 and n. 4, for Charles's letters of December 1444 in Brézé's favour. For Brézé's bewitching speech see the 'Dépréciation pour Messire Pierre de Brézé' in Chastellain, VII, 37–65, 72, and III, 347.

[2] Beaucourt, III, 292.

[3] See ibid., III, 293, and below, 108–9.

[4] Basin, II, 282.

[5] Escouchy, III, 282, and below, 108–9.

[6] Ibid., 268.

[7] Chastellain, IV, 365.

[8] Beaucourt, IV, 174.

[9] Ibid., 174; V, 322; VI, 26, 188.

[10] Olivier de la Marche, II, 55.

lead to *ribaudise* and dissoluteness in the matter of costume, she was the begetter and inventor'.[1] But the most furiously moralistic outburst came from the ubiquitous Jean Juvenal des Ursins. In his advice to his brother, on his becoming chancellor in 1445, Jean Juvenal wrote indignantly:

> . . . that, in his own household itself, the king should prohibit openings in front through which you can see the women's nipples and breasts, and the great furred trains, girdles and other things, because they are so displeasing to God and the world, and not without reason; and that in his household and that of the queen and his children, he shouldn't tolerate men or women tainted with whoredom and ribaldry and all sorts of sins, because by tolerating them all too many setbacks and divine punishments have come about. I've seen the robes of the king's grandmother, which had trains which were hardly a foot long. . . .[2]

Perhaps Jean Juvenal had not seen the king's mother's robes. Or, if he had, he was keeping quiet about it. Such clerical denunciations of the extravagance and obscenity of courtly costume were not unprecedented. A hundred years earlier, Jean de Venette had attributed the disasters of the 1350s to the indecency of contemporary aristocratic dress.[3] At a later date, Jean Juvenal could tell the king that the great headdresses and trains of the women of his court were nothing but meretricious tricks. They looked like 'old mules or old mares got up in fine harness to be more marketable; and then they display their breasts or nipples: one must give the courtiers an appetite somehow. . . .'[4] Whether Charles VII's court was any more immoderate in its dress than that of Isabella of Bavaria is uncertain. There had always been court tarts, some of noble birth. Accusations about the corruption of the court fill the works of Eustache Deschamps and Alain Chartier.[5] It was an established literary convention. As for extravagance of costume, it could be argued from the evidence of household accounts that the workaday clothing of the court was not so. Black, grey and russet seem to have been the most popular colours, as they were before about 1470 at the court of Anjou.[6] The household of France may reflect more general tendencies towards greater luxury and extravagance of costume at the top of the hierarchy, especially on ceremonial

---

1 Chastellain, IV, 366.
2 B.N. MS. fr. 2701, fol. 55ᵛ.
3 See *The Chronicle of Jean de Venette*, ed. R. A. Newhall (New York, 1953), 34, 62–3.
4 B.N. MS. fr. 2701, fol. 99ʳ.

5 See Chartier's *Le Curial*, ed. F. Heuckenkamp (Halle, 1899), and Eustache Deschamps's *Poésies*, ed. G. A. Crapelet (Paris, 1832), 16–17, 28–9, 45–6, 106–7.
6 See Piponnier, op. cit., 212–13, 291–2.

occasions. The courts of Burgundy and Anjou seem to follow this pattern.[1] Jean Juvenal's remarks may thus be less a commentary on what was peculiar to Charles VII's court than an attack on the allegedly declining morals of the age. It was perhaps as a result of the Angevin hegemony – represented by the presence of Charles of Anjou and Pierre de Brézé – at court that such alleged excesses were tolerated. The household of Marie of Anjou was, perhaps, the exception which proved the rule. Vogue and fashion, expressed by gay costumes and a taste for jousts, may have erupted into the court of Charles VII in the 1440s.[2] It would be tempting to attribute this to the influence of the 'young men' in the *ambiance* of Agnès Sorel and Brézé. But there was at least one young man who became increasingly estranged from the court at this time.

The story of the dauphin Louis's growing antagonism towards his father's court has often been told, and it is not intended to repeat it here.[3] Charles had employed his son on lieutenancies since 1440 – in Ile de France, Guyenne, and on the expedition to support the Habsburgs against the Swiss in Alsace and Lorraine in the summer and autumn of 1444.[4] On that campaign – partly devised as a means of ridding France of the worst of the *écorcheurs* – he was wounded at the siege of Lambach in September 1444. An arrow was shot through Louis's knee and pinned him to his saddle.[5] The king's alarm is indicated by the stream of letters sent to his only son, ordering him to return from Alsace to the court. It has been asserted that this was a mere pretext on Charles's part to regain the control which he had, allegedly, lost over his son.[6] But it was at the king's command that Louis had left for Alsace in the first place. Paternal affection, and the natural desire to safeguard his heir, might better explain Charles's concern. The king was conducting an expedition in Lorraine at the same time, reasserting the sovereignty of René of Anjou, as duke of Lorraine, over the city of Metz.[7] Both the Alsace and Lorraine expeditions of 1444–5 could also be seen as a blow against Philip the Good of Burgundy. The *écorcheurs* in Louis's companies openly insulted the Burgundians, who were garrisoning the town of Montbéliard in the name of their ally, the duke of Württemburg.[8] Metz had also made an alliance with Philip. By occupying Alsace, Louis's *écorcheurs* were allowed to winter off the

---

[1] See O. Cartellieri, *The Court of Burgundy* (London, 1929), 59–64; Piponnier, op. cit., 61–79, 195–212, 290–3.

[2] Beaucourt, IV, 90–101, 182–4.

[3] See Thibault, *Louis XI*, 551 f; Beaucourt, 188–201; Kendall, *Louis XI*, 52–68.

[4] Beaucourt, IV, 7–46.

[5] Ibid., 41.

[6] Kendall, *Louis XI*, 60.

[7] Beaucourt, IV, 47–76.

[8] See Vaughan, *Philip the Good*, 115–18; also the depositions of witnesses printed in A. Tuetey, *Les Ecorcheurs sous Charles VII* (Montbéliard, 1874), 301–80.

country before being unleashed again. It was a question of whether Burgundy or Milan would be the next to suffer.[1] The problem of occupying the troops bulks large in these years. If there was a truce with the English – as there was in 1444 – where should the companies find employment? The rival claims of the English war, the war of attrition against Burgundy, or the pursuit of the dynastic claims of the houses of Orléans and Anjou in Italy provided a source of debate and conflict at the court of France.

At the age of twenty-one, Louis was an unprepossessing figure.[2] He had his father's poor legs and awkward walk. He was nonchalant to the point of shabbiness in his dress. He entered Toulouse in 1443 in such mean attire that he was not recognised.[3] It was not the last time on which he was mistaken for a servant or a messenger of the king's *écurie*. He suffered from a slight speech impediment and his pronunciation was indistinct.[4] He must have hated Pierre de Brézé for his eloquence. There was a vulgarity about Louis which his father never shared. Unlike him, he was a great eater and drinker, in both high and low company. Charles usually ate alone.[5] Both could be cruel – Louis's behaviour towards prisoners at Dieppe, and towards Jean IV, count of Armagnac, suggests unnecessary harshness towards the vanquished.[6] Despite the legendary picture of Louis as a 'universal spider', he was, perhaps, not as subtle, nor as clever, as his father. He talked too much, and made enemies through the viciousness of his tongue. His father's recorded utterances tend to suggest extreme caution, and a circumspection which Louis never seems to have shared. Above all, Louis had come to detest the wife to whom he had been wed, without his consent, by his father's wish. Margaret of Scotland was sterile, her dower had not been paid, she was consumptive, she was melancholic, and she was a target for insinuation at court.[7] But both Charles and his queen appear to have had considerable affection for her. When she fell seriously ill, after contracting what seems to have been pneumonia in August 1445, the king was deeply concerned. His doctor, Robert Poitevin, was sent to attend her. But she died on 16 August, aged twenty-one, allegedly worn out by her over-fertile poetic imagination.[8]

On the morrow of her death, Charles left Chalons 'suddenly, sad, angered and troubled' – perhaps as much by the indifference of his son as

[1] Beaucourt, IV, 33–46, 62–6.
[2] For what follows, see Thibault, *Louis XI*, 458–91.
[3] Ibid., 461.
[4] Ibid., 491, citing Basin as evidence for this.
[5] Beaucourt, IV, 87. Henri Baude, Basin and Chastellain concurred on his sobriety at table.
[6] See Thibault, *Louis XI*, 468–9.
[7] See Beaucourt, IV, 106–11.
[8] Ibid., 110; Thibault, *Louis XI*, 546.

by his own personal grief.[1] He was sufficiently disturbed by the affair to order an inquiry into it, which began at Chalons in October.[2] At the centre of the issue stood Jamet du Tillay, *bailli* of Vermandois, one of Louis's chamberlains. It was alleged that Louis had been using him to spy on Margaret's activities at court while he was away campaigning. No proof was adduced, either at the inquiry of October 1445 or a subsequent series of interrogations between June and August 1446.[3] Jamet du Tillay remained in office, and continued to attend meetings of the king's council.[4] The state of affairs at court in the summer of 1445 is described by the ambassadors of Filippo Maria Visconti, duke of Milan, who were at Nancy in May. On 26 May they wrote:

> As to the state of affairs over here, we inform your Lordship that, as far as we can discover, there are in the heart of the house of France great jealousies and burning disputes. None could be more violent than those between the illustrious lord dauphin and the king René. This springs from the fact that King René is the one by whom everything is done in the kingdom. It is he who has had this *ordonnance* for the reduction of men-at-arms issued, of which we have sent a copy to your Lordship. Besides this, there is little contact between the duke of Orléans and King René, always through jealousy on the subject of government.[5]

The Milanese were probably attributing too great an influence to René, neglecting the important role of Charles of Anjou, count of Maine, at this time. But there was sufficient truth in what they said for the king to remove the Angevins from court later that summer. Charles told them 'by word of mouth, that they should not return until they were sent for'.[6] It was a complete reversal of the tendency towards Angevin ascendancy, first traced at Nancy in the previous year. René's name does not appear in the surviving lists of counsellors after September 1445, and Charles of Anjou disappears from them in December.[7] Exile was evidently not absolute, nor was it permanent. But the waning of Angevin power at court had important implications. First, the claims of the house of Orléans to the duchy of Milan and the county of Asti could be more seriously entertained as a result of the departure of the Angevins.[8] French interven-

[1] Beaucourt, IV, III, and Vaesen, *Lettres*, I, 200.

[2] Beaucourt, IV, 181–2; Duclos, IV, 24–49.

[3] Duclos, IV, 38–49.

[4] Beaucourt, IV, 182.

[5] Ibid., 102.

[6] Escouchy, I, 68.

[7] Beaucourt, IV, 103.

[8] For these claims, see E. Jarry, *La vie politique de Louis de France, duc d'Orléans, 1373–1407* (Paris, 1889), 25–43. The marriage treaty by which Orléans gained Asti was approved by Pope Clement VII in May 1387.

tion in Italy could now turn away from supporting the abortive attempts of René and his family to realise their claim to the throne of Sicily and Naples. Secondly, the dauphin Louis might be reconciled to the situation at his father's court. He disliked the Angevins greatly, and was no doubt glad to be rid of them.[1] But there was a stumbling-block which could not be eliminated. Pierre de Brézé had convinced himself (whether sincerely or not there is no means of telling) that a new Praguerie was forming among the lords at court in the summer of 1445. The marriage alliances between the house of Luxembourg and those of Brittany and Anjou may perhaps have given rise to his suspicions. Richemont married Catherine of Luxembourg, and Charles of Anjou, deprived of a Burgundian heiress, married Isabella of Luxembourg.[2] Brézé, it was alleged, began to spread rumours – rumours which reached the king's ear. He had turned against his former employers. The way was now clear for him to render himself indispensable to the king.

The composition of the king's council at this period can be established from a number of sources – lists of witnesses appended to the king's ordinances, depositions of witnesses under interrogation, and so on. A key to the code by which Charles's closest advisers were identified in letters written to Philip the Good of Burgundy in February 1445 gives the names of five men who were often with the king 'in his retreat'.[3] They were Brézé, Bertrand de Beauvau, lord of Précigny (another old servant of the house of Anjou), Jamet du Tillay, Jean du Mesnil-Simon (son of the king's governess when a child) and Master Jean Bureau. As one might expect, those most often in close contact with the king were the courtiers and civil servants. The more formal means of taking counsel – a meeting of the *grand conseil* – was dominated by the chancellor. On 16 June 1445 Guillaume Jouvenel des Ursins was appointed to that high office.[4] It was on this occasion that his brother Jean Juvenal composed his treatise on the chancellor's duties. The council must be seen as a committee, in which the king presided, with the chancellor chairing the meeting.[5] Only the king and the chancellor were allowed to interrupt a speaker. No council minutes or memoranda survive for this part of the reign. What actually went on in the council is thus a topic of pure speculation. But Jean Juvenal was anxious to tell his brother that business did not end at the end of a session of the council. The suspicion that some members of the council spoke merely 'in order to please those who put them there' led the chan-

[1] See Thibault, *Louis XI*, 469–70.
[2] Beaucourt, IV, 101–2.
[3] Escouchy, III, 318–19.
[4] Beaucourt, IV, 410.
[5] B.N. MS. fr. 2701, fols 42^r–44^r, and see Lewis, op. cit., 128–32.

5 Title page of a sermon preached before Charles VII on 10 June 1442 by Bernard du Rozier, bishop of Bazas. The MS. was presented to Charles VII on 1 January 1451 (*Bibliothèque Nationale, MS. lat. 6020, fol. 85*)

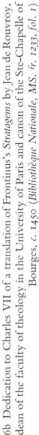

6a Jean Le Bègue presents his translation of Leonardo Bruni's *History of the First Punic War* to Charles VII. The MS. is dated 9 June 1454 (*Bibliothèque Nationale, MS. fr. 23085, fol. 1*)

6b Dedication to Charles VII of a translation of Frontinus's *Stratagems* by Jean de Rouvroy, dean of the faculty of theology in the University of Paris and canon of the Ste-Chapelle of Bourges, c. 1450 (*Bibliothèque Nationale, MS. fr. 1233, fol. 1*)

cellor to take preventive action. The king would go into a little closet (*un petit retrait*), and the chancellor would see that the right people were called to see him secretly. Robert le Maçon did this all the time. The chancellor should not scruple to withhold some kinds of business from the council, and he should talk to the king, and other counsellors, privately about them. Jean Juvenal warned his brother about his manner when doing this.

> I know that you'll stop yourself from doing it in the council . . . but outside the council, when someone comes to talk to you, you're sometimes a bit irascible, even though you have a good complexion. And I've seen, when you were young, that it appeared from your face and manner that you were angry. And as for me, I'm a hundred times more like that, and so take care and stop yourself doing it. And you can always look at your face in a mirror in your chamber when you're angry, and this should hold you back.[1]

There was evidently at least one choleric man in Charles VII's council. His portrait, perhaps, confirms his brother's view.[2] As chancellor, he was well advised to dissimulate, to play for time, to keep his temper. The council, it has been observed, was 'a world in which the force of personality was paramount'.[3] But sometimes personality had to be kept on a tight rein. To chair the king's council required more skills than mere industriousness. An astute chancellor could more or less control the business of conciliar government by carefully drawing up the council's *agenda*. He had his allies – in 1445, Guillaume Jouvenel could perhaps rely on the support of his two brothers, Jean and Jacques, both civil-servant bishops, as he steered an issue or scheme through a rough passage. A show of temper was hardly likely to make headway against the gilded eloquence of a Brézé or a Dunois.

The two 'fine talkers' had assumed a leading role in court and council by the summer of 1445. Both were on good terms with the dauphin Louis. There is evidence that the dauphin was effectively placing members of his household in the king's council at this time. Guillaume Cousinot, counsellor of the Dauphiné, and Etienne Chevalier, *maître* of Louis's *chambre aux deniers* since 1443, appear in the *ordonnances* from this time.[4] Chevalier, who was to have a distinguished career as a royal civil servant,

[1] B.N. MS. fr. 2701, fol. 45ᵛ.
[2] Now Musée du Louvre, no. 288, attributed to Jean Fouquet. For a reproduction see G. Ring, *A Century of French Painting, 1400-1500* (London, 1949),

Plate 72. The portrait dates from *c.* 1455.
[3] Lewis, op. cit., 131.
[4] See Thibault, *Louis XI*, 498–501; *Ord.*, XIII, 425, 427.

witnessed many of the documents emanating from the secretariat.[1] But such apparent harmony did not last. In October 1445 Louis fell out with Dunois, and purged a number of his 'familiars' from his household, among them Louis de Bueil, his counsellor and chamberlain, brother of Jean de Bueil, later admiral of France.[2] The reasons for this move are utterly obscure. As yet, there was no rupture between Louis and Brézé. In January 1446 he presented Brézé with a consignment of Rhine wine, while the court was at Chinon for the New Year.[3] If Louis was aiming to capture the council, then he was obviously prepared to work through Brézé at this stage. But the seneschal of Poitou's connection with Agnès Sorel was not likely to assist Louis. Initially, Louis had no quarrel with Sorel. At some time after the expedition which he led against Jean, count of Armagnac, in January 1444, he presented her with tapestries which he had removed from Armagnac's castle of L'Isle-Jourdain.[4] If Louis, as well as his father, was her lover, then she might have been the principal cause of the estrangement between them. Some contemporaries certainly thought that she was, and devised stories of Louis threatening her and being thrown out of his father's presence as a result.[5] Thomas Basin believed that she was by no means faithful to the king.[6] Whatever the truth really was, Louis's next move seemed unequivocal. He began, it is asserted, to conspire against his father.

The instrument chosen by him was the former écorcheur, Anthoine de Chabannes, count of Dammartin. Knowledge of Louis's behaviour at this time is largely derived from depositions made by Chabannes.[7] These must be treated with caution. They are *ex parte* statements by an interested party, attempting to clear his name of a possible charge of treason. They probably do not contain enough truth to be used as evidence for relations between Charles VII and his son. Chabannes was interrogated on 27 September 1446, at Candé, by Guillaume Jouvenel des Ursins and Adam Rolant, one of the king's secretaries. He gave evidence about events of the previous April, when the court was at Chinon. Louis, he alleged, had spoken with him 'in his retreat' overlooking the moat of the castle of Chinon.[8] They had talked about the king's guard of Scots

---

[1] Thibault, *Louis XI*, 501. Chevalier had previously served the constable Richemont from at least 1426 onwards. See Cosneau, *Richemont*, 126, 522. Also Godefroy, *Chartier*, 884–6.

[2] Beaucourt, IV, 189–90.

[3] Ibid., 190.

[4] Vallet de Viriville, op. cit., 308.

[5] See Beaucourt, IV, 190 nn. 4 and 5; Kendall, *Louis XI*, 67.

[6] Basin, II, 281.

[7] B.N. MS. fr. 20427, fols 3ʳ–6, and MS. fr. 15537, fols 8ʳ–11ʳ (27 September 1446).

[8] B.N. MS. fr. 20427, fol. 3ʳ; Beaucourt, IV, 192–3.

archers, who, Louis remarked, 'keep the kingdom of France in subjection'.[1] He intended to win them over, or, if that failed, to overpower them by force, using Chabannes's and his own archers. Chabannes refused to be party to the scheme, and then deposed that Louis had promised him 1,000 *livres* rent in the *comté* of Valentinois, and sent him on a mission to Savoy. On his return, while riding in Louis's company on the road to Razilly, where the king was, Louis took him aside and they rode together through the fields.[2] A plan to seize power was still on the dauphin's mind. He tried to enlist Chabannes's support, asking him to find certain men-at-arms and archers for him. Razilly was relatively unguarded, and access to it was easy. Louis claimed that he had allies within the king's entourage – Charles of Anjou, out of favour at court, had told him that he could get him the services of Nicholas Chambers, captain of the Scots guard. Bertrand de la Tour, lord of Montgascon, was already his. The Laval family, lords of Châtillon and Lohéac, were also behind him. Louis then made an interesting observation. He wished, he said, to be there in person when the *coup* was made, for 'everyone fears the king's person when they see him'.[3] Unless he was there himself, he could not trust his men to do what they had been told. An attack on the person of the king was unthinkable – Louis merely intended to put him in the tutelage of 'good and sure men'. Only the English killed their kings.

Chabannes may have been lying. A solemn oath may have meant little to a former captain of *écorcheurs*. Louis might have said nothing of the kind to him. There were plenty of people around Charles VII who were anxious to smear his son's name and have him exiled from the court. Chabannes slept in the king's chamber, and was therefore privy to everything that a *mignon* might know. Louis was content for this to continue, he claimed, and also for Brézé to remain supreme at court. 'But,' he said, 'it will be under me', not under his father.[4] At this moment they were interrupted, and the matter rested for a time. Unsuccessful (allegedly) with Chabannes, Louis tried other means.[5] His counsellor and chamberlain Jean de Daillon was brought into play, sent back and forth between king and dauphin. Louis de Bueil, recently dismissed from Louis's household, was his accomplice. They were seen talking together in low voices, and raised them when they saw Chabannes. The latter knew that Louis suspected him, and it was suggested to him that he had been unwise to play tennis

[1] B.N. MS. fr. 20427, fols 3ʳ, 3ᵛ. For the guard see Beaucourt, IV, 179 ff, 63–4, and above, 33.
[2] B.N. MS. fr. 20427, fol. 3ᵛ.
[3] Ibid., fol. 4ʳ.
[4] Ibid., fol. 4ʳ. Beaucourt, IV, 194–6.
[5] B.N. MS. fr. 20427, fol. 4ᵛ.

with Renaud de Dresnay, *bailli* of Sens, an intimate of his father's.[1] Business was evidently combined with pleasure at the court of Charles VII. One of Louis's 'familiars', called Jupilles, told Chabannes that 'you know he [Louis] is the most suspicious man in the world, so behave yourself in such a way that he won't be displeased with you'.[2] Despite pouring rain, Louis sent Chabannes to Savoy once again, then to Chinon, to collect some money for him. He was being treated badly, and Jupilles said that Louis had told him that he would not speak to Chabannes again. Louis's extraordinary lack of discretion seems patently obvious from these depositions – if, that is, they can be trusted. Even his attempts at bribery were overheard.

Chabannes evidently thought that Louis had maltreated him. He was, perhaps, anxious to discredit him throughout his depositions. Amaury d'Estissac, Louis's chief counsellor, told him that the dauphin thought that Chabannes was in his household merely 'to spy on everything that was done, and to report it to my lord the seneschal [Brézé], and that he was his'.[3] Chabannes denied this, but, given his concern to win back the king's favour after his dismissal from the army,[4] he may have been so employed. Most of the courtiers at this time appear to have served at least two masters. 'Loyalty' is an extremely ambiguous concept. Louis appears to have believed that he could gain the unqualified and absolute loyalty of these men by buying up their services. His father was perhaps better aware of the inconstancy of the men around him. He had learnt from experience that there was no one whom he could trust. Favour and disgrace, arbitrarily meted out, were the only effective means of controlling the self-seekers who were his servants. They were all informing on each other. A servant of Louis de Bueil, called Galchault, was said by another of his servants, Guillaume Benoist, to have told him about the views of their master. From his words it could be concluded that there was an attempt under way to dislodge Brézé from power.[5] He was the scapegoat for many things – a dishonourable truce with the English, the procuring of Agnès Sorel for the king, the sending of the dauphin to Alsace, and an alleged subsequent withdrawal of support. An unlikely alliance between the Angevins and Louis would end all this. The king himself, so the deposition claimed, 'does not like the seneschal [Brézé] at all, and the principal reason is that he reproves him too much in front of people'.[6] Whether

[1] B.N. MS. fr. 20427, fol. 4ᵛ. For Renaud see below, 112.
[2] Ibid., fol. 4ᵛ.
[3] Ibid., fol. 6ʳ.
[4] See Contamine, op. cit., 400, 596–7.

Jean, bastard of Armagnac, and Jean de Salazar were also purged from the army in 1445 (ibid., 401).
[5] B.N. MS. fr. nouv. acq. 1001, fol. 37.
[6] Ibid., fol. 37, and Beaucourt, IV, 195–6.

the man was merely telling his interrogators what they wanted to know, or not, can never be discovered. But the picture of Brézé taking the king up on issues in the presence of his entourage is not a wholly implausible one. A 'fine talker' can presume too much.

The testimonies of these witnesses seem to confirm the view that there was a plot to unseat Brézé in the summer and autumn of 1446. The exact part played by the dauphin Louis in that conspiracy is by no means clear. He preserved an outward affection for the seneschal. It was perhaps his servants, and their servants, who were after Brézé's blood. Louis de Bueil (whose loyalty to Louis was in any case dubious), his unpleasant servants Benoist and Galchault, and Jean de Daillon – Louis's agent at court – may have been the real instigators of the plot against Brézé.

On 18 October the king was sufficiently disturbed by events to order Blanc Barbin, counsellor and *maître des requêtes* of his household, to examine certain witnesses on the subject of 'certain slanders . . . uttered by some against certain great lords of his *grand conseil*'.[1] There was one 'great lord' given particular mention. Thibaud Gounin, esquire, living at Le Plessis-Rideau, near Tours, said that Jean de Daillon came to Le Plessis 'recently', riding very fast. Daillon was reported to have said that 'there were some people who would soon lose their lives', and the esquire assumed that this referred to Brézé.[2] A rumour had spread that the seneschal had been ousted by the dauphin. Daillon was also said to have remarked that both Jean and Louis de Bueil, and Louis de Laval, lord of Châtillon, had been dismissed from the dauphin's household.[3] This is important evidence. A second witness, Jeanne Poussine, a *damoiselle* of eighteen, enjoyed Daillon's company at Le Plessis for two hours that day. He amused her with jokes, but also said that he was fleeing, because both he and Louis de Bueil had been sent away from court for plotting Brézé's death.[4] To another *damoiselle*, Jacquette Poussine, aged twenty-four, Daillon said that Châtillon and Louis de Bueil thought that he was dead, and he wished them to be told that he was alive.[5] This evidence was confirmed by an esquire called Jean le Texier, who had heard it from certain unnamed people in Louis's household.[6]

Louis had thus taken the initiative against his servants. Brézé remained where he was. Perhaps the dauphin – if he was in fact plotting in the way that his biographers have claimed – saw that Brézé was too valuable to

---

[1] B.N. MS. fr. nouv. acq. 1001, fols. 40ʳ–41ʳ.
[2] Ibid., fol. 40ʳ.
[3] Ibid., fol. 40ʳ.

[4] Ibid., fol. 40ᵛ.
[5] Ibid., fol. 41ʳ.
[6] Ibid., fol. 41ʳ.

lose. He had, after all, it was alleged, said that he would keep him in favour and use him.[1] Yet his position, like that of the king's previous co-adjutors – was a precarious one. Like them, he made enemies. Even his fellow-*mignon*, André de Villequier, was said to be against him in the summer of 1446.[2] A confidant of Charles VII had to pick his way through what has been aptly compared to a minefield.[3] Brézé lasted for a remark-ably long time, but he was as dispensable as the rest of them. His devious-ness – which could sometimes go to absurd lengths – saved his skin for a while.

Apart from personal antagonisms, a political issue divided the court. The truce of Tours (1444) had left the English war suspended for twenty years. This was further cemented by the marriage of Henry VI and Margaret of Anjou. The English administrations of Normandy, Maine and Guyenne thus survived. Brézé had played a leading part in negotiating the truce and the marriage. It was alleged that he had personally profited from them, just as it was to be alleged that, on the other side, Suffolk had sold out to the enemy.[4] Charles VII's military *ordonnance* of June 1445 had created a standing army from the ranks of the unoccupied men-at-arms, without employment because of the truce.[5] The problem of utilising this potenti-ally anarchic force again plagued the king and his advisers. In the event, a scheme was planned, using a proffer of aid by Filippo Maria Visconti of Milan in November 1446.[6] In return for military assistance against Venice, the Milanese would help Charles VII to seize Genoa, abetted by the house of Orléans. The county of Asti would also be handed over to Charles of Orléans, through the title inherited by him from his mother, Valentine Visconti.[7]

Asti was an imperial fief, and Orléans did homage, by proxy, for it in 1444.[8] A series of diplomatic exchanges between Milan and the French court took place during the following year. René of Anjou was hoping to gain Genoese support against the Aragonese in Naples. Two of the greatest lords of France thus stood to gain from an aggressive policy in Italy. It could be argued that the cessation of hostilities with the English in 1444 accommodated the ambitions of the houses of Anjou and Orléans. An Italian campaign would also keep the standing army occupied. If the lords could lead the companies out of France, a second Praguerie would be

[1] B.N. MS. fr. 20427, fol. 4ʳ.
[2] Beaucourt, IV, 195–6.
[3] See Lewis, op. cit., 125.
[4] See Escouchy, III, 325, 336; for Suffolk, *Rot. Parl.*, V, 179–81 (March 1450).

[5] Contamine, op. cit., 277–319; Beaucourt, IV, 387–404.
[6] Beaucourt, IV, 233–7.
[7] See above, 97–8.
[8] Beaucourt, IV, 220–1. Charles of

less likely to arise. The dauphin could be employed as his father's lieutenant, marching from the Dauphiné across Savoy to Genoa.[1] In the event,
Alsace was to be his theatre of war. A decisive change seems to have
taken place in the autumn of 1446. On 28 September Michelotto Attendolo,
captain-general of the Venetian republic, was victorious at the battle of
Casal Maggiore over the troops of Filippo Maria Visconti of Milan.[2]
Visconti dispatched Théaude de Valpergue, one of his vassals, as ambassador to seek aid from France. Charles and Louis would be helped to gain
Asti and Genoa in return for aid in the recovery of Milanese territories
– Bergamo, Brescia, and so on – recently conquered by the Venetians
on the mainland. A treaty was signed with Milan on 29 December 1446.
Charles was to provide 4,000 troops, to recover Brescia and Bergamo
after being invested with Genoa, and Théaude de Valpergue was to become governor of Asti in Charles's name.[3]

But Filippo Maria was not satisfied with the terms, and procrastinated.
Genoa provided a more promising objective.[4] The republic was in a state
of near-anarchy, and a faction of the council appealed for aid to France,
against the supporters of Alfonso V of Aragon. At Nice, one Janus de
Campo Fregoso, leader of the faction, negotiated with Jacques Cœur,
the shipowner and financier who was Charles's *argentier* and chief creditor
at this time. A fleet was amassed, Cœur's experience obviously being fully
exploited in the provision of galleys for an expeditionary force.[5] The
aptly named Janus entered Genoa, with a galley manned by 300 troops,
on 30 January 1447. Once he had unseated the rival Adorno faction, he
performed a *volte-face* and turned against the French and Angevin claim.
The dauphin Louis had been sent to the Dauphiné by his father in January,
to hold himself ready to join the projected French expedition into Lom-
bardy for the recovery of Asti. Nothing happened. Early in March,
French ambassadors, including Jean Juvenal des Ursins, embarked for
Genoa at Villefranche, near Nice. They found Janus de Campo Fregoso
entrenched there, ready to defend his title against all comers. Lacking
forces, they were compelled to return to Provence. The 'Affair of Genoa'
was a fiasco. Discontent was rife at the French court, and Brézé's hegemony

Orléans could also claim the duchy of
Milan through his mother. Filippo Maria
Visconti had no legitimate heirs. For the
succession crisis, in which Charles VII
supported Orléans's (unsuccessful) claim,
see ibid., 248–51 (August 1447).
[1] Ibid., 223–9. For the origins of the claim
of the house of Orléans to Genoa and

other lordships in Piedmont, see E. Jarry,
*Les origines de la domination française à
Gênes, 1392–1402* (Paris, 1896), 44–51.
[2] Beaucourt, IV, 230–31.
[3] Ibid., 231–7.
[4] Ibid., 237–8.
[5] Ibid., 239–40; Escouchy, III, 252; for
Jacques Cœur see below, 127–34.

seriously threatened.[1] On 30 April, Jean de Dresnay, another intermediary between Charles and Louis, testified before Guillaume Jouvenel des Ursins, Bertrand de Beauvau, lord of Précigny, and Master Guillaume Cousinot that, at Easter, he had been in Louis's household at Romans in the Dauphiné. His interrogators were anxious to discover the climate of opinion there. The record stated:

> Asked if he, being with . . . the dauphin, had ever heard the king's affairs spoken of to the people of his household, he said that he had heard it said to my lord of Estissac and also to Master Regnier [de Bouligny], while supping and dining . . . that one could clearly see how the king was governed, in as much as he intended to have the towns and lordships of Genoa and Asti, and, in order to do this, to spend a great sum of money, and neglected to recover the land of Normandy, which the English hold at present, and that the money would have been far better spent on the recovery of . . . Normandy, where the king has a far better cause than elsewhere. . . .[2]

The implication was that the king was 'governed' by Orléans, Anjou (now represented at court by the reinstated Charles of Anjou) and Brézé. Obviously there was resentment of the fact that Italian ambitions were impeding the reconquest of Normandy and other areas still held by the English. The quarter from which these resentments may have most forcibly come will be examined later.[3] Louis's household, now geographically remote from his father's court, provided a favourable climate in which the malcontents could intrigue. He was, perhaps, as much a victim of his servants as their master. The events of the following year are, again, obscure. But they can be traced through the bundle of lies, half-truths and intentional falsifications which form the record of another inquiry of this period – the *procès* of Guillaume Mariette.[4]

Guillaume Mariette served Louis as a *maître des requêtes* of his household. In October 1447 he was arrested at Bourges, on charges of falsifying letters, and was imprisoned at Loches.[5] After a hearing before Jacques Cœur and others, he was transferred to the jail at Lyon, where further interrogations took place. On 6 February 1448 Mariette escaped from his prison, and took sanctuary in the cathedral cloister at Lyon.[6] After an altercation with the dean and chapter, the royal *commis* – Jacques Cœur and Pierre

[1] Escouchy, III, 288, 323.
[2] B.N. MS. fr. 15537, fol. 15ʳ.
[3] See below, 118–19.
[4] Printed by Beaucourt from B.N. MS. fr.

18440 in his edition of Escouchy, III, 265–341.
[5] Beaucourt, IV, 211–12.
[6] Ibid., 212; Escouchy, III, 265–7.

Buyer – interrogated Mariette further in the house of Louis Prévost, which was attached to the cloister. He then contrived to escape once more, and fled to the Dauphiné. The dauphin's officers recovered him at Eyrieu, and, despite offers of bribes to his gaoler, he was then sent to the dauphin's prison at La-Côté-St-André. On Friday 1 March 1448 Louis empowered four *commis* to inquire into the case, anxious to know what Mariette's part had been in the intrigues of his father's court.[1] From Saturday 2 March until Wednesday 13 March, Mariette was subjected to interrogations, some of them under torture. A bundle of memoranda had been found in the box which Mariette carried with him. Both royal and delphinal interrogators were anxious to discover the meaning of these, their provenance, and the use to which they were to be put. Mariette at first concocted a story. He had found them while riding from Tours to Montils-lès-Tours, picked them up off the road, and put them in his box.[2] It was not until 4 March, after he had been tortured, that he admitted to having written them himself at the instigation of Pierre de Brézé.[3] Some of the memoranda and letters were addressed to Philip the Good of Burgundy, others, apparently, to Brézé. Mariette was not a very efficient espionage agent, and his papers seem to have been in considerable disorder. The addressee of some letters is thus not always certain. But there is much valuable information to be gleaned from them about the political situation in 1447.

Mariette's confessions essentially reflect the political technique of Brézé. They fall broadly into two categories – those concerned with Burgundy, and those concerned with Brézé's position *vis-à-vis* the king. Both series indicate a similar technique. Mariette confessed, for instance, that the letters addressed to Philip the Good had been written at Brézé's behest. His interrogators were puzzled. When asked how this could be, given that the letters were damaging towards Brézé, Mariette said 'that he [Brézé] wished that the said Mariette should speak thus to my lord of Burgundy, to sense and discover what intention and wish my said lord of Burgundy had against the said my lord the seneschal'.[4] Similarly, when interrogated about two memoranda apparently addressed to Brézé, concerning the dauphin's intentions, Mariette said:

> . . . that the said seneschal made him write them, pretending that he was speaking to the said seneschal; saying also that he wished that . . . Mariette should speak thus to the king, because he said that the king was very subtle in understanding, and that the king would tell him many things

[1] Escouchy, III, 265-6.
[2] Ibid., 268.
[3] Ibid., 301-2.
[4] Ibid., 305.

in reply; and that the . . . seneschal knew the king's manner of speaking well enough, and for this reason made him write them in this way and then speak them in front of the seneschal, as if he were the king; he [Brézé] answered Mariette with the words with which he thought the king would reply. . . .[1]

This curious dress rehearsal suggests that Brézé was taking no chances, and was going to almost comically absurd lengths to achieve his ends. Brézé had concocted the scheme at Bourges in the late spring or early summer of 1447, and Mariette saw the king soon afterwards. If we make the necessary alterations of addressee, Mariette would have said to Charles:

My said lord [the dauphin] has decided to give the seneschal [Brézé] good cheer, when he shall be with you, in order to arrive sooner at what he wants, which is to take over the government from you, and to do the seneschal down in every way; and this good cheer is advised by Châtillon, Estissac and Regnier de Bouligny. The latter boast that it's not necessary to get rid of the seneschal, saying that they have the greater part of the council for them, such as the chancellor [Guillaume Jouvenel des Ursins], Précigny, Xaintrailles [?] and Cousinot [?]; who say that they are on good terms with the seneschal, and he does not suspect anything: and if it fails by this means, then an Agnès up to the hilt will put things right; and Jean de Daillon will be present for this, who says that he wishes to be the instrument of it; and my said lord [the dauphin] has decided with those above that by one means or another it would come about.[2]

In the event, Mariette was told by Brézé to omit the passage about Agnès Sorel. This was because the king would then realise that the report was a fabrication.[3] Mariette was to refer only to the counsellors around Charles. The exact implication of this is unclear. Brézé claimed to know the king's mind better than any other. From Mariette's account of the interview his claim was not an entirely vain one. To couple Agnès's name with his own, thought Brézé, would arouse the king's suspicions.

[1] Escouchy, III, 307; cf. 282-3.
[2] Ibid., 282-3. Beaucourt's reading of line 6 of article XLIX on p. 282 would make better sense if it were not 'une dague' but 'une dagne'. I have rendered it thus in my translation in the light of the subsequent interrogation of Mariette on this point on p. 307. Agnès Sorel is called 'La Dagne' in this document. Cf. Basin, II, 282.

[3] Escouchy, 307. In Beaucourt's transcription there is no reference to Sorel in articles XLVIII and XLIX of the interrogations. As Mariette was quite specific on the question of omitting a passage relating to 'La Dagne', I can only conclude that Beaucourt's reading is inaccurate – a most unusual occurrence.

Why? Charles would have viewed Mariette as a man in the service of his son. The assumption that an informer from Louis's household would not refer to Agnès Sorel is puzzling. It can only be assumed that either Louis's servants were very badly informed about events at the court of France, or that Brézé was trying to protect himself. To tell Charles that Agnès could be used in the manner reported might not be very politic for one who had perhaps procured her for the king in the first place. Brézé may, or may not, have been correctly reading the king's mind, but his intention, as Mariette confessed, was clear – it was 'to separate my said lord the dauphin ever more and more from the king'.[1]

Brézé had given Mariette further 'articles' which he was to state to the king. These concerned relations between the dauphin and Philip the Good of Burgundy. Burgundy, it was alleged, was urging Louis to put an end to the king's 'bad government, of which the seneschal is entirely the cause'.[2] Louis was said to be plotting to seize his father and put him in a hermitage – he could join Felix V of Savoy as a recluse.[3] When Louis was back at court he would contrive to take over the government. If a *coup* was out of the question, he would agree to serve his father in Italy or elsewhere, but would use the troops in his charge to depose Charles. Burgundy would probably aid him. Mariette was then told to implicate Amaury d'Estissac – evidently no friend of Brézé's – in Louis's dealings with Burgundy. Estissac was in the game only for the money which he might receive. Questioned by the dauphin's *commis* about these matters, Mariette said that Brézé had made him write them, and rehearsed him as before, 'saying that the king was very subtle and that . . . Mariette did not know his ways'.[4] Most of the script was acted out in front of the king, and, on 9 March 1448, Mariette told his interrogators what had happened. They thought he was going to die. The torture which he had undergone on the previous Saturday could hardly have improved his condition. Louis was alarmed enough to send a doctor to him, lest he die before confessing to the truth.[5] He had already told his interrogators that he had tried to dissuade Brézé from implementing the ruse. But the seneschal, speaking with him in a gallery in the house of Guillaume Jouvenel des Ursins at Bourges, had told him not to be a fool.[6] The king suspected Louis's intentions already, and his suspicions would merely be confirmed by the testimony of a member of his son's household. No harm would come either to Brézé or to Mariette, because the king would tell no one

[1] Escouchy, III, 307.
[2] Ibid., 285–6; cf. 308, 315–17.
[3] Ibid., 286.
[4] Ibid., 308; cf. 285–8.
[5] Ibid., 312.
[6] Ibid., 310–11.

what he had heard. Brézé went on: 'the king is well advised . . . not to reveal, nor tell, what is said to him; for, since he has disclosed and told what has been said to him on other occasions, he has not been informed about many things, by which he's come to a lot of harm'.[1] Brézé did not specify what those occasions were. But a taciturn circumspection was obviously highly desirable.

Mariette's words were intended to strengthen the king's resolution. He had been warned that Louis's reappearance at court would bring discord in its wake. If one of his son's servants could confirm that warning, then Louis would be exiled from the court for a very long time. Whatever the dauphin might profess, his intentions could only be suspect. Brézé was, in effect, poisoning the king's mind against his son. It may already have been badly disposed, but Mariette's testimony was intended to deliver a *coup de grâce* to any remaining shred of paternal trust. The ploy seems to have been moderately successful. Charles was alleged by Mariette to have told him that it was hardly likely that the dauphin would come to him unless he was ordered to do so.[2] Mariette replied that he would come in any case, order or no order, and would purge the king's household. Charles asked Mariette who of his advisers were in favour with Louis. Mariette told him that Guillaume Jouvenel, Précigny, Charles of Anjou, Louis de Laval, lord of Châtillon, and André de Laval, lord of Lohéac, were willing to help Louis on his way.[3] There is no way of testing his statement. It is known, however, that Jean Juvenal des Ursins received a gift from Louis of 300 *écus d'or* on 18 September 1447.[4] We have no evidence for his brother's stance at this time. A letter found among Mariette's papers, however, addressed to Philip the Good, suggests that he was as susceptible to bribery as the rest of the entourage. If Burgundy wanted his services – and those of Brézé and Jean Juvenal – he would have to pay dearly for them.[5] In June 1447, it was claimed, Brézé, Précigny, and the brothers des Ursins, might agree to a renewal of the truces with the English only if they were well enough paid.[6] But it would be difficult to show that any of them was supporting a *coup d'état* by the dauphin.

The inclusion of their names by Mariette was probably part of Brézé's ruse. He certainly did his best to blacken Brézé's own name when he spoke to the king at Bourges. Charles replied just as Brézé had anticipated.[7] It was, in its way, an impressive piece of mind-reading. The king asked

[1] Escouchy, III, 311.
[2] Ibid., 314.
[3] Ibid., 314.
[4] Beaucourt, IV, 207 n. 3.

[5] Escouchy, III, 325-6.
[6] Ibid., 328.
[7] Ibid., 313-15.

Mariette to put what he knew in writing. But he then thought for a moment, and told him to write to one of his household. In reply to Mariette's question about this, the king suggested Brézé. But, well rehearsed as he was, Mariette remarked that he was 'the most double-dealing man in the world, who talked recklessly'.[1] The king, with an oath of 'By St John!' agreed and told him to write to the count of Tancar-ville instead. Mariette furthered his deception by telling the king that Gaston IV, count of Foix, hated the dauphin, and that he and Brézé were in alliance. But this was quite untrue, because Foix had told him 'many times' that he was for the dauphin, and his alliance with Brézé was merely a feint.[2] Whatever the truth of the allegations, Foix continued to receive his pension of 6,000 *livres* a year in 1447.[3] These men were masters of the techniques of insinuation, double- (if not triple-) dealing, and subterfuge. The impression which emerges from the *procès* of Guillaume Mariette is that, at the court of Charles VII, no one told the truth. Perhaps the accusations against the court were not so very wide of the mark. Some of the courtiers and their agents came to grief. Wooed by Brézé with promises of pensions, offices and a good marriage, Guillaume Mariette was deserted by each of his patrons – the dauphin Louis, Philip the Good, and Brézé – in turn. He was handed over by Louis's officers to the king's justice, imprisoned in the Bastille, and executed at Tours.[4]

It was a testimony to his capacity for survival that Brézé emerged from the affair unscathed. Temporarily disgraced, and denounced by the dauphin, his case was brought before the *Parlement* of Paris at the end of April 1448.[5] Brézé, though 'out' at court, was demonstrating his usefulness in the negotiations and military operations by which Le Mans was re-covered from some recalcitrant English captains.[6] There is no surviving record of the case before the *Parlement*. A letter of pardon from the king, however, made play with the value of Brézé's past, present, and future services.[7] It was said that Brézé had not intended to alienate Charles from his son by using Mariette in the way in which he did. The king claimed that there was no rancour in his heart against Brézé, and that Mariette's words had been shown to be false. They had not led to mistrust between the king and dauphin, or the lords of the blood and members of the king's household. It was a public statement, issued for general consumption. The king could hardly do otherwise if Brézé was to be retained. Mariette was

[1] Ibid., 313–14.
[2] Ibid., 314–15. For letters of alliance between Gaston IV and Brézé see ABP, E.440 (18 May 1445).
[3] Beaucourt, IV, 407.
[4] Ibid., 213; Escouchy, I, 137–8.
[5] Beaucourt, IV, 214–15.
[6] See ibid., 284–308.
[7] Printed in Duclos, IV, 67–74.

dispensable. There were plenty of ambitious men willing to act as agents in the hope of getting a good position in the *Chambre des Comptes* or the *Requêtes*, as Mariette hoped.[1] Brézé, in the political circumstances of April 1448, was thought to be indispensable. He had his supporters at court – above all, Guillaume Jouvenel and Jean Juvenal des Ursins. On such issues as an Anglo-French peace, all three were together, bound, it was tartly observed, in an alliance of cupidity.[2] With the failure of the Genoese affair in March, all three were perhaps anxious to regain lost credit at court. At the end of April, during the hearing of Brézé's case before the *Parlement*, another potential supporter arrived in Paris. Agnès Sorel came, ostensibly on a pilgrimage to Ste-Geneviève, and remained until 10 May.[3] Was she there to plead Brézé's cause with the king?

It is possible only to speculate on the motives which led Charles to reinstate the seneschal of Poitou. By 14 May 1448 he was sufficiently in favour to be styled 'counsellor and chamberlain of the king' in a quittance.[4] But he did not yet reappear in the council. His name is lacking from the lists of counsellors appended to the king's letters from mid-May to late August 1448.[5] He was given business outside the court – his knowledge and talents were employed in preparing for the forthcoming invasion of English-occupied Normandy. This was to be the arena in which the energies of the courtiers were now to be harnessed. The Italian schemes of the previous year had failed. In October 1447 an attempt by Regnaud de Dresnay, with a force of French troops, to gain the lordship of Asti for Charles of Orléans, had been decisively defeated by a joint Milanese-Venetian army.[6] Italy, though not completely set aside, was now replaced by Normandy and Guyenne as the primary political objective. Campaigns of reconquest might serve many purposes and further many interests. The companies of the standing army would find employment, and so would the magnates – as lieutenants in the king's war. There were people at court who would stand to gain from the invasion of Normandy.[7] It is not necessary to adduce, with Beaucourt, the notion that the king 'burned with the desire to chase the English from the land'.[8] The presence of Agnès Sorel at this time might suggest that his desires were of a rather different kind. But Normandy was a viable political objective, as long as a good pretext could be found for a breach of the truces with the English. That pretext was to be offered to him in March 1449.

[1] Escouchy, III, 315, 317–18.
[2] Ibid., 328.
[3] Beaucourt, IV, 215–16.
[4] Ibid., 216 n. 1.

[5] Ibid., 216.
[6] Ibid., 250–1.
[7] See below, 118–20.
[8] Beaucourt, IV, 217.

The intrigues of Brézé were, at least temporarily, at an end. Relations between him and the king, despite the letters of pardon, were never again so close as they had apparently been before the storm over Guillaume Mariette's case broke. The records of that affair – whatever the truth about it really was – at least give credence to part of Chastellain's later assessment of the king. That Brézé was forced to adopt such tactics in order to discover where he stood with the king suggests that, as Chastellain wrote, 'no one, however great he was, had the faintest idea where he stood'.[1] One result of Mariette's interview with Charles was that Brézé knew that the king was aware of his duplicity. That he, and those named in Mariette's depositions, were retained in the king's favour suggests that Charles was merely acknowledging a commonplace of his time. The *gens de la cour* gave their services to those who paid for them. Loyalty was negotiable in terms of hard cash. A king could only control them by ensuring that he could outbid his rivals in the giving of rewards. Without his pensions, his offices and his gifts, Brézé would have been a nonentity.

But a king, or a prince, could sometimes be the victim of his own servants. There can be little doubt that the dauphin Louis was particularly susceptible to the pressures of his entourage. When he became king in July 1461, he recognised that things had been done in the past 'against the truth, and on my account'.[2] One of these was the handing over of Guillaume Mariette, and the issue of letters of pardon to Brézé. As dauphin, he had been acting on the advice of his council. It is difficult to see Louis's own initiative constantly at work behind his behaviour in the 1440s. It could be argued that the hostility which grew up between father and son was, in part, a creation of their respective servants. Both were in this sense victims of the men around them. It was only when those men became entangled in the web of their own intrigues that a prince could rid himself of them. A treason trial, or a sequestration of their property, would serve to discredit or eliminate the more dispensable of these double-dealers. The weapon of arbitrary disgrace had been used before by Charles VII – it was to be used again, and again, until the end of the reign.[3] It was unanimously agreed that the king was subtle. He was perhaps only following a well-known Aristotelian counsel in his dealings with his servants: 'deliberate slowly, but then act very fast'.[4] In October 1446 one of Louis de Bueil's servants claimed that he knew the king's manner of behaving. 'When he wants to get rid of someone who "governs" him, he makes his

---

[1] Chastellain, II, 184.
[2] B.N. MS. fr. 20490, fol. 36ʳ.
[3] See below, 131-2, 154-62.

[4] See E. Wind, *Pagan Mysteries in the Renaissance* (London, 1967), 100, citing the *Nicomachean Ethics*.

alliances little by little, first with one person, then with another, a year or six months before he throws him out.'[1] Charles of Anjou and Brézé may have suffered as a result of this technique. Brézé apparently knew that he would not enjoy the king's favour for very long. He was alleged to have told Guillaume Mariette at Chinon that 'he [Brézé] would not last long with the king', but, as long as he lasted, he would see that Mariette was well rewarded.[2] These men, therefore, acknowledged that their success would be short-lived. Acute insecurity was something with which they were obliged to come to terms. To become indispensable, to be in the right place at the right time, to build up a 'practice' which was one's own – these were the only forms of insurance against total shipwreck. The motto of Alfonso d'Este of Ferrara – *A Lieu et Temps*[3] – was as relevant for the servants of a prince as for the prince himself. To be in Charles VII's entourage was indeed dangerous. Surprisingly, it was a contemporary observer – Georges Chastellain – who was, for once, telling the truth. The lions' den contained at least one Daniel.

[1] See Beaucourt, IV, 196.   [3] Wind, op. cit., 108, and Plates 81 and 82.
[2] Escouchy, III, 315.

Chapter 5 ✤ The Later Years 1449–1461

I Reconquest

1 The expulsion of the English and the case of Jacques Cœur

Oh! Please God that your son, the present king, inheriting your blood, shall inherit your very commendable principles also, such as not being quick to take revenge, nor to shed blood.[1]

Chastellain's address to the deceased Charles VII could thus express the wish that the dauphin Louis should, in one respect, follow his father's political usages. The notion of Charles VII as an appeaser – and as one merciful to his enemies – was evidently current among his contemporaries.[2] How far that notion was borne out by the king's actual behaviour is less clear from an examination of the evidence. Recent work has endorsed this view – historians have looked to the reign of Charles VII in order to find evidence of the 're-establishment of peace in French society' on the morrow of the Hundred Years War.[3] It is the purpose of the following pages to investigate, firstly, the manner in which the king recovered Normandy and Gascony from the English between 1449 and 1453, and, secondly, to examine the means by which the costs of reconquest were met. Once these measures have been described, the scene is set for a glimpse of the king at work during this period, and for an assessment of his role in the process of pacification and appeasement in the aftermath of victory. The alleged inactivity of the king will also be discussed. The nature of his political technique and handling of the everyday business of government can be established – if only momentarily – from the surviving evidence. Without reconquest, pacification was impossible. It is to the situation in the early months of 1449 that one must turn to examine the means whereby that reconquest was achieved.

Why, on 31 July 1449, was the truce with the English, negotiated at Tours, broken? Who was responsible for its breach, and on whose instiga-

[1] Chastellain, VII, 45.
[2] See Beaucourt, VI, 448–51. Considerable play was made with Charles's 'clemency' in his dealings with the dauphin Louis. See Duclos, IV, 101 (8 June 1456).
[3] Bossuat in *Recovery of France*, 80–1.

tion were they acting? It was a matter which the king apparently had very much at heart. At a meeting of his *grand conseil* at Les Roches Tranchelion on 31 July 1449,

> The king said and demonstrated how, after many great attempts and excesses done and committed by the English against the truce, as much in the takings of St-Jacques-de-Beuvron, St-Guillaume-de-Mortain, and recently the seizure of the town and castle of Fougères, as in many other attempts done and perpetrated by the said English, the king has conducted many inquiries with the English, to seek reparation of the same; which they have not in any way done. . . .[1]

The king's words were borne out by the payment of Osbern Munde-ford, esquire, from the English receiver-general of Normandy, for journeys 'to communicate, treat and appoint with the ambassadors on the side of [Henry VI's] uncle of France . . . on many abuses, attempts and controversies committed and perpetrated as much on the side of the king . . . as . . . of his said uncle during the present truces and abstinences from war'.[2] These proceedings took place between 13 and 30 June 1449. It was acknowledged that responsibility for acting against the truces was shared by both sides. Why then did Charles VII take the initiative one month later, and invade Normandy? The answer which has normally been given to this question is that the taking of the town and castle of Fougères – a frontier stronghold on the Breton border – in March 1449, gave the king no alternative but to adopt reprisals.[3] Fougères was seized by the Aragon-ese mercenary captain François de Suriennes, in the pay of the English, at the instigation of the dukes of Suffolk and Somerset. It was therefore the English with whom the primary responsibility for breaking the truces lay. But, in a *mémoire* prepared for Louis XI in 1464, the capture of Fougères was not considered to have been the major point at issue. An alleged attempt by the English to detach François I, duke of Brittany, and his brother Gilles, lord of Champtocé, from French allegiance was thought to be 'twenty times greater an enterprise and breach of truce than the said taking of Fougères'.[4] François de Suriennes's offence was thus considered to be comparatively venial.

In a letter written by Charles on 2 April 1451 a similar *rationale* is

[1] Escouchy, III, 245.
[2] B.N. MS. fr. 26079, no. 6137 (9 August 1449).

[3] See A. Bossuat, *Perrinet Gressart et François de Suriennes, agents de l'Angleterre* (Paris, 1936), 324-35, 348-9.
[4] Ibid., 330.

given. Informing the king of Castile and Leon of the reasons for his invasion of Normandy in August 1449, the king wrote:

> . . . [the English], to demonstrate their will and intent more clearly, have . . . attempted, by certain means, to withdraw and attribute to themselves *the subjection and obedience of our said nephew of Brittany* and of his land and duchy, although, in truth and as is well known, *he is our man, vassal and subject*, and that, since the commencement of the truces, the same our nephew, as our subject . . , had been named and included, with his lands and lordships, in the same, which is a very clear demonstration of a notorious and manifest breach of the said truces on the part of the English. . . .[1]

It was a declaration of royal sovereignty at its most extreme. The concept of subjection was not an invention of Louis XI's.[2] To Charles VII and his advisers, the question of Breton obedience to the Crown of France was of paramount importance. Its denial was sufficiently grave a matter for it to serve as a pretext for a breach of the truces and a consequent re-opening of the war with the English. The evidence for English attempts to seduce Gilles de Bretagne is clear. In December 1443 he was given two books, a pension of £666 13s. 4d. per year, and a gift of a gold chest with £100 in it by Henry VI.[3]

The failure of his government to retain the province of Maine may have led Henry VI's advisers to attempt to 'reassure public opinion' in England by securing an alliance with Brittany against France.[4] Gilles de Bretagne, as an English pensioner, was a useful weapon. But, on 26 June 1446, he was arrested in Charles VII's name by his enemies Arthur de Montauban and Prégent de Coëtivy.[5] He was kept in his brother's custody during the king's pleasure. It was inevitable that the English should take steps to recover their ally and pensioner. François de Suriennes, in a statement made in March 1450, could assert that the English captain Matthew Gough, and others, tried to gain the services of his escalader, Thomassin du Quesne, 'to find means of recovering my lord Gilles de Bretaigne'.[6] A less direct method of recovery was to persuade a captain in English pay to take a Breton place, in order to force François I to release his brother. It was here that François de Suriennes was

[1] Cosneau, *Richemont*, 620.
[2] *Pace* B. A. Pocquet, 'Une idée politique de Louis XI: la sujetion éclipse la vassalité', *RH*, ccxxvi (1961), 383–98 (tr. in *Recovery of France*, 196–215).
[3] Stevenson, *Letters and Papers*, I, 439–41.

He was also a knight of the Garter. He was assassinated in April 1450 (Cosneau, *Richemont*, 377–90).
[4] Bossuat, *Suriennes*, 308–9.
[5] Ibid., 309; Cosneau, *Richemont*, 382–3.
[6] Stevenson, I, 281.

brought into play by the English, and, ultimately, Fougères was chosen. But the latter was secondary to the major point at issue. On 14 March 1446 François I had done homage to Charles VII for the duchy of Brittany.[1] That homage was not to pass uncontested.

On 29 March 1448 François I of Brittany was included in a letter of Henry VI among *his* 'allies and vassals'.[2] In the summer of 1449, after a series of fruitless negotiations over truce-breaking, Somerset's ambassadors were informed in Charles's name that Fougères was a possession of the duke of Brittany, who, 'together with his lands and subjects, was, and is, included by name on the king's side, in the said truces'.[3] They were also told that 'it appears clearly that the subjection and obedience of the said land of Brittany belongs to the king, without any question or dispute. And to make it a contentious issue at present would be to do far greater damage to the king than the restitution of Fougères could be to his profit.'[4] In other words, even the handing back of the place to François I would not compensate the king for the attempt against his sovereignty. The terms were harsh. They suggest either that Charles VII was determined to establish once and for all the much-contested claim to sovereignty over Brittany, or that he was under some degree of pressure from the vested interests of the men around him. His behaviour at Chinon in March 1446, and at Montbazon in November 1450 – when Pierre II of Brittany paid homage – suggests that he was content with a compromise solution.[5] Liege homage, though requested, was not formally paid on either occasion. Such willingness to come to terms contrasts oddly with the trenchant observations of June and July 1449. One clue to the intransigence shown towards the English at that time may be found in the reply given by Charles to Somerset in July 1449. If the breach of the truces was not repaired, he wrote,

> trouble would arise, for the said my lord of Brittany was his nephew and subject, expressly included in the truce, and he had many great lords, relatives and friends in great abundance, his subjects [as] war captains, such as the constable, a marshal and the admiral, a captain of men-at-arms, and others, who, if they took the trouble to repair the said breach, no one should be surprised. . . .[6]

[1] Beaucourt, IV, 183; V, 313–14.
[2] See *Foedera*, XI, 207.
[3] Stevenson, I, 249, misdated April 1449. It should be 31 July (Escouchy, III, 251).
[4] Stevenson, I, 256.

[5] See Beaucourt, VI, 350–1.
[6] Stevenson, I, 251, 261; 268–9 for Brittany's inclusion in the truces on the French side.

The allusion to a group of Bretons at the court of France is significant. Men such as Arthur de Richemont, the constable, André de Laval, lord of Lohéac, one of the marshals of France, and Prégent de Coëtivy, the admiral of France, may have formed a vested interest at court.[1] Charles VII was thus extremely cautious about consulting the Bretons in the summer of 1449. He had to make sure that the support of the duke, and of his subjects, relatives and friends at the court of France, would be forthcoming if an invasion of English-occupied areas was to be mounted. He informed the duke and his relatives of all that the English ambassadors had said and offered. By July, the Breton captains were outside Fougères, intent on forcing Suriennes to surrender.[2] Why were they so zealous in this cause? Their previous loyalty to the dukes of Brittany was not outstanding. Prégent de Coëtivy, for instance, had wrested the lands of the executed sex-murderer Gilles de Rais from the hands of Duke Jean V.[3] It was Coëtivy who gained the rights to Gilles de Bretagne's lordships when they were confiscated by Charles VII's order in June 1446.[4] The arrest of Gilles de Bretagne, moreover, had arguably greater significance than has previously been claimed. His arrest could have been a device initiated by the Breton lords who had come to Charles's court in the following of Richemont. It could have been intended to provoke English retaliation in defence of their ally and pensioner. By attempting to withdraw Brittany from French allegiance, the English incurred the hostility of those Breton lords who owed their political power and their pensions, not to the court of Brittany, but to the court of France. Three of the most competent military officers at court were Bretons. Their influence with the king was considerable – Prégent de Coëtivy's brother, Olivier, could be given the hand in marriage of the king's illegitimate daughter, Marie.[5] The Breton courtiers thus stood to lose as a result of any change in the status of the duchy. The king stood to gain from any act of English aggression which would enable him to resume the war, and, in the process, recover Normandy. The interests of the king, and of an influential group of his courtiers, coincided.

The courtiers stood to gain, and did gain, from other aspects of the

---

[1] For their behaviour in 1449 see Cosneau, *Richemont*, 394–403.
[2] Ibid., 395–6; Bossuat, *Suriennes*, 337–9.
[3] See G. Bataille, *Le Procès de Gilles de Rais. Les Documents* (Paris, 1965), 198–9; Cosneau, *Richemont*, 378.
[4] Cosneau, *Richemont*, 382.

[5] Beaucourt, VI, 432–3. The marriage contract was made on 25 November 1458. Charles's two other surviving illegitimate daughters – Charlotte and Jeanne – were married to Jacques, son of Pierre de Brézé, and Anthoine, son of Jean de Bueil, respectively (ibid., 434), in 1461 and 1462, by Louis XI.

reconquest. A roll of payments from the king's 'domain and confiscations of Normandy' in 1450 cites gifts and rewards from confiscations granted to Pierre de Beauvau, Pierre de Brézé, and Jean d'Estouteville, lord of Torcy, for their services in the recovery of the duchy.[1] Norman revenues also rewarded Dunois and Culant, the *grand maître d'hôtel*, for their services in the work of reconquest from the English.[2] On 11 August 1450 the recently appointed admiral of France, Jean de Bueil, received the Norman *vicomté* of Carentan, and André de Villequier had been given that of St-Sauveur-le-Vicomte in July.[3] The spoils of Gascony were similarly employed. In January 1450 the lordship of Lesparre 'at present held and occupied by our . . . enemies and adversaries the English' was given to Prégent de Coëtivy.[4] It was an effective means of whetting the courtiers' appetites for the work of reconquest. But Coëtivy was killed by gunshot at the siege of Cherbourg in August 1450, and Lesparre was offered to the loyal Gascon, Arnaud-Amanieu d'Albret, lord of Orval.[5] The lordship of Blanquefort, in Médoc, was given by the king to Anthoine de Chabannes, for his services 'about our person' on 17 June 1451.[6] The courtiers thus had a vested interest in the recovery, and retention, of Normandy and Gascony. Pierre de Brézé was set up as *grand sénéchal* of Normandy and was given the duke of Somerset's house at Rouen.[7] It was one means of employing his talents, but of keeping him away from court. The lavish endowment of those close to the king with confiscated lands and revenues might not, on the face of it, seem a very effective device in the promotion of 'peace in society'. In the aftermath of war came problems which were only partially solved.

That the king was much exercised by these problems is evident from his creation of special officers to administer forfeitures and confiscations in Normandy. A letter of Jean Hardouin and Jean le Boursier, *commissaires* for confiscations, to the *vicomte* of Gournay, written at Rouen on 10 February 1450, is significant.[8] They told the *vicomte* that the king had appointed one Jean Acart to deal with confiscations in the Norman *vicomtés* of Arques, Neufchâtel and Caudebec. Acart had 'laboured there without ever finishing the job. And as . . . the king has this matter very much at heart', he had empowered them to order Acart and the *vicomte* to complete the operation. They were to be paid from the proceeds of

[1] Escouchy, III, 384–5.
[2] Ibid., 391–2.
[3] Beaucourt, V, 309–10.
[4] A.N., JJ.180, no. 19.
[5] A.N., JJ.182, no. 139.
[6] A.N., JJ.182, no. 67.

[7] See Bernus, 'Le rôle politique de Pierre de Brézé au cours des dix dernières années du règne de Charles VII (1451–61)', *BEC*, lxix (1911), 316–17.
[8] B.M., Add. Ch. 12417.

the movable goods and real estate which were confiscated. Their zeal was no doubt prompted by such methods of reward. Master Jacques Charrier, money-changer in the king's treasury, was set over the *ad hoc* department thus created, assisted by men such as Jean Rogier, king's clerk, who was also paid from the proceeds of the confiscations which he administered.[1] To employ such means of recompensing one's civil servants could put a premium on the over-zealous discharge of their duties. The interests of both courtiers and civil servants lay in a strict application of the legislation relating to forfeitures and confiscations.[2] The king reserved certain lands and revenues to himself, to be disposed of at his own pleasure. Revenues at Bourg, Blaye and Langoiran, in Guyenne, fell under this category in July 1453 and May 1454.[3] The remissions granted to their holders were only partial in their application. The king was careful to deprive them of a certain amount of their income so that his loyal servants might be adequately rewarded for their patriotic deeds.

Public service in the fifteenth century was stimulated and encouraged by the hope of private profit.[4] As has been seen, the king's servants, whether in court or office, were in the business largely for what they could get out of it. By claiming, and realising, his sovereign rights over the duchies of Brittany, Normandy and Guyenne, Charles VII was not merely serving the interests of the abstract Crown of France. He was also acting in the interests of his servants and of his accomplices in the work of government. Since the military and diplomatic measures which he took after the breach of the truces in July 1449 have often been narrated, it is not intended to re-tell the story here.[5] There were other means besides military force with which to achieve a reduction of English-held areas. Without the active support and participation of members of the Norman and Gascon nobility, for instance, the conquest of each of those duchies would have been much retarded.[6] Bribery was sometimes an alternative, sometimes a supplement, to the use of military force. There can be little doubt of the superiority of Charles VII's army to that of his adversaries at this time.[7] Yet brute force was tempered by subtler weapons. First, the king's spies were at work in both Normandy and Gascony.

[1] Escouchy, III, 377-8.
[2] See below, 151-4.
[3] A.N., JJ.182, nos 62, 67, 101.
[4] See Lewis, op. cit., 140-53.
[5] See Beaucourt, V, 3-56; E. Perroy, *The Hundred Years War* (London, 1962), 315-22; Cosneau, *Richemont*, 391-423. See Table of Events for résumé.

[6] See Vale, op. cit., 206-15, and my article 'The last years of English Gascony, 1451-53', *TRHS*, 5th series, xix (1969), 119-38. For a Norman case see Escouchy, III, 374.
[7] See Contamine, op. cit., 313-14, and my article cited above, 125, 132-6.

He had retained at least one espionage agent on a permanent basis from about 1440 onwards. In a petition to Louis XI, which probably dates from soon after his accession in July 1461, a certain friar Pierre claimed that

> . . . it is true that I am the friar who was a prisoner of the English for twelve years, who was tortured seven times so that they should discover from me the secrets which I made known to your late father the king, on whom God have pity and mercy; but they could discover nothing from me, for I would rather have died, all alone under the tortures, than have been the cause of the deaths of many. Having escaped from prison twenty-two years ago [i.e. in 1440?], I came to Lusignan, to the said late king, who received me kindly, and gave me a surname which is not my own, which you call *Samedi passé*, and of his grace granted one hundred pounds *tournois* to support me; but, because of the war, which was great, my lords of the *grand conseil* withdrew half from me . . . and he [the king] made me his chaplain. . . .[1]

Friar Pierre went on to say that Charles VII had sent him to Calais 'many times', and to other places 'to discover the enterprises of the English'. His petition ended on a suitably mendicant note. He asked Louis to confirm the 'alms' granted him by Charles, and his letter of appointment as chaplain. The result of his petition is not known. But the usefulness of members of the mendicant orders – moving from one house of friars to another with ease – as spies is evident from other sources. One Jean Convyn, an Augustinian friar at Rouen, was paid by the king for his 'services . . . to the said lord since his entry into this land of Normandy for the recovery of the same from the hands of the English'.[2] The Augustinian had 'come many times, to the great danger of his person, leaving Rouen, to Louviers and Pont-de-l'Arche, to the said lord in order to tell him the state of the said town of Rouen, and what measures he would have to take to recover the same'. An annual pension of 20*l*. 12*s*. 6*d*. *tournois* followed, beginning on 1 October 1449. Charles's informants within the enemy camp were not always clerical. A certain Thierry de Ravaige, servant of a Gascon nobleman, Bérard de Lamothe, lord of Roquetaillade, was recompensed for 'a certain journey which he lately made from the . . . land of Bordelais, coming from his said master to the said lord [the king] in the month of February last [1450], to the town of Bernay in Normandy . . . to inform the same lord of certain matters

[1] B.N. MS. fr. 20485, no. 76.   [2] Escouchy, III, 383.

from the said land of Bordelais'.[1] A gift of 30*l. tournois* followed. Charles VII was evidently well served by his agents. Without them, the process of reconquest might have been much less rapid.

Secondly, the king resorted to bribery. In September 1449 Richard des Epaules, esquire, captain of Longny in Perche for Henry VI of England, surrendered that place to Charles VII.[2] Brézé, who received the surrender in the king's name, had promised to pay him 450*l. tournois*, 'to distribute among twelve French-speaking companions of war, who were in the said place with and under [him] . . . and of his alliance, both for having been the cause, with him, of the reduction of the said place, as for having reduced and put themselves in the king's obedience . . . and performed the oath. . .'.[3] Richard des Epaules let the French into the keep of Longny castle, and his captaincy was confirmed – now in the name of Charles VII. Treachery was commonplace in Normandy. One Jean de la Mote, an English esquire, was rewarded by the king for services which were of such import that 'the said lord has not wished, and does not wish them to be declared in this present roll, nor anywhere else'.[4] The clerk who wrote these account rolls of November 1450 must have been tantalised by such instructions. A similar formula was used to describe the services done to the king by John Merbury, esquire, son of Richard Merbury, captain and *bailli* of Gisors. He had been going from Rouen on secret business 'which greatly touches the good of the king . . . and his lordship'.[5] A later account roll contains the information that Richard Merbury had delivered Gisors to the king.[6] A total of 58*l. tournois* had been paid to John Merbury by November 1450.[7] Another account roll, certified and signed by the king on 2 April 1451, describes how others besides Merbury *père* and *fils* had aided the king to recover Gisors. Brézé had given 687*l.* 10*s. tournois* to a certain 'Reynfoks', and Englishman, for the reduction of Gisors to the king's obedience.[8] Brézé got his money back from Master Etienne Petit, who paid him from the revenues of Languedoc and Guyenne. It was hardly misappropriation of the taxation granted by the Three Estates of Languedoc. The war effort had to be maintained. It was understood that French money might consequently flow into Englishmen's purses.

[1] Escouchy, III, 387.
[2] Ibid., 374. He was lord of Ste-Marie-du-Mont.
[3] Ibid., 374, and Bossuat, *Suriennes*, 342.
[4] Escouchy, III, 375.
[5] Ibid., 380. For Richard Merbury, knight, captain of Pontoise under the English administration, see Stevenson, II, 436, 543. He was at Verneuil in 1424 (ibid., II, 394).
[6] Escouchy, III, 387, and cf. Stevenson, II, 622.
[7] Escouchy, III, 380, 387.
[8] See *ABSHF*, cxxiv (1864), ii, 147.

Since François de Suriennes surrendered Fougères to the marshal of
Brittany in November 1449, a pattern of reduction by payment, as well
as by agreement or assault, was established. Suriennes was given 10,000
écus and honourable terms under which he and the garrison marched
out.[1] He told Henry VI in March 1450 that he could have had 50,000
écus from the duke of Brittany to surrender the place, but he would not
have done so 'for all the treasure in the world'.[2] As it was, he did not
leave Fougères empty-handed. Others assisted the king's cause in Gascony. Gadifer Shorthose, the English mayor of Bordeaux, was rewarded
for his services in the reduction of the city by a gift and a pension from
Charles VII in June 1451.[3] In the previous year the town of Bergerac
had fallen to the king, and its captain, one Maurigon de Bideran, esquire,
was said to have been 'the means of the said reduction'. A letter of pardon
from Charles VII to him, his son, and the garrison, followed in February
1452.[4] It was essential for a native Gascon to make his peace – as did so
many after the recovery of Bordeaux in June 1451 – with the French
régime. For Englishmen, it was desirable to be paid by the French to go
away. At Gisors, Harcourt and La Roche-Guyon, English (or Welsh)
captains were bought out by the French. At La Roche-Guyon, John
Edwards, a Welshman, made the large sum of 4,500l. tournois from his
agreement with Charles VII to surrender the place.[5] It was an ill wind
that blew nobody any good. In defeat, as well as in victory, some Englishmen still took their profits of war. Others, such as Somerset at Rouen,
found the terms of the indemnities which they were expected to pay to
the French extremely harsh.[6] But that was, perhaps, an exceptional
case. On the whole, the terms upon which the English surrendered to
Charles VII in Normandy and Gascony between 1449 and 1451 were
not crippling. But the costs of reconquest to the king's financial resources
were potentially so. The outlay of liquid capital necessitated by these
campaigns was immense. To the costs of bribery, those of the standing
army, the artillery, the sappers, miners, and pioneers had to be added.[7] In
whatever manner the king fought his war, he could never let it pay for itself.

What was more, conquests had to be retained. Writing to James II,
king of Scotland, in January 1457, Charles VII observed:

[1] Bossuat, *Suriennes*, 344–5.
[2] Stevenson, I, 296.
[3] B.N. MS. fr. 32511, fol. 142ʳ (account of
Mathieu Beauvarlet, receiver-general of
Languedoïl).
[4] A.N., JJ.181, no. 25. He had also
surrendered the important castle of Biron

for money (ABP, E.702, no. 8).
[5] B.M., Add. Ch. 4069 (29 January 1451);
Stevenson, II, 619–34, for these, and other,
surrenders.
[6] Stevenson, II, 607–18.
[7] See A.N., K.69, nos 4ᵃ and 7.

... although his obedience is ... much enlarged, and all the kingdom ... more valued and renowned in many places, nevertheless the king's responsibility, both for his troops as for the costs of paying them, is no less than what it was beforehand. For, at the time when the English occupied Normandy and Guyenne, the king had only to defend certain frontiers and places, which were known and ordained, and were well provided for and established, as the case required. And if the English decided to conduct greater campaigns, the king was informed of them early and in good time, and knew their strength, and which way they would come, so as to prepare for them as was necessary. But at present the king has to watch all the coastline daily ... from Spain to Picardy, which amounts to more than 450 leagues of land; in which he has continually to keep men-at-arms in great numbers and in great strength, pay their wages, who do not move from the said places, and in such a way that all the revenue of Normandy (which is one of the finest parts and greatest revenues of this kingdom) could not suffice, by 100,000 francs, to pay the men-at-arms detailed to guard the same. ... [1]

The king's purpose was, in part, to convince the king of Scotland that he was unable to assist him in invading England. But his words, written at St-Priest in the Dauphiné, were a realistic assessment of the problems which followed reconquest. Apart from anxiety about the dubious loyalty of recently regained areas, he was obliged to meet the costs of watching the coastline and keeping the standing army in garrisons and billets in Normandy and Gascony. The army had either to be employed or demobilised. If it was disbanded, anarchy might follow. Men whose lives had been given over to acts of violence could not be expected to retire peacefully to their places of origin. After the recovery of Guyenne, in June 1451, the king was entertaining the possibility of an Italian campaign in order to employ the companies of *ordonnance*.[2] As it was, the taking of Bordeaux by Talbot in October 1452 demonstrated that the retention of reconquered areas was not to be considered a cause for complacency.[3] So sudden and unexpected was that reversal of fortune that his advisers seem to have become almost obsessed with the possibility of further English descents. In October 1452 even the espionage service had failed in its task. In subsequent years the king's officers were only too

[1] Stevenson, I, 341–2.
[2] See V. Ilardi, 'The Italian League, Francesco Sforza and Charles VII (1454–61)', *Studies in the Renaissance*, vi (1959), 137.
[3] Vale, *TRHS*, 5th series, xix (1969), 124–6.

eager to tell him the 'news of the English army' which was constantly about to descend on the Norman coast. In September 1454, for example, such news was brought to the king on behalf of the constable, the archbishop of Narbonne, 'and others of the council of the said lord being in Normandy'.[1] Such fears were to outlive Charles VII. From the surviving documentation, an impression of the king's reaction to less disturbing news can be gained. The accounts of Mathieu Beauvarlet, receiver-general in Languedoïl, list the rewards given to those who brought news of the victories over the English.

In November 1450 Orval, the herald of Charles II, lord of Albret, was given 41*l. tournois* for bringing the first news of the defeat of the English outside Bordeaux, known to the Gascons as the *Male Journade*, to the king at Montbazon.[2] In May 1451 Guyenne Herald received 27*l.* 10*s. tournois* for bringing the news of the fall of Blaye to the king at Poitiers.[3] Esperance, pursuivant of Jean de Bourbon, count of Clermont, was given the same reward as Albret's herald, for telling the king of the surrender of Bayonne in August 1451.[4] He learnt of the taking of Bourg from Angoulême, herald of the count of Angoulême, and also of the capitulation of St-Macaire, Duras and Sauveterre from a servant of the count of Armagnac.[5] The magnates were evidently anxious to assure him of their active participation in the work of reconquest. In turn, the king had messengers riding post-haste to carry the good news to those of his loyal (and not so loyal) subjects who were less directly concerned with the campaigns. In August 1451 Briant, pursuivant of the count of St-Pol, was dispatched to the dukes of Burgundy and Orléans, bearing news of the fall of Bayonne.[6] Others were sent on far-flung missions to bring the glad tidings to the princes and powers of Christendom. On 17 October 1453, for example, one Louis Tondart was dispatched from Toulouse to Rome, 'carrying to certain of my lords of the household of our Holy Father the news of the surrender of the city of Bordeaux and of all the land of Bordelais and Guyenne'.[7] It was fitting that thanks should be given to God for His favourable judgement on behalf of the Valois claim. Hence, on 31 August 1450, the king wrote to the chapter of the cathedral at Chartres. To celebrate and give thanks for the reduction of Normandy,

[1] See B.M., Add. Ch. 4074. Also 4075, 4087–8, 4090; A.N., K.67, no. 13.
[2] B.N. MS. fr. 32511, fol. 142ᵛ.
[3] Ibid., fol. 143ᵛ.
[4] Ibid., fol. 144ʳ.
[5] Ibid., fol. 145ᵛ.

[6] Ibid., fol. 146ʳ. In a letter to the king from Dunois it was said that the surrender of Bayonne was preceded by a 'miracle' in the shape of a white cross in the sky. See MS. fr. 5028, fol. 183ᵛ, and Beaucourt, v, 52 n. 1.
[7] B.N. MS. fr. 26082, no. 66164.

processions and masses were to be said throughout the metropolitan churches and cathedrals of the kingdom.[1] An annual procession and mass was founded in perpetuity by the king, to take place on 12 August – the day on which Cherbourg surrendered, thereby bringing the recovery of Normandy to its conclusion. Similar commemorations followed the reduction of Gascony in 1453.[2] Amid the euphoria of victory there was no room for doubts or fears.

Yet the circumstances in which victory was achieved could give the king and his advisers cause for concern. The strains imposed by the costs of war could not be effectively absorbed by his revenues. The absence of a financial budget for the 1450s means that exactly how much the campaigns of reconquest actually cost Charles VII is not known. In an assessment of contributions to an *aide* granted by the Three Estates of Languedoc at Montpellier in the spring of 1453 it was observed that the tax was justified by the king's evident necessity.[3] He intended to make war in order to recover Gascony that summer. But he had also, it was said, to 'provide for other frontiers, both in Normandy and elsewhere, which things will not be possible for him to undertake nor finance, given the very heavy extraordinary expenses which he must bear . . .'. These were incurred in paying his 'great lords', as well as the troops of the companies of *ordonnance* and the artillery. Hence heavy taxation was unavoidable in both Languedoïl and Languedoc in 1453.[4] To hold Normandy, while undertaking a campaign of reconquest, for the second time, in Guyenne, imposed a tremendous strain on a financial administration which did not permit the speedy raising of large sums of liquid capital. The war effort could not wait for the inevitable delays which attended the collection of taxation – the bargaining, haggling and administrative laggardness which that process had always involved. A recourse to more direct methods of realising vast amounts of liquid capital was highly desirable in the spring and summer of 1453. It was to the person of his *argentier* – the keeper of the office responsible for the day-to-day supply of his household – that the king turned.

Jacques Cœur had been appointed *argentier* in 1438.[5] An obscure early

[1] Stevenson, I, 307–9.

[2] See B.N. MS. fr. 26081, no. 6592. Also *Documents historiques sur la ville de Millau* (Millau, 1930), 328–9; *Mémoires de la Société des Antiquaires de l'Ouest, 1840* (Paris, 1844), 408, for a 'great fire' and other loyal demonstrations at Poitiers on 20 July 1453.

[3] A.N., K.69, nos 4–4ᵈ.

[4] B.N. MS. fr. 26081, nos 6514 and 6560; A. Spont, 'La Taille en Languedoc', *AM*, v (1890), 478–85, 495–7.

[5] For what follows see M. Mollat, 'Jacques Cœur', in *Citta Mercanti Dottrine nell'Economia Europea dal iv al xviii secolo*, ed. A. Fanfani (Milan, 1964), 191–206.

career in the royal mint at Paris led him into the service of the king's household. As *argentier* he set up 'a sort of bazaar' where the king and his court provided themselves with clothes, jewels, plate, arms and armour, tapestries, and with liquid capital.[1] The *argenterie* was the pawn-shop of the court. Its warehouse was permanently established at Tours, while the *argentier* himself accompanied the king on his constant travels, serving on diplomatic and financial missions as occasion arose. By the late 1440s his fortune was immense, and he was engaging in production of silks, and of arms and armour, for which the *argenterie* acted as a marketing department. His company, with its agents and branches at Florence, Genoa, Bruges and London, possessed a capital of 3,500 florins. The Medici *Bottega di Sieta* had capital assets of about 5,000 florins.[2] The scale of Jacques Cœur's enterprise was thus considerable. He was the greatest shipowner in France, sending his galleys into the Levant from the ports of Provence. From 1447 he was exploiting the mineral deposits of the Lyonnais and Beaujolais, striking silver coin with them, and exporting it to the Levant. His house at Bourges has been aptly described as a palace, and still stands to bear witness to his affluence. As a royal commissioner on finances, he had been made responsible for the farming out of the king's revenues in Languedoc. This was, perhaps, the key to his fortune. It has been said that it was as if he possessed 'a current account on the finances of the provinces of the Midi'.[3] In 1441, it was alleged, he had robbed the king of over 2,000l. *tournois* by farming out the revenues from the fairs of Pézenas and Montignac for less than the sum for which the lessees actually rendered account.[4] Above all, he was thought to have been lending the king his own income, and charging interest for it.

The value of such a fortune at a time of crisis was obvious. By marshalling his reserves, Jacques Cœur could supply liquid capital to the king in very much less time than the normal machinery. As Professor Mollat has pointed out, Cœur had amassed by 1449 'the enormous capital necessary for the liquidation of the Hundred Years War'.[5] His subordinates in the king's financial administration were often his agents in his private enterprises. Men such as Guillaume de Varye held offices in the finances, and there were six receivers of the king's *tailles* and *aides* among his servants.[6]

[1] Mollat, op. cit, 194. For Cœur as a supplier of arms and armour to Charles VII's court see *ABSHF*, ii (1864), 32.
[2] Mollat, op. cit., 202. For the scale of his fortune see *CEH*, iii, 488-9.
[3] Mollat, op. cit., 204.

[4] Dauvet, I, 10-11.
[5] Mollat, op. cit., 195.
[6] See Mollat, 'Une Equipe: les commis de Jacques Cœur', *Hommage à Lucien Fèbvre* (Paris, 1953), II, 178-9.

The extent to which he was conducting his own business with royal revenues is evident from an account roll showing the sums paid by Etienne Petit, treasurer-general of Languedoc, from the proceeds of the royal salt granaries there. Between February 1449 and March 1450, Cœur had received 10,000*l. tournois* to meet the costs of building and maintaining his ships and galleys in the ports of Languedoc.[1] The only other recipient listed in the account was the king himself. Charles had also taken 10,000 *livres* from this source, for unspecified purposes, at Tours, at 'the abbey of Grestain near Honfleur', and at Alençon, between February 1449 and March 1450.[2] King and *argentier* were in league as holders of current accounts on the finances of the kingdom. As long as Cœur could supply the king with what he wanted – ready money – the fount of royal favour flowed. In the spring and summer of 1451 he lent Charles the very large sum of 70,680*l. tournois* to finance the first expedition to Guyenne.[3] He was to have been repaid by an assignment on the revenues of Poitou. But, late in July of that year, Cœur was arrested on the king's order and imprisoned at Taillebourg.[4]

The charges levelled against him were singularly nebulous. He was said to have been responsible for the death of Agnès Sorel on 9 February 1450. The rumour was that he had poisoned her.[5] He was also accused of 'conspiring against the king's person', although no evidence appears to have been adduced in support of the charge. It was not until 29 May 1453 that a formal condemnation was issued by the king.[6] From August 1451 until May 1453 Cœur was kept in jail – at Taillebourg, Lusignan, and Poitiers. All the while, his resources were in the king's hands. His enemy, the Florentine Otto Castellain, was appointed *argentier*.[7] Not only did the king gain from Cœur's deposition. The edict of condemnation stipulated that all his goods were to be put up for sale at what amounted to public auctions, in which they were to be sold to the highest bidder.[8] The proceeds were to go to the king. Jean Dauvet, the king's proctor-general in the Paris *Parlement*, was empowered to conduct a full inquiry into the whereabouts and state of all Cœur's possessions. This began on 1 June 1453 and was not completed until July 1457.[9] The value of the former *argentier*'s possessions is evident from many pages in Dauvet's detailed *Journal*, in which he recorded his day-by-day business during the

[1] B.N., MS. fr. 26079, no. 6145.
[2] Ibid., no 6145.
[3] Dauvet, II, 564–5.
[4] See Beaucourt, V, 104–6.
[5] Ibid., 106–7.
[6] Dauvet, I, 5–14.
[7] Beaucourt, VI, 119.
[8] Dauvet, I, 15.
[9] Ibid., v–x.

conduct of the inquiry. Most revealing, perhaps, is an entry for 5 July 1453. Dauvet wrote:

> It was commanded that Jean de Neufbourg, *bourgeois* and merchant, Gilbert, the king's goldsmith, Jean Boudenier and other money-changers of Tours, should come to me, and their opinion was sought on what should be done with the salt-cellars and other gold jewels . . . [owned by Cœur] and if it would be more profitable to keep them . . . or . . . to break them up and send them to the Mint and have money made from them; and Neufbourg, Boudenier, Gilbert and the other money-changers, and also . . . Otto Castellain, Briçonnet and I with them – seeing that the king is at present at his conquest of Guyenne, and demands every day that all the money that can be found should be sent to him – were all agreed that all the above-mentioned salt-cellars, except that which has the figure of the Moorish girl, and that made of mother of pearl, should be broken up. . . .[1]

To the salt-cellars were added some gold chains and other objects of precious metal. The precious stones were removed from them, and the rest sent to be melted down at the Mint.[2] It was by such acts of fiscal vandalism that the second Guyenne expedition was financed. The charges drawn up against Cœur in May 1453 attempted to justify the arbitrary act by which he had been arrested and deposed two years previously. He had struck 'false' money; he had trafficked with the Saracens; he had forged a matrix of a small seal identical to the king's secret seal; and he had swindled the king of the revenues in Languedoc.[3] It was, perhaps, hardly fortuitous that the king had allowed him to behave in this way until the summer of 1451. His enemies, especially Anthoine de Chabannes, were quite prepared to testify against him.[4] Some of his factors and servants were not conspicuous for their loyalty to him after his fall. It was easy to produce evidence of corrupt practice and use it against the king's principal creditor. Louvet had suffered that fate in 1425.[5] In the financial emergency of 1451–3, such methods must have seemed a simple means of solving the problems of meeting the costs of reconquest. But Cœur may well have been riding for a fall, whatever the direction of the king's policy. There was a growing danger that he would run out of liquid capital. His investments in land, ships, and other assets could have led to a locking up and 'freezing' of his capital assets. Most dangerously of

[1] Dauvet, I, 34.
[2] Ibid., 34, 35–6.
[3] Ibid., 7–11.

[4] See Beaucourt, 'Le Procès de Jacques Cœur', *RQH*, xciv (1890), 466–7.
[5] See above, 38.

7 The inner courtyard of the *hôtel* of Jacques Cœur at Bourges. Known as the *Grande Maison*, it was begun in 1443 and seized by Charles VII after Cœur's arrest late in July 1451

8 Charles VII's reply to the dauphin Louis, at Bourges, 21 March 1461. This document has important alterations in the hand of one of the king's secretaries (*Bibliothèque Nationale, MS. fr. 15537, fol. 55v*)

all, his agents were being forced to make advances with their own money.[1] It was hardly surprising that men such as Otto Castellain, his factor, did nothing to help their master after his fall from grace.

In the king's edict of condemnation of 29 May 1453, Cœur was declared guilty of financial peculation, breaking of royal ordinances, lèse-majesté, 'and other crimes'.[2] The principal charge upon which he had been initially arrested – the poisoning of Agnès Sorel – was not substantiated. Charles's edict merely stated that 'with regard to the poisoning, because the case is not yet ready to be judged for the moment, we make no judgement on it at present'.[3] Almost two years had elapsed since the accusation was brought. If evidence could not be adduced by that time, it would never be. When Louis XI came to reopen the case, in May 1462, Cœur's defenders claimed before the Parlement that Charles VII had promised to exonerate him if he was found innocent of the charges of conspiracy and poisoning. But the prosecuting advocate replied that 'he knew nothing of this, and no mention was made of it in the entire procès, and it is not acceptable for anyone to allege something which comes from the king without letters patent on the matter'.[4] The king's views on the affair can only be deduced from his public utterances. Charles acknowledged Cœur's services to him, and took into account a letter from Pope Nicholas V in his favour. He was not condemned to death. He was to perform a penance before the king's proctor; to buy back a Christian slave whom he had, allegedly, sold to the Saracens; and to restore to the king, 'for the sums extorted, taken and unduly exacted from our land and subjects', the sum of 100,000 écus. He was also fined a further 300,000 écus, and banished perpetually from the kingdom.[5] When the proceeds from the sale of his goods and the seizure of his plate and jewels were added to these enormous sums, the extent of the king's profit from Cœur's deposition was clear.

Charles's personal involvement in the affair remains difficult to assess. It is known that he personally presided over the meetings of the grand conseil and other notables summoned to deliberate on the affair in June 1452 and May 1453.[6] He had no qualms about keeping the argentier in prison without formal trial for the better part of two years. But it was characteristic that neither gratitude nor justice was shown by him to servants of whom he had decided to rid himself. It was alleged, moreover, that Cœur had raised money by false pretences which involved the king

[1] Mollat, in Hommage à . . . Fèbvre, 181.

[2] Dauvet, I, 13–14.

[3] Ibid., 14.

[4] See Beaucourt, op. cit., 465.

[5] Dauvet, I, 14, 20.

[6] Beaucourt, V, 117–18, 124–5.

personally in his dealings. In the edict of condemnation, endorsed 'by the king in his council' at Lusignan, it was said that

> . . . it was also discovered . . . that while the marriage of our very dear and much loved daughter Jeanne was being negotiated with our very dear and loved cousin, the count of Clermont, the same Jacques Cœur, moved by great avarice and not having our interest and honour before his eyes, as he should, had said to the lords of Canillac and La Fayette, and others who had come to our town of Chinon . . . on behalf of our very dear and loved cousin the duke of Bourbon, for the negotiation of the said marriage treaty, that they would get nowhere with us . . . unless we first were given 2,000 écus with which to play at dice and take our pleasures at the Christmas feasts which were then about to take place; and that for the said sum . . . he had taken obligations and sealed letters from the said lords. . . .[1]

But it was said that the king had never entertained any such notion. His honour was gravely compromised by Cœur's behaviour. Perhaps the slight was deeply felt. Cœur had at least convinced the two lords. The fact that they had agreed to the proposal might suggest that it may have conformed to what they knew, or suspected, about the king's behaviour on such occasions.[2] That his behaviour towards Cœur himself was in keeping with what is known of Charles's character is revealed by the manner of his arrest. It was extremely sudden. Only on the very eve of his arrest was Cœur aware that his future was in jeopardy. His wife, his son, Jean Cœur, archbishop of Bourges, and his servants knew nothing of his impending downfall. They had received letters from Cœur only two or three days before the royal commissioners responsible for making an inventory of his goods arrived at Bourges early in August 1451. In them he wrote that 'he was as much in the king's favour as he had ever been, whatever was said about it, and for this reason one should not fear his arrest'.[3] This may have been a reassuring gesture on his part. The tenor of the king's edict of condemnation suggests that he had been informed upon at some time before that date. Charles had had 'certain inquiries' made into Cœur's behaviour before the end of July 1451. The upshot of these investigations was the scrutiny of their findings by the king, his council and other officers 'for a long time' when he was at Taillebourg between 7 and 30 July.[4] According to his heirs, Cœur was

[1] Dauvet, I, 9. The marriage took place in 1447.
[2] See below, 183-4.
[3] Dauvet, I, 152.
[4] Ibid., 5-6.

arrested on 31 July.[1] His letters to them, despite their evident concern to allay any fears about the future, suggest that he was just becoming aware of what was happening at Taillebourg. It is curious that the accusation of poisoning Agnès Sorel was made by Jeanne de Vendôme, lady of Mortagne, almost eighteen months after that event.[2] That the allegation was a fabrication appears likely from the fact that she too was fined and banished by the king. As a *fille d'honneur* of the queen's household, she was no doubt privy to the secret intrigues of the court. The fact that she held her tongue until July 1451 must give rise to suspicion. In the event, Cœur was condemned, as Louvet had been condemned, merely for financial and administrative malpractices.

But Jeanne de Vendôme and her husband, François de Montbéron, may have had less disinterested motives for testifying against the *argentier* in the summer of 1451. Both were Cœur's debtors. He had lent Jeanne de Vendôme the sum of 500 *écus* on 26 March 1448.[3] This was still unpaid in January 1457. Cœur possessed some kind of hold over the goods of Jeanne and François de Montbéron – probably an assignment for the repayment of their debts to him.[4] There was, perhaps, good reason for their behaviour towards their creditor. The king, by deposing his *argentier* at a time when he was greatly in his debt, was behaving in a similar fashion. Foreclosure had become the prerogative not of the creditor, but of the debtor. There was, perhaps, a grain of truth in the tart observation of Cœur's sons at a later date: they alleged that the king had taken 100,000 francs from Cœur's fortune 'for the conduct of his wars'.[5] Ultimately, a very much greater sum had been realised from the affair. The king was keeping a watchful eye on Jean Dauvet's conduct of the business. He gave Dauvet an audience on three occasions. On 22 June 1455 Dauvet came to the king at Bois-Sire-Amé, near Bourges, to 'make his reverence' and tell him of the progress which the inquiry was making.[6] Charles told him that he would summon him to hear more fully about the matter. This seems to have been done on 4 September 1456, when Dauvet came to see the king at Châtelard.[7] He told him of the remaining business to be concluded, the accounts to be settled, and the debts to be recovered in the king's name. Charles ordered him to Bourges so that the affair might soon be over. Cœur's children were assigned sums of money for their upkeep, but his house at Lyon was taken into the king's hands.[8]

[1] Beaucourt, v, 106 n. 6.
[2] Dauvet, I, 5–6; Beaucourt, v, 106–7.
[3] Dauvet, II, 494.
[4] Ibid., I, 185; II, 579.
[5] Beaucourt, v, 107 n. 1.
[6] Dauvet, II, 455.
[7] Ibid., 482.
[8] Ibid., 482–3.

On the same day the king settled the problem of what should be done about the ransoms of certain English prisoners to which Cœur was entitled. His treatment of the case provides an instance of his ability to realise a large sum of money at little or no cost to himself. It is with a picture of Charles, surrounded by six of his civil servants, on a September day in 1456, that an account of the king at work can begin.

11 *The king at work*

The month of September 1456 was an eventful one for Charles VII. In its first week the storm broke over the head of the dauphin Louis when the king learned of his flight to the court of Burgundy.[1] The king had been in the Bourbonnais during the summer months, and, early in September, was at the castle of Châtelard, near Montluçon. At Paris, his officers were conducting interrogations of the servants and accomplices of Jean II, duke of Alençon, who had been arrested on 31 May.[2] Meanwhile, the inquiry into the affairs of Jacques Cœur was in full spate. Jean Dauvet was interviewing witnesses and collecting information at Gannat, near Nancy, in July and August.[3] On 4 September he came to see the king at Châtelard. It is his Journal that gives a fleeting impression of the king at work. On that day Charles sat in council with some of his financial officers.[4] Master Pierre Doriole, Master Laurens Girard, Otto Castellain, Jean Briçonnet, Master Jean de la Loère, his secretary, and Dauvet himself were present. They were there to discuss the ransoms of two English prisoners-of-war – George Neville, lord Bergavenny, and John Butler, son of the earl of Ormond. It had been found that Jacques Cœur and Dunois had shared the ransoms between them.[5] Cœur held three parts of each ransom to Dunois's one part. The king had taken Bergavenny into his own hands, giving Ormond to Dunois. But Dunois asserted that his one-part share in Bergavenny's ransom was worth far more than Cœur's three-part share in that of Ormond. It was also discovered that Dunois owed Cœur the sum of 3,000 écus, and Dauvet showed the king an obligation of debt which he had found among the *argentier*'s papers. To complicate matters further, Cœur owed Dunois 700l. *tournois*.

The king's decision was a simple one. To compensate Dunois for the

[1] See Beaucourt, VI, 95-6, and below, 169-70.
[2] B.N. MS. fr. 18441, fols 1-125ᵛ.
[3] Dauvet, II, 480-1.
[4] Ibid., 483.
[5] Ibid., 483; I, 194.

loss of his valuable share in Bergavenny's ransom, Charles merely wrote off and pardoned his debt of 3,000 *écus* to Cœur. This was to be done on condition that Dunois did not claim any part of the 700*l. tournois* owed him by Cœur. The king, disposing of Cœur's credit in this way, lost little in comparison to what he gained. Bergavenny was his prisoner, and Dauvet was ordered to sell him to whomever would buy him. By the end of the day he had been sold to Jean de Bueil, the admiral of France, for the very large sum of 24,000 *écus*. The king agreed to these terms, after speaking to Dauvet, and hearing that the prisoner was in danger of death. By wiping out a relatively minor item of debt, the king had used his prerogative over prisoners to good effect. It was in such matters that astuteness was a particularly valuable asset for a king. There were other items in Cœur's possession on which he was eager to lay his hands. On 5 and 6 October 1456 Dauvet had some tapestries valued which were hanging in Cœur's great house at Bourges.[1] The king's predilection for 'chambers' of tapestry – that is, complete sets of hangings for beds – is known from various sources.[2] Cœur had two of these at Bourges. One set showed scenes from the life of 'Nabugotdenozor', and the other was 'sown' with winged stags and the king's arms. There were also wall hangings and covers for seats and benches, sewn with the king's arms. The lot was valued at 1,465¼ *écus*, and, in default of bidders, went to the king at that price. He paid nothing for the tapestries. The cost was merely to be deducted from the fines imposed on the unfortunate *argentier*.[3]

Dauvet had acted on a direct mandate from the king. Such interventions suggest considerable application to, and knowledge of, the business in hand on the king's part. The conventional picture of his behaviour during his later years has been derived from the accounts of polemicists, such as Thomas Basin, rather than from the records of government. From the rumours and insinuations of Basin and the Burgundian Jacques du Clercq, allegations of a 'moral collapse' have been made against Charles VII.[4] Since the death of Agnès Sorel in February 1450, the place which she had filled was vacant until April 1454. André de Villequier then died, and his widow, Antoinette de Maignelais, was alleged by contemporaries to have 'given the king what he wanted'.[5] She

[1] Ibid., II, 505–6. See Plate 7.
[2] See B.N. MS. fr. 6750, fol. 9ᵛ (purchase of cord and hooks on which to hang the 'rooms, chambers and retreats of the king' in 1458).
[3] Dauvet, II, 506.
[4] See Beaucourt, VI, 7–9; Vaughan, *Philip the Good*, 132.
[5] Beaucourt, VI, 8–10.

was Sorel's cousin german – her critics may have been only too determined to argue that she must, therefore, have acted likewise. Remarkable
diagnoses of 'perversions' have been made for the king. Antoinette de
Maignelais, it is argued, acted as procuress for the king's *seraglio*, which
accompanied him everywhere. On the basis of gossip recounted by
Jacques du Clercq, the king has been accused of using Antoinette de
Maignelais to procure 'teenage girls . . . from among the French nobility'.[1] But du Clercq contradicts himself. At one point he writes that the
'five or six *damoiselles*' whom she kept were 'of humble birth', but were
dressed as queens.[2] He then goes on to tell a story about a nobleman's
eighteen-year-old daughter from Arras who was sent to court by her
evil father.[3] The insinuation is that Antoinette was acting as the *madame*
of a royal brothel. To say that is not necessarily to imply any 'perversions' on the part of the king. The moral of the tale was drawn by du
Clercq in terms of paternal meanness on the part of the nobleman rather
than royal perversion.

A further allegation made against the king at this time was his inaccessi-
bility. Thomas Basin set out the charge in his vituperative prose:

> He [Charles VII] disliked staying in large towns, especially Paris; he
> did not willingly live in towns or in places where there were many
> people, but in little towns or castles around Bourges or Tours, where
> there was little and scanty accommodation, except for himself and his
> entourage. He sought out such retreats so that he could keep the troop
> of whores which surrounded him more freely and quietly, and so that
> he could more fully pursue his pleasures, taking care that he should be
> disturbed only by the least troublesome of matters. Great harm came
> to the kingdom in this way; the people of the kingdom and the provinces
> were rarely granted audience or access to his presence; but the gnawing
> dogs of the court acted as intermediaries, those flatterers and ministers
> to his pleasures, by whose work the truth rarely reached his ears, and
> even more rarely was advice given by them in the public interest. . . .[4]

Basin was writing during the winter of his discontent – as an exile from
France, twenty years after the events which he purported to describe.[5]
After all, there could be other reasons for a prince to shun large centres
of population, and to prefer the security of his retreats. The image of

---

[1] Vaughan, op. cit., 132.
[2] Quoted in Beaucourt, VI, 9.
[3] Ibid., 10.
[4] Basin, II, 306.

[5] Ibid., I, viii–x, xvi, where his *Histoire de
Charles VII* is dated by its editor to
1471–2.

an idle, negligent king, devoted only to his pleasures, must be modified by the use of less vivid sources than the works of Thomas Basin. From the sheer volume of Charles's ordinances, the known facts of his itinerary, his surviving letters, and the scanty records of the work of his council, an impression of constant and unremitting assiduity seems to emerge. With so many cares and concerns before him, the king perhaps deserved at least some of his pleasures. Chastellain, although making the statutory condemnation of his morals and of his 'days of recreation . . . with women', admitted that he possessed 'marvellous industry'.[1] He saw all kinds of men at preordained hours, and their attendance was obligatory. He spent, said Chastellain, 'one hour with ecclesiastics, another with nobles, another with foreigners, another with artisans, armourers, siege-engineers, bombardiers and similar people; he remembered their business and their fixed day; no one dared to put them off'.[2] It is a picture which can be substantiated from the surviving evidence.

First, in order to gain some impression of the king's activities at this time, his itinerary for one year can be established.[3] In 1451 – the year of the first reconquest of Guyenne – he spent his time in, broadly, two areas of the kingdom. With the exception of a few days in Paris, and a pilgrimage to the shrine of Ste-Catherine-de-Fierbois, the first four months of the year were passed at Montils-lès-Tours and in the surrounding countryside. With the onset of the Guyenne expedition, the king went southwards in the wake of his troops, spending May and June at Poitiers, Lusignan and St-Jean-d'Angély. From July until late September he was at Taillebourg, where he remained until the end of the campaign. Most of the remainder of the year was spent in Poitou, at St-Maixent and Villedieu, near Lusignan, until he returned to Montils-lès-Tours for the Christmas period. Throughout the Guyenne expedition he had been kept away from the fighting. It was a sensible decision. There was no possibility of a recurrence of the threats to his safety which had attended the Norman campaign of the previous year. During that expedition he had been in the front line with his troops on a number of occasions. When he was outside Rouen in November 1449, a lawyer called Vincent de Druy had offered to gain possession of his person and hand him over to Somerset and Talbot if they would grant him the chancery of France.[4] A far

---

[1] Chastellain, II, 184, 185.
[2] Ibid., 184.
[3] The only attempt to construct a complete itinerary for Charles VII was made by Vallet de Viriville. It is now in B.N. MSS. fr. nouv. acq. 5083 and 5084.

Unfortunately it is full of contradictions and internal inconsistencies. I have selected material from MS. 5084, fols 191ʳ ff. in this instance.
[4] See Bossuat, Suriennes, 346.

more serious threat to the king's security was made at the siege of Caen in June 1450.

One means of gaining access to Charles VII was by means of his body-guard – the Scots archers and German crossbowmen who slept fully armed in the king's lodgings every night, taking their turn to go on sentry duty. As has been seen, they were thought to be susceptible to sub-version in 1446.[1] Four years later an attempt was alleged to have been made by the English to seduce five of their number during the siege of Caen. Robin Campbell, lieutenant of Robert Cunningham, captain of the king's men-at-arms and archers, was accused, with four other Scots of the bodyguard, of conspiring against the king's person.[2] Somerset had promised them 4,000 écus and fifty pounds sterling if, with the aid of four Englishmen, they took one of the following: Dunois, André de Villequier, Jacques Cœur, or Jean Bureau, treasurer of France. They were also to guide a force of 1,500 English out of the town. Of these, five hundred were to be mounted, and would descend on the king's lodging 'in order to seize him, and take him to Cherbourg, and put him to flight'.[3] The remaining thousand troops were to go on foot among the king's artillery, putting torches into the powder kegs and spiking the bom-bards. As Charles wrote to James II of Scotland in January 1457, the matter was important enough – as it concerned the persons of the king, his lieutenant-general, and the principal officers of his army – to warrant proceedings for treason.[4] These were brought in August 1455 and both Robin and John Campbell were condemned to death by beheading and quartering.[5] Despite the pleadings of James II, through his ambassadors, Robert Cunningham was not spared banishment from the king's presence, though he escaped death.[6] With such designs influencing those whose function it was to provide for the king's personal security, suspicion fell on all those around him. He knew that he could trust no one. With the onset of his first proven bout of illness – in September 1455 – the ques-tion of survival may have begun to exercise his mind more vigorously than it had done for some time past. Natural mistrust was prompted by the course of events.

The king's appearance in the front line was thus fraught with dangers – not only from his 'ancient enemies', the English, but from members of his own entourage. His normal practice seems to have been to retire to

---

[1] See above, 100–1.
[2] B.N. MS. Dupuy 38, fol. 89ʳ.
[3] Ibid., fol. 89ᵛ.
[4] Stevenson, I, 346–51.

[5] B.N. MS. Dupuy 38, fols 88ʳ, 89ᵛ.
[6] Beaucourt, vi, 28–9. For the arrests of two more Scots in 1459 see ibid., 435 n. 2.

a religious house some distance from the actual fighting. During the Norman expedition he was lodged at the abbeys of Grestain and Jumièges (where Agnès Sorel died) in February 1450.[1] At the time of the threat to his safety at Caen, in June, he was at the abbey of Ardenne, just outside the town.[2] These Norman monasteries must have been chosen for their size and their supposed wealth. They suffered from the descent of the king and his entourage upon them. To house the court adequately was no mean achievement. His household accounts show that messengers were sent ahead of the king and his train, proclaiming his movements and requisitioning billets and lodging.[3] In February 1450, during his month's sojourn at Grestain, while his troops were besieging nearby Honfleur, the abbot of the house had to be compensated for the costs of the visitation. He was also given money 'to rebuild . . . his church' – whether its deterioration was due to the war, or to the presence of the king's troops, is unclear.[4] But the monks had little choice. Entertainment of great nobles was one of their functions, and the presence of the court – with its licentious inmates – was probably no revelation to them.[5] Others suffered more directly from the king's campaign. The abbot and monks of St-André-de-Gouffier, near Falaise, were recompensed for the loss of the timber taken from their woods by the king's artillerymen for the siege of Falaise.[6] The parishioners of Léry, Val-de-Rueil, Vauvray and Portejoye were similarly compensated for unspecified 'losses and damages' sustained by them during the passage of the king's companies of *ordonnance* through the *vicomté* of Pont-de-l'Arche.[7] Appeasement began on the very morrow of reconquest.

But reconquest was thought to be difficult to achieve without the presence, if not the participation, of the king. On 27 July 1453, during the second Guyenne expedition, when Charles was some way from the theatre of war, he received letters from Guillaume Jouvenel des Ursins and Jean d'Estouteville, lord of Torcy, master of the crossbowmen.[8] The king was at Angoulême. Guillaume Jouvenel and Torcy had left Angoulême on 24 July, and had been empowered by Charles to inquire into irregularities in the taking of the town of Castillon by his troops.[9] On

[1] See *Ord.*, XIV, 84, 86, 89; Beaucourt, V, 26–7.

[2] *Ord.*, XIV, 98; see above, 138.

[3] B.N. MS. fr. 6750, fol. 7ᵛ.

[4] Escouchy, III, 384–5.

[5] See the extracts from the household book of Richard Beauchamp, earl of Warwick, in Normandy (1431–2), printed in

J. Harvey, *Gothic England* (London, 1947), 173–5.

[6] Escouchy, III, 390.

[7] Ibid., 391.

[8] B.N. MS. Dupuy 761, fol. 21; Beaucourt, V, 465–6.

[9] B.N. MS. fr. 18442, fols 46ʳ–47ᵛ, and MS. Duchesne 108, fols 35ʳ–42ʳ.

26 July they began to hear the complaints of the discontented, and wrote to the king from Libourne. By nine o'clock on Saturday the 28th, the king's reply was in their hands. It was an impressive testimony to the distance which the *chevaucheurs*, or messengers, of the king's stable could cover in a short time, Libourne being about sixty miles from Angoulême. In his letter the king expressed his satisfaction at their labours over the commission which he had given them.[1] Torcy had obviously written a separate letter, dealing with the urgent necessity for the king to be present among his troops. Perhaps it was thought that his presence might prevent the dispute over the manner in which Castillon was taken. Whatever the reason, his appearance, he wrote, 'has seemed among you over there to be necessary for the cutting short of our conquest'. Consequently, Charles was ready to leave Angoulême for the abbey of La Couronne on the next day. He said that he intended to stay there until Tuesday the 31st, in order to collect provisions for the next stage of his itinerary. It was not easy for the royal household to move speedily. Owing to scarcity of victuals, the king anticipated remaining at Blanzac, about twenty miles from Angoulême, for some time, while food and drink was gathered, and carts provided. If it was a matter of real urgency the king would do his best to come sooner, but victualling was alleged to be a serious problem.

Meanwhile, the chancellor and Torcy were to arrange lodgings for the king, and supervise the siege of Fronsac. The king's quartermasters would soon be sent to assist them in their task of finding suitable accommodation. Charles was as good as his word in one respect, for he was at the abbey of La Couronne, a few miles from Angoulême, on 30 July, and wrote from there to the duke of Savoy.[2] By 8 August he had reached Libourne, and was present at the capitulation of the castle of Fronsac. The garrison, claimed Martial d'Auvergne, surrendered 'for fear of his person'.[3] From there he moved to Montferrant, in the Entre-deux-Mers, and supervised the laying of siege to Bordeaux.[4] His presence was vital to the course of operations. On 17 September the penalties of resistance to his sovereignty were made plain to the garrison of Cadillac, who were withstanding siege, although the walls of the place had been battered by his guns.[5] On his arrival at the place, they surrendered. The captain was executed on his orders. His sovereignty was no longer to be mocked.

[1] MS. Dupuy 761, fol. 21.

[2] Beaucourt, v, 464-5.

[3] Martial d'Auvergne, *Vigilles*, II, 150.

[4] Beaucourt, v, 278.

[5] Leseur, II, 19; Escouchy, II, 56; MS. fr. 32511, fol. 165ᵛ, for payment to an esquire 'for having guided the king and his crossbowmen, and a bombard . . . to the siege before Cadillac'.

Throughout September the king remained in the forefront of the reconquest, granting letters of pardon and confirming the agreements by which
the Gascon towns had surrendered to his captains.[1] By October, an
epidemic had broken out among his troops. Jacques de Chabannes, the
grand maître of the household, and Pierre de Beauvau, died of it.[2] A speedy
conclusion to the campaign was essential. On 19 October Bordeaux
finally capitulated. The king did not enter the city in person, but left
Gascony for Poitou. It was the last time that he was to appear at the
head of his troops.

It can be surmised that the active waging of war was not to his taste.
He was, as Chastellain wrote, not bellicose by nature.[3] His talents lay
rather in the council, and the counting-house, at this period of his life.
There is, however, evidence that he was something of an armchair
soldier. During the conquest of Normandy, the Genoese Louis Giribault,
one of his gunners, was experimenting with a design for a new gun-
carriage for the king's artillery.[4] Between August 1449 and February
1450, Giribault had been making the gun-carriage at Tours. Owing to
the king's departure for the campaign of conquest, he could not see work
in progress. Such was his interest in the project that a model of the invention was made for him at Rouen. The object of the experiment was to
create a gun-carriage which was not drawn by horses, thereby economis-
ing on the costs of transporting the guns from siege to siege. Giribault
followed the king from Rouen to Tours, Bernay and Alençon in February
and March 1450. Charles perhaps saw the advantages of ceasing to re-
quisition horses to draw the artillery. The detrimental effects of such
practices on his loyal subjects who lived in the path of his armies were
obvious.[5] Financial advantage was perhaps accompanied by solicitude –
loyalty had, especially in areas of reconquest, to be encouraged and sustained. But it was in the financing of war that the king's abilities – as has
been observed from the case of Jacques Cœur – were more productively
employed. War was best left to the soldiers. 'The facts of war,' Charles
wrote in January 1457, 'are matters which must be understood and
appreciated by the eye.'[6] The advice of captains and counsellors should
be sought on such affairs. But the scrutiny of finances was one means
whereby tactics and strategy were rendered possible. A king's successes
in battle were not gained exclusively by his generals.

---

[1] For letters issued by him at St-Macaire
see A.N., JJ.182, nos 1, 13 (September
1453).
[2] Beaucourt, v, 281.

[3] Chastellain, II, 180–1.
[4] Escouchy, III, 381–2.
[5] See Contamine, op. cit., 311–12.
[6] Stevenson, I, 338–9.

Henri Baude, poetaster rather than poet, but one of the king's financial officers in Bas-Limousin, could testify to his concern for his finances. He inspected 'the complete state of his finances,' wrote Baude, 'and had it calculated in his presence, for he understood it very well.'[1] He reserved part of Wednesday, and all of Friday and Saturday, for the expedition of financial business. Account rolls, certificates, warrants and quittances were signed by him personally. Baude's statement is borne out by surviving documents. Each page of a register recording the distribution of *aides pour le fait de la guerre* between October 1454 and September 1455 is signed in the king's hand.[2] Sometimes the king's signature served as a certificate of authenticity, whereby a financial officer's disbursements were warranted by the king. Payments made by Macé de Launoy, receiver-general in Normandy, were thus authenticated in April 1454 by the king at Montils-lès-Tours, Charles having scrutinised the account roll which was drawn up for audit by the higher officers in the *Chambre des Comptes*.[3] Similarly, Pierre de Janouillac rendered his account for the distribution of the king's New Year's Day presents (*étrennes*) in 1452, citing 'a roll of parchment signed at the end in the king's hand' as sufficient warrant for the payments which he had made.[4] At Montsoreau, in December 1459, Charles certified to his *gens des comptes* that Jean Artaut, constable of Bordeaux, had been ordered to disburse revenues from Guyenne, largely in order to pay for building work on the castles of Hâ and Trompette at Bordeaux. As late as 13 March 1461 Charles was signing Artaut's account rolls at Bourges, although his signature shows every sign of debility.[5]

These accounts were perhaps among the last that he signed. They ran from September 1459 until September 1460, and were authenticated for the Easter audit of 1461. When the account for expenditure on the king's household between 1 October 1460 and 31 March 1461 came to be rendered, it was said that certain payments which were normally recorded 'in a roll signed in the king's hand' were not warranted.[6] This was because Charles had suffered a 'severe illness' during the period covered by the account. He was unable to sign warrants, and, from the shakiness of his signature on 13 March 1461, had then only just sufficient strength to hold a pen.[7] The clerk's entry in the household account suggests that

[1] Vallet de Viriville, *Nouvelles recherches sur Henri Baude* (Paris, 1855), 10, 11; cf. Chastellain, II, 186.
[2] B.N. MS. fr. 2886, fols 3ʳ–25ʳ.
[3] B.N. MS. fr. 26083, nos 45–6.

[4] B.N. MS. fr. 10371, fol. 5ʳ.
[5] B.N. MS. fr. 26086, nos 7322, 7428.
[6] B.N. MS. fr. 6754, fol. 5ᵛ.
[7] B.N. MS. fr. 26086, no. 7428.

such an omission was accounted for only by exceptional circumstances. But he enjoyed sufficient respite from his illness to be able to sign his last surviving letter-missive on 15 May, two months before his death.[1] What this evidence seems to point to is the fact that Henri Baude's statement was not merely part of a tendentious panegyric on the virtues of the king. His physical health is a subject to which further discussion will be devoted.[2] Until the autumn of 1455, it was relatively sound. It is from the months before that illness afflicted him that some of the most precious evidence for his actual behaviour is to be derived. The survival of a register recording the business of his *grand conseil* for the months of April to June 1455 provides a unique picture of the king at work.[3] It offers a test case against which to set other evidence. The accusations of both contemporaries and later critics can be evaluated in the light of the cold facts which it discloses.

A *prima facie* case for the king's retirement from the business of government could be made from the fact that he presided in person over his council only twice during these three months.[4] But such evidence is deceptive. A number of notes made by the secretaries who wrote up the register suggests that he was consulted, presumably in his 'retreat', on many of the more important issues before the council. His observations have been preserved in the form of marginal annotations.[5] Where no royal assent, or dissent, is recorded, the name of the secretary responsible for expediting the council's decision is recorded in the margin of each of the forty folios.

Medieval government presupposed delegation. On many matters, the small, workaday council was adequate to deal with routine business without the king's presence. A disputed election to the bishopric of Alet was discussed on 18 June 1455 by a council of five, and a similar, though more serious, incident at Albi by six councillors on 21 April.[6] The need to ensure the safekeeping of the bishop of Albi's fortified places – no doubt excluding the cathedral – led to an intervention by the king. He warned the council that if an error was found by the Paris *Parlement* in the judgement given against Robert Dauphin, one claimant to the see, recovery of the fortified places from the other party might be very difficult.[7] Such interventions presuppose the submission of the small council's decisions to the king for advice and approval. His presence was, however, deemed

[1] See Plate ii.
[2] See below, 172 ff.
[3] Printed in Valois, *Conseil*, 231–323.
[4] Ibid., 264–7 (19–20 May 1455).

[5] Ibid., 232, 241, 260–1, 278, 284, 287–8, 289, 297, 301, 303–4, 305, 313.
[6] Ibid., 320, 233, 241.
[7] Ibid., 241.

essential on occasions of greater significance. On 19 and 20 May he presided over the council at Bourges.[1] A large body of secular lords, clergy
and civil servants made up the council on these days. They were gathered
together in order to receive the ambassadors of James II of Scotland.
When the bishop of Galloway gave him letters from his sovereign,
Charles said that he would be heard on the following day. This was done.
A very large assembly – including the counts of Foix, Etampes, Maine,
Nevers, Richemont, La Marche, Sancerre, Dunois and the lord of Albret
– was gathered.[2] The ambassadors then requested a private audience with
the king. This was granted, and they were asked to confer with Dunois,
Pierre Doriole and the Scots captain of the king's guard, on the prickly
question of the Campbell–Cunningham plot.

It has been observed that 'a crude counting of attendances is hardly an
assessment of influence'.[3] This must hold good, above all, when the
attendances of the king in his *grand conseil* are computed. A Scottish
embassy was on a different level from a disputed election, appointment
or resignation from an office or benefice. The 'influence' of the king can
more accurately be measured by his recorded observations, whether he
was present or not in the council. It is worth examining each of those
observations. On 31 May 1455 eleven members of the council were discussing complaints brought by Pey Berland, archbishop of Bordeaux,
against the behaviour of the king's officers in his recently reconquered
diocese.[4] Ecclesiastical courts were being prevented from hearing cases
on real estate and contracts. The archbishop also objected to certain
points in the ordinances issued recently on the administration of justice
in Guyenne by the king's commissioners.[5] Charles's reaction was noted
by the secretary in the following manner:

> The king makes a certain amount of difficulty over this reply, because
> those of his *grand conseil* are not informed of what rights the archbishop
> of Bordeaux, from ancient times, has been accustomed to enjoy, nor
> whether he has been accustomed to do so from times past, nor whether
> he can do so by law. And, because the said lord [the king] would not
> wish to remove anything from the Church, he wishes that this point
> should be well debated, so that nothing is done about it which would
> be on his conscience. . . .[6]

[1] Valois *Conseil*, 264–7.
[2] Ibid., 266–7.
[3] Lewis, op. cit., 128.
[4] Valois, *Conseil*, 303–4.
[5] Ibid., 303; G. Hubrecht, 'Jurisdictions et

compétences en Guyenne recouvrée',
*Annales de la Faculté de droit de l'Université
de Bordeaux, série juridique*, iii (1952),
63–79 (tr. in *Recovery of France*, 82–101).
[6] Valois, *Conseil*, 303.

Accordingly, the council referred the complaint to Jean Bureau, commissioner on the exercise of justice in Guyenne, to discover what moved the commissioners to make such ordinances. The king approved this step. An appearance of concern for the liberties of the Church was always politic. Past precedent was a sound basis for present action, especially in a conquered land. Similar caution was exercised by the king on the question of tax exemption for lay tenants of the Church at Bordeaux. They were, the council decided, to be taxed with the other inhabitants, but the king would only assent if it was found that, by law, they were no more exempt 'than the others of this kingdom'.[1] Taxes on wine which the council wished to impose on the clergy were, again, only to be taken 'according to ancient custom'. Without the king's assent, the council could evidently do nothing. Further information was to be gathered from Jean Bureau, who was at Bordeaux and knew the situation there. In another case, a firm negative greeted a decision of the council. On 12 June 1455 nine members of the council heard a petition from the inhabitants of Narbonne.[2] They desired the king's permission to levy a tax on salt, the proceeds of which would help to keep the bridges over the river Aude in good repair. Jacques Cœur had prevented them from levying it previously. The council agreed that they could levy the tax for a period of ten years. But the king's reply took the form of a veto. 'The king,' wrote the secretary, 'has not mandated this action, and has said that he will not do so without his officers of Languedoc, and that one should wait to speak with them about it when they are over here.'[3] Four months later, on 10 October, the petition was granted, 'by the king in his council', and Adam Rolant drew up the formal letters which confirmed it.[4] The influence of the royal officers in Languedoc might be discerned in the stipulation that the receivers of the tax were to be appointed by, and to render account to, 'the people of our council in the land of Languedoc'.[5] The king's *domaine* and taxes were to be in no way diminished as a result of the grant. Council, civil servants, and subjects had each staked their respective claims. But the driving force behind such actions lay with the king.

In many cases the king was content to endorse the council's decision, and the secretary simply wrote, 'It seems well to the king'.[6] His interventions, when they dissented from the council, seem to have been moved largely by two considerations. First, the necessity of observing past precedent and former legislation – even that of his enemies; and

[1] Valois, *Conseil*, 304.
[2] Ibid., 313.
[3] Ibid., 313.

[4] *Ord.*, XIV, 367–9.
[5] Ibid., 368.
[6] Valois, *Conseil*, 303, 297, 301.

secondly, a desire on his part to see that those of his officers who would be particularly concerned with the affair should be properly consulted. Such actions on his part served as a brake on the resolutions of the council. Implementation of decisions on certain important issues could thus be retarded by royal initiative. 'It seems well to the king,' wrote his secretary opposite an entry relating to certain demands made by Charles II, lord of Albret, 'as long as one takes time.'[1] To deliberate slowly, and then to act quickly, was a commonplace maxim of medieval and Renaissance state-craft. As has been argued, the king's behaviour might conform to this notion. But what actually happened during those thirty-six sessions of his council of which some record has survived? First of all, who were the most regular and assiduous attenders? As was to be expected, the chan-cellor – Guillaume Jouvenel des Ursins – was present at every session.[2] So was Olivier de Longueil, bishop of Coutances, a hard-working civil servant if ever there was one. As a result, the diocese of Coutances did not see its bishop at this time. He was to reply for the king to the pleas for clemency towards Jean II, duke of Alençon, made by Philip the Good of Burgundy's proctor at Alençon's trial in September 1458.[3] After him came François Hallé, one of the Chancery staff, whose views on the king's sovereignty were known to be equally uncompromising.[4] He attended thirty-one sessions in 1455.

Last among the most industrious members of the day-to-day council was Master Etienne Lefèvre, one of the four *maîtres des requêtes* of the king's household. He had twenty-nine sessions to his credit.[5] The purpose for which he attended the council is indicated by his title. As one who was responsible for receiving requests, or petitions, the *maître des requêtes* of the household was a crucial figure in the king's conduct of affairs. It has recently been remarked, in the context of Richard II of England's system of patronage, that

> the importance of the petition in medieval government can hardly be over-emphasised: patronage as much as justice was founded upon it. It was the subject's means of gaining access to government, of bringing local and particular grievances and requests to the notice of a govern-ment which was bound otherwise to remain ignorant or indifferent, and of obtaining all kinds of acts of grace from the crown or those to whom the crown's powers of patronage were delegated.[6]

1 Valois, *Conseil*, 297.
2 For an analysis of attendances see ibid., 150.
3 See below, 160-2, 205-9.
4 Valois, *Conseil*, 160.
5 Ibid., 150. See below, 147-8, 207.
6 J. A. Tuck, 'Richard II's system of patronage', in *The Reign of Richard II* (London, 1971), 4.

The same can be said for France under Charles VII. If this was the means of 'gaining access to government' then the king's accessibility must be measured by the volume of petitions which were heard and adjudicated upon by him. A crude computation of appearances in the royal presence is no measure of anything – least of all 'accessibility'. It had been a commonplace of French medieval government since the thirteenth century that a petition to the king was normally made before letters patent were issued.[1] By the fourteenth century these were usually written requests, upon which the king acted with the advice of his council. The *maîtres des requêtes* of the household were so called because they received and examined all petitions addressed to the king. Their function was crucial to the business of government.

In the fifteenth century the office was still no sinecure. Etienne Lefèvre was paid his wages 'for the time he has served at court' during this period, together with Masters Girard le Boursier, Jean Tudert and Georges Havart.[2] The indefatigable Henri Baude bore witness to the importance of the petitioning process as it reflected on the king's aptitude for government: 'when requests were delivered to him, he had them taken and looked at, and, when one had given him an account of them, he sent the petitioners to the right place. . . .'[3] It was the function of the *maîtres des requêtes* to receive and scrutinise the petitions. Sometimes the king was subjected to importunate suitors, which led him to issue letters in their favour. It is not known if Charles VII was preyed upon by suppliants in person, as was his predecessor Philip V, as he walked from Mass in his chapel to his private apartments.[4] The existence of the *maîtres des requêtes* must have protected him from such troublesome calls upon his time and judgement. Henri Baude was anxious to assure his readers that the king acted, not impulsively, but only upon the advice of his council.[5] That the *maîtres des requêtes* were trusted members of that body appears from the other jobs which they were sometimes given by the king. In May 1459, for example, Master Georges Havart was given a silken robe by the king to wear while he was on an embassy to Constance.[6] Jean Tudert was given robes of scarlet and grey cloth for an embassy to Aragon in March of the same year.[7] Sometimes the king dealt with petitions in what were evidently more formal sessions. It was during these public sessions, known as

---

[1] See G. Tessier, *Diplomatique Royale Française* (Paris, 1962), 269–71.
[2] B.N. MS. fr. 6750, fol. 5^v; 6751, fol. 3^v; 6752, fol. 4^v.
[3] Vallet, *Nouvelles recherches*, 9.
[4] Tessier, op. cit., 270.

[5] Vallet, op. cit., 9.
[6] A.N., KK.51, fol. 109^r.
[7] Ibid., fols 113^v, 115^r. He became first *président* of the *Parlement* of Bordeaux on its foundation in 1462.

C—F

requêtes générales, that he exercised one of his most important prerogatives – that of mercy.[1]

If the volume of petitions for pardon, and for remission from crimes of all kinds, is any indication of Charles VII's accessibility to his subjects, then it seems that he was very accessible indeed. It had long been common for such petitions to be presented to the king personally on certain occasions, especially Good Friday.[2] There seems to be evidence of Charles VII acting in this way at Eastertide 1458. For their part in causing the death of one Thomine l'Effrayte, an old woman reputed to be a witch, at the village of Andillé, near Loudun, three men were pardoned by the king. She was obviously a lunatic, who 'ran madly on the roads, stark naked'. But the king, preferring mercy to harshness, pardoned her murderers 'in honour and reverence of the Passion of Our Lord Jesus Christ, who on this day suffered death'.[3] The letter of remission was endorsed 'by the king, holding his *requêtes*, at which you [the chancellor], Masters Jean Tudert, Georges Havart, François Hallé, and many others, were present'. It was the team as before, wearing rather different hats, but performing one of their allotted tasks. Unlike his predecessor, Charles VI, and his successor, Francis I, Charles VII did not on this occasion appoint a deputy to grant his Good Friday pardons.[4] In April 1461 he was still holding sessions 'of his *requêtes*', at which his favoured younger son, Charles of France, was present – no doubt gaining valuable experience for the future.[5] A wife driven to murder her husband's lover through hatred and jealousy was pardoned during that session.[6] It is difficult to see how the king, given his own alleged behaviour, could sympathise with her. But it was the lower orders of society who made a habit of the *crime passionel*. From the contents of the letters which he granted – and which are preserved in the registers of his *Trésor des Chartes* – Charles must have learnt much about the behaviour of his subjects from them.[7] The stories which they told were *ex parte* statements, designed to justify their actions and get them off the penalties which often hung over them.

Apart from the Easter remissions, the hearing of petitions must have been one of the most common activities in Charles's working life as king. The constant presence of at least one *maître des requêtes* at court throughout the year implies regularity in the discharge of this duty. The king's reaction to such supplications is unknown. Only those which he granted

---

[1] Tessier, op. cit., 272.
[2] Ibid., 272 and n. 2.
[3] Printed in *AHP*, xxv (1906), 60.
[4] Tessier, op. cit., 262 n. 1, 272 n. 2.

[5] *AHP*, xxv (1906), 289.
[6] Ibid., 288–9.
[7] For the registers see A.N., JJ.179–94.

have survived, slightly altered during transmission from *requête* to letter of remission. His reasons for rejecting petitions, as he rejected – or delayed – decisions of his council cannot now be discovered. If the letters of remission which he granted to petitioners from the province of Poitou at Mehun-sur-Yèvre in January 1455 are taken as specimen cases, some impression emerges of the kind of cases upon which he was required to adjudicate.[1] These were crimes of violence, the legacy of war and of the presence of the standing army. Tavern brawls, crimes of passion, rapes, bestiality, soldierly excesses – such were the staple items among the gloomy tales to which he listened. His mercy was infinite, to judge from some of the extremely dubious cases which he remitted. But sometimes matters came to his notice which concerned him more directly than these village vendettas. He had never seen most of the people involved in them, and they might in any case have appeared to him as inhabitants of another world. In other, rarer instances, men whom he *had* seen were making claims upon his mercy and magnanimity. For example, in March 1454 he pardoned a former valet of one of the archers of his guard for theft.[2] The crime had been plotted when the king was at Poitiers after the surrender of Bordeaux in October 1453. In the hope of becoming a member of the king's guard, a cook had conspired with Guillaume Comin, the valet, to steal jewels from his master. These were to be offered as a bribe to Thomas Halliday, the Scots captain of the guard. Comin, of course, denied that Halliday was involved. But, as he was only an accomplice, he was pardoned. He did his best to incriminate his master, Alexander Baste, archer of the guard. The king took him at his word.

Occasionally the king himself was referred to in these petitions. In May 1459 Mathurin d'Appelvoisin, knight, and Jacques Jousseaume, esquire, were pardoned for their part in the death of a lawyer, in the *sénéchaussée* of Guyenne.[3] The lawyer, Master Hector Rousseau, was alleged to have withstood a minor siege of his house by them. He was already known for his contempt of the king's officers, and was well provided with culverins and other instruments of war. It was claimed that he 'cursed God, and said that he would do nothing for the king nor for the queen, and called the said lord, and also . . . Jousseaume, who are noblemen, of great honour and estate: "Villains, traitors, ribalds, robbers"' and suchlike terms of abuse.[4] The aggressive advocate was killed by a crossbow shot as a result. Whether this was merely the culmination of a private feud we shall never know. But his contempt for the king's sovereignty and for his

[1] See *AHP*, xxii (1903), 398–402.   [3] Ibid., xxv (1906), 125–44.
[2] Ibid., 364–73.   [4] Ibid., 128.

officers led to the pardon of his killers, at Razilly, by 'the king in his council'.[1] On a second occasion, the king's mercy was sought by an archer in
the company of *ordonnance* commanded by Anthoine de Chabannes.[2]
He said that he had met one Jean Guilloteau, *franc-archer*, at a fair in the
town of Thors, in Saintonge. François Queret, the archer, asked Jean to
exchange daggers with him. Jean refused, claiming that 'we [the king]
had given it to him, but the said petitioner told him that we did not know
who he was'. He went on: 'When the king loses us, he'll lose his kingdom.'[3]
Jean then turned on him and François killed him. Such acts on the part of
the soldiery were commonplace. Scuffles between the *franc-archers* and the
archers of the *ordonnance* were one product of the institution of a standing
army. There was no chivalry in their ranks. Nor was there much in the
way of *cavalleria rusticana*, if the sordid record of village crimes is an
accurate reflection of fifteenth-century rural life. The king could have
found little with which to console himself as these pathetic, bizarre, and
often horrifying cases were presented to him.

His clemency was constantly sought. On 22 May 1455 his council discussed the case of a poor old woman called Jeanne Mynute, aged eighty
or thereabouts.[4] She had been condemned by the *Parlement* to pay two
fines, but, given her poverty and age, and the length of time which her
supporter had devoted to her case, the king was asked to reduce the fines
by half. This he apparently did. On the following day the council were
discussing a petition from the duke of Bourbon.[5] Charles VII's subjects, of
whatever social group, were hardly denied access to his mercy and his
judgement. Although the *Parlement* and the *Chambre des Comptes* might
claim sovereign justice and the control of finances, the king remained the
last resort, the final court of appeal. Both institutions could act as watchdogs on his behaviour. On 3 June 1455, for example, a discussion in the
council led to the question of François II of Brittany's powers to grant
Norman confiscations being referred to the *Parlement*.[6] The king, it was
pointed out by four of the councillors, had prohibited the *grand conseil*
from taking cognisance of such cases. His relations with the sovereign
court of the realm were not stormy. But his freedom of action was
curtailed by its decisions and rulings. In the work of pacification in the

[1] See *AHP*, xxv (1906) 136, 144.
[2] Ibid., 202–8 (November 1459).
[3] Ibid., 203.
[4] Valois, *Conseil*, 280–1.
[5] Ibid., 283–4.
[6] Ibid., 290–93; for an example of a
confirmation by the king of such a grant
by Brittany see B.N. MS. fr. 20417, no.
19, endorsed 'By the king, the admiral,
Jacques Cœur, Master Etienne Chevalier
and others present', at the 'abbey of
Ardenne near Caen', 30 June 1450. This
was the grant of the receivership of *aides*
for war at Avranches to Pierre Burdelot.

aftermath of war its role was a vital one. The king has been observed at work in a variety of areas. His contribution to the process of appeasement and the 're-establishment of peace in society' remains to be considered.

III *Appeasement or revenge?*

'Charles VII,' it has been said, 'affirmed for his part his desire to keep his subjects and safeguard them in peace and concord, "without finding cause to recall the misfortunes and the evils done and perpetrated by one camp upon the other". This was his constant and sincere preoccupation.'[1] A letter of January 1457, written by Charles to James II of Scotland, set out the problems with which he was faced on the morrow of victory over the English. He wrote:

> . . . recently some of the lords of this realm, men of great estate and renown, and even close relatives of the king, have made some attempts against the king, to the prejudice of this kingdom and in favour of the English. . . . And besides this, all the divisions within this realm are not appeased . . . but they will soon be, at God's pleasure; and the king's intention is to give such good heed to this that no trouble shall result from it. . . .[2]

To take the second point first, what were the 'divisions within this realm'? Some of these have already been described, particularly in the context of the case of Joan of Arc's rehabilitation.[3] The problem was primarily one of rights to property. The king had shown concern for his own rights over the confiscations taken as a result of the recovery of the duchies of Normandy and Guyenne.[4] Confiscation led inexorably to litigation. Litigation was to some extent controlled by legislation. The edict of Compiègne, which was issued on 29 August 1429, sought to return the property of the king's supporters to them in the condition in which it was when they had lost it after the Burgundian *coup d'état* of 1418.[5] All that would have become theirs by inheritance since that date was also to be returned to them. This was partisan legislation, and the Burgundian *volte-face* of 1435 gave rise to disputes over the condition in which such property was to be returned. The treaty of Arras met Burgundian objections by returning it in its current condition. This contra-

[1] Bossuat in *Recovery of France*, 80–1.
[2] Stevenson, I, 344–5.
[3] See above, 60–1, 64–5.
[4] Above, 120–1.
[5] *Ord.*, XIV, 102–5.

dicted the edict made at Compiègne six years previously. The history of 'appeasement' and 'pacification' during the reign of Charles VII is largely a commentary upon that contradiction. As Professor Bossuat has shown, 'the courts thus found themselves faced with contradictory legislative principles, difficult to apply'.[1] They attempted to solve the problem through proceeding by a form of case-law. Above all, the *Parlement* of Paris, as supreme court of appeal, 'judged each case on its individual merits'.[2] The scope offered to the avarice of lawyers, who throve on the litigation, and to the corrupt practices of clients, was considerable. Law-suits dragged on in the *Parlement*, to the profit of no one but the coun-sellors and advocates. If appeasement was the king's aim, then it was appeasement at a price. That price was lawyers' fees. The high-mindedness discerned by Professor Bossuat in the behaviour of the *Parlementaires* had its other face.

The king's legislation about property held during English occupation was contradictory. The amnesty issued to the inhabitants of Rouen, upon its surrender in November 1449, was in flat opposition to the terms of the Compiègne ruling.[3] The clergy, nobles, burgesses and other inhabitants of Rouen were confirmed in possession of their inheritances, revenues and all rights to property, as long as they remained in the king's obedience. Such clemency was perhaps designed to gain the affection of the people. But on 28 October 1450 the edict of Compiègne was confirmed by the king at Montbazon.[4] It was registered by the *Parlement* on 15 February 1451, not without remonstrance, and for the first time. This, observed Charles, was because certain persons had challenged the edict in the *Parlement* and in other courts after the reduction of Normandy. This was 'in great irreverence of us, and . . . to the damage of our subjects who have always kept on our side, and remained in our obedience'.[5] How many of these there were in Normandy during the English occupation of 1419–50 is still unclear.[6] But there were obviously enough people who claimed to

---

[1] Bossuat, op. cit., 71.

[2] Ibid., 80.

[3] *Ord.*, XIV, 75–7.

[4] Ibid., 105–6. The amnesty of November 1449 to Rouen was, however, registered by the *Parlement* on 16 July 1454, 'without prejudice to the declaration made by the king at Montbazon' (Bossuat, op. cit., 366, n. 45).

[5] *Ord.*, XIV, 105.

[6] The evidence presented by R. Jouet in *La résistance à l'occupation anglaise en* *Basse-Normandie (1418–50)* (Caen, 1969) needs to be set beside B. J. H. Rowe, 'John, duke of Bedford, and the Norman "Brigands"', *EHR*, xlvii (1932), 583–600, and A. Dupont, 'Pour ou contre le roi d'Angleterre . . .', *Bull. Soc. Antiq. Normandie*, liv (1957–8), 164–6. The 'patriotism' of the Norman brigands is by no means proven, nor is that of the middle and lower nobility – at least in the *vicomtés* of Carentan and Orbec.

have been loyal to render the registration and confirmation of the edict desirable. The king ordained that it should be observed throughout the entire kingdom, 'perpetually and inviolably'. Sentences to the contrary were declared null and void. Letters of remission, amnesties and pardons were not to affect the ruling. It was, again, a direct contradiction of such acts as the amnesties granted to Paris in 1436 or to Rouen in 1449. What were the lawyers to do? They seem to have done their best to ignore the legislation, and acted as the case (or the clients) deserved. In his edict of October 1450, Charles expressed the wish that he had issued it 'desiring to keep and hold good peace and union between our subjects, without their having reason to remember, one against the other, the evils and troubles done and perpetrated during the wars and conflicts which have taken place in our kingdom, wishing [also] to prevent litigation and court cases between our said subjects'.[1] To confirm the partisan edict made at Compiègne, with its exorbitant terms on the restoration of property, and its refusal to provide for repayment of debts, was hardly conducive to perpetual oblivion among his subjects.

Litigation could become the continuation of civil war by other means. The evidence for a restoration of peace is not yet substantial enough for a generalisation to be made. Many cases were no doubt settled out of court, but the volume of litigation concerning confiscations showed little sign of slackening by the king's death in 1461. His behaviour towards the Gascons, after the revolt of the Bordelais in October 1452, was, perhaps justifiably, harsh.[2] Heavy indemnities were imposed, but local customs seem to have been largely confirmed. The major point at issue was the conflict of ecclesiastical and secular jurisdictions. There was little doubt about which side would ultimately win. The king's seneschal in Guyenne gained considerable extension of his judicial competence from the dispute.[3] Ancient enemies had become rebels as a result of Talbot's recovery of part of the duchy. But they were privileged rebels. Harshness was not practicable in the circumstances which surrounded the reconquests of 1449–53. Too many people were compromised by their past careers – not least the clergy involved in the affair of Joan of Arc.[4] Too many interests were opposed to a vindictive stance on the part of the king. The government of Normandy, and the functioning of the Paris *Parlement*, would have been

[1] *Ord.*, XIV, 105.
[2] See R. Boutruche in *Histoire de Bordeaux*, IV: *Bordeaux de 1453 à 1715* (Bordeaux, 1966), 9–29; Vale, *English Gascony*, 222–8.

[3] See *AMB*, v, *Livre des Coutumes*, 642–80, for the ordinances of Charles's commissioners on justice in Guyenne (28 January 1455).
[4] See above, 60–9.

quickly rendered impossible if a witch-hunt had been operated against the ecclesiastical, and secular, *collaborateurs*. Despite the partisan and patriotic rhetoric of the king's edicts, savage reprisals, had he wished to adopt them, were not feasible. The contradictions in his legislation left much to the discretion of his lawyers – men like François Hallé and Jean Tudert who served on his council. Appeasement meant business to one of the most acquisitive groups in fifteenth-century French society.

The second point which Charles made to James II of Scotland in January 1457 concerned the behaviour of certain unspecified members of the nobility. Uppermost in his mind at that time was, probably, the case of Jean II, duke of Alençon. Alençon's part in the Praguerie of 1440 has already been described.[1] The companion of Joan of Arc, he was sentenced to life imprisonment for *lèse-majesté* by the king at Vendôme on 10 October 1458. The trial was a landmark in the process by which the relationship between king and prince of the blood was transformed from the bilateral feudal contract to unilateral subjection.[2] That relationship was becoming based more upon fear than upon mutual trust. Loyalty was no longer negotiable. The king's sovereignty was inviolable. The trial therefore set precedents for future legal processes to be brought against the very highest nobility of the kingdom. The constable of St-Pol, Jacques d'Armagnac, duke of Nemours, and, in the early sixteenth century, the constable Bourbon, suffered from such proceedings.[3] The climate in which the king's lawyers could bring charges of treason and conspiracy against a peer of France can be appreciated from the recorded remarks of François Hallé, king's councillor and advocate in the *Parlement* of Paris. In the course of pleadings before the court, Hallé said that 'it is not possible . . . to have a peer and companion for the monarchy'. Referring to certain usurpations of the king's rights by some lords, he continued: 'if the other lords wished to assume the said rights, which are the *fleurons* of the crown, only a hat would be left'.[4] The *gens du roi* could be more royal than the king when they so wished. Only the king could be 'emperor in his kingdom'. He could not tolerate violations of his supreme authority by the peers – they were merely their own equals, never the equals of the king.

Why then was Alençon tried at Vendôme in 1458? Were the accusations made against him justified, and what purpose was the trial intended to serve? Its scenario and stage-management will be described in detail

---

1 Above, 76-82.
2 See Pocquet in *Recovery of France*, 196-215.

3 For these trials see B.N. MS. Dupuy 76, fols 1-14[v].
4 Valois, *Conseil*, 160; *Ord.*, XIV, 450.

later,[1] but its motivation and significance must be assessed at this point. If the charges of vindictiveness and a desire for revenge cannot be sustained when the king's dealings with recently recovered areas are considered, how far can they be proven from his treatment of this prince of the blood? First, Alençon was tried for conducting negotiations with the English. The thirteen witnesses who were interrogated by the king's officers at Paris and Rouen after his arrest in May 1456 provided incriminating evidence.[2] Most of them alleged that he had attempted to persuade both Henry VI and Richard, duke of York, to invade Normandy in 1455 or 1456. How far the English were prepared to take Alençon's proposals seriously is less clear from the documents. Henry VI was said to have told one of those interrogated, Master Esmond Gallet, that 'he wished that his uncle of France and those of his kingdom would make a good peace with him and with those of his [i.e. Henry's] kingdom, so that his uncle of France might help him to chastise his enemies, and . . . he his'.[3] There was little hope in that quarter. The plot had been betrayed by one of Alençon's tenants, Pierre Fortin, who had been sent by him on a mission to England. Fortin's information was passed to the king by the archbishop of Narbonne.[4] The king remembered Fortin's good services as an informer, and he received the gift of a robe from him in 1459.[5] Chastellain thought that the prime motive for Alençon's arrest was his agreement to deliver certain of his castles in Normandy to the English, so that they might recover the duchy.[6]

What had moved the duke to such an act of treason? It was known that he dabbled in the occult, consulting astrologers 'to discover why he had been so ill-fated and what was in store for him in the future'.[7] But this was a normal practice among the fifteenth-century nobility. The king himself did likewise. There was no mention of such activities in the treason trial of 1458, although the king's officers were busily collecting evidence of Alençon's interest in the occult two years previously.[8] The duke was not in good physical, nor, apparently, mental health. He seems to have suffered from a painful kidney complaint, had fears that he was sterile, and was considered by some of his servants to be 'a man possessed by the Devil'.[9] He was convinced that Charles of Anjou, count of Maine, had poisoned the king's mind against him. He was, he remarked, 'the man in

[1] See below, 204-9.
[2] B.N. MS. fr. 18441, fols 1ʳ-125ᵛ, for the interrogations.
[3] Ibid., fol. 112ᵛ.
[4] Beaucourt, VI, 59-60.
[5] A.N., KK.51, fol. 105ʳ. Fortin's

deposition is found in MS. fr. 18441, fol. 21ʳ.
[6] Chastellain, III, 100.
[7] MS. fr. 18441, fol. 2ʳ.
[8] Ibid., fols 1ʳ-3ᵛ, 10ᵛ-16ᵛ, 75ᵛ, 83ᵛ-88ʳ.
[9] Ibid., fol. 110ʳ.

the world who hates me most and who always contrives harm for me'.[1] Alençon had suffered from a ransom after his capture at Verneuil in 1424, which had forced him to alienate some of his lands, including the lordship of Fougères.[2] Worse still, some of the lordships of the count of Maine, including those in Perche such as Nogent-le-Rotrou, lay as enclaves within his lands. Alençon wanted them all. He claimed that Maine's hegemony at court had 'put him in the ill-will of the king' so that he had not dared to go to court for two years.[3] Maine had also caused his pension to be reduced by half, from 12,000 to 6,000 francs.[4] He had taken Alençon's assignments of taxes on his lands, and had overburdened them so that his own would be relieved from the king's taxes.[5] To what extent were these accusations justified?

Since the revolt of 1440, Alençon had undoubtedly been in bad odour with the king. Charles refused to help him to recover Fougères, which he had been forced to pledge to the duke of Brittany in order to pay his ransom. It was worth 15,000 *écus* a year, he claimed, and Brittany had a mortgage of 80,000 *écus* on it.[6] The king declined to assist him to repay the debt, and he had decided to revenge himself on Brittany, Maine and Charles himself. He sought English aid, and, one of his servants deposed in October 1456, swore that 'if the English would not help him to do this, he would seek aid from the Turks . . .'.[7] His servants considered the balance of his mind to be disturbed. The action which the king took in 1449 merely reaffirmed Brittany's title to Fougères. Alençon's appearances at court became rarer, and by 1452 he was said to be seeking a Yorkist marriage for his daughter, Catherine.[8] It would be a slight on the house of Anjou, now linked to the house of Lancaster by Henry VI's marriage. In the following years he was constantly plotting with the English, especially with Richard, duke of York, and intended to take advantage of the absence of many companies of the standing army from Normandy to allow the English into the duchy. The king had gone to the Dauphiné, Brézé had 'only a hundred lances' in Normandy, the constable Richemont was not there, and no one would resist them.[9] Alençon told one of his envoys to Richard Woodeville, Lord Rivers, lieutenant of Calais, that the king's 'subjects of Normandy were more heavily burdened with *tailles* than they had ever been and were all weary of being in the king's obedi-

---

[1] MS. fr. 18441., fol. 52ᵛ.
[2] See Bossuat, *Suriennes*, 313; Escouchy, II, 318-19, 323-4; Chastellain, III, 487, for the next sentence.
[3] MS. fr. 18441, fol. 106ᵛ. Maine was his 'mortal enemy' (ibid., fol. 112ʳ).

[4] Ibid., fol. 106ᵛ.
[5] Ibid., fol. 106ᵛ.
[6] Ibid., fol. 107ʳ; Beaucourt, VI, 194.
[7] MS. fr. 18441, fol. 107ʳ.
[8] Chastellain, III, 478.
[9] Ibid., 479; MS. fr. 18441, fols 42ʳ, 47ᵛ.

ence'.[1] At this point the royal clerk who drew up the record of the interrogation in which this observation was made wrote in the margin: 'Note the lord's [i.e. Alençon's] malice.'[2] When the English invaded, they were to abolish all taxes and issue pardons, but should reimpose taxation three or four years after the reconquest. As Charles VII had already shown, it was necessary – as at Rouen in November 1449 – to 'gain the hearts of the people . . .'.[3]

The picture which Alençon's envoys painted of the state of affairs in Charles's recent conquests was, of course, an intentionally gloomy one. It was designed to induce the English to recover Normandy and restore him to the places of which he felt he had been defrauded. Brézé would turn traitor, and the English were to have no fear of the king because, if he left the Dauphiné in order to fight them, 'the land of Guyenne and other parts would rebel'.[4] The standing army was split into three units, and Alençon was optimistic about the ease with which Normandy might be regained. He told Huntingdon herald at his castle of La Flèche in the summer of 1455, that 'he had both cannon and bombards, culverins and serpentines to the number of nine hundred, all prepared, and that he would never cease to make them until he had a thousand, and that he would have two bombards made which would be the finest in . . . France . . . which he would give to the duke of York'.[5] Given his financial state such statements should be treated with the scepticism they deserve. But from the material provided by the interrogations of the summer and autumn of 1456, Alençon's guilt was, in one respect, clear. He had been conspiring with the English. Perhaps the implicit endorsement of François I of Brittany's title to Fougères by the king in 1449 transformed resentment into deep hatred. There is no evidence for any participation by Alençon in the raid by which François de Suriennes had taken the place for the English in March 1449. But it is known that at least one of his agents was in touch with him, and owed his prebend of Coutances to him. Suriennes, on hearing of Alençon's scheme in 1455 or 1456, merely remarked that 'he did not believe that the said lord . . . would be able to bring it off'.[6]

[1] Ibid., fol. 42ʳ.
[2] Ibid., fol. 42ʳ.
[3] Ibid., fol. 59ʳ, see above, 152–3.
[4] Ibid., fol. 60ᵛ.
[5] Ibid., fols 57ʳ–57ᵛ.
[6] Ibid., fol. 123ʳ. John Fermen, Alençon's English *valet de chambre* deposed on 20 August 1456 that he had heard Esmond Gallet say that Suriennes was to descend on Normandy with 10,000 English 'and then the said lord of Alençon said . . . to . . . Esmond Gallet that he would rather have the said my lord François l'Aragonais [Suriennes] with him because he was a wise soldier and knew the land of Normandy well' (ibid., fol. 33ʳ). It would obviously have been to Alençon's advantage if Suriennes had managed to hold Fougères in 1449.

In the event, there was no English invasion of Normandy. Internal dissensions at home, if nothing else, were sufficient to scotch any such plan. In any case, Alençon's enthusiasm for the notion of his paying liege homage for his lands to Henry VI was lukewarm enough to give rise to doubts among York and his supporters. He told Huntingdon herald that the time was not yet ripe, and that it would be more profitable if he feigned allegiance to Charles VII.[1] This he continued to do, but with evident distaste. In one of his more abandoned moments, at Chinon or Tours in 1452, it was alleged, he spoke of a powder which could be used to desiccate the king if it was put into his laundry basket. The informer, Alençon's English *valet de chambre*, professed himself unable to remember whether Charles would die as a result of this bizarre scheme.[2] Again, nothing happened. It was only in May 1456, as a result of Pierre Fortin's activities as an informer, that the king proceeded to arrest Alençon. On 3 May the duke had testified in favour of Joan of Arc before the tribunal of rehabilitation.[3] On the 31st he was taken into custody by Dunois, his former companion in the company of the Maid. The irony was crude and heavy. When Alençon's conspiracy with the English was revealed to him, the king told his entourage that he was most displeased when it appeared that he had to defend himself against those of his own blood.[4] He would not know whom he could trust. Such was the public utterance recorded by the chronicler Mathieu d'Escouchy. It has to be treated with caution. The king, as has been argued, had known for a long time that he could trust no one implicitly. His action against Alençon in 1456 was one of a series of *démarches* conducted by him since he had imprisoned Jean IV, count of Armagnac, in 1444.[5] But how far had he moved against Alençon before his arrest in 1456? The question of Alençon's pension and its alleged reduction is germane to this issue.

He had certainly been deprived, temporarily, of his pension of 12,000 *livres*, given him by the king in 1432, after the Praguerie.[6] This was soon restored to him. But he subsequently claimed, in the presence of his agent Master Esmond Gallet, that it had been halved. 'Here,' it has been said, 'rancour had forced him into complete untruth; it was never cut.'[7] A receipt signed by him on 31 July 1453 acknowledged that he had been paid 12,000 *livres*.[8] On 20 August, however, Jean Dauvet's Journal recounts

[1] Ibid., fol. 61ʳ.
[2] Ibid., fol. 38ʳ.
[3] Doncœur and Lanhers, *Rédaction*, 210–16; Beaucourt, VI, 61–2.
[4] Escouchy, II, 322.

[5] Escouchy, III, 112–43; Vale, *English Gascony*, 198–201.
[6] Beaucourt, VI, 42. See above, 81.
[7] Lewis, op. cit., 228; cf. MS. fr. 18441, fol. 106ᵛ.
[8] B.N. MS. fr. 20373, no. 29.

that Dauvet and Jean Briçonnet went to recover a debt of 4,261*l.* 9*s.* 7*d.* *tournois* from Alençon.[1] This was owed by him to Guillaume de Varye, former agent of Jacques Cœur, 'for silks and other things taken by him [Alençon] and his servants from the *argenterie*' while Cœur was *argentier.* Alençon contested the sum due, and Dauvet told the duke's chancellor, Jean Lenfant, that he would recover it by taking the profits of the salt-granaries in Alençon's lands into the king's custody.[2] These were the warehouses in which the salt to be compulsorily purchased under the terms of the *gabelle* was stored. It was apparently common practice for the king to assign at least part of the proceeds of the tax to the magnates in whose lordships it was taken. By 1 September 1453, Dauvet had decided to recover the debt by seizing the sources of revenue upon which Alen-çon's pension had been assigned.[3] These included the salt-granaries of Alençon itself, Exmes, Verneuil and Bellême, as well as other revenues which had not yet been assigned for the purpose by the *trésorier.* Dauvet had taken action at Rouen by 27 September, when he drew up a com-mission in the king's name for the stopping of Alençon's pension.[4] The *receveurs des aides* and *grenetiers* of Normandy were to withhold payment until the sum owed to Varye and Cœur had been raised. Alençon was alleged to have said early in 1456 that the count of Maine had taken 'all his assignments on his lands in order to displease him'.[5] He may have had the Norman salt-granaries in mind. From the available evidence, it appears that his pension was not permanently reduced by the king. But his debts to Jacques Cœur meant that, in 1454, he received only 7,740 *livres* of his 12,000 *livres* annuity.

Alençon's grievances against the king were thus exaggerated. They were a product of almost twenty years of self-imposed isolation, and of the bitterness which so often accompanies ineffectuality. He had suffered from the war – his ransom was a heavy burden on a magnate whose lordships lay on the 'frontier of war'. His physical health was poor and the stone which he may have had in the kidneys a constant source of pain. It was hardly surprising that he felt ill-used by the king. He came close to the practice of necromancy in his despair. He resorted to taking a drug called *martagon*, and to having an astrological talisman and a magic powder made for him.[6] These were produced by the celebrated astrologer, Master

---

[1] Dauvet, I, 102–3.
[2] Ibid., 103.
[3] Ibid., 109–10.
[4] Ibid., 119–20.
[5] B.N. MS. fr. 18441, fol. 106ᵛ.
[6] Ibid., fols 10ᵛ, 11ᵛ, 12ʳ–12ᵛ, 14ᵛ–16ᵛ.

For *martagon*, see P. Robert, *Dictionnaire alphabétique et analogique de la langue française* (Paris, 1959), IV, 458. It was a herb extracted from the martagon lily, named after a turban adopted by the Sultan Muhammed I (*OED*, VI, 189).

Michel Bars, *prévôt* of Wastines in Flanders, under a favourable constella-
tion.[1] These would act as a panacea for all his ailments, and would
ingratiate him with the king. He was not cured. At Easter 1455, while
riding with one of his household esquires, he was said to have remarked
that he was 'fat and sluggish, and couldn't do what he used to be able to
do'.[2] He told Michel Bars that he

> had a serious 'accident' to his person, that's to say, great pain sometimes
> in the kidneys and sometimes in the head, and sometimes in other parts
> of the body. And when this illness afflicted him he suffered such great
> pain that he could hardly bear it. And the said lord also said that since
> this 'accident' had happened, he had had no children. And he believed
> that he never would have any until this illness was cured. . . .[3]

It was probably in 1447, or thereabouts, that this 'accident' had struck
him. His behaviour became more reckless and his absences from court
more frequent from that time onwards. His trial followed a period of two
years' imprisonment – a similar lapse of time as that which had passed
between the arrest and condemnation of Jacques Cœur. He was arrested
at a well-timed moment. The knights of Philip the Good of Burgundy's
order of the Golden Fleece were about to hold a 'chapter' of the order in
May 1456, at The Hague. Alençon was a member of the Burgundian
order, and Chastellain drew the obvious conclusion from the king's
behaviour.[4] The herald *Toison d'Or* was sent to intercede for Alençon
with the king, but he would not depart from his resolution to keep the
duke in prison. According to Chastellain, Philip the Good thought the
lit-de-justice, which was initially summoned to Montargis in the summer of
1458, was the product more of malice than necessity. He was summoned
to attend, but was given only three weeks' notice. His dislike of the pretensions of the Paris *Parlement* exacerbated his anger. *Toison d'Or* was sent
to the king to plead his master's exemption from such summonses under
the terms of the treaty of Arras. Charles accepted Philip's excuses, but
insisted on the sending of a Burgundian embassy to the *lit-de-justice*.
Philip had been ill, and personal attendance was deemed to be out of the
question. Chastellain analysed the king's motives for proceeding against
Alençon in the following terms:

[1] MS. fr. 18441, fols 14ᵛ–16ᵛ; for such
cures see Thorndike, op. cit., 122, 318–21,
574–85.
[2] MS. fr. 18441, fol. 90ʳ.
[3] Ibid., fol. 14ᵛ. His son René was born in

1440 and a daughter soon after that date;
Odolant-Desnos, *Mémoires historiques sur la
ville d'Alençon . . .* (1787), II, 162–3, 165,
167.
[4] Chastellain, III, 101, 422–3.

. . . he thought and intended to frighten the duke of Burgundy, whom he maintained was a rebel. He hoped to gain advice and remedy by putting the matter to an assembly of the peers, where, if the said duke of Burgundy had been found guilty with . . . Alençon, he would have summoned the *lit-de-justice* to condemn him as well as the other. . . .[1]

Attempts were made during the interrogations of Alençon's accomplices in 1456 to gain incriminating confessions implicating Philip the Good in his treasonable designs. These had failed, although torture had been employed.[2] All that the king's officers could gain was the information from Esmond Gallet that he had told Henry VI that Alençon and Burgundy were on good terms.[3] Henry had, he alleged, replied that he wished that Alençon and Charles of Anjou, count of Maine, were on good terms – for obvious reasons. He would rather hear that Alençon and Burgundy were on bad terms, because Philip the Good was 'the man in the world whom he would most willingly fight, because he had abandoned him in his youth, although he had sworn an oath to him, without his having ever done wrong, and that if he lived long enough he would make war on him'.[4] The memory of the Burgundian defection of 1435 still rankled with Henry, and the promptings of Margaret of Anjou no doubt increased and fed his vindictiveness. York was adopting a friendly stance towards Burgundy, who, on the eve of the *lit-de-justice*, sent his ambassadors to meet a Yorkist delegation at Calais.[5] The king was at Montils-lès-Tours, biding his time, sending spies to discover what was afoot. One of them – the herald Normandy king-of-arms – was seized between Bourbourg and Gravelines, disguised as a merchant.[6] Incriminating letters were found upon him, and he was imprisoned by Philip's officers at Lille. Charles was obviously consumed with the suspicion that Burgundy was plotting a similar enterprise to that of Alençon two years previously. There were rumours of open warfare between France and Burgundy throughout the summer of 1458.[7] Philip conciliated the inhabitants of the troublesome city of Ghent, allegedly so that they would remain loyal to him in the event of a war with France. Chastellain claimed that both Charles and Philip were mobilising their military resources, calling up the *ban et arrière-ban* in their respective territories on the

---

[1] Chastellain, III, 422-3; Beaucourt, VI, 180-5.
[2] Chastellain, III, 101, 430-31.
[3] MS. fr. 18441, fol. 112v.
[4] Ibid., fol. 112v. He was said to have

spoken these words in Gallet's presence at Westminster early in 1456.
[5] Chastellain, III, 428.
[6] Ibid., 428; Beaucourt, VI, 187 and n. 1.
[7] See Vaughan, *Philip the Good*, 351-3.

frontiers of France and Flanders.[1] The hot summer was a time of cold war.

In the event, Alençon was tried and convicted of *lèse-majesté* at the *lit-de-justice* held, because of the outbreak of an epidemic at Montargis, at Vendôme in September and October 1458. The conditions and terms in which he was condemned – and pleaded for – will be described in a subsequent chapter.[2] But it was not only Alençon who was on trial. The *lit-de-justice* effectively put the notions which had been developing among the king's servants – especially among the members of the *Parlement* of Paris – to the test. It was a trial of strength between monarchy and oligarchy. The sentence was severe, although mitigated from death to imprisonment during the king's pleasure. Alençon was to be deprived of his *pairie*, and lost his lands and movable goods.[3] But the king allowed his wife and children to enjoy his movables, excepting his artillery, armour and instruments of war. The lordships of Alençon, Verneuil and Domfront were annexed to the royal *domaine*, with other rights and dues. What was left went to his heirs. It must have been very little, to judge from the payments made to Marie d Armagnac, duchess of Alençon, from her husband's exiguous revenues.[4] But the duke was to come into his own again. On 10 October 1461, three months after his father's death, Louis XI pardoned and restored him.[5] During the proceedings against Alençon, Louis's name had been on many lips. Was he in any way associated with the duke in his treasons? In August 1456 Louis had fled to his uncle, Philip the Good. If it could be shown that both Louis and Philip were implicated in Alençon's plots, then the king could make war on both of them with inviolable justification. He could, if he so wished, recover his son by force from the camp of a man in league with his enemies.

[1] Chastellain, III, 423–5.

[2] Below, 204–9.

[3] Chastellain, III, 478–87.

[4] B.N. MSS. fr. 26084, no. 7036; 26085, no. 7119, for the payment to Marie d'Armagnac, duchess of Alençon, of 12 *livres tournois* per day (6 November 1457). It was not a generous allowance, giving her 4,980 *livres* per year when an allowance for her *argenterie* was added. Cf. the figures for pensions, below, 225–6.

[5] Alençon agreed to Louis's terms at Tours on 12 October 1461. He was pardoned, but Louis kept the wardship of his children. See B.N. MS. fr. 18439, fol. 278ᵛ.

Chapter 6 ✤ The Later Years 1449–1461
II The Problem of the Dauphin

I *Estrangement and its implications*

Charles VII, it has been recently observed, 'was an excellent judge of all men except his son'.[1] Between January 1447 and his death in July 1461, the king did not see the dauphin Louis. The origins of their estrangement have been traced elsewhere,[2] and what follows here is a discussion of the implications of that estrangement. Louis has been described as a 'complex, nervous, amused creature', the dynamic *alter ego* of his weak, passive father.[3] That father, it is argued, did not understand his son's nature. The argument rests partly upon current psychological explanations, which seek to analyse fifteenth-century people in twentieth-century terms. The over-emphasised 'generation gap' cannot always be so crudely applied to men who inhabited a different world.[4] Such a 'gap' has not always prevented good relations between grandparents and grandchildren, especially in countries such as France where the grandparents have played a vital role in bringing up their children's children.[5] Personal relationships between fifteenth-century people lie obscured in the murkiness of the few surviving sources. It is only possible to investigate them at the level of kings and great nobles. Even then, there is much that can never be known. The facts of estrangement can, however, be chronicled, and speculated upon. They must be considered against a background of the king's ill-health. From the autumn of 1455 Charles suffered from bouts of illness – some of them severe – followed by periods of remission. The nature of his illness will be discussed later. What is relevant here is that the king must have been in acute pain at certain times during these years.

[1] Kendall, *Louis XI*, 399.
[2] See above, 75–82.
[3] Kendall, *Louis XI*, 72.
[4] See ibid., 44, for Louis as a teenage rebel, at the age of thirteen, 'too energised against submissiveness to accept the role of deference which convention prescribed'. His letters to his father suggest otherwise.

As his first surviving act, signed in his own hand, dates from 1438, when he was fifteen, Professor Kendall's assessment appears to be based on hindsight.
[5] For this practice see Marc Bloch, *The Historian's Craft*, tr. P. Putnam (Manchester, 1954), 40–1, 185–7.

There is little evidence before March 1451 for a deterioration in relations between father and son from the working agreement between them which gave Louis the government of the Dauphiné. Both exchanged New Year's presents. In January 1449 Louis sent his father a leopard.[1] As late as January 1451, Louis sent Charles a diamond.[2] Charles had a gold chain made, from which it was to hang as a pendant. One assumes that the king wore this token of filial affection. But the accounts of *étrennes* given from 1452 onwards do not mention the exchange of such gifts between father and son.[3] If such evidence can be used as an index of personal attitudes, then it may be that Louis's marriage to Charlotte of Savoy on 9 March 1451 irreconcilably alienated Charles from him. In November 1450 Louis's envoys had told the king and his council at Tours that the dauphin was seeking a second wife.[4] An English marriage – to a daughter of the duke of Buckingham – had previously been mooted for Louis. But he was now seeking a wife in the houses of La Marche, Savoy or Laval, because he liked the look of their women. From Savoy, he would gain 260,000 *écus* as his future wife's dowry, as well as valuable information on the recovery of the duchy of Milan, Genoa, and other Italian lordships. Louis also desired his father to grant him a lordship. He offered to recover Guyenne from the English if he was given it as an *apanage*. Nothing came of this request, and Louis took the initiative himself. He married without gaining the prior consent of his father.

On 20 March 1451 Charles heard the report of his envoy to the duke of Savoy – the herald Normandy king-of-arms.[5] Presiding over his council at Montils-lès-Tours, the king read two letters in their presence, one from the duke, the other from his council. The duke's letter informed the king that he had received his letters protesting about the marriage on 10 March, one day after the ceremony had taken place. He claimed that Charles had in fact agreed to the union between Louis and Charlotte of Savoy, giving his consent to the papal legate.[6] Normandy king-of-arms was then ordered to give his report. He said that Dunois had told him the contents of the letters which he was carrying to Savoy. They contained the king's 'astonishment' that the marriage should be negotiated without his approval. His major objection to the union was that the twelve-year-old Charlotte was not of child-bearing age. This 'the king greatly desired'.[7] A

---

[1] *ABSHF*, cxxiv (1864), 138–9.
[2] Ibid., 146–7.
[3] See B.N. MS. fr. 10371, fols 1ʳ–41ʳ (1452–8).

[4] B.N. MS. fr. 15537, fols 5ʳ–5ᵛ (23 November 1450).
[5] Printed in Duclos, IV, 74–80.
[6] Ibid., 80–2.
[7] Ibid., 76–7.

girl who was not yet husband-high could not give heirs to the house of Valois. However sincere his opposition to the marriage on these grounds, the king could not view the prospect of Louis's remaining childless for very long with equanimity. Given the dauphin's apparent desire to put himself to grave personal risks on campaigns, there was no guarantee that he would survive until Charlotte was of an age to bear him heirs. Normandy king-of-arms then described the dauphin's behaviour towards him. He granted him no audience, but attempted to induce him to hand over his father's letters to him. Bribery was applied. It failed, and Normandy gave the letters to Louis of Savoy's chancellor.[1] He spoke neither with the duke, nor with the dauphin. Louis's attempts to intercept the letters to the duke suggest that he was anxious lest Savoy should change his mind about the marriage. In the event he succeeded in wedding Charlotte of Savoy, dressed in a crimson robe trimmed with ermine, before the duke saw them.

Louis had, in a sense, succeeded in his designs. He had married as he wished, and had gained a foothold in the duchy of Savoy from which to mount campaigns for the conquest of an Italian lordship. But he was soon to be disillusioned. On 27 October 1452 Louis of Savoy came to terms with Charles.[2] He put himself under French protection and renounced the dauphin. Charles was moving with an army towards the duchy of Savoy in order to punish the duke if he would not come to heel. It was rumoured that the king also intended to recover his son by force.[3] But the scheme was thwarted by Talbot's descent upon Bordeaux. The king's army turned towards the south-west. Louis, obviously very scared, wrote to his father, offering his services in the recovery of Guyenne. Writing from Vienne on 25 October, two days before Charles's treaty with Savoy, he pleaded with his father in the humblest of terms. He wrote:

> . . . and because I was previously told that you were rather displeased that, during your conquest of Normandy and of the said Bordelais, I did not offer you my services – but which I did, through Estissac, Remon and Benoist, addressing myself to [my] fair cousin of Dunois, notwithstanding the fact that I was in a pitiful state, and would be most displeased, with all my heart, if it did not come to your notice – now, my very redoubted lord, I am sending you my . . . councillor and chamberlain, the lord of Barry, to offer you my service and to put my body and goods at your disposal, if it is your pleasure to do me

[1] Ibid., 78; for these events see Beaucourt, v, 134–53.

[2] Beaucourt, v, 178–81.

[3] Ibid., 171–3; Kendall, Louis XI, 76.

the honour of giving me the responsibility and thus employing me. . . .[1]

Louis's reference to his servants might suggest that he was as much their victim as he had ever been. In the replies which he was to make to his father over the remaining nine years of the latter's life, the statement that he would not abandon any of his servants constantly recurs. In fact, he was not employed in Guyenne during the campaign of recovery in the summer of 1453. Before that event took place, the king had received disturbing accounts of his behaviour from Gérard le Boursier and Louis de Fontaines, who had been sent to the dauphin in December 1452.[2] At Moulins, on 8 January 1453, the two envoys reported back to the king. They had found Louis at Pierrelatte, hunting. When he had read the letters from his father which they gave him, he asked them how many of Charles's counsellors were present when they were drawn up. They told him that only the king, the admiral, the lord of Torcy, the *trésorier*, Master Etienne Chevalier and Jean Bureau were there. Louis then hedged, and sent off to Valence to get advice. He quibbled over the sureties which were to be offered, and feared that he would be disinherited in favour of his younger brother, Charles of France. The envoys then spoke to Louis's council, without his being present. His counsellors told them that when the king would draw Louis towards him 'in sweetness', and properly establish the sureties or pledges of good faith which Louis should give him, then something could be achieved. The emphasis on sureties is of note. It was later denied by the king that such pledges had ever been requested by him.[3] The ways of Louis's servants were, again, all too scrutable. Louis's offers were then read to the king.[4] Louis asked the princes of the blood of France, and other lords, to give the king their sealed letters, guaranteeing that he would keep his promises. If any of these was broken by him, they were to serve the king, presumably against him, at their own expense. It was perhaps doubtful that the great lords would ever have done so. Louis also promised to swear 'on the arm and relics' of his favourite saint, St Anthony, to do what he had promised. If he defaulted, he would 'renounce all such title that he could have to the crown of France'.[5]

These offers are curious. The king maintained that he did not require such assurances of his son's good behaviour and trustworthiness. He was

[1] Escouchy, III, 429–30.
[2] B.N. MS. fr. 15537, fols 21ʳ–28ʳ.
[3] Ibid., fol. 55ᵛ (March 1461); below, 181 and Plate 8.

[4] Ibid., fol. 27ʳ.
[5] Ibid., fol. 27ʳ. His vow may refer to relics kept at the abbey of St-Anthoine-de-Viennois.

'confident enough of the lords of the blood', he replied.[1] Louis, under the influence of his advisers, was obviously temporising. It was odd that he, the weaker party, should be offering sureties which had never been demanded by his father. Such proposals indicate that the situation was moving towards deadlock. Both sides were dependent for information upon the reports of their respective envoys and the insinuations of their respective servants. In this instance, both were at their mercy. That the crucial question was that of Louis's return to his father's court is evident from the abortive negotiations which were to follow the offers of January 1453. Neither party was prepared to accept the other's servants—the inmates of court and household. Louis, according to Chastellain, would not come back to court because of the 'indignation which he had against certain people'.[2] Among them must have been Anthoine de Chabannes, Brézé, and Charles of Anjou. Louis wished his father well, it was said, and desired to be in his favour. But he would not come to court and would not dismiss any of his own servants. Charles, on the other hand, was grieved by his son's behaviour, because he saw him employed in unrewarding business and was not able to use him for any of his 'enterprises'. The recovery of the Somme towns from Burgundy was one such 'enterprise'.[3] Mutual suspicion, exacerbated by lack of personal contact of any kind, was leading both parties more deeply into an *impasse*. Suspicion was fed by rumour, hearsay, and the tendentious reports of servants and 'familiars'. If only because they had no idea of what would happen to them, the servants of both king and dauphin did all they could to prevent a reconciliation.

On 8 April 1457 the king resumed direct government of the Dauphiné. He revoked all grants by Louis from the *domaine*, and all gifts of 'extraordinary pensions'.[4] On 9 April, when the king was at St-Priest in the Dauphiné, his chancellor addressed the Three Estates of the province. They had already agreed to obey him and 'to accomplish whatever it pleases the king to command them'.[5] Loyalty to the dauphin was thus non-existent in April 1457, even within the land which, according to his biographers, he had governed so well.[6] Louis de Laval, lord of Châtillon, remained governor, serving directly under the king. Louis was alarmed, and wrote to his father expressing his distress that he should have such great suspicions. He confessed that he had 'great fears'.[7] Chastellain

[1] Ibid., fol. 28ʳ.
[2] Chastellain, III, 52.
[3] Ibid., 52–3, 55–6.
[4] *Ord.*, XIV, 426–7; Duclos, IV, 83–6.

[5] B.N. MS. fr. nouv. acq. 1001, fols 43ʳ, 45ᵛ.
[6] See Kendall, *Louis XI*, 69–72.
[7] Duclos, IV, 88–90.

claimed that Louis felt 'a savage fear of his father, and a suspicion that
if by chance he found himself with him, he would have punished him
. . . by imprisonment or otherwise'.[1] Louis was in an extremely weak
position. Harried out of the Dauphiné, *persona non grata* in Savoy, he was
homeless. He had sent three embassies to his father between April and
August 1456.[2] He offered to swear such oaths and offer such sureties
as his father desired. He would renounce all his alliances, and would not
cross the Rhône, nor enter the kingdom of France, without his father's
permission. Once again, there was no question of his father having either
demanded sureties, or refused him such permission. There was obviously
no way to bring Louis back except by force. The king's testy reply to
Louis's envoy, Guillaume de Courçillon, suggests a hardening of attitude.
The king was losing his patience. He told Courçillon, through his
chancellor, that he intended to do nothing about Louis's most recent
terms. The affair 'had lasted too long' and he wished to see an end of it.[3]
Courçillon went back empty-handed.

Two months later, Courçillon and the prior of the Celestines at Avignon
were at Châtellard as envoys of the dauphin.[4] Louis repeated his offers,
but Charles replied that they were still unacceptable. Only when Louis
did as a 'good and obedient son' should do would the king act towards
him as a 'good and natural father'.[5] He would never approve Louis's
self-imposed exile from court, nor would he agree to Louis's terms on the
question of his servants. But his son had no reason to fear him, and he
stressed the 'great benignity, sweetness and clemency' which he possessed.[6]
On 20 August 1456 he repeated his terms.[7] The papal legate, Cardinal
Guillaume d'Estouteville, was to be present when they were announced
to Louis's envoys. The king's 'greatest pleasure', he said, would be that his
son might be disposed to serve him, obey him, and 'employ himself for
the good of the public weal of this kingdom'. Gabriel de Bernes, Louis's
envoy, was to tell him that the king now consented to his master's terms
on the question of sureties and passage into France, but could not accept
the two-fold conditions proposed. The king, it was stated, 'has not been
and is not advised' to grant them.[8] Behind a father's words lay the insinuations of his advisers. If he agreed to let Louis remain away from court, he

[1] Chastellain, III, 53.
[2] Duclos, IV, 90-101, 112; Beaucourt, VI,
76-90.
[3] Duclos, IV, 91; Chastellain, III, 56.
Chastellain claimed that the king did not
even ask Courçillon how Louis was.
[4] Duclos, IV, 93-101; Chastellain, III, 160-9.

[5] Duclos, IV, 95.
[6] Ibid., 101.
[7] B.N. MS. fr. 15537, fols 19ʳ-19ᵛ.
[8] Ibid., fol. 19ʳ. For the presence of
Guillaume d'Estouteville, the papal legate,
see above, 64-5.

would merely approve his absence and the situation which already pre-
vailed. If Louis would not accept his terms, then he would 'proceed against
those who thus guide and advise him'.[1] It was a threat of armed intervention. Louis replied by gathering troops together at Valence, and
appointed the bastard of Armagnac as his marshal.[2] But, according to a
letter written to the king by Anthoine de Chabannes, the inhabitants of
the Dauphiné would not support Louis.[3] They put their trust only in the
king, and, thought Chabannes, the duke of Savoy would also come to
heel. Meanwhile, the king empowered Chabannes – Louis's inveterate
enemy – to march into the Dauphiné with a royal army.[4]

Louis was terrified. If his actions are any indication of his state of mind,
his fears of capture and assassination at the hands of his father's servants
were intense. He fled from the Dauphiné to the court of his uncle, Philip
the Good of Burgundy. Riding furiously, he paused at St-Claude, on the
frontier of the *comté* of Burgundy, and there wrote a letter to his father on
31 August.[5] His reason for going to join his uncle, he claimed, was to aid
him in the crusade which he was to lead against the Turks. Philip would
also, thought Louis, try to find a way in which to reconcile him with his
father. This, Louis claimed, was 'the thing which I most desire in this
world'. Such claims were patently insincere. In a letter to Chabannes of
2 November Charles observed that Louis had been 'seduced and coun-
selled' to flee by the bastard of Armagnac and Jean de Garguesalle, his
servants.[6] Louis's subsequent appointment of Armagnac as governor of
the Dauphiné, in place of the dispossessed Louis de Laval, at Bruges in
January 1457, and his gift of a pension of 600 *livres tournois* to him, may
endorse Charles's suspicions.[7] Jean, bastard of Armagnac, lord of Tournon,
has been named in connection with Alençon's plots by some of those
interrogated in the summer and autumn of 1456.[8] Alençon claimed that a
certain priest called Mathieu, a servant of Armagnac, had brought him
letters of credence from the dauphin and his master. But the king's officers
considered this a contrivance on Alençon's part.[9] The dauphin could not be

[1] Ibid., fol. 19ᵛ.
[2] Duclos, IV, 108–9.
[3] Ibid., 109.
[4] Ibid., 111.
[5] Printed in Beaucourt, VI, 89.
[6] Duclos, IV, 126–7; Beaucourt, VI, 479–80.
At a meeting of the Estates of the
Dauphiné in October 1456, Charles spoke
of those who 'governed' his son, including
the bastard of Armagnac, who 'was not
Armagnac at all, but English, and an old

enemy of France' (Beaucourt, VI, 96–7).
[7] Duclos, IV, 142–7. For his pension see
B.N. MS. fr. 20491, no. 102.
[8] Chastellain, III, 484–5.
[9] Ibid., 484–5; B.N. MS. fr. 18441, fol.
114ʳ, 117ᵛ. Alençon intended that Henry VI
should assist Jean V of Armagnac, his
brother-in-law, to recover the lands he had
lost after the king's expedition against him
in May 1455. See Beaucourt, VI, 34–6.

associated with him in any way. But the mission of Armagnac's servant was not in doubt. In November 1456 Charles was instructing Chabannes to seize the bastard if he could, as he was said to be journeying towards the Dauphiné.[1] He told the inhabitants of Strasbourg that the dauphin was wilfully disobeying his father, and that any warlike acts by him were quite contrary to his wishes.[2] The possibility of reconciliation was now extremely slim.

On 8 April 1457 Charles had deprived Louis of the Dauphiné. This was a flat refusal of Louis's terms offered on 22 December 1456.[3] Writing from Genappe, in Flanders, Louis had asked his father for the Dauphiné, and for a very large pension of 24,000 *livres*. He wanted his suspicions of the king's designs on his person, and on those of his servants, allayed. He said that he would be happy to pardon certain of his father's servants if they agreed to serve him. He also required a pardon signed in Charles's hand, but refused to collect it himself. Louis was obviously terrified at the prospect of coming to court. He feared assassination. His entourage told him that he would be disinherited in favour of Charles of France.[4] The king's views on the matter are not known. Chastellain analysed the king's attitude towards Louis's exile after 1458 in terms of the predicament in which some of Charles's servants and counsellors found themselves.[5] During the 'cold war' of 1458–61 between France and Burgundy, now harbouring the dauphin, the court of France was divided. Some of the greater lords – Bourbon, Richemont, Orléans – argued that the king should not attempt to recover Louis by force from Philip the Good. The counts of Nevers and Etampes acted as intermediaries between the two sides, and were related to both.[6] But others – presumably Chabannes, Jean de Bueil, Anthoine de Laval, Dunois, Charles of Anjou, Brézé, and Gaston IV, count of Foix – opposed this pacific stance. They urged the king to seize Louis, even if this meant war with Burgundy. 'They feared nothing,' wrote Chastellain, 'as much as falling . . . into the hands of the dauphin, who hated them.'[7] If the king regained control of his son, then they could be received into Louis's grace. If not, Louis would succeed to the throne and they would be dimissed. Their fears, in the light of the events of August 1461, were justified.[8] If Louis could not be recovered from Burgundian hands, then he should be disinherited by his father.

[1] Beaucourt, VI, 479 (2 November 1456), 480 (3 November 1456). Charles was at Vienne, in the Dauphiné.
[2] Ibid., 482–3 (3 November 1456).
[3] Duclos, IV, 138–41.
[4] Chastellain, III, 441.

[5] Ibid., 440.
[6] Ibid., 440–1; Armstrong, *AB*, xl (1968), 16–18.
[7] Chastellain, III, 440.
[8] See below, 188, 191.

Charles never did this. He was independent enough of the self-interested counsels of his entourage to ignore their advice on certain issues. Perhaps the recollection of his own disinheritance made him exceptionally wary of depriving Louis of the right to succeed him. His own legitimacy rested on a denial of the right of his father to disinherit him under the terms of the treaty of Troyes.[1] There was no solution but to keep open the door to further negotiations with Louis and his new protector. This did not preclude the putting of pressure on Burgundy. As has been shown, Franco–Burgundian relations between 1451 and 1461 reveal Charles as a *provocateur*, allying himself with Burgundy's enemies, trying to buy the duchy of Luxembourg, and encouraging the estrangement which had developed between Philip and his son Charles, count of Charolais.[2] The Croy family – those objects of Charolais's hatred – could be relied upon to act in Charles's interests.[3] The Paris *Parlement* attacked Burgundy on the juridical front, attempting to withdraw appeals from the duke's courts. A growing nervousness among Charles's counsellors may be discerned from the record of a resolution by the council 'meeting at Villefranche in Berry in the house of my lord the count of Maine' on 28 July 1460.[4] The council recommended the king to proceed by force of arms against Burgundy, so as to ensure obedience to royal orders and the judgements of the *Parlement* in all Burgundy's lands 'within the kingdom of France'.[5] The *venue* of the meeting is perhaps significant. Charles of

[1] See above, 32.

[2] Vaughan, *Philip the Good*, 347, 349–53; cf. B. de Mandrot, 'Etude sur les relations de Charles VII et Louis XI . . . avec les cantons suisses, 1444–83', *Jahrbuch für Schweizerische Geschichte*, v (1880), 93–9; A. Leroux, *Nouvelles recherches critiques sur les relations politiques de la France avec l'Allemagne de 1378 à 1461* (Paris, 1892), 309–13.

[3] Vaughan, op. cit., 352. They had succeeded the Chancellor Rolin as exponents of a policy conciliatory towards France.

[4] See Plancher, IV, ccxxxv–ccxxxvi. The meeting took place in two sessions, on 26 and 28 July. Charles of Anjou, Bernard d'Armagnac, count of La Marche, André de Laval, lord of Lohéac, Anthoine de Chabannes, count of Dammartin, Masters Etienne Chevalier and Pierre Doriole were present. It was said that Burgundy was acting against the king's

sovereignty, 'which the king, as much by his coronation oath . . . as otherwise, is held and obliged to guard and defend'. It was concluded that Charles had 'just cause to proceed by *voie de fait* and force of arms' but should ensure that areas such as Guyenne were well defended. He was to find out how many of the companies of *ordonnance* he could use against Burgundy and was to make ready his artillery 'and all other things necessary for . . . war'. In order to avoid a 'general war' he was to first make quite sure that Burgundy could be easily defeated (ibid., ccxxxvi).

[5] Ibid., ccxxxvi. It was claimed that the king's letters and ordinances, as well as the decisions of the *Parlement* of Paris, were 'in no way obeyed' in Burgundy's lands. Truces had also been made with the English, but without royal licence. For the 'nuisance value' of the Paris *Parlement* to Philip the Good, see Vaughan, op. cit., 350. Appeals from Flanders, though

Anjou might be among the first to be removed from power if Louis was not recovered before his father's death. The possibility of Charles's dying before then made war with Burgundy increasingly likely during the last three years of his life.

II *Illness and death*

Until the winter of 1453-4 Charles VII appears to have enjoyed relatively good health. His sobriety at table, noted by the chroniclers, no doubt contributed to this at a period in which princes were not noted for their abstinence.[1] But, early in 1454, information was received by Francesco Sforza, duke of Milan, that the king was ill.[2] His indisposition was serious enough for Sforza to think in terms of the king's death. The report may have been a false alarm, for there was no mention of it in the dispatch which Sforza's ambassador sent from the court on 12 March.[3] More secure evidence for ailment is contained in a letter which the king wrote to Anthoine de Chabannes from Bois-Sire-Amé on 26 September 1455. Charles wrote:

> . . . concerning what you have written to us about your sending Master Pierre Burdelot over here to know for certain the state and condition of our person – because there has been news over there that we have been rather indisposed, as we have recently made our . . . counsellors Master Jean Bureau, *trésorier* of France, and Pierre Doriole, write to you at length on our behalf – we have been for two or three days a little indisposed on one side, but, thanks to Our Lord, we have fully recovered, and are in as good health as we have been for a long time past. And, as we have lately written to you, we are all ready and well disposed to go forward and do everything that will be necessary for the good of [our] affairs. . . . And because of this do not be downcast for fear of the condition of our person, but always . . . employ yourself actively in the execution of those things for which we have given you responsibility. . . .[4]

The stilted style, and the reassuring words, could not hide the fact that the king's health was failing. Bureau and Doriole had been forced to write

prohibited by Charles in 1445 and 1455, were still being heard by the *Parlement* in 1448, 1449, 1451 and 1459.
[1] See above, 96.
[2] Beaucourt, VI, 27 n. 1. A previous rumour of illness was circulating in July 1438. His apothecary was seized, but later released (ibid., III, 56-7).
[3] Ibid., VI, 27 n. 2.
[4] Printed in ibid., VI, 470-1.

to Chabannes on the matter. The trouble with his side cannot, given the vagueness of the reference, be diagnosed. The king was at that time trying to recover Louis by force, but had first to gain the aid of Louis of Savoy.[1] Chabannes was his instrument in this affair. A letter of 19 September written by Pierre Doriole to Chabannes had expressed thanks that the king 'is on good form and makes good cheer'.[2] This would put his 'indisposition' to the first two weeks or so of September. It was not followed by further ill-effects. Early in October, Charles was well enough to leave Bois-Sire-Amé for the Bourbonnais.[3] According to the available evidence, it was not until December 1457 that he was to fall ill once more. On this occasion his illness dogged him until his death four years later. The circumstances in which he fell ill made the Christmas festivities of 1457 at Tours into an occasion for mourning. On 8 December an embassy from Ladislas, king of Hungary and Bohemia, had arrived at Tours in order to negotiate his marriage with Madelaine, daughter of Charles VII.[4] Charles was to aid Ladislas to obtain the duchy of Luxembourg from Philip the Good. It was not until 18 December that the king was sufficiently fit to see the ambassadors.[5] Chastellain wrote that he was suffering from an 'incurable disease in one leg', which constantly discharged pus.[6] The astrologers predicted that he would be dead before the end of March 1458. Processions and prayers were offered for his recovery. Chastellain's account is borne out by the interrogation of a Breton esquire, Guillaume de Tiercain, by the king's officers on 15 November 1459.[7]

That Charles's condition became a chronic one is evident from Tiercain's depositions. He was asked if he knew a barber called Symonnet, who, it was alleged, had been charged to take one of the dressings for the king's leg.[8] This move was apparently instigated by the dauphin. Tiercain replied in the negative. The king's attack in December 1457 was made worse by the news of the sudden death of Ladislas of Hungary. Charles had dreamt of the king's death, and his entourage considered it dangerous

---

[1] Ibid., 70–4.
[2] Ibid., 72. He told Chabannes that 'my lord of Dunois, whom the king calls the "hunter of fish", and also my lord of Maine, have done the worst that they can against you; but the birds that sing in the night haven't forgotten you . . .'. The allusions are tantalising, but give scope for speculation about the role of *mignons* and mistresses.
[3] Ibid., 477.

[4] Ibid., 166. For the negotiations see ibid., 156–66; Leroux, op. cit., 280–85.
[5] Beaucourt, VI, 167.
[6] Chastellain, III, 444. Philip the Good of Burgundy was ill at the same time and astrological speculation was rife about whether one, or both, of them would die (ibid., 446–7).
[7] B.N. MS. fr. 15537, fols 169ʳ–170ʳ.
[8] Ibid., fol. 169ᵛ. He was the barber of Jean, lord of Montauban, one of Louis's servants.

to inform him of the tidings.[1] In the event, Brézé was chosen to tell the king, because he was 'a man of very fair and pleasant speech' who 'knew how to manage the king better than any other'.[2] Preparations for the celebration of a Requiem for Ladislas had been kept secret. It was only on 30 December, on the morrow of the ceremony, that Brézé went to Charles at Montils-lès-Tours.[3] The fact that the news had been so success-fully kept from him suggests that he was confined to his sickbed. He was much distressed by the news, but the 'profound moral depression' into which he might have fallen does not seem to have struck him down. He attempted to take Luxembourg into his own hands, and wrote a threaten-ing letter to Philip the Good.[4] His persecution of Burgundy was perhaps made all the more savage by his illness.

The disease is difficult to diagnose. On 3 March 1459 half-length hose (*ung chaussons jusques a my jambe*) was made for him.[5] In April of the same year, cloth was delivered to his hosier 'to make nine stockings, laced up at the back, with a false opening', for the king to wear on his bad leg.[6] At about the same time, green cloth was bought to cover the foot-rest which the king used when at table.[7] From October 1458, the bread which he ate was cut into small pieces.[8] This suggests an infection of the mouth. Charles was thus unwell at the very moment when Alençon was tried at Vendôme. His goldsmith, Jean Sevineau, made a little bowl at that time which he delivered to Jean Roy, the king's apothecary, in which to pre-pare medicines for him.[9] The harshness of Charles's treatment of Alençon may therefore have been in part a result of ill-health.

There can be little doubt that Charles was in more or less constant pain during the winter of 1458–9. In January, Jean Sevineau made a palette on which the constituents of potions and drugs were ground for him.[10] His appearance at the trial of Alençon on 10 October 1458 in a long robe – an unusual dress for him, if the *argenterie* accounts for his clothes are taken into account – may have been necessitated by his condition.[11] His leg may have been swollen, and swathed in bandages. It was hardly a reassuring sight for his subjects to contemplate in the public arena. The making of

[1] Beaucourt, VI, 169–70. Filippo Maria Visconti also seems to have been afflicted with a phobia about hearing news of sudden death (Burckhardt, II, 54). Cf. Brachet, op. cit., 70–1.
[2] Chastellain, III, 380–1. No one was to tell the king of Ladislas's death, under pain of death, lest Charles himself died as a result of the news.

[3] Beaucourt, VI, 171.
[4] Ibid., 171–4; Vaughan, op. cit., 348.
[5] A.N., KK.51, fol. 16ʳ.
[6] Ibid., fol. 36ᵛ.
[7] Ibid., fol. 78ᵛ.
[8] Ibid., fol. 69ʳ.
[9] Ibid., fol. 64ᵛ (October 1458).
[10] Ibid., fol. 64ᵛ.
[11] See Plate 10 and below, 223–4.

half-length hose and special stockings in March and April 1459 carries the implication that he could not bear to wear the normal tight garments on his leg. A laced stocking suggests that the leg had become badly swollen. What was Charles's illness, given these symptoms? As in the case of Henry VIII of England, no definitive answer can be given to this tantalising question.[1] There seem to be at least three possibilities. First, Charles could have been afflicted with a varicose ulcer of the leg. The ungainliness of his walk, commented upon by Basin and Chastellain, could conceivably have been caused by varicose veins.[2] It has been said of a potential fellow-sufferer, Henry VIII, that 'inadequate and often savage treatment, together with lack of sufficient rest, would have caused the veins to become thrombosed, the leg to swell and an extremely painful chronic ulcer to develop on his thigh'.[3] A second possibility would be osteomyelitis. It would explain the discharge of pus from the chronic ulcer on Charles's leg. A severe fall, such as the one which Charles experienced when a floor collapsed at La Rochelle in October 1422, can lie at the root of this septic infection of the bone.[4] But a fall sustained almost forty years before the first onset of the disease is, perhaps, not worthy of consideration.

Neither of these diagnoses, however, takes into account the infection of the mouth with which Charles was probably afflicted from October 1458 onwards. It was this which was ultimately to kill him. The combination of sores and abscesses in the mouth with a festering, malignant ulcer on the leg points in another direction. His disease could have been syphilis: a complaint which, it has been said, 'was not then unknown, as is sometimes alleged'.[5] Both of Charles's symptoms were well-known secondary symptoms of the disease. Although the *morbus venereus* only reached the proportions and virulence of an epidemic in the Mediterranean world during the 1490s, that does not mean that individual cases were not found beforehand.[6] Even if surviving accounts of Charles's sexual behaviour in his later years are only partially acceptable, the possibility that he contracted 'the sickness of Venus' can never be entirely ruled out. The common Renaissance cure for syphilis – mercury treatment –

---

[1] See A. S. MacNalty, *Henry VIII: a difficult patient* (London, 1952), 159–65.
[2] Basin, II, 280: 'the slenderness of his legs and shins, with each knee swollen and bent towards the other . . . gave him a deformed look'; Chastellain, III, 178, for his 'peculiar walk'. He was obviously knock-kneed.

[3] J. J. Scarisbrick, *Henry VIII* (London, 1968), 625.
[4] See ibid., 625 n. 79; also above, II, 32–3.
[5] K. B. McFarlane, *Lancastrian Kings and Lollard Knights* (Oxford, 1972), 103, referring to Henry IV of England.
[6] See R. Lewinsohn, *A History of Sexual Customs* (London, 1958), 167–71.

was not yet devised.[1] No assistance is forthcoming from the *argenterie* or household accounts which survive which might permit a diagnosis from the records of treatment which was administered to the king. He presumably endured the fevers and the pain which accompanied an ulcerated leg as best he could. His physicians could provide only palliatives. That he continued to move from place to place (though his itinerary became increasingly restricted to the valley of the Loire) suggests that he enjoyed periods of respite from his illness. In the winter of 1458–9 he remained, unwell, at Montils-lès-Tours; during that of 1459–60, he was able to move from Vernou in Touraine, to Le Tusseau, to Montils-lès-Tours again for Christmas, and to Montbazon; and it was only in April 1461 that he finally came to Mehun-sur-Yèvre, where he was to die three months later.[2]

There can, of course, be no proof that Charles suffered from any disease known to modern men. The medical history of the fifteenth century is still obscure. But, if he did suffer from the disease which was to become a scourge to Renaissance Europe, then its contemporary name – *morbus gallicus* – was apter than the physicians realised. It was widely believed that Charles of France, his younger son, died of an illness provoked by his sexual licence.[3] But that illness could have been an hereditary one. Whatever it was, the dauphin Louis seems to have escaped its ravages. If Charles of France did inherit a disease from his father, then it would have had to have been contracted by Charles VII before December 1446. No such evidence is to be found, and the facts cannot bear too great a burden of hypothesis. They can be recorded, but interpreted only with great caution. It has been seen that the king was unable to sign certain documents between 1 October 1460 and 31 March 1461 because, for part of that period, he was gravely ill.[4] During that time the household account shows that one Henryet Gaudete was sent, with a *chevaucheur* of the king's stable, from Chinon to Bordeaux to choose and fetch wine. This was to be the king's table wine when he was ill.[5] It was a sound choice. Bordeaux wine

[1] Ibid., 171; Scarisbrick, op. cit., 625. François II, duke of Brittany, also appears to have suffered from an ulcerated leg. In March 1461 the dauphin Louis was alleged to have remarked that he had 'a fistula in the leg – and he has no doubt that the duke has another in the head' (Kendall and Ilardi, II, 222). Antoinette de Maignelais had become François II's mistress by this time. What is known of her career would not rule out the possibility

that she may have been a carrier of syphilis. See Beaucourt, VI, 438; above, 135–6.
[2] Beaucourt, VI, 423–4. It will be noticed that these were all within very easy reach of either Tours or Bourges.
[3] See H. Stein, *Charles de France* (Paris, 1919), 452–4.
[4] See above, 142.
[5] B.N. MS. fr. 6754, fol. 7ᵛ.

was, and is, thought to be good for invalids. Other sources lend their support to a royal illness in the winter of 1460–1. He had been ill in June and July, and, in December, letters of remission were issued merely with the endorsement 'by the council, meeting in the *Chambre des Comptes*'.[1] But his complaint was episodic enough to be compatible with periods of remission. He continued to concern himself with the business of government until a few weeks before his death.

On 3 March 1461 Prospero da Camogli, Sforza's ambassador at Genappe, wrote to his master that 'the news here is that the king of France has been gravely ill for six days'.[2] On 9 March Prospero told Sforza that 'the dauphin has been in close negotiations about reconciling himself with the king of France . . . and I fear an agreement will be reached, on the part of the king of France, because he is a sick old man, and to an aged father the recovery of a son is a great consolation, especially in circumstances of such high political importance'.[3] The Milanese ambassador regretted this possibility, as Sforza was planning to use Louis and Burgundy to join a Yorkist invasion of France. This would be a response to Charles VII's support of Angevin intervention in Naples, where Sforza was supporting Ferrante, the Aragonese claimant.[4] But by early March 1461 a Yorkist invasion was deemed to be out of the question. Louis, thought Prospero, was being forced to reach an agreement with his father. His patience was 'almost exhausted'.[5] The Milanese ambassador at the court of Genappe reported Louis's terms: Charles was to give him Genoa, the governorship of Asti, control of Savoy, the Dauphiné, and lands between it and Burgundian territory. In return Louis would 'restrain' Sforza from giving aid to Ferrante in Naples. His ambitions to rule in Italy, controlling a large principality on the north-western boundaries of Sforza's domain, caused concern to the Milanese at Genappe. His father might forget the past and, in remorse, might endow his son once again with lands. By 11 March Prospero was writing to tell Sforza the bad news that Louis had sent an envoy, Jean Wast, lord of Montespedon, to his father's court.[6] This was done at the instigation of Charles of Anjou.

[1] *AHP*, xxv, 278. He was, however, still present at the hearing of petitions and granting of remissions in May 1461 (ibid., 297).

[2] Kendall and Ilardi, 11, 142.

[3] Ibid., 148.

[4] Ibid., xiii–xx; Ilardi, 'The Italian League, Francesco Sforza and Charles VII (1454–61)', *Studies in the Renaissance*, vi (1959), 129–66. Charles delayed the sending of representatives to the Congress of Mantua, summoned by Pope Pius II in 1459, because of papal support for Ferrante (ibid., 153). The Angevin claim to Naples and Sicily was, of course, to be used as one justification for the French invasion of Italy in 1494.

[5] Kendall and Ilardi, 11, 148.

[6] Ibid., 168; Beaucourt, vi, 312–22, for Wast's two missions.

The count of Maine was evidently trying to safeguard his own position as well as the public weal of the kingdom.

It was hardly surprising, given their fears of the king's imminent death, that the dauphin's envoy was 'honoured by the whole court'.[1] Wast had returned from a previous mission on 7 February, bringing with him two replies from the king. The first asked Louis to come to his father, so that he could see him alone.[2] But Charles refused to receive Philip the Good. The second was not written down. Wast told Louis by word of mouth that Charles had offered him, if he still refused to see his father, the lands which he had asked for in his previous terms.[3] But these were to be granted only on condition that Louis supported the designs of John, duke of Calabria, the Angevin claimant to Sicily and Naples. The Angevin interest at the court of France was thus sufficiently strong to dictate the conditions upon which a partial reconciliation between father and son was to be founded. Charles of Anjou was absent from the court at the time – perhaps by design – and the negotiations were in the hands of Gaston IV, count of Foix.[4] But he assured Louis of his good offices, claimed that he would be 'master of the king', and that Louis's enemy, Chabannes, would be 'reduced to a cipher'.[5] So far, so good. But there was a stumbling block to such an agreement. The king gave no promise of any kind about his behaviour towards Philip the Good, off whose bounty Louis was living. War between France and Burgundy was thought to be imminent. One way out of the trap would be for Louis to renounce Burgundian aid. His relations with Philip the Good were no longer so amicable. Prospero da Camogli could tell Sforza on 15 March that, at Brussels, 'I find here hardly less war between the duke of Burgundy and *his* son than between the dauphin and the king of France'.[6] Louis had incurred Philip's suspicion and jealousy, because he was thought to be supporting Charles, count of Charolais, against his father. Philip was also unhappy about Louis's behaviour towards his favourites, the Croy family.[7] Louis was resentful of his own existence as a parasite on the court of Burgundy. Pressures from many directions were forcing him to think in terms of a reconciliation with his father.

Wast was sent back to the king at Bourges, where he stated Louis's terms in two letters which he read out on 20 March.[8] The extreme weakness of Louis's position led him to ask Charles to forget the past, and to

1 Kendall and Ilardi, II, 168–9.
2 Ibid., 169–72.
3 Ibid., 170; Beaucourt, VI, 314–15.
4 Beaucourt, VI, 315.
5 Kendall and Ilardi, II, 172.

6 Ibid., 188; for Charolais, see Vaughan, op. cit., 340–3.
7 Kendall and Ilardi, II, 188, 212.
8 B.N. MS. fr. 15537, fols 87r–78v, 18r–18v; Beaucourt, VI, 318–19.

9 Charles VII as St Louis, with St John the Baptist, from the *Retable du Parlement de Paris, c.* 1455-60 (*Musée du Louvre, Paris*)

10 Trial of Jean II, duke of Alençon, at Vendôme, October 1458. The illumination,
from the MS. of a French translation of Boccaccio's *De casibus virorum illustrium*,
dated 24 November 1458, is attributed to Jean Fouquet (*Bayerische Staatsbibliothek,
Munich, Codex Gall. 6, fol. 2v*)

provide for him a lordship which would enable him to subsist. Anthoine de Croy, Philip the Good's favourite, told Francesco Coppini, bishop of Terni, at Brussels on 23 March that Louis was in acute financial difficulties.[1] These were partly the result of lavish pious endowments and gifts. In the second document which Wast read out, the question of treason on Louis's part if he came back to his father was raised.[2] One gains the impression that the dauphin and his envoy were trying desperately to assure the king of his good intentions. Although Prospero da Camogli claimed that Louis had told him that he would never go back to his father, for fear that he would be imprisoned or worse, and Francesco Coppini endorsed this, the diplomatic documents may suggest otherwise.[3] Wast told the king:

> . . . I begged you that you would be pleased to give him [Louis] a place which would be agreeable to him and secure for his residence, but you were not pleased that he should remain there, because the first malcontents would take themselves to him, and so the trouble would be even worse than before. So, sire, although he's well disposed and determined not to do this, or anything else, which would cause you displeasure, he wants to fulfil these two articles in such a way that you would advise. . . .[4]

Wast then concluded by advising the king orally to 'make yourself sure about him and all the other fears which you may have on this matter . . . and don't give him anything that you can't take away next morning if you repent of it. And if you do that, no one can ever say that he's bound to you.'[5] The king's own views appear from the unique record, in the hand of one of his secretaries, of the words which he spoke at Bourges on 21 March 1461.[6] There can be little doubt of the authenticity of this document. It is contained in a collection of drafts and memoranda emanating from the secretariat.[7] No one but the king, some members of the council, and, in its final form, Louis's envoy, would have seen so confidential a document. It was, according to a note on its last folio, raw material for a reply to the dauphin.[8] The writer seems to have written out a draft of the king's spoken words, corrected them, crossed out some passages,

[1] Kendall and Ilardi, II, 214.
[2] B.N. MS. fr. 15537, fol. 18ʳ.
[3] Kendall and Ilardi, II, 173–4, 222.
[4] B.N. MS. fr. 15537, fol. 18ʳ.
[5] Ibid., fol. 18ᵛ.
[6] Ibid., fols 55ʳ–57ᵛ, and see Plate 8.

[7] It contains material relating to the dauphin during the period from 1446 to 1461.
[8] B.N. MS. fr. 15537, fol. 57ᵛ, in a different hand. It is printed in Beaucourt, VI, 319–22, but without sufficient attention to alterations and emendations.

and inserted alternative readings into the margins. It is thus a very messy document. It bears all the marks of dictation, and has an immediacy which is all too rare. It is also the last surviving statement of the king's attitude towards a relationship which was clearly a personal, as well as a political, embarrassment. It is therefore worth citing in full. Charles, sick as he was, said in reply to Wast's proposals:

I have heard what you told me yesterday on behalf of my son the dauphin, and today I have seen what you have given me in writing concerning the said business, which I've had read in the presence of those of my council who are here; and I'm amazed that you said that my son has taken the reply which I gave you last time so strangely, and that he has been angered and displeased by it. For it seems to the lords of the blood and the people of my council that the said reply was so sweet, so gracious and so reasonable, that he ought to welcome it, be content with it, and accept it.

You have touched on two points in the things you've said to me; and it seems to me that it's just the same old story again, and that my son wishes that I approve of his absence and of the reasons which he holds for not returning to me, which would be to nourish the error which has existed in this kingdom for a long time, where people say that I don't wish him to come back; this, as anyone ought to know very well, doesn't come from me, and I'd have been very happy if, some time ago, he'd been here to lend a hand with the others in recovering the kingdom and in booting out its enemies, having his share of the honour and the spoils, just like the others. And I've wanted him back not so much for myself as for him; because, although it would be a very great joy and pleasure for me if he was here so that I could see him and talk to him, and say . . . those things that I would not write to him nor command him through someone else, I believe that he'd be very happy and contented, and would never want to go away again; and if it so happened that he did want to go away after I'd spoken to him, he could certainly do so, as I've told you before. And also, if it so happens that he doesn't wish to come, but wishes to absent himself for ever from me, as he's done up to now, I'd rather that he did it himself and of his own free will, and by the advice of those who recommend it, than give my consent to it. And I'm puzzled as to where these fears of which you've spoken come from; because it seems to me that, all the time he's been away from me, he's had plenty of time to make himself sure and provide for his case. How has this [fear] come about? And one must

say that it's a true devilry[1] that he refuses to come to him from whom
good things and honours should flow. . . . Alas, he has the finest estate
of this realm, after me, and still has capable hands – which I have not –
and when he comes back here, my good and loyal subjects, who have
so honourably and bravely conducted themselves in the recovery, and
to the profit, of this kingdom, resisting the enterprises of its ancient
enemies and others, will all be comforted and overjoyed; and, because
he is so far away, and they cannot have any conversation with him,
they cannot have the love for him which they should have. . . .[2]

My enemies trust my word and my bond, and, when I have had them
in my power – and when they were abandoned by their own side –
everyone knows that I did nothing cruel to them.[3] And now my own
son doesn't trust my word to come back to me, in which it seems to me
that he does me little honour: for there's no great lord in England,
although they are my enemies, who doesn't trust me so well. And I'd
be most displeased if, under my surety, anything was done which was
harmful to him. And even if I should have such a wish, do you think
that I'm so powerless, and my kingdom so badly provided for, that I
couldn't have done it to him where he now is? How does it seem to
you? Think about it![4] You tell me that I should take such surety as I
wish from my son, after the things that you've told me. I've had no
need of it so far, and I still can't see that it would be necessary to do so,
thank God.

And as to the provision which you've asked for him, as I've told you
previously, when he comes to me to do his duty, or even less than duty,
and to take his share for the good of the public weal, as he should, I
shall . . . give him such good provision that he'll be very contented
with it; and if I should do as you ask, that would be to nourish the
separation which he's had for so long . . . and I'll not do that at all.
And when the lords of the blood and the people of the Three Estates
will be with me soon, I think that they won't advise me to do that;

[1] This phrase and the following sentence
(fol. 55ᵛ) are deleted in the MS. and
replaced by a marginal passage which is
reproduced in a fairer copy on fol. 56ʳ.
This is printed by Beaucourt, VI, 320–1.
The omission of 'cest une droicte deablerie'
and the sentence beginning 'Helas, il a le
plusbel estat . . .' are interesting. Perhaps
these possessed a little too much candidness
for the consumption of Louis and his
envoy. See Plate 8.

[2] B.N. MS. fr. 15537, fol. 56ʳ, for the
alternative, and perhaps final, reading
ending in the words 'dont je maquite'.
[3] Ibid., fol. 55ᵛ. The English seem to be
the 'enemies' here.
[4] Loc. cit. The words 'Or y pensez' are
underlined in the same manner as 'cest
une droicte deablerie'. They would also be
omitted from the final draft submitted to
the dauphin's envoy. See Plate 8.

but if they do advise it, then I'd rather that they did it by themselves than give my consent to it. And it's up to those who advise it and are of this opinion to give him such provision, not to me.

These were the words of a very sick man. The Three Estates never met before his death on 22 July. The dauphin never saw his father. Charles's refusal to endow Louis with a lordship within France until he had come to see him at court may have been prompted by paternal affection as much as by policy. Given the dauphin's financial straits, and his uncertain position at the court of Burgundy, the provision of a lordship was undoubtedly a pressing concern. If his father would provide him with one, then he would have to return to him. It would require only a single visit, thought Francesco Coppini, for a reconciliation to be effected between them.[1] But in the event, Louis waited for his father to die. News from England late in March was reassuring – the cause of Margaret of Anjou had suffered a disastrous setback at Towton.[2] Charles had been about to send a fleet to aid Margaret. He was mobilising troops on the Flemish border, and was preparing to invade Burgundian territory.[3] The Yorkist victory scotched his plans. Louis, his alliance with York vindicated by the victory of the Yorkists over the Lancastrians at Towton on Palm Sunday, 1461, and his alliance with Milan by the ejection of the French from Genoa on 9 March,[4] had less need to play the prodigal son. By 4 April, Philip the Good had sworn an oath of allegiance to Louis as future king of France. He also gave him a supplementary gift of 1,200 *livres*.[5] They had now merely to wait for his father's death. The astrologers' predictions were comforting. On 8 May Coppini wrote to Sforza from St-Omer, telling him that he had spoken with them, especially with a 'skilled one, a prelate of an order'.[6] Although Chastellain denied the fact, Philip the Good also had sufficient trust in their prognostications to consult the astrologers in May 1461. The religious had predicted that 'the king of France will this summer stand in the greatest danger of death, and if he escapes it will be a miracle rather than the course of nature. Around August the result will be seen.'[7] It was a guarded prognostication, allow-

[1] Kendall and Ilardi, II, 222.
[2] Beaucourt, VI, 328.
[3] Kendall and Ilardi, II, 214-16. The members of the Order of the Golden Fleece were to appear at their chapter at St-Omer fully armed. Cf. Chastellain's comment about Charles's prejudice towards those of his relatives, including

Alençon, who were members of the Order (III, 185). In the light of these events his rancour, which increased with age, is perhaps more explicable.
[4] Beaucourt, VI, 332-3.
[5] Ibid., 333-4.
[6] Kendall and Ilardi, II, 328.
[7] Ibid., 328; cf. Chastellain, III, 448.

ing for the intervention of God by means of a miracle. The astrologer was wrong in his calculation – but only by one month.

The lack of a Milanese ambassador at the king's court – owing to the hostility of France and Milan – means that knowledge of the king's behaviour at this time is gained at second-hand. Prospero da Camogli and Coppini wrote from the Burgundian lands, acting as filters through which information brought north from Bourges and Mehun-sur-Yèvre was passed to Sforza. But there is some first-hand evidence of his activity during these last months of his life. The more prosaic of this is found in the household accounts, and in a roll of payments made by Etienne Petit from the revenues of the salt-granaries in Languedoc.[1] The latter shows that, between 1 September 1460 and his death, the king was receiving no less than 27,500 *livres tournois* 'for his pleasures and desires'.[2] This was set beside an expenditure on the household as a whole of 20,889 *livres* between 1 April and 1 August 1461.[3] Sums of this magnitude are striking. The dauphin Louis's financial officers were particularly struck, and embarrassed, by the enormous sum spent on 'pleasures and desires'. When they came to examine the accounts after Louis's accession, they reported in a marginal note: 'with regard to the 27,500 *livres tournois* a lot is still owing, about a half, which is 13,700 *livres tournois*, and the truth can be discovered from Master Laurens Girard'.[4] Such assignments could impose an intolerable strain on revenues which – as was the case in Normandy in 1460 and 1461[5] – were often already overburdened. On what 'pleasures and desires' were such sums spent? It seems that the pensions, gifts and rewards to the favoured around the king were not included in them. The king was at liberty to spend this very large sum – from the yield of the *gabelle* in Languedoc – on whatsoever he pleased. It disappeared in the deeper recesses of the privy purse, lost from sight by both the *gens des comptes* and the historians of French royal finances. But we can hazard a number of guesses about the use to which such sums were put.

The king was unwell for much of the time to which this account relates. With his ulcerated leg, he could hardly enjoy the May Day festivities as he had done in the past.[6] At the Christmas feast of 1460, he spent a mere 2,700 *livres tournois*.[7] Wine was bought for him at Bordeaux

[1] B.N. MS. fr. 20498, fols 77ʳ–80ᵛ.
[2] Ibid., fol. 77ʳ.
[3] Douët-d'Arcq, *Comptes de l'hôtel*, xxxiv. Receipts were a mere 4,160 *livres*.
[4] B.N. MS. fr. 20498, fol. 77ʳ.
[5] Ibid., fol. 79ʳ, for a marginal note recording that the king had advanced the wages of the companies of *ordonnance* a month before his death. This had been done 'as best as one could' and revenues from Toulouse assigned for the purpose. For Normandy see MS. fr. 6754, fol. 8ʳ.
[6] See below, 223.
[7] B.N. MS. fr. 20498, fol. 77ʳ.

when he was ill at this time, but the cost is not known.[1] The lack of an *argenterie* account for 1460-1 means that there is no longer an exact record of expenditure, but the lavish spending presupposed by Etienne Petit's disbursement can be speculated upon further. There is evidence that the king had a number of pursuits in his last years. He played chess. In July 1459 two ivory chessboards, with chessmen, were bought for his 'diversion and pleasure'. Three further chessboards made of cypress wood were also purchased.[2] But he was also sympathetic towards more expensive games. Between May and September 1458 he ordered the controller of his household to surrender the green cloth from his *bureau* to the ladies of the court so that they could 'play at *martres* and *glic*'.[3] Dicing and gaming was a common pursuit of the fifteenth-century nobility.[4] If Charles was a gambler himself, then the pretext on which Jacques Cœur had raised money from two of the duke of Bourbon's clients may have been genuine. It was said that he had lifted 2,000 *écus* off them so that the king could 'play at dice and take [his] pleasures at the Christmas feast'.[5] He certainly borrowed 2,200 *livres tournois* from Jean de Bueil with which to gamble at the Christmas feast of 1445.[6] The inclusion of dicing with the king's 'pleasures' might imply that this was a pursuit in which the king was especially free to do as he wished. It could be an extremely expensive pleasure. If it was coupled with lavish spending on women, then the reckless pillage of his revenues to the tune of 27,500 *livres* might be more easily accounted for. Both pursuits were compatible with the more sedentary existence which illness was forcing him to lead. He may have known that he had little time left to him. But there were less costly pursuits open to him. His near-contemporary, Piero de Medici, smitten by arthritis and hence debarred from hunting, hawking and jousting, sought his pleasures among his books 'as if they were a pile of gold'.[7] Charles's literary tastes were applauded by Chastellain, and it is known that he received Robert Blondel's *Oratio historialis* in a French translation

1 Above, 176-7.
2 A.N., KK.51, fol. 82ʳ.
3 B.N. MS. fr. 6750, fol. 9ᵛ.
4 See, for some English instances, K. B. McFarlane, *The Nobility of Later Medieval England* (Oxford, 1972), 101, 246.
5 Dauvet, I, 9, and above, 132.
6 Escouchy, III, 257. He played for high stakes. See Beaucourt, IV, 86, and B.N. MS. fr. 23259, fols 4, 11, 21. In January 1453 he was given a pack of cards as a

New Year's Day gift, and in January 1454 a board on which to play games of chance (B.N. MS. fr. 10371, fols 24ʳ and 35ᵛ). For the practice of giving *étrennes*, see below, 226-7.
7 See E. H. Gombrich, 'The early Medici as Patrons of Art', *Italian Renaissance Studies*, ed. E. F. Jacob (London, 1960), 302, quoting from Filarete's treatise on architecture.

during 1460.[1] His library, as well as his women, perhaps provided some consolation in what must have been a fight for survival.

Alongside these intellectual pleasures Charles possessed certain interests which might be described as scientific. Technological inventions interested him.[2] Although there is no contemporary evidence for it, it is likely that he knew of the innovations introduced by Gutenberg in the science of printing. Whether he actually sent a spy to discover Gutenberg's 'secret' in 1458 is unknown.[3] The block-books and woodcuts produced at Paris towards the end of his life are innocent of the invention of movable type.[4] There are better grounds for attributing an interest in the mechanisms of clocks to him. In July 1459 he bought no less than five clocks from a master-clockmaker of Paris.[5] Four of these were chiming clocks, with a counterpoise, while the fifth was a 'half-clock', without a counterpoise. The clockmaker had brought them to Razilly and the king had inspected them. A fascination with the measurement of time is sometimes common in later years. At fifty-six, Charles was an elderly man by fifteenth-century standards. He had also the consolations of religion. By what appears to be the operation of a double standard, fifteenth-century princes were able to reconcile their licentiousness with their piety. Absolution was cheap, and the confessors of both Charles VII and Philip the Good must have spent much of their time absolving them from their mortal sins. The king at least went through the motions of the conventional devotional religion of his time. He heard three Masses a day, one of which was sung.[6] At the head of the eighteen chaplains of the chapel royal in 1458–9 was the celebrated composer Jan Ockeghem.[7] To the consolation of religion were added the pleasures of some of the finest church music of the age.

Ockeghem had left Antwerp cathedral for Charles's service by 1453, when he received a New Year's gift from the king in return for his own – a song book.[8] That the king enjoyed music, and could read its notation, is evident from his purchase, in 1459, of 448 richly illuminated vignettes, each with a gilded initial letter, which were painted into two song books 'for his pleasure'.[9] When he was at Vendôme in the autumn of 1458 to

[1] Beaucourt, VI, 402–3.
[2] His interest in artillery dated from an early stage in his career. See Beaucourt, I, 246, for payment to a cannoneer for 'a cannon which we have had from him' (20 December 1419). Also above, 74, 141.
[3] Ibid., VI, 409–10.
[4] See P. Meyer, 'Les Neuf Preux', Bull. Soc. anc. textes fr. (1883), 45.
[5] A.N., KK.51, fols 96ᵛ, 97ʳ, 97ᵛ.

[6] Vallet, Henri Baude, 8. He got up in the mornings, unlike Philip the Good, who did not hear Mass in his later years until 2 or 3 p.m. (Vaughan, op. cit., 128).
[7] A.N., KK.51, fol. 129ᵛ. For his career see M. Brenet, 'Jean de Ockeghem, maître de la chapelle des rois Charles VII et Louis XI', Mém. Soc. hist. Paris, xx (1893), 1–32.
[8] B.N. MS. fr. 10371, fol. 35ʳ.
[9] Beaucourt, VI, 408 n. 5.

try the duke of Alençon, the news of Pius II's election to the papacy arrived. The king ordered the singing of a *Te Deum* by Ockeghem and his chaplains in the castle chapel at Vendôme on 5 November.[1] This was a common occurrence. On 17 May 1455, for instance, after receiving a letter from the College of cardinals, the king entered his chapel 'and had the *Te Deum laudamus* sung, as he is accustomed to do'.[2] Ockeghem was well rewarded for his services. In 1454–5 he was receiving, above his normal wages, an additional 180 *livres tournois*, assigned on the *aides* for war in the *haut pays d'Auvergne*.[3] The peaceful arts thus benefited from war taxation. Under Ockeghem's directorship the chapel royal grew – from seven singers in 1452 to thirteen in 1461.[4] Each of these, with Ockeghem, was paid at the rate of 15 *livres tournois* per month – the monthly wage of a mounted man-at-arms in one of the king's companies of *ordonnance*. Between 1456 and 1459 Ockeghem was given the office of treasurer of St-Martin of Tours, and was given dispensation from residing there on 18 April 1461 because he was 'in the service of the court'.[5] Three months later he was to appear with the singers of the chapel royal, dressed in mourning vestments for the king's funeral. Besides the formal set-pieces of church music—masses and motets—Ockeghem evidently composed secular music for the king. In January 1459 he presented Charles with a New Year's present of a richly illuminated song.[6] Some of his twenty surviving masses and eight motets must have been written for the chapel royal during Charles's lifetime. But the attribution of a given work to a specific event is a hazardous undertaking. Ockeghem continued to serve the house of France under Louis XI and Charles VIII, dying in about 1495. Apart from his own work, posterity is indebted to Charles VII's patronage of Ockeghem for the fact that he taught Josquin des Près.

But such pleasures can hardly have been appreciated by the king during the last few months of his life. His last letter-missive was signed by him on 30 May 1461.[7] His last public appearance was probably his reception of an embassy, led by a Franciscan, Louis de Boulogne, from some princes of

1 Brenet, op. cit., 6. For Pius's election see Beaucourt, VI, 241–2. There was a strong possibility in August 1458 that a French pope might be elected. Cardinal Guillaume d'Estouteville was a candidate, but the Italian cardinals in the Sacred College were swayed by the future Pius II's harangue on the subject of foreign popes and the likelihood of French intervention in Italy which would follow Estouteville's election. See Ilardi, op. cit., 148–50. There was thus little cause for celebration at Vendôme in November 1458.

2 Valois, *Conseil*, 262.
3 B.N. MS. fr. 2886, fol. 20ʳ.
4 Brenet, op. cit., 4, 7.
5 Ibid., 7.
6 A.N., KK.51, fol. 122ʳ.
7 Beaucourt, VI, 437 n. 5. I have been unable to trace this letter. For a letter of 15 May 1461, signed by his own hand, see Plate ii.

the East.[1] They arrived in the course of May at Mehun-sur-Yèvre, hoping that Charles VII would support their campaign against the Turks. They left with nothing more than assurances of goodwill. The king was perhaps less concerned about the fate of Christendom than about his own survival. In the first two weeks of June rumours of open war between France and Burgundy were circulating. A spy had been sent by the *bailli* of Hainault on 27 May to Laon 'to gain news of the French, because it was rumoured daily that the king had decided to make war on my lord the duke'.[2] Troops were being assembled in Normandy, and a double invasion—of England as well as the Burgundian lands—was rumoured. On 18 June Coppini wrote to Sforza from Bruges.[3] He discussed the possibilities of war. The king had his sovereignty on his side, and, more tangibly, the counts of Maine and Foix. But, at Bruges, people thought little of the rest of his lords, 'since they would probably neither aid nor be loyal to him'.[4] Paris and its surrounding countryside, Normandy, Brittany and Gascony, thought Coppini, were also of dubious loyalty in the event of a war. They were 'suspect to the king of France, as all of them would foment disorders if there were war'.[5] The Milanese agent predicted that there would be. The men around Charles, he observed, 'know that his Majesty is old and feeble'. Active campaigning on his part was out of the question, for he could not ride ten leagues in armour. But his entourage knew that they were hated by the dauphin, and 'may perhaps be more ready to persuade the king to make war'. If the king died, they would have forces enough to secure good terms from Louis if war had been declared.

In the event, nothing happened. Messengers rode back and forth between Philip the Good and the king on 1, 6 and 9 July.[6] On receipt of news from France on that day, Philip sent them immediately to Louis and to Charles, count of Charolais. These concerned the king's most recent bout of illness.[7] A few days later Louis was writing that he had 'had news from my lord [the king] in many and various ways, and all say, in effect, that there is no hope'.[8] Louis's informants were, however, a little over-confident. The king was said to have rallied, and went to Mass a few days later.[9] The drone of public prayers filled the churches of

---

[1] Ibid., VI, 345.

[2] Vaughan, op. cit., 353. Preparations for war may be inferred from the advancing of wages to the king's troops in June 1461. See above, 183 n. 5.

[3] Kendall and Ilardi, II, 428–32.

[4] Ibid., 430.

[5] Ibid., 430–2. For these fears at other times see above, 124–6, 157.

[6] Beaucourt, VI, 338–9.

[7] Ibid., 339.

[8] Vaesen, *Lettres*, I, 143.

[9] Beaucourt, VI, 439, n. 3.

France from 10 July onwards. But they were to no avail. Charles's last, and fatal, relapse came about a week later. On 17 July his council wrote to the dauphin Louis. They told him that

> . . . a certain illness has, for some time, afflicted the king your father, which began with a toothache, by reason of which his jaw and part of his face was very swollen, and gave off a great deal of matter, and his said tooth was then extracted, and the wound closed up, so that, because of this, and of the bulletins which the doctors gave us every day, we had high hopes that he would soon be cured. However, as the affair has gone on longer than we thought it would, and, as it seems to us, he is weaker than he has ever been, we, as those who, after him, wish to serve and obey you, have decided to write to you and let you know . . . in order to have such advice on all this as shall be your pleasure. . . .[1]

The letter was signed by Charles of Anjou, Gaston IV of Foix, Guillaume Jouvenel des Ursins, Jean, lord of Lorraine, Anthoine de Chabannes, Jean d'Estouteville, lord of Torcy, Mathelin Brachet, Tanneguy du Chastel, Jean Bureau and Guillaume Cousinot. The councillors were reconciled to a situation which had previously horrified some of them. They were, at the last possible moment, trying to make their peace with the dauphin. That they failed is evident from the fact that, at his accession, Louis dismissed all of them except Charles of Anjou and Jean Bureau.[2] At Genappe, the news that the projected army which was to aid Margaret of Anjou had again been called off served to confirm the council's letter.[3] At last it looked as if the king really would die. It is one mark of his stamina that he had survived so many previous attacks. On 18 July he was thought to be beyond all help.[4] At Genappe it was noted that, on 20 July, Louis's men were already furbishing up their armour as if they were about to embark on a crusade to the Holy Land.[5] It was rumoured that he had already distributed some of the offices in the kingdom to his servants. There is no means of proving this, but the careful record of the offices held by such of his father's servants whom he retained suggests that some appointments had at least been ear-marked before his accession.[6] The Bureau brothers could perform useful services for him. Antoinette

---

[1] B.N. MS. fr. 20855, fol. 21ʳ; Beaucourt, VI, 440.

[2] Beaucourt, VI, 435–6; cf. MS. fr. 20487, fol. 96, for Bureau.

[3] Kendall and Ilardi, II, 448. Letters from Rouen reported that the fleet which was to carry the expedition had been disbanded.

[4] Beaucourt, VI, 441.

[5] Kendall and Ilardi, II, 444.

[6] Ibid., 444; B.N. MS. fr. 20487, fol. 96, where Bourré, Louis's secretary, noted that Jean Bureau held the offices of *trésorier* and *maître des comptes*, mayor of Bordeaux, captain of Meaux and governor of Pons.

de Maignelais's services, for which she received a pension of 6,000 *livres* from him, can more easily be assumed.[1] As he himself wrote, intelligence from his father's court came to him 'in many and various ways'. One of those upon whom he relied for information was Louis, count of St-Pol. On 20 July St-Pol wrote to him from Male, near Bruges, that his men, of whom one had left Mehun-sur-Yèvre on Thursday the 16th and the other on Friday the 17th, had both told him that 'the king is . . . in great danger [of death] unless God finds a remedy'.[2] It was 6 p.m. on the Monday before the Wednesday on which the king died.

News was travelling very fast indeed, if a rider could cover the 300 or so miles from Mehun to Bruges in under three days. On the previous evening, at about 7 p.m., the bishop of Paris had received letters from the king's council, telling him that the king was extremely ill.[3] No attempts were being made to disguise the fact. The bishop ordered solemn processions, in which relics were to be carried, in the church of Ste-Geneviève on the next day – the Monday on which St-Pol wrote to the dauphin. Meanwhile the king's condition steadily worsened. He was unable to eat, or, according to some sources, refused to eat for fear that he would be poisoned by his own servants.[4] Given his symptoms, the thesis that he was poisoned is an unconvincing one. Although the removal of his diseased tooth appears to have been moderately successful, an abscess seems to have formed on the gums. Accompanied, as it probably was, by acute inflammation of the mouth and of the upper digestive tract, any form of feeding would have been intolerably painful. Before the advent of antibiotics, it was apparently quite common for patients afflicted with septic infections of the jaw and mouth to be unable to swallow even a few drops of liquid without terrible suffering.[5] The chroniclers might introduce the actuality, or suspicion, of poisoning into their accounts for dramatic or partisan effect. But the medical evidence, such as it is, would explain the king's enforced inability to take any kind of nourishment for something like a week. Jean Chartier tells us that after eight days or so of total abstinence, his doctors tried to feed him, but he could not swallow because his digestive tract had closed up.[6]

Gaspard, his brother, held the offices of *maître* of the artillery, captain of the Louvre (by purchase) and captain of the bridge at Poissy. Both kept their offices.

[1] Beaucourt, VI, 436; 438 for her intrigues with Louis.

[2] B.N. MS. fr. 20485, no. 1; printed in Escouchy, III, 449–50.

[3] Escouchy, III, 450–1.

[4] Beaucourt, VI, 441–2.

[5] Ibid., 457–9, for a medical opinion of 1891.

[6] Chartier, III, 113: 'Et adonc mist paine de menger, mais ne peult, car ses conduits estoient tous rettraitz.'

If he could not eat or drink, it was unlikely that he could have spoken. All *obiter dicta* are to be viewed with the deepest suspicion. According to the *Chronique Martinienne*, the king was supposed to have remained conscious until the end, asking the clergy around him on Wednesday 22 July what day it was.[1] They told him that it was the feast of the Magdalene. The king was alleged to have replied that he thanked God that he, the greatest sinner in the world, should die on the day of the greatest female sinner. Imagination perhaps got the better of the writer on this occasion. While the king lay on his deathbed at Mehun, his son was making ready for the journey to Rheims. His faithful (and not-so-faithful) subjects were gathering their retinues together so that they might meet the dauphin on the road.[2] Louis was getting news every day, as he waited to move with his household towards the French border. One letter which he received may have given him especial pleasure. On the day of his father's death, his mother wrote to him in her own hand. Marie of Anjou's letter bears the endorsement 'written at Chinon, this Wednesday, the day of the Magdalene'.[3] She could therefore not have been with Charles when he died at Mehun between noon and 1 p.m. on 22 July.[4] The long-suffering wife was clearly not prepared to suffer the long hours at the bedside. Charles died without the consolations of his two closest – yet emotionally most distant – relatives. The queen wrote to her son:

My son, you should know at this moment the illness and trouble [which has] afflicted the person of my lord, who, as you may imagine, is very weak. May God, by His grace, come to his aid! My son, my brother of Maine and others being with my lord send the *grand sénéchal* to you to tell you the condition in which he has left my said lord, and they have given him full responsibility to speak to you. You must listen to his credence and believe it, for they are all resolved to serve you, even in the affairs of this kingdom when the case arises.[5] In which case, my son, I beg you that you be advised to enter it in a good and sweet manner, so that, through lack of good advice, there is no trouble anywhere, as I have ordered Janilhac, the carrier [of these letters] to tell you more fully . . . and on all these things, I beg you, pay attention to your uncle, my brother of Maine. . . .

These maternal counsels, with their impressive testimonial for Charles of Anjou, were not entirely ignored by Louis. If he had not listened to her,

1 Beaucourt, VI, 442.
2 Kendall, *Louis XI*, 111; Champion, *Louis XI*, II, 2–4.
3 Printed in Beaucourt, VI, 495–6.
4 Ibid., 443. Chinon is about 120 miles, as the crow flies, from Mehun.
5 Ibid., 495, i.e. when Charles died.

the count of Maine's behaviour when he was in a tight corner at Mont-lhéry on 16 July 1465 might have been even more ambiguous.[1] There is no record of what the *grand sénéchal* Brézé told Louis, if the latter received him at all, but it clearly did nothing to reduce the dauphin's suspicions about him. He was dismissed from the council, and temporarily im-prisoned.[2] Soon after his accession, Louis wrote of Brézé that he was 'so variable in his defences' that his officers were contemplating putting him to the torture.[3] He had not forgotten Brézé's behaviour in the case of Guillaume Mariette. Nor had he forgotten Anthoine de Chabannes's treachery towards him. Chabannes was, according to the *Chronique Martinienne*, with the king when he died.[4] The chronicler told the story that Chabannes implored him to take some nourishment, saying that if he suspected anyone of attempting to poison him, he would have that person tried and torn apart by four horses. The king was alleged to have replied: 'I resign the retribution for my death to God.'[5] It was a most unlikely utterance, indicating a presumption in the chronicler's mind that the king was in fact suspecting an attempt at poisoning. Chabannes's loyalty was made to appear all the greater by the writer – a staunch defender of the house of Dammartin. His loyalty cost Chabannes his pensions and offices in August 1461.[6]

The news that the king was dead reached Paris on Friday 24 July.[7] The previous day had seen solemn processions in the city by both clergy and people. A Parisian journal tells how the news from Mehun was brought to the king's officers of the *Chambre des Comptes* while they were assembled in the Ste-Chapelle.[8] They were about to set out on a procession, barefoot and carrying candles, praying for the king's recovery, when a messenger brought letters into the chapel. Immediately their procession was aban-doned, and they had requiem masses said. The canons and chaplains of the Ste-Chapelle had a busy day, celebrating masses for the dead and for the salvation of the king's soul. At Mehun, the barber-surgeons and apothecaries were about to begin their macabre task of eviscerating and embalming his body.[9] Once it had been sealed in its great leaden coffin, Charles VII's ravaged and wasted corpse was not to be seen again for

[1] See Commynes, *Mémoires*, I, 20; cf. La Marche, III, 8 n. 5; Champion, *Louis XI*, II, 24.
[2] Bernus, *Revue de l'Anjou*, lxiii (1911), 355–71.
[3] B.N. MS. fr. 20490, fol. 36r. But he was killed, on Louis's side, at Montlhéry.
[4] Beaucourt, VI, 442–3.
[5] Ibid., 443. Charles, wrote the chronicler, advised Chabannes to serve the *petit seigneur* well. He was referring not to Louis but to Charles of France.
[6] For his dispossession, and that of others, from the standing army, see Contamine, op. cit., 406.
[7] Escouchy, III, 451.
[8] Ibid., 451.
[9] *ABSHF* (1864), 179–80, and below, 210.

three hundred years. On Thursday 17 October 1793 the tomb which contained his body, and that of Marie of Anjou, was opened, together with all the other royal tombs in the church of St-Denis.[1] Their mortal remains were taken out and thrown into a common ditch, which was immediately covered up. Their tomb had already been robbed, and only the fragments of a crown and a silver-gilt sceptre were found by the revolutionaries. The effigies of both Charles and Marie of Anjou were smashed to pieces in an orgy of vindictive iconoclasm. Had it not been for the diligent antiquarianism of the seventeenth-century writer Gaignières, no record would have survived of what the king's tomb was like. A drawing in one of his vast collections shows a marble effigy under a canopy, with its feet resting upon a lion, its head resting on a cushion sown with *fleurs-de-lys*, wearing the appropriate vestments. But, apart from the bust, it was destroyed before it could be saved by Alexandre Lenoir for his *Musée des Monumens Français*.[2]

The news of his father's death reached Louis on about 25 July, at Genappe. He left for Avesnes, in Hainault, on the French border, very soon afterwards.[3] There he found a large gathering of the lords of France and their clients, royal officers and civil servants, each one hoping for confirmation of his office. Before his father was even buried, Louis was granting offices in the kingdom of France. On 4 August, four days before Charles's last Requiem in St-Denis, he was giving away offices in the administration of the town of Laon, surrounded by his Burgundian servants.[4] It was not until 15 August that he was crowned at Rheims. The sackings and purgings had already begun. He was, he told Philippe de Commynes, to repent of them later in his life.[5] His hatred of his father's servants, nourished by fourteen years' exile, led him to make mistakes. Prospero da Camogli's report that he replied to requests at Avesnes 'without taking counsel with anybody' was ominous.[6] In this respect he was

[1] See A. Lenoir, *Description historique et chronologique des Monumens de Sculpture réunis au Musée des Monumens Français* (Paris, 1802), 347.

[2] See Bodleian Library, MS. Gough, Gaignières 2, fol. 45ʳ, for the tomb, and Plate 12a. Also J. E. Biet, *Souvenirs du Musée des Monumens Français* (Paris, 1821-6), 21-8; Lenoir, op. cit., 174, for the busts of Charles and Marie of Anjou. The bust of the king was restored 'with much skill and care' by the Citizen Beauvallet, the rest of the effigy having

been 'smashed by some malicious persons' (ibid., 174). See Plate 12b. For the influence of the *Musée* on French nineteenth-century artists and writers see Francis Haskell, 'The Manufacture of the Past in nineteenth-century Painting', *Past and Present*, liii (1971), 114-15.

[3] Beaucourt, VI, 441.

[4] B.N. MS. fr. 20490, fol. 23ʳ: 'commanded at Avesnes in Hainault, the fourth day of August 1461'.

[5] Commynes, *Mémoires*, I, 20.

[6] Kendall, *Louis XI*, 107.

decidedly not his father's son. By dismissing his father's officers, those 'wise and notable knights, . . . notwithstanding the fact that they had served his father well in the recovery and pacification of the kingdom', Louis found himself confronted by rebellion in the summer of 1465. Dunois, André de Laval, Chabannes and Jean de Bueil were singled out by Commynes for particular mention.[1] If nothing else, they were good soldiers. In the circumstances of July 1465, Louis needed as many good soldiers as he could get. His father had employed such men according to their talents. When old rancours were allowed to triumph over such pragmatic considerations, a king could be in great difficulties. It was ironic that Louis was soon to become the perpetuator of his father's behaviour towards Burgundy. In one respect at least, Charles's death did not have the cataclysmic effects which some desired, and others feared.

[1] Commynes, I, 20; confirmed in Contamine, op. cit., 406. Dunois was not dismissed, but was exiled to defend Asti. Louis's motives in giving Brézé, his 'mortal enemy', the command of his vanguard at Montlhéry were perhaps suspect. Brézé was among the very first to be killed (Commynes, I, 21–2). It was perhaps less Louis's desire to 'avoid battle' (ibid., 21) than to be rid of Brézé that may have moved him.

Chapter 7 ✤ The Ceremonial King

I *The office and mystique of kingship*

> Some wore their robes of red,
> In token of one thing:
> That Justice is never dead
> Through death or change of King. . . .[1]

Martial d'Auvergne's description of the four *présidents* of the Paris *Parlement*, wearing their scarlet robes at the funeral of Charles VII, is noteworthy. Here the concept of the immortality of royal Justice is expressed in the most tangible of ways. Not only did Justice never die, but the king's office, or dignity, was thought to be immortal. Dynastic, as well as judicial, continuity had been established by what Professor Kantorowicz called 'the crucial fifteenth century'.[2] Amid the mourners and weepers in the church of St-Denis on 8 August 1461, the brilliantly attired lawyers of the *Parlement* must have contrasted strangely with the black draperies and funereal tapers with which the king's last earthly appearance was attended. *Dignitas non moritur* – despite the evident fact that the king was a mortal man like other men, his 'dignity never dies'. From the reign of Charles V – that crucial time of change in French royal ceremony and iconography – the notion of 'twin-born majesty' pervaded the works of those who speculated upon the nature of kingship.[3] The king was not one, but two, persons: he was the God-made man, destined to perish; and he was the man-made God, personifying the 'mystical body' of the kingdom, which was immortal. Charles VII was therefore, on certain public occasions of very great solemnity, seen by his subjects as an icon.

Such notions required a willing (or unwilling) suspension of disbelief.

[1] Martial de Paris, dit d'Auvergne, *Les Vigiles de Charles VII*, in *Poésies*, ii (Paris, 1724), 170. This section is intended to serve as a study of the public image of Charles VII, as well as of royal ceremonial during the reign.

[2] E. H. Kantorowicz, *The King's Two Bodies* (Princeton, 1957), 6.
[3] See B. Guenée, *L'Occident aux xive et xve siècles. Les Etats* (Paris, 1971), 133–59; M. Bloch, *Les Rois Thaumaturges* (Paris, 1961), 185–215, 478–89.

Those who knew the king as a politician, and as the unprepossessing figure with poor legs and a peculiar walk, were obliged to venerate him on such occasions. At his coronation, at his entries into the towns of his kingdom, at his *lits-de-justice*, and, lastly, at his funeral, the king was presented as an ideal type. That ideal was compounded of many elements – by the 'crucial fifteenth century' these were beginning to fuse to produce an image of French monarchy which was to survive until the Revolution. The king was king 'by the grace of God', he administered Justice which was undying, and, most importantly, his worldly success might excuse many transgressions. Charles VII, by his victory over the English, was excused many things in the minds of his contemporaries. A king, to be a successful king, did not need to be 'virtuous'. A 'good' king was an effective one. 'If you cannot live chastely,' wrote John of Viterbo, 'you should act cautiously.'[1] The notion of the cunning, circumspect prince was often on the lips of those around him. In the dedication to Charles VII of his translation of Frontinus's *Stratagems*, Jean de Rouvroy, dean of the faculty of theology in the University of Paris, wrote:

> . . . in this book, of all the stories which are known, both Greek and Roman, are recounted all the most notable examples of all the ruses (*cautelles*) and subtleties which have been performed in war by sea and land in all the three parts of the world. . . . He who would search through all the histories would find more battles to have been won by ruses and subtleties . . . than by greater numbers. . . .[2]

Such sentiments would not have been disowned by Machiavelli. Charles VII, by his 'subtlety', was realising at least one of the attributes of kingship set out by his contemporaries. But there were other, more tangible attributes which a king possessed. Above all, there were the regalia. These changed according to the nature of the occasion. On the most solemn, such as the coronation, the king wore his open crown of *fleurons*, and carried the sceptre and the *main-de-justice*.[3] Having been anointed with the holy oil which had descended to Clovis, contained in the sacred *ampoule* kept at Rheims, the king received a robe of blue cloth, sewn with golden *fleurs-de-lys*, and trimmed with ermine. We have no equivalent of the *Coronation Book of Charles V* for the coronation of Charles VII in

---

[1] Guenée, *L'Occident*, 142.

[2] B.N. MS. fr. 1233, fol. 1ʳ. See Plate 6b.

[3] Guenée, *L'Occident*, 147. For the coronation ritual see E. S. Dewick, *The*

Coronation Book of Charles V of France (London, 1899); C. R. Sherman, *The Portraits of Charles V of France (1338–80)* (New York, 1969), 33–7. See Plate 9.

1429, but it would be surprising if the ceremony was not closely similar. A letter of 17 July 1429 refers to the event as if it were a drama.[1] It was a 'beau mystère', conducted with the greatest pomp, and three observers thought the royal regalia so fine, and the arrangements so well made, that it was as if the ceremony had been prepared a year previously. In the circumstances, of course, this would have been out of the question. From nine o'clock in the morning until two in the afternoon, the ceremony moved towards its climax, the unction. Throughout those five hours, Joan of Arc stood beside the king, holding her banner. Once the holy oil had been poured upon his head, and also applied by the archbishop of Rheims to his hands and chest, the crown was placed on the king's head. At that moment 'everyone cried *Noël!* and trumpets sounded so that it seemed that the vaults of the church would crack'.[2] The significance of the act was quite clear to contemporaries. At Rheims, for the first time, Charles received not only the unction, but 'by divine miracle, the royal insignia [*enseignes roialles*] with which you are marked'.[3]

To those who remembered the brief ceremony at Mehun-sur-Yèvre in October 1422, the events of July 1429 must have seemed miraculous. On the former occasion, the dauphin's officers and a few loyal nobles and churchmen acclaimed him as his father's heir.[4] A banner of France was raised in the chapel of the castle, and the cry of *Vive le roi!* was given. It was a shabby enough performance. Charles was not anointed, because there was no *Sainte Ampoule* to be had. This, the 'unique source of the supernatural powers of the French kings', made the king a priest, a *sacerdos*, who took Communion in both kinds.[5] Without this, so many of his subjects believed, the king was not fully empowered. Joan of Arc was adopting the strictest interpretation of the nature of French kingship when she insisted on referring to Charles only as her 'dauphin' until the coronation at Rheims. Once anointed, the king could perform priestly and therapeutic functions. He could touch those afflicted with the 'king's evil' – the skin disease known as scrofula[6] – and could claim a degree of control over the Church within his kingdom denied to other sovereigns. He was, said Bernard du Rozier, provost of the cathedral of Toulouse in 1442, 'the right hand of the Holy Church of God, and the continual defender and protector of all churches and churchmen of all [the] king-

[1] Quicherat, *Procès*, v, 128; above, 51.
[2] Ibid., 129.
[3] Bloch, op. cit., 251, citing Robert Blondel's *Des droiz de la couronne de France* of 1459 or 1460.
[4] See Beaucourt, II, 55. He wore a red robe for the ceremony.
[5] See Lewis, op. cit., 81–4; Bloch, op. cit., 212–13.
[6] Ibid., 27–8.

dom . . .'.[1] His ambassadors to Pope Pius II were adamant ont he issue in
November 1459. The healing power of the kings of France, they argued,
proved the peculiar sanctity of the house of France, and hence the
sovereignty of the king over the Church.[2] If the Gallican Church needed
a head to be set over its members, it found one in the person of the
Lord's Anointed.

But there were other insignia besides the unction. The series of royal
coronations in a mid-fifteenth-century manuscript of the *Grandes Chroniques
de France* show contemporary visions of the ceremony at their most vivid.[3]
Lothar is depicted in an illumination receiving the archbishop's benedic-
tion at Rheims.[4] Among the lords spiritual and temporal in attendance,
one holds the sceptre, another the *main-de-justice*, another the sword
Joyeuse, another the vessel containing the oil, and another the spurs which
the king will wear when he has been dubbed knight. Charles VII received
knighthood from Jean, duke of Alençon, at his coronation in 1429.[5] In
another illumination, Philip Augustus is shown at his *sacre*, where the
archbishop pronounces the blessing, the king of England (as duke of
Aquitaine) holds the crown, the constable carries the sword, and one of
the spiritual peers holds the sceptre and *main-de-justice*.[6] The sovereignty
of Charles VII over the peers of France is made quite explicit. In the altar-
piece which was made for the chapel of the Paris *Parlement* late in his
reign, the king is shown as St Louis, bearing the sceptre, wearing the
sleeveless chasuble sewn with *fleurs-de-lys* over the scarlet robe which was
the symbol of dynastic continuity.[7] He is shown in the company of St
John the Baptist to whom he gestures with his left hand. The Baptist in
turn points to the lamb which he cradles in his arms. The king thus
receives his judicial power from Christ, transmitted by the saint. The hand
which normally held the staff topped with the ivory *main-de-justice* here
extends towards the source of all regal power. The king, as the head of the
'mystical body' which was the realm, thus stood before his lawyers at
their devotions, an icon to be venerated rather than a mere mortal to be
respected.

At his coronation, the king appeared only to those few gathered to
witness the 'beau mystère' at Rheims. For the majority of his subjects,
the king's likeness was known only through the painted or sculpted image,

---

[1] B.N. MS. lat. 6020, fol. 87ʳ. See Plate
5 for the MS of this sermon.
[2] Bloch, op. cit., 140–1.
[3] *Grandes Chroniques de France*, ed.
H. Omont (Paris, 1906), for a facsimile of
this MS. (B.N. MS. fr. 6465).

[4] Ibid., pl. 17.
[5] Beaucourt, II, 229.
[6] *Grandes Chroniques*, pl. 24.
[7] Now Musée du Louvre no. 998A. See
Plate 9.

such as the statues in the Grande Salle du Palais de la Cité, or the 'galleries' of French monarchs at Notre Dame, the Sainte-Chapelle of Bourges, and the cathedrals of Rheims and Chartres.[1] Perhaps the most common occasion on which one might see the king was on the road, or at his ceremonial entry into one of the towns of his kingdom. Some were privileged to see him in less formal circumstances. Master Esmond Gallet, licentiate in laws, native of Paris, told his interrogators on 22 October 1456 that he had seen Charles VII only twice in his life. He said that 'he had only once seen him on horseback, and he seemed to be a fair prince, and another time he saw him in the abbey of Ardenne, near Caen, where he was reading a chronicle, and he seemed to him to be the best reader that he had ever seen'.[2] Such opportunities were denied to the majority. The king was not normally caught unawares by them. The image which he presented on his comparatively rare public appearances was carefully moulded by his advisers. Above all, the royal entries into the loyal (or not so loyal) towns of the realm were carefully stage-managed. It has recently been observed that these elaborate ceremonies were 'expressly conceived to impose a certain image on him and his power'.[3] From being an occasion on which simple hospitality was shown, the royal entry had become, by the fourteenth century, a highly theatrical piece of royal propaganda. The towns themselves met the expenses of the entry and provided the necessary scenario – streets hung with tapestries, *tableaux* representing allegories and didactic scenes, and the canopy under which the king rode in triumph.

Accounts of Charles VII's entries into Paris in 1437, Limoges in 1439, Toulouse in 1442, and Rouen in 1449 supply enough evidence to form an impression of the impact of such ceremonies on the spectator.[4] It is obvious that the king's entry to Paris, recently recovered from Anglo-Burgundian hands, would be an opportunity for lavish and elaborate ceremony. The king had come into his own once more, and neither he nor his Parisian subjects were allowed to forget that fact. The king was presented in full armour, mounted on a 'fine hunting horse', which was covered with blue velvet, sewn with gilded *fleurs-de-lys*.[5] Before him rode his first esquire of the stable, on a horse covered with a cloth sewn with the device of the winged stag (*cerf volant*). The esquire carried the

[1] See B. Guenée and F. Lehoux, *Les Entrées Royales Françaises de 1328 à 1515* (Paris, 1968), 8 n. 3.
[2] B.N. MS. fr. 18441, fol. 120ʳ.
[3] Guenée and Lehoux, 8.
[4] See ibid., 70–86, 156–60, 160–2; A. Leroux,

'Passages de Charles VII et du dauphin . . . à Limoges en 1439', *BEC*, xlvi (1885), 303–14.
[5] See T. Godefroy, *Le Cérémonial français* (Paris, 1649), 653–8; Guenée and Lehoux, 73.

king's great helm on a staff, with a gold crown above it, in the centre of which was a great gold *fleur-de-lys*. His king-of-arms carried the king's surcoat, of blue velvet, embroidered with three gold *fleur-de-lys* garnished with pearls. Another esquire of the stable carried his sword, worked with gilded *fleurs-de-lys*. The archers of the king's guard and those of Charles of Anjou, count of Maine, followed, and the king himself was surrounded by the archers of the constable Richemont and the count of Vendôme. His advisers were evidently taking no risks. Behind him rode the dauphin Louis, flanked by Charles of Anjou and the count of La Marche, followed by the pages of the king, dauphin and lords. Dunois came next, riding a horse covered in cloth of gold down to its feet, holding a staff in his hand as an emblem of his military authority. Behind him rode an esquire of the stable, bearing the banner of St Michael, its field sewn with golden stars. At the rear of the procession came the army – eight hundred lances, all gorgeously attired. The riot of colour evidently fascinated the chroniclers. Both Gilles le Bouvier and Monstrelet devoted meticulously detailed passages to the occasion.[1]

Two crucial moments can be isolated from their garrulous narratives. When the royal *cortège* reached the chapel of St-Denis, it was met by the representatives of the city of Paris – the provost of the merchants, the *échevins*, and a number of the burgesses.[2] The provost presented the keys of the city to the king, who gave them to the constable. It was a gesture of submission. On 12 November 1437 – apparently for the first time – a great city had offered its keys to its sovereign as a token of its obedience. The ceremony was to be repeated at Rouen in 1449 and from that date was to become an indispensable part of royal entries into the most loyal of loyalist towns. Secondly, as Monstrelet noted, the surrender of the keys was immediately followed by a further symbolic act. 'The same provost and *échevins*,' he wrote, 'then raised up a blue canopy covered with *fleurs-de-lys* over the king, and thenceforth carried it above his head.'[3] From the entry of Charles VI into the town of Lyon in October 1389, references are found to such canopies, or baldaquins.[4] They resembled the canopies found over the thrones of the Valois monarchs, represented on their seals, their coins, and in illuminated manuscripts. By the end of the fourteenth century, canopies had become the common property not only of the king, but of the greater magnates. But the use of the canopy, carried

[1] Printed in ibid., 72–5, 75–9.

[2] Ibid., 76.

[3] Loc. cit.

[4] Ibid., 13–14. He also entered Montpellier and Beziers in November 1389 under canopies. Climatic conditions on all these occasions are not recorded.

on four poles by the councillors of the town, perhaps contained further layers of meaning. It was possible to conceive of the processional canopy as a part of a moving throne. But it has been shown that its probable significance did not end there. By the fourteenth century it had become usual to carry the Sacrament under a canopy which was remarkably similar to those used in royal entries. In the *Corpus Christi* processions through the streets of a town, the Host was borne in such a manner.[1] Given the notions held in the fifteenth century about the divine and priestly attributes of kingship, the transfer of the canopy from the Sacrament to the king is highly illuminating. Once again, the God-made man was becoming the man-made God.

Such processions also provided occasions for the display of more traditional allegories. In the *cortège* of November 1437, people dressed as the Seven mortal sins and the Seven virtues rode, appropriately, behind the custodians of Justice – the councillors of the *Parlement* and members of the *Chambre des Requêtes*.[2] Of the scenes enacted in the *tableaux* along the route of the procession, most showed religious subjects – the Passion, Resurrection, Annunciation and the Baptism of Christ. But, beneath the gate of the *Châtelet*, the king was greeted by a *tableau* which strove – in a way which the chronicler does not make at all clear – to represent 'the *Lit-de-justice*, Divine Law, Natural Law and Human Law'.[3] More opportunity to the imagination was perhaps afforded by the groups on the other side of the gate. They depicted Judgement, Paradise, and Hell, with St Michael in their midst, weighing souls in his scales. Suitably edified, no doubt, by such scenes, the king arrived at the great West door of Notre Dame, where he was met by the clergy and the University of Paris. The *collaborateurs* among them were perhaps anxious to demonstrate their newly found loyalty to the house of Valois.[4] It was at four o'clock in the afternoon that the king dismounted from his horse before the closed doors of Notre Dame and took the oath to maintain the privileges of the Church. Touching the Gospels which the bishop of Paris held out to him, Charles said: 'As my predecessors have sworn it, I swear it.'[5] Having kissed the Gospels, received a sprinkling of holy water from the bishop, and kissed the Cross, the king was admitted to the cathedral. The organs and bells sounded, and an 'innumerable crowd' cried '*Noël! Noël!*' as the royal entourage entered. The king, suitably attired, prayed before the statue of the Virgin, venerated relics, and heard the children of the

[1] Guenée and Lehoux, 16–17, and Fig. 1.
[2] Ibid., 76.
[3] Ibid., 77.

[4] See above, 59–60, 67–8.
[5] Guenée and Lehoux, 85; 79–86 for these ceremonies.

choir sing the *Te Deum* in his honour. He then retired to the *Palais de la Cité*. The entry was over.

The pattern followed at Paris in 1437 served as a model for subsequent royal entries. Distinctions of degree, rather than of kind, marked off the ceremonies staged by the *bonnes villes*. On 2 March 1439 the king entered Limoges.[1] Although on a far less elaborate scale, the pattern of the ceremony at Paris two years previously was repeated. Charles 'found a fine canopy [*papilionem*] prepared, with his arms, which the consuls and burgesses of the said town carried; and the king was alone beneath it . . . and the people cried aloud *Noé, Noé, Noé!*'[2] As he had kissed the cross offered to him by the bishop of Paris, so he kissed the cross offered by the bishop of Limoges, before entering the great church of St-Martial. It is notable that the kind was alone granted the canopy – although accompanied by the dauphin Louis, that privilege was claimed by the burgesses only for the king. During his visit to the town, he venerated the head of St-Martial at the high altar, and then rode to the abbey of St-Martin, where he was shown other relics, including the shirt of Ste-Valérie. It was normal on such occasions for the king to be subjected to a sermon, or harangue, from a local ecclesiastical or secular dignitary. At Limoges, Charles heard one Master Martial Barmondet, consul of the town, on the subject of depredations by a local garrison. The Limousin chronicler recorded that he 'heard all of it freely and benignly, as did his council, promising to provide remedy within a short time'.[3] The town then supplied entertainment in the form of an archery contest (*trahentes de arbalista*) – the king's predilection for shooting at the popinjay was perhaps well known.[4]

A royal entry was also an occasion for gift-giving. At Lyon, in June 1434, the chapter of the primatial church of St-Jean intended to offer a lavish gift of six dozen torches, fifty pounds of spices, and three hundred measures of oats to Charles VII.[5] According to the receiver of the chapter, Hugues de Noyer, master of the king's household, told him to present only a small portion of the gift to the king. Noyer and the receiver had a brief audience with the king in his lodging. Charles thanked them for the gift, and retired to his chamber. At that very moment, the spices and torches were 'devoured' by the king's men. The rapacity of the household was notorious. Hugues de Noyer could remark to the receiver: 'Good

[1] Leroux, op. cit., 305–6.
[2] Ibid., 305.
[3] Ibid., 308, and cf. the sermons preached before him in B.N. MS. lat. 6020 (see Plate 5).

[4] Ibid., 309; Beaucourt, IV, 86; Grandeau, *BPH* (1967), 840, for Charles VI's children playing at 'papegaut' in their early years.
[5] Guenée and Lehoux, 157.

host, see what would have become of your gift if you'd brought it all!'[1]
But perhaps he had designs on the gift himself. Whatever the case really
was, the chapter's gift cost them over 80 francs, excluding sixty of the
measures of oats. Gifts also went to the chancellor – capons, geese and
chickens – and to the archbishop of Vienne. The ancient custom of giving
hospitality to the king and his officers was evidently not yet dead. At
Lyon, the Church also supplied part of the king's costume as he entered
St-Jean. The *biretta* which he wore was paid for by the chapter, and, as
was customary, he wore priest's vestments in which to enter the church
and pray before the high altar.[2] The mounted figure of the *miles Christi*
was thus transformed into that of the *sacerdos*, in cap, amice, cowl and cope.

A number of pictorial representations of Charles VII's entries survive.
During the campaign for the reconquest of Guyenne in the summer of
1442, the king entered his loyal town of Toulouse. An illumination in the
communal register for that year depicts him riding under a canopy carried by eight of the *capitouls* (town councillors).[3] He holds a *bâton* in his
left hand, is preceded by the communal banner, and followed by the
dauphin. Again, the king alone rides beneath the canopy, which is
adorned with shields bearing the *fleurs-de-lys*. Another illumination, in
the *Chronicles* of Monstrelet, shows a somewhat schematic version of the
next important entry of the reign – into a newly recovered Rouen in
1449.[4] The king is shown in full armour, wearing a hat crowned with
fleurs-de-lys, receiving the keys of the town from the *échevins*. The accounts
of the entry into Rouen are not entirely consistent. An eye-witness
account, now in the *Bibliothèque Municipale* at Poitiers, does not quite
tally with that given by Monstrelet.[5] But the ceremony was, in almost all
essentials, the same as those which have already been described. In one
respect, however, there is an innovation. Guillaume Jouvenel des Ursins,
chancellor of France, rode in the procession. Before him, a riderless white
hackney was led, with the king's great seal on its high saddle.[6] The concept of 'twin-born majesty' was given further tangible expression by this
device. The king's seal – the emblem of undying authority – was separated

[1] Guenée and Lehoux, 158.
[2] Ibid., 157. For his wearing of vestments
on other occasions see above, 43; also
Lewis, op. cit., 81, for the king's
coronation tunic 'in the fashion of a tunic
that a sub-deacon wears when he serves at
Mass' and his mantle which was to be
'raised on the left, as one raises the
chasuble of a priest'. Cf. Bloch, 482, and
above, 197 n. 7. Also Plate 9.

[3] Guenée and Lehoux reproduce this as
Fig. 129.
[4] B.N. MS. fr. 2679, fol. 322ᵛ, and
Guenée and Lehoux, frontispiece.
[5] MS. 267, fols 2ᵛ–3ᵛ. Printed in Guenée
and Lehoux, 160–2. Cf. Godefroy,
Cérémonial, I, 659–62.
[6] Guenée and Lehoux, 160–1; Godefroy,
I, 660.

from the mortal king. Charles VII's presence was no doubt all too cor-
poreal. But the ungainly figure in armour (to which it was not accustomed) was merely one of the king's two bodies. The seal symbolised
the *corpus mysticum* of the kingdom. It was an assertion of the undying
quality of the State.

To those of the English and their recent suporters among the Normans
who witnessed the procession, the meaning of such devices must have been
obvious. A victorious Valois monarchy was asserting its inalienable
sovereignty over the duchy of Normandy, as it was to do, by an identical
practice, over its duchy of Guyenne in June 1451.[1] From a window above
the route, the *cortège* was viewed by Talbot and other English hostages.
They were, wrote Monstrelet, 'very pensive and down at heart' as they
looked on at the *mystère* enacted before them.[2] For its splendour, the
entry to Rouen outdid the entry to Paris in 1437. At the head of the procession were the archers of the king's guard, clad in their livery of red, white
and green. With them marched the archers of René of Anjou, wearing
their livery of grey, white and black. Monstrelet reckoned that there
were six hundred archers in the procession.[3] Behind them came the
heralds, trumpeters and minstrels – sounding their instruments as they do
in illuminations of previous royal and imperial entries. Next came the
king's seal, followed by the chancellor in his red robe, trimmed with fur –
a bulky figure. An esquire of the stable called Pierre Fontenil rode behind
Guillaume Jouvene, holding the king's cloak. Behind him was Poton de
Xaintrailles, *grand écuyer*, bearing the sword *Joyeuse*. The king's appearance was thus carefully prepared. He rode on a horse covered with cloth
of gold, sewn with *fleurs-de-lys*. He wore plate armour, and, at the Porte
Beauvoisine, was met by three or four hundred burgesses, all dressed in
blue, with red hoods. They 'offered to the king their bodies and goods',
and presented the keys to him in the presence of the count of Dunois, his
lieutenant, and the chancellor. Pierre de Brézé, seneschal of Poitou, was
entrusted with them by the king. The clergy had gathered to revere the
king outside the town walls, and the *échevins* had been careful to hang the
Porte Beauvoisine, through which the king entered, with *fleurs-de-lys* and
the king's livery colours.

He received the keys, and, as at Paris, the four burgesses bearing the
canopy moved into position. Four esquires of the stable took the four

---

[1] See *Bordeaux sous les Rois d'Angleterre*,
ed. Y. Renouard (Bordeaux, 1965), 513.
[2] Godefroy, I, 662.

[3] Ibid., 659. See also Martial d'Auvergne,
Vigilles, I, 70, and my article, 'The livery
colours of Charles VII in two works by
Fouquet', *GBA*, lxxiv (1969), 243–8.

corners of his horse-cloth – a practice which was to some extent paralleled
in the funeral ceremony.[1] The *cortège* moved slowly through the streets of
Rouen towards the cathedral of Notre Dame. Behind the king rode Jean
Havart, bearing his pennon with three *fleurs-de-lys*, and he was followed
by the great magnates of France. After them came the king's pages, the
grand maître Culant, and Rogerin Blosset, who bore the king's standard.
At the rear of the procession came the companies of *ordonnance*, to the
number of two or three hundred lances. Along the route the images of
submission were presented by the burgesses. Over one doorway was a
tableau showing the Church, the burgesses, the nobles and the common
people who presented to the king a woman, signifying the town of Rouen,
kneeling with her hands clasped.[2] Near the cathedral there was a contrivance consisting of a winged stag, worked by two girls, which had a
crown around its neck. This fantastic beast 'knelt . . . before the king as
he passed by'.[3] One of the solemn emblems of Valois monarchy had been
appropriated and vulgarised as if for a carnival or *Kermesse*. But the
ceremony at which it appeared may have shared the atmosphere, as well
as the audience, of a mystery play and a popular pageant. In this sense,
French monarchy of the fifteenth century was dramatised. It had become a
part of the popular theatre.

There were other, less public, occasions on which the king's appearance
was carefully prepared. A seventeenth-century writer could speak of the
royal *lit-de-justice* in the following terms: 'one sees *Lex et Rex* reposing
under the canopy . . . sees them together on that bed of Justice'.[4] By the
early fifteenth century the *lit-de-justice* had become the most solemn
assembly of the *Parlement* of Paris. It was a plenary session of the sovereign
court, convened to mark some especially formal occasion. Since the first
issue of *lettres de jussion* (letters of coercion) in 1392, the ceremony had
been used by the king as a means whereby the *Parlement*'s right of remonstrance against unwelcome legislation could be over-ruled.[5] It was the
only occasion in the court's procedure over which the king presided in
person. A *lit-de-justice* might be convened on a second occasion – that of
the trial of a great magnate or peer of France. Such an occasion took
place in October 1458, when Jean II, duke of Alençon, was tried for
treason at a series of plenary sessions of the *Parlement* which were held at
Vendôme.[6] With the presidents, counsellors, advocates and notaries of the

[1] Below, 211–12.
[2] Guenée and Lehoux, 162.
[3] Godefroy, I, 662.
[4] Quoted in Kantorowicz, op. cit., 414.

[5] J. H. Shennan, *The Parlement of Paris*
(London, 1968), 161.
[6] See above, 154–62; Chastellain, III,
466–90.

Parlement sat the lords spiritual and temporal. Their presence was essential when one of their number was on trial. Fortunately a visual as well as a written record of this assembly exists. In an illumination, attributed to Jean Fouquet, which forms the frontispiece to a manuscript of Boccaccio's *De casibus virorum illustrium*, the scene at Vendôme is set.[1] The manuscript – a French translation by Laurent de Premierfait – was completed on 24 November 1458. It was commissioned, so the argument runs, by Laurens Girard, controller of finances, notary and secretary to Charles VII.[2] He had replaced Master Etienne Chevalier as controller in 1453, and lived on to serve Louis XI as controller of the *argenterie* from 1463 to 1464. His manuscript is prefaced by a frontispiece which was both apt and topical. A treatise on the fall of famous men and women – Adam, Eve, Nimrod, Samson, the daughters of Cadmus, Meleager, Agamemnon, Dido, Saul, Manlius Capitolinus, Jugurtha, Hannibal, Mithridates, the Templars and Filippa la Catanese – thus begins with an allusion to an event of the very recent past. It was an event of which a civil servant such as Laurens Girard might have approved.

The artist opens a window upon the scene. Chastellain's written record bears out the visual image:

> So was the hall where the king sat richly furbished and arranged with benches and seats covered with *fleurs-de-lys*, and where they were all sitting according to order and degree. My lord Charles of France [was there] and between him and the king was a vacant seat laid aside for the king's eldest son, the dauphin, who was not there. After [him] were the other dukes and counts just as they should sit in the correct order according to their peerage; then the bishops and the prelates; the chancellor of France sitting at the king's feet, then all the members of the *Parlement* in their appointed place, and all those employed in the *Parlement*, that is, the *maîtres des requêtes*, advocates, secretaries; a multitude of high and noble barons in their appointed places, such as the two marshals of France, the admiral, the *grand sénéchal* of Normandy, the lord of Torcy, the count of Dammartin, and many others like them, of whom the number is far too great to name them all. The hall was made public and open to all to go in and to hear the king's sentence....[3]

The sentence was in fact given on 10 October, and the illumination shows some point during one of the later sessions of the trial. The king

[1] Munich, Bayerische Staatsbibliothek, Codex Gall. 369, fol. 2ᵛ. See Plate 10

[2] P. Durrieu, *Le Boccace de Munich* (Munich, 1909), 14–15.

[3] Chastellain, III, 477.

sits 'en son siège royal' at one angle of the chamber.[1] He is enthroned on a dais, under a canopy or *pavillon*, both of which are covered with blue cloth sewn with gold *fleurs-de-lys*. A prodigious expenditure of such cloth was required, for the benches around the enclosure, and its floor, are also covered with it. Since the early fourteenth century this had been normal for royal *lits-de-justice* whether they were held in the *Grande Salle* of the Paris *Parlement* or elsewhere. The walls of the chamber are hung with great tapestries. They, like the painted border which frames the scene, are composed of alternating vertical bands of red, white and green, sewn with roses. Here the juxtaposition of the king's personal livery colours with the cloth of *fleurs-de-lys* is perhaps a telling one. It could be argued that the concept of the king as a great, though mortal, prince – expressed by his livery colours – is here offset by that of the king as the immortal embodiment of the undying Crown. Dressed in a blue robe, the king seems almost to merge into the blue drapery of the throne. King and Crown are as one.

The scene represented by the painter was not unprecedented in French art. In 1372 an Augustinian canon, Jean Corbechon, presented his book called *Les propriétés des choses* to Charles V.[2] In an illumination he is shown giving the book to the king who sits enthroned under a canopy, in the angle of a square enclosure. To his right sits the constable du Guesclin, to his left the chancellor Jean de Dormans. The existence of an earlier example than the manuscript of 1458 of this manner of representing the king at a plenary session of the *Parlement* imust make one think again about the convention within which the artst was working. There was nothing novel about the stylistic device which he adopted.[3] But he innovates in one respect. The depiction of the trial scene is in no way schematic. It is faithful to the event in a meticulous way. It supplies a portrait gallery of the politically powerful of mid-fifteenth-century France and an almost photographic image of the king in circumstances of the greatest solemnity. The figures of king, chancellor and constable are iconic. *Rex*, *Lex* and military power form the central triangle of the composition to which the eye is inexorably led.

If, as contemporaries believed, 'Justice . . . is the principal member of his Crown, by which he reigns and has lordship', then the presentation of the instruments of the king's justice on such occasions was of the greatest significance.[4] Both the chancellor, Guillaume Jouvenel des Ursins, and the

[1] Godefroy, II, 448.

[2] See B. de Montfaucon, *Monumens de la Monarchie Française* (Paris, 1734), III, pl. viii.

[3] Cf. O. Pächt, 'Jean Fouquet: a study of his style', *JWCI*, iv (1940–1), 92.

[4] *Chroniques des règnes de Jean II et de Charles V*, ed. R. Delachenal (*SHF*, Paris, 1910), I, 343.

first *président* of the *Parlement*, Pierre de Scépeaux, are similarly dressed in the painting. They wear scarlet robes lined with miniver, with three bands of white fur trimmed with gold on their shoulders. This was the *bouton d'or*, alleged to descend from the pendants of the Roman imperial *fibula*, or shoulder-clasp.[1] The purple (i.e. red) robe and the *bouton d'or* may thus have alluded to two of the 'four insignia of imperial majesty', the others being the sceptre and the diadem. The other members of the *Parlement* are less splendidly attired. They sit on the lower benches, wearing green, blue, pink and violet robes, with lined miniver capes and hoods. Some wear the black *pileus*, or *mortier*, which was to become the distinctive mark of a member of a *Parlement* in *ancien régime* France.[2] The iconography of the law, as well as of the Crown, was beginning to formalise.

Identification of the other individuals shown in the illumination is not easy. The surviving accounts of the *assiette*, or seating-plan, at Vendôme in October 1458 do not always tally with the artist's depiction of the scene.[3] The closest similarity yet found is with a contemporary manuscript list headed 'The seating-plan made in the *Parlement* assembled and held at Vendôme for the ending of the trial of my lord of Alençon'.[4] It is reproduced, with slight differences, in a second manuscript,[5] and one can work from both of these sources to try to establish the identity of the persons represented. On the king's right hand, at a suitably measured distance, sits Charles of France, twelve years old, in the absence of the exiled dauphin. Next to him, at an appropriate distance, sit the lords temporal: Charles of Orléans, poet and ex-prisoner, aged fifty-one; Jean II, duke of Bourbon, aged about thirty-one; Charles of Anjou, count of Maine, aged about forty-four; the count of Eu, an elderly man of sixty-five; and, in front of them, the counts of Angoulême and La Marche. The two figures at the extreme left of the row are probably Gaston IV, count of Foix, and the count of Vendôme. Below them, on the second row, sit the three *présidents* of the Parlement, some household officers, and the four *maîtres des requêtes*. The lay councillors of the *Parlement* occupy the third row of benches. On the king's left hand sit the lords spiritual. In the back row, from the left, Jean Juvenal des Ursins, archbishop of Rheims and first ecclesiastical peer of France; the bishops of Laon, Langres, Noyon, Chalons, Beauvais, Paris, Viviers, Agde and Coutances (who

[1] Kantorowicz, op. cit., 415–17; W. N. Hargreaves–Mawdsley, *A History of Legal Dress in Europe* (Oxford, 1963), 21–3.
[2] Ibid., 20–2.
[3] See Godefroy, II, 441–9.

[4] B.N. MS. fr. 5943, fols 33ᵛ–34ʳ.
[5] B.N. MS. fr. 5738, fols 17ʳ–19ʳ. Both contain contemporary documents relating to the trial.

played a leading role in the prosecution of Alençon), and, lastly, the abbot of St-Denis, in his black hood and cowl. In the next row, from the left, sit more of the king's household officers and courtiers: the lords of La Tour d'Auvergne, of Torcy (*maître des arbalétriers*), of Vauvert (*premier chambellan*), the *bailli* of Touraine, the lords of Prie and Précigny, the *bailli* of Rouen and the lord of Quars. On the next bench sit (at right-angles to the lords spiritual) the civil servants: Jean Bureau, *trésorier*, Etienne Chevalier, *trésorier*, Pierre d'Oriole, *général des finances*, Pierre de Reffuge, *général*, Tristan l'Hermite, *prévôt des maréchaux*, and the *prévôt* of the household. Below all these sit the clerical counsellors of the *Parlement*, each according to his degree. On the lowest benches sit the advocates and proctors of the king, and, in the centre of the scene, his no-taries. The figure to their left, wearing a beaver hat, with arms folded, has been identified as Jean duke of Alençon himself. If this is correct, the scene cannot be the reading of the sentence against Alençon, because he was not present at the end of the trial. Outside the enclosure stand the crowd, trying to gain a glimpse of the proceedings, one of them caught in the act of being arrested by one of the king's *huissiers* who guard the chamber.

In the event, Alençon was condemned, not to death, but to life im-prisonment. Charles's reply to the Burgundian ambassadors who pleaded for mercy was exemplified by his action. 'Kings', he observed through the bishop of Coutances, 'reign through Justice . . . and if there were no good Justice of kings and princes, kingdoms and lordships would be merely dens of thieves.'[1] Charles of Orléans had also spoken in Alençon's favour. His modest disclaimer of learning was hardly borne out by his speech, which contained many Scriptural and other learned allusions. He com-pared his relationship to the king with that of a dog 'at the feet of his master', who would 'always remain loyal' in that master's obedience.[2] He told Charles VII in his speech to the assembly at Vendôme:

When I ponder deeply on what this word 'sovereign' means, it must be some great thing. For you are only a man as I am, of flesh and blood, subject to the hazards, perils, adversities, illnesses and tribulations of this world as I am, and as we all are . . . but . . . for a long time past none of your predecessors have had the kingdom so entirely in their hands as you have it. And when I consider whence comes this word 'sovereign' I see clearly that it must come from the sovereign place, that is, God, who is sovereign over all. . . . And you are called 'very Christian king', whom He has sent to be lieutenant in the kingdom of France, and

[1] B.N. MS. fr. 5738, fol. 10ᵛ.   [2] B.N. MS. fr. 1104, fol. 49ʳ.

representative of his presence, by reason of which all Frenchmen are bound to serve, obey and advise you loyally. . . .[1]

It was a statement of God-given kingship which would not have sounded out of place on the lips of Joan of Arc. The doctrine of sovereignty and subjection was not a notion introduced by Louis XI. But the prerogative of Justice was accompanied by that of Mercy. Orléans recalled 'a treatise which I once saw in a book' where it was said that God has two courts – one of Justice, the other of Mercy.[2] He cited the case of David, who put Mercy before Justice in the Psalm. Alençon and his ancestors had loyally served the Crown, and Orléans appealed to the king's conscience. The Burgundian ambassadors at Vendôme similarly played upon the concepts of Justice and Mercy. They cited Justinian, Policratus and Seneca on the subject, and stressed the proximity of lineage between the king and Alençon. In his speech of 14 September 1458, Jean l'Orfèvre, *président* of Luxembourg and proctor of Burgundy, pleaded for clemency.[3] He littered his discourse with classical and biblical allusions, but more than hinted that if such trials continued there would be no telling where they might stop. It would be as if there was a witch-hunt among the nobility. One senses the depth of Burgundian apprehension in the speech, which was delivered at a time of 'cold war' between France and Burgundy.[4] After Alençon, would Philip the Good himself be the next to suffer? The treason trial, realised in the form of a *lit-de-justice*, was becoming the formal expression of the king's control over his nobility. Louis XI had good precedent for his elimination of the constable St-Pol.

The few who were privileged to witness the king at a *lit-de-justice*, in which they themselves also participated, appeared again in the most solemn ceremony of all – the king's funeral. The facts of this elaborate and protracted event are known from a number of sources – the chroniclers, especially Mathieu d'Escouchy, and the surviving account which was rendered for its cost by Tanneguy du Chastel, first esquire of the stable.[5] A total sum of over 18,200 *livres tournois* was spent on the lavish series of ceremonies. On 22 July 1461 Charles VII had died at the castle of

[1] Ibid., fol. 49ʳ.
[2] Ibid., fol. 49ᵛ.
[3] See B.N. MS. fr. 5738, fols 1ʳ–8ʳ; Chastellain, III, 468–71.
[4] See above, 170–2; Vaughan, *Philip the Good*, 351–2.
[5] Printed in *ABSHF*, cxxiv (1864),

178–98; R. E. Giesey, *The Royal Funerary Ceremony in Renaissance France* (Geneva, 1960), and Kantorowicz, op. cit., 409–37, for discussion of these funeral ceremonies. Tanneguy was nephew of the king's former servant.

Mehun-sur-Yèvre, where he had been first acclaimed king in October 1422. The first task among the preparations had, by its nature, to be done quickly. Over two weeks were to elapse between the king's death and his entombment in St-Denis. His corpse was thus eviscerated by Jean Rousseau and Jean Moreau, barber-surgeons, and the entrails put into a special vessel.[1] A shroud of cloth of Troyes was made. The death mask was taken, and one Pierre Hennes was dispatched from Bourges to Paris with an impression of it. He was to seek out 'Fouquet the painter', who was to colour it so that it could be used for the king's effigy, to be carried in the cortège which was to enter Paris.[2] A leaden coffin weighing 390 pounds was meanwhile made at Bourges. This was sealed with plaster, bound with thongs, lined with grey cloth, and placed in a wooden outer coffin.[3]

Since 1327 it had been customary in England to bear a life-like effigy of the king during the royal funerary ceremony. This practice was adopted in France as a result of the proclamation of the Lancastrian double monarchy in 1422.[4] There were, once again, two bodies carried in this royal ceremony. Both were dressed in the appropriate royal vestments – the robe (manteau), dalmatic (diacre) and shoes (cendales or houssetes). Charles VII wore the blue robe sewn with fleurs-de-lys spun from gold wire of Florence and Cyprus. He wore the crown, and carried the sceptre and main-de-justice, both of silver gilt except for their staves. The regalia were thus buried with him. The whole process was duplicated so that the visible effigy might be properly presented to the people. A second crown, garnished with jewels, a sceptre and main-de-justice were therefore provided by Jean Sevineau, the king's goldsmith. The effigy was placed on a cart, covered with a great black hood bearing a white velvet cross and nine shields of France, embroidered in blue and gold. The cart was open at each end, so that one could see the effigy as it passed on the journey from Mehun-sur-Yèvre to Paris. Behind it rode some of the king's nearest relatives, including Charles of Orléans, with the household officers and servants on foot, weeping and dressed in mourning.

The cortège reached Paris on the evening of Wednesday 5 August, and the king's body was to be placed in the church of Notre-Dame-des-Champs, in the faubourg of the city. As it approached its first resting-place, one hundred people bearing tapers assembled outside the church. A further 160 mourners carrying candles came out of the city to join the

[1] ABSHF, cxxiv (1864), 179.
[2] Ibid., 180.
[3] Ibid., 181. For the description which follows I have used this source and the

account by Mathieu d'Escouchy in Escouchy, II, 422–44.
[4] Kantorowicz, op. cit., 419–21.

11 Last surviving letter of Charles VII, signed in his own hand, 15 May 1461. It concerns the sending of Odet d'Aydie, *bailli* of Cotentin, with instructions on the recovery of Genoa, to the king's officers there (*Beaucourt*, VI, Pl. VI)

12a Tomb of Charles VII and Marie of Anjou (now destroyed) in the abbey of St-Denis, Paris (*Bodleian Library, Oxford, MS. Gough, Gaignières 2, fol. 45*)

12b Bust of Charles VII from his tomb in St-Denis (*Musée du Louvre, Paris*)

cortège and escort it as far as the church. Before the effigy rode one of the king's *huissiers*, carrying his coat of arms, a horse bearing his sceptre, and a man on foot carrying a *bâton*. The hooded cart was drawn by five great horses decked out in black horse-cloths which reached to the ground, led by five grooms. Of the horses, only the eyes, muzzles and feet could be seen. Between the effigy and the king's mortal body, which followed in a second cart, were the lords who had escorted it from Mehun, and six pages, dressed in black mourning robes, mounted on horses similarly caparisoned. The separation between the king's two bodies was thus preserved. As the procession reached the *faubourg*, outside the city walls, Anthoine Viguier, prior of the church of Notre-Dame-des-Champs, led a large company of clergy to meet and receive the king's corpse. The coffin was lowered on to a bier with three wheels, and, flanked by four great candles, the body lay in state for the night as vigils were kept.

These observances were merely the prelude to the more elaborate ceremonies of the next day. At eleven o'clock on the morning of Thursday 6 August the town criers of Paris, in mourning, with shields of France on the front and back of their robes, went through the streets, crying:

> Say your *paternosters* for the very high and very excellent prince King Charles, seventh of that name; and, at three o'clock, come to the vigils, in the church of Notre Dame of Paris.[1]

The procession began to assemble for the entry to Paris. The first to arrive at Notre-Dame-des-Champs were the lords of the blood, the courtiers and household officers. Then came the provost of Paris, with most of the counsellors and advocates of the court of the *Châtelet*, all on foot, escorted by the serjeants of the court. After them came the members of the *Parlement*, preceded by six *huissiers* dressed in scarlet, bearing their maces. The four *présidents* wore their scarlet robes, followed, two by two, by the counsellors and advocates of the court, similarly dressed. Behind them were the *échevins* of Paris, the counsellors of the *Chambre des Comptes*, the indigent poor from the *Hôtel-Dieu*, and two hundred paupers dressed in mourning, carrying two hundred tapers, each weighing three or four pounds, embellished with two shields of France. Then there were fourteen or so blind men, walking two by two, dressed in black, each with a *fleur-de-lys* embroidered on the front of their robes, helped on their way by guides. The sixty-four men who were to carry the coffin and effigy then arrived, and, with the arrival of the clergy in force, bearing crosses from the churches, the *cortège* was complete.

[1] Escouchy, II, 428.

C—H

At five o'clock the procession began its slow progress to Notre Dame. The mendicants went first, followed by the two hundred paupers with their tapers. Then came the parishes of Paris with their clergy. After them the criers of Paris, sounding their bells, followed by more clergy, on the left side of the street, chanting, and, on the right, the University. Louis de Harcourt, bishop of Bayeux, and the rector of the University walked behind them. Surrounded by his serjeants, the provost of Paris came next, preceding four heralds-at-arms, clad in black velvet. Around the king's corpse marched the members of the *Parlement*, privileged, as representatives of Justice, to be nearest to the king's body. Bearing the great weight of the leaden coffin, surmounted by the effigy, the porters – invisible save for their feet – performed their traditional task. The funeral pall of cloth of gold and blue velvet, sewn with great *fleurs-de-lys*, was held at each corner by the four *présidents* of the *Parlement*. At royal entries, the four corners of the king's horse-cloth had been held by four esquires of his stable. Now the instruments of Justice stressed judicial continuity by their proximity to the effigy representing undying kingship. On the pall lay the effigy itself, a masterpiece of realistic portraiture, according to Mathieu d'Escouchy.[1] It was crowned, wore a robe of violet silk, with sleeves 'in the ancient manner, very large', over which the royal vestments were borne. The 'great royal habit' was sewn with *fleur-de-lys*, and lined with ermine. Over the effigy was carried the canopy 'as one carries it over the *Corpus Christi*'.[2] The six poles were held by the king's proctor at the *Châtelet* 'and others', and the canopy was carried a little behind the effigy, so that the people could see the king's likeness better.

Immediately behind this centre-piece, the aged Charles of Orléans, weeping copiously, rode on a little mule led by two men. He led the princes of Deep Mourning, who were followed by the royal household *en masse*. Finally, the empty cart in which the king's coffin had been carried from Mehun brought up the rear of the *cortège*. Once inside Notre Dame, vigils began to be said for the king. His body was placed in a small wooden 'chapel', painted black, and surrounded with candles. Orléans, Angoulême, Eu, Dunois and other great lords were present for the vigils. The church was hung with cloth bearing the *fleurs-de-lys*, its high altar was draped in black, and shields of the arms of France were affixed to the pillars. The expenditure on tapers and candles was prodigious. Even the prolix Mathieu d'Escouchy claimed that 'no man could have written about it'.[3] At six in the morning of Friday 7 August the

[1] Escouchy, II, 432.   [3] Ibid., 437.
[2] Ibid., 433.

bells of Notre Dame began to toll, under the supervision of Master
Nicholas Conne. Between eight and nine the *Grande Messe des Morts*
commenced, at which five of the higher clergy of France officiated in the
choir. The offertory was brought, first, by the king's four heralds. Then
Charles of Orléans was helped to the 'chapel' where the king's body lay,
and made his obeisance. Master Jean de Châteaufort then preached a
sermon on the text: *Memento judicii mei, Domine* – a relevant theme, given
the large number of the king's lawyers who were present in the choir of
Notre Dame that morning. At the end of the Requiem, as the lords departed,
prayers were said by the clergy over the body. Throughout the day, no less
than 275 chaplains each celebrated a mass for the king's soul in Notre Dame.

At half-past ten the preparations for the next stage in the king's last
journey began. Since 1271, when St Louis's remains had been brought to
the vigils in Notre Dame, the kings of France had then been carried in
funerary pomp across Paris to the abbey of St-Denis.[1] It was a distance of
five miles. To carry the weighty coffin and catafalque on foot for that
distance was no mean achievement. The task was apparently performed in
relays, by the twenty-four *hanouars* (or salt-porters, accustomed to bearing
great weight on their backs) of Paris.[2] But in August 1461 even they
could not do the job without assistance. A further forty porters were
enlisted. There were a number of resting-places along the route, at which
crosses had been set up. The first of these was on the *Pont des Changeurs*,
which linked the Ile-de-la-Cité to the right bank of the Seine. Here the
hanouars handed over their charge to the salt-carriers of the rue St-Denis,
together with their robes of mourning. The *hanouars* were surly, troublesome men, who demanded not only payment, but food, gifts and the
privilege of bearing off the funeral pall of cloth of gold on which the
king's effigy lay. In 1422, at the funeral of Charles VI, they claimed it, but
it was granted to the monks of St-Denis, after an altercation which
threatened to disrupt the ceremony.[3] In 1461 they proved less tiresome to
the authorities. But they had their revenge on the monks of St-Denis. As
the procession came to the place at which the jurisdiction of the city of
Paris gave way to that of the abbey of St-Denis, the salt-carriers put down
their burden. The corpse and effigy was laid on two trestles, and the monks
of the abbey attempted to put their rights into practice by carrying it
through their jurisdiction. But so heavy was the whole cumbersome
apparatus that they could not lift it. A dispute broke out, and Dunois was
forced to intervene, commanding the *hanouars* to take up the load once

[1] Giesey, op. cit., 35–7.   [3] Ibid., 33, 64.
[2] For them see Giesey, op. cit., 33–4, 64–5.

more and carry it the remaining distance to St-Denis. This they did, as they had done in 1422, but not without compensation. The monks of St-Denis were obliged to pay the twenty-four porters 'for having carried the said late lord to burial through the jurisdiction of the same monks, and also for having carried the said corpse through many other places and boundaries which they were not obliged to do'.[1] The *hanouars* had exacted their revenge.

So long had the *cortège* taken to reach St-Denis, having left Notre Dame at three o'clock in the afternoon, that it was dark by the time it arrived. It was too late for vigils, so prayers and responses were said over the corpse. Once again, the coffin was placed in a 'chapel' of mourning. The nave of the church was hung with black satin, with blue cloth sewn with *fleurs-de-lys* above it. The king's painters – Jacob de Littemont, Colin d'Asnières and Pierre Hennes – had been at work on the decorations for both Notre Dame and St-Denis. *In toto*, they had produced no less than 750 small shields of France, 350 larger shields and 125 very large shields for both churches. Jean de Monbuxon, a painter living at Bourges, had contributed a further 15 large and 150 smaller shields. The larger shields were hung on the pillars of the churches, the smaller were fixed to the tapers which the weepers bore, and to the candles with which the churches were festooned. At St-Denis, there were 55 great torches around the body, which was flanked at each corner by enormous candles, each weighing twenty pounds. A further four great candles were placed around the open grave. Thirty-eight candles were distributed over the altar of the 'corps sains', the altar 'in front of king Dagobert's tomb', and to the children who processed before the clergy. Seven hundred torches were set up in the church, and a double rank of 2,300 tapers ran around its walls, pillars and chapels. The black draperies, the flickering tapers, and the gilded *fleurs-de-lys* combined to produce a scenario just as impressive to the spectator as that at Notre Dame.

The final Requiem began at eight on the morning of Saturday 8 August. Master Thomas de Courcelles, the former *collaborateur*, allegedly moved the congregation to tears by his sermon.[2] Once the Requiem was at an end, the burial itself could at last take place. The coffin was lowered into the vault, while the king's chamberlains pulled off the cloth of gold, 'to prevent the people from seeing it'.[3] For a space of thirty minutes prayers

[1] *ABSHF*, cxxvii (1964), 189. But in the event the cost was met by Tanneguy du Chastel; Giesey, op. cit., 64.
[2] See above, 68.

[3] Escouchy, II, 443. The cloth had been disputed between the *hanouars* and the monks of St-Denis at Charles VI's funeral in 1422 (Giesey, op. cit., 33).

were said, to the accompaniment of weeping from the spectators. The premier herald – Berry – then cried aloud: 'Hear ye!' But the prayers were not yet over, and the Church was allowed even longer in which to discharge its duties. As the bishop of Bayeux threw earth into the tomb, the herald cried, weeping all the while: 'Pray for the soul of the very excellent, very powerful and very victorious prince, King Charles, seventh of that name.'[1] It was the first time on which the epithet 'the very victorious' was formally used. He laid his staff of office on the tomb-chest, and, after enough time had elapsed for a *Pater Noster* to be said, he took it up again. The cry 'Long live King Louis!' was given, and was taken up by the king's secretaries. Then the *huissiers* and royal serjeants threw their maces and *bâtons* into the tomb. It was a symbolic act. With the king's burial, the household was disbanded. It is from the funeral of Charles VII that the first evidence of this practice is derived. After the dinner which followed the last Requiem, the first chamberlain addressed the household. He said that 'he and all the other servants had lost their master, and that every man must think for himself, and each one should provide for himself'.[2] Martial d'Auvergne echoed his words: the household was no more, and, in the circumstances of 1461, its members had no guarantee whatsoever that they would be retained by the new king. The very body which had played so conspicuous a part in the funeral ceremonies had no claim to immortality.

Yet the king had such a claim. It was expressed throughout these ceremonies. The king's successor was not present at them, because the fiction was maintained that the dead king was still alive. The notion that 'the King never dies' was, perhaps, contained in the last cry which the herald made over Charles VII's mortal remains. Though lacking the impersonality of the later formula: 'The King is dead: long live the King!', the notion of perpetuity in the dignity of kingship seems to underlie the herald's cry.[3] Dynastic continuity was also presumed by such a practice. Louis XI did not need to be crowned before he was recognised as king. The coronation no longer 'made' the king in the fifteenth century. Hence the funerary ceremony became all-important. It was perhaps the most dramatic of the ceremonies in which the king – or his likeness – was displayed to the people. As with all such public occasions, it was apt to be a victim of the more anarchic aspects of human nature. The behaviour of

---

[1] Escouchy, II, 443; Godefroy, *Chartier*, 320, 480.
[2] Chartier, III, 120; Giesey, op. cit., 74, 76.

[3] Guenée, *L'Occident*, 87; Kantorowicz, op. cit., 412. The impersonal cry was established in France at the funeral of Louis XII in 1515.

the *hanouars* was always unpredictable. At one point in the solemnities of Charles VII's funeral, the old Adam broke through the constraint of that highly formal ceremony. It was customary for alms to be given to the poor on the day of the king's burial at St-Denis. Each indigent pauper was to receive 10*d. tournois* outside the abbey. In the event, although 300*l. tournois* had been set aside for the purpose, only 50 *livres* were actually distributed on the day. As the paupers gathered to extend their palms towards this source of bounty, a band of roughnecks broke through their ranks and tried to seize the alms.[1] They mobbed and terrorised the paupers, and the remaining 250 *livres* were withdrawn. These were then given to the provost and *échevins* of Paris, to be distributed to the inmates of the *Hôtel-Dieu*, to poor widows, pregnant women, unmarried girls and other needy people. The king's soul would then, it was thought, be more assured of salvation.

The desire to present the king in the ways which have been described was, it has been argued, inseparable from fifteenth-century assumptions about the office and mystique of kingship. These essays in dramatised political theology impressed an image of divine and legitimate monarchy upon the spectator. The king was king by the grace of God, he was the vicar of God, and, above all, he was seen under a canopy 'as one carries it over the *Corpus Christi*'. Anointed, crowned, endowed with therapeutic powers, ruling with his sceptre and doing Justice with his *main-de-justice*, Charles VII was undoubtedly seen by his subjects as the incarnation of sanctified kingship. Those who denied this might have to pay dearly for their mockery of his right. The aged Jean Batiffol of Bialon, who denied the king's legitimacy in June 1457, was let off with a pardon. 'The king is king,' he said, 'but he ought not to be king, because he's not of the royal line; for when he was born, he didn't bear the royal birthmark [*enseigne*], and didn't have the *fleur-de-lys* like a true king'.[2] But Jean Batiffol was very old, and very drunk. Others cast doubts on the king's powers when not in their cups. A certain Henri Payot, blacksmith, living at Persay-le-Petit, in the *bailliage* of Sens, brought his sister to Langres, where the king was, to be touched for the scrofula.[3] The king's men who examined her claimed that she was not suffering from the disease. Henri Payot had suffered from the wars, as Jean Batiffol and his drinking friends had suffered from taxation. He cursed the king and queen, calling them fools. But he was let off with a pardon at Romorantin on 23 October 1454.

[1] *ABSHF*, cxxvii (1864), 196.
[2] Quoted in Bloch, op. cit., 250. See A. Thomas, 'Le "signe royal" et le secret de Jeanne d'Arc', *RH*, ciii (1910), 278-82, and above, 51-2.
[3] Bloch, op. cit., 96 n. 1.

He no doubt paid a fee for it. On the morrow of the victory over the English, there were, perhaps, fewer people who had to be convinced of the birth and sanctity of their Valois sovereign. If there were such – in Normandy and Gascony – a royal ceremony might serve to allay their fears.

To mock or deride the king's sovereignty was becoming increasingly dangerous. Jean Batiffol was evidently informed upon by his supposed friends. Treason was less easily masked under the cloak of legitimate choice between rival allegiances after the expulsion of the English in 1453. To mock the awkward figure who occupied the throne was not something which could still be done with impunity. To plot against him was, as Jean II, duke of Alençon, discovered in October 1458, no longer so effective a weapon in the armoury of a great magnate. In this process, the public celebration of the office and mystique of kingship no doubt played its part. In a climate of loyalism, disloyal behaviour was all the more culpable. A doctrine of resignation to the inevitable was being developed. Those who witnessed a royal entry, a *lit-de-justice*, or a royal funeral may have had private doubts about the king's title. The former servants of the Lancastrian double monarchy were many. Men such as Raoul Roussel, archbishop of Rouen, Master Thomas de Courcelles, dean of Notre Dame of Paris, and even Thomas Basin, bishop of Lisieux, had much to forget. But they resigned themselves to the incontrovertible fact that Charles VII was not merely 'Well Served and Well Loved'. He was *Le Roi Trèsvictorieux*. The abstract notion of sovereignty, which now extended from the king's rights to the territory over which he exercised them, was largely realised in his reign. To be victorious was, in itself, both an attribute, and a justification, of the office of kingship. It furnished the foundation upon which more elaborate and less credible mystiques were to be built.

11 *The court and its functions*

The arena in which Charles VII ruled was his court. It has been said that 'the court [of France] is rarely dignified by the label "institution". Yet in some senses it was the most vital political institution. . . . It was a power-complex of influence and favour.'[1] Influence and favour, in a time of essentially personal monarchy, were perhaps among the most vital of all political attributes in fifteenth-century France. The way to that influence and favour was *via* the king's ear; and the way to the king's ear lay through

[1] Lewis, op. cit., 122.

the servants and officers of his household. The court was, in essence, the royal household. Its offices provided both sinecures and sources of employment for its inmates. Of what then did the court consist? First, its internal sub-division is significant. The distinction between the 'upper' and 'lower' household – the *domus magnificencie* and the *domus providencie* – operated in France as it did in Lancastrian and Yorkist England.[1] 'Above stairs' lay the sphere of the politically powerful; 'below stairs' lay that of the domestic officers and servants, whose job it was to service the daily needs of the court. All told, there could be as many as 800 people in the household – a figure much in excess of the total personnel of the formal departments of Chancery and *Chambre des Comptes*. The *domus magnificencie* was concerned with ceremonial and with politics, staffed by the gently born. Between 1418 and 1422, Charles's household as dauphin consisted of 4 *maîtres d'hôtel*, 24 esquires of the stable, one esquire *d'honneur*, one first breadbearer (*pannetier*), 12 other breadbearers, one first cupbearer (*échanson*), 12 other cupbearers, 4 carving esquires, 30 counsellors and chamberlains, and 37 chamberlains.[2] It was a large establishment.

Besides these members of the upper household, there were the *menus officiers*, or 'below stairs' population. In 1458 there were at least 99 of these receiving, and wearing, liveries of red cloth.[3] Between October 1458 and September 1459 the king's lower household consisted of 5 chamber varlets, 8 breadbearers, 7 cupbearers, 14 king's cooks (*cuisiniers de bouche*) under the head cook, Guillaume Raguier, 12 ordinary cooks (*cuisiniers de commun*), who cooked for the lesser members of the household, 4 porters, 2 doorkeepers, 6 *fruitiers*, 5 kitchen officers (*saulsiers*), 10 varlets of the chapel, 3 messengers of the stable (*chevaucheurs d'écurie*), and 18 varlets of the baggage. In attendance on the king there were the bodyguards[4] – his 25 Scots archers of the guard, all in livery of the king's colours of red, white and green; the 31 men-at-arms of the guard under the Scots captain Patrick Foulquart; the 27 French archers of the guard; and the 24 crossbowmen (*crannequiniers*), some of them Germans, all specialists in the use of their weapon. Without the Scots, said Anthoine de Chabannes in April 1446, 'people would have done many things which they have not dared to do'.[5] Also in attendance 'above stairs' were the king's physicians and surgeons, his astrologer Master Arnoul des Marez,

[1] See D. A. L. Morgan, 'The King's Affinity in the Polity of Yorkist England', *TRHS*, 5th series, xxiii (1973), 1–25.
[2] Beaucourt, I, 351.
[3] A.N., KK.51, fol. 126ʳ.

[4] See above, 33, 101, 138; A.N., KK.51, fols 123ʳ–125ᵛ, for their liveries, and fol. 128ʳ for their names; Vale, *GBA*, lxxiv (1969), 243–4.
[5] B.N. MS. fr. 20427, fol. 3ʳ; above, 101.

and his apothecaries, all of whom received New Year's Day gifts from him.[1] His tailors, hosiers, shoemakers, goldsmiths and so on were listed among the varlets of the chamber. All held office in the lower household, and were supplied by men such as Jean de Beaune, merchant draper 'following the court'.[2] It was from his activities that the great Semblançay fortune was to derive.

This household organisation is reflected in the description of the Burgundian household drawn up by Olivier de la Marche in 1474, and in the Black Book of Edward IV's household.[3] But the Burgundian establishment was larger than that of the king. Both were costly. Receipts of money for the expenses of Charles VII's household rose from 17,200l. *tournois* to 27,830l. *tournois* between October 1450 and September 1460.[4] From 1 October 1460 to 31 March 1461 receipts rose to 38,778 *livres*.[5] The accounts of the *argenterie* reveal a similarly high level of expenditure. Charles VII lived, despite his sobriety at table, in the very greatest luxury. Between October 1458 and September 1459 the ordinary receipts of the *argenterie* totalled 12,000 *livres*, while the extraordinary receipts came to no less than 37,900 *livres*.[6] The former sum derived largely from the proceeds of the *aides* for war in Languedoc; the latter from other Languedoc revenues, such as the *gabelle* and the other much-plundered taxes on the transport and sale of salt. In 1460 and 1461 the household was funded from more varied sources, among them the revenues of Normandy, a tax on wines at La Rochelle, the *aides* in Poitou and Limousin, and assignments on the receivers of *aides* at Paris, Melun, Noyon, Soissons, Laon, Amiens, Troyes, Tonnerre and Mantes.[7] Taxes for war were being diverted to pay for the luxuries of the court. On New Year's Day 1459 the king spent 14,580l. *tournois* on gifts (*étrennes*) to its members.[8] This was almost as much as the total annual expenditure on the household in 1450 and 1451. None of these disbursements was called in question, although the receiver-general of Normandy claimed that he was already overburdened.[9] There was no Parliament in France, and therefore no Commons to call for a reduction in the costs of the king's household.

For Yorkist England, it has recently been observed that 'what made the household a political institution was the group of some 250–300 knights,

[1] B.N. MSS fr. 10371, fols 8ᵛ, 9ʳ; KK.51, fols 120ʳ, 120ᵛ; Beaucourt, VI, 399–400.
[2] A.N., KK.51, fol. 3ʳ (1458–9).
[3] La Marche, IV, 1–82; A. R. Myers, *The Household of Edward IV* (Manchester, 1959); for later medieval households in general see Guenée, *L'Occident*, 148–50.

[4] See Douët-d'Arcq, *Comptes de l'hôtel*, xxxiv; B.N. MSS fr. 6750–4.
[5] MS. fr. 6754, fols 1ʳ–4ʳ.
[6] A.N., KK.51, fols 2ʳ, 99ᵛ.
[7] B.N. MS. fr. 6754, fols 1ʳ–4ʳ.
[8] A.N., KK.51, fol. 122ᵛ.
[9] B.N. MS. fr. 6754, fol. 8ʳ; above, 183.

esquires, gentlemen and clerks whose function was not technical and official but personal and variable'.[1] Their French equivalents were those men who held such titles as carving esquire, esquire of the stable, and 'counsellor and chamberlain of the king'. Among the *baillis* and *sénéchaux* appointed under Charles VII, many were thus styled.[2] The *sénéchaux* of Beaucaire–Nîmes kept their *sénéchaussée* loyal to the king even through periods of acute political crisis.[3] Who were they? First, there was Guillaume de Meulhon, lord of Valbarat, servant of the house of Anjou and household retainer of Charles as dauphin. He held the *sénéchaussée* from 1418 to 1429. Then there was Raymond, lord of Vilars, counsellor and chamberlain of the king, who held it from 1429 to 1455. He was followed by Jean Daulon, *maître d'hôtel* to the king, between 1455 and 1458. Finally, the great Southern *sénéchausée* was held by Joachim Rouault, esquire of the king's stable, counsellor and chamberlain, constable of Bordeaux and marshal of France, from 1458 to 1461. These men could be courtiers first, and royal officers second. The register of the king's council between March and June 1455 certainly shows the household *baillis* and *sénéchaux* attending its sessions.[4] Anthoine d'Aubusson, *bailli* of Touraine, counsellor and chamberlain, was there. The king wrote to the pope in favour of his brother, Louis, bishop of Tulle, who had refused to accept translation to a poorer see.[5] Such favours were among the perquisities of the courtier. Louis de Beaumont, *sénéchal* of Poitou, also styled counsellor and chamberlain, was there as well.[6] Joachim Rouault, *sénéchal* of Beaucaire–Nîmes, was evidently a favoured member of the court in 1458, because, in November of that year, the king ordered a fantastic dress to be made at his expense for 'the female fool of Joachim Rouault, called Dame Jeanne'.[7] Those who made the king laugh were well rewarded.

Yet it is by no means clear that the domestic duties implied by the titles attached to certain great household offices were ever performed by their holders. Unlike the court of Charles the Rash of Burgundy, where the gently born officers such as the first breadbearer, the first carving esquire, and the first cupbearer actually served the duke at table, these greater offices were honorific.[8] In the king's household accounts of 1450–1 and 1460, the *grand pannetier* (Anthoine de Chabannes), the *grand*

1 Morgan, op. cit., 4.

2 See G. Dupont-Ferrier, *Gallia Regia*, (Paris, 1942), I, *passim*.

3 For what follows see ibid., 270–2.

4 Valois, *Conseil*, 150.

5 Ibid., 320.

6 Ibid., 255.

7 A.N., KK.51, fol. 87ʳ. Also further gifts to fools and jesters on fols 85ʳ, 86ʳ (October–November 1458); 90ʳ (June 1459). The fool of the duke of Brittany was given a robe of red, white and green – the king's livery colours.

8 Cf. La Marche, IV, 20–40, 43–8.

chevalier tranchant, the *grand échanson* (Louis d'Estouteville), and the *grand queux* were not paid their annual wages of 40 *l. tournois* each, because 'they have not served the said lord at all' at the four great feasts of the court.[1] The recurrence of this entry in the household accounts suggests that the domestic organisation of the upper household merely provided titles for the politically important. Alain Chartier, at the beginning of the reign, could complain in *Le Curial* that 'we relish . . . titles and the name of "Master" far too gluttonously and are proud of them . . . but such titles and names are more often meaningless . . .'. He went on: 'and always among us, the courtiers . . . we pursue the names of offices rather than their functions. . . . We are verbose and relish words rather than things . . .'.[2] It is from the reign of Charles VII that some of the greater household offices were suppressed, having outlived their former usefulness. On 29 May 1449 the offices of *grand bouteiller* and *grand pannetier* were suppressed 'to relieve the burden on our subjects', but their holders conserved their titles on an honorific basis.[3] The office of *grand aumônier* fell vacant on the death of Jean d'Aussy in 1453 and remained so until the end of the reign.[4]

It can therefore be argued that offices of this kind were sinecures. They no longer required the performance of domestic duties, beyond a 'personal and variable' attendance on the king. But they remained to be sought after as indices of royal favour and of political significance. To hold the office of *maître d'hôtel* or *grand échanson* demonstrated that a courtier had reached the summit of the patronage system. To be a counsellor and chamberlain of the king was becoming a prerequisite for holding a *bailliage* or *sénéchaussée*. In this sense, Charles VII's government was household government. The *bailli* or *sénéchal* would normally act through a lieutenant – generally a lawyer – and would reside at court. Like the Burgundian *baillis* under Philip the Good, the royal *bailli* was primarily a courtier. He might consider Montils-lès-Tours or Chinon as his arena of political activity. In ducal Burgundy, for example, the *bailli* of La Montagne had no less than four lieutenants by 1450.[5] In 1453 the *bailli* spent only one month presiding over the assizes in his *bailliage*. The example can be paralleled by analogies drawn from royal *bailliages* such as that of Senlis.[6] The court at Tours, Bourges, or Chinon was becoming the real

---

[1] Douët d'Arcq, *Comptes de l'hôtel*, 326–7, 344.
[2] Chartier, *Curial*, 17, 19.
[3] Beaucourt, v, 314–15.
[4] Ibid., 315.
[5] See J. Bouault, 'Les bailliages du duché

de Bourgogne aux xive et xve siècles', *AB*, ii (1930), 15–16.
[6] See B. Guenée, *Tribunaux et Gens de Justice à la fin du Moyen Age* (Paris, 1963), 7; Lewis, op. cit., 146–7, for plurality and absenteeism at this level (and below).

centre of political power – a centre in which men's careers were made or broken. The monarchy had succeeded in adapting the old household offices to new purposes – the chancellor, the constable, the chamberlains and the *maîtres des requêtes* survived the vicissitudes of the later Middle Ages to emerge at the head of new administrative structures.[1] But to speak of administrative structures renders formal an establishment which was haunted by a paradox. The court was indeed a formal body – its ceremonies were highly formal – but the manner in which political business was done within its bounds could be remarkably informal.

Apart from the receipt and hearing of petitions in formal sessions, or *requêtes*,[2] there were other occasions which called for the household to discharge its ceremonial duties. At Epiphany and on May Day the king held court in festive splendour. A full court was held on those occasions, as well as at the more traditional feasts of Easter, Whitsun, All Saints' Day and Christmas. On these days, a solemn Mass was said, followed by a feast, and the festivities ended with music and dancing.[3] In January 1447 the king referred in a letter to 'the feast of the Kings, which we should perform as is the custom every year'.[4] This was the celebration which took place from 8 p.m. on the eve of Epiphany (6 January). A visual record of part of one of these ceremonies has survived. In the Book of Hours of Master Etienne Chevalier, *trésorier* of France, which must have been illuminated between August 1452 and July 1461, the page depicting the Adoration of the Magi includes a portrait of Charles VII.[5] He kneels before the Virgin and Child, offering a chalice to the infant. As the eldest of the Magi, he is followed by the figures of the other two Kings, which may, or may not, be portraits.[6] The scene takes place at night, and part of the Epiphany celebrations – a mock attack on a partly fortified *château* – is shown in the background. Burning braziers hang from the windows of the place, from which spectators look down on the scene of sham battle

---

[1] See R. Cazelles, 'Une problème d'evolution et d'intégration: les grands officiers de la couronne de France dans l'administration nouvelle au Moyen Age', *Annali della Fondazione . . . Storia Administrativa*, i (1964), 183–9.

[2] See above, 147–8.

[3] Beaucourt, IV, 77–8. There is no evidence from this period to support Zeller's statement that the elaborate ceremonies of the French court under Charles VIII and Louis XII contrasted sharply with the 'completely bourgeois simplicity of preceding sovereigns'. See

G. Zeller, *Les institutions de la France au xvie siècle* (Paris, 1948), 94.

[4] A.N., JJ.178, no. 110.

[5] See frontispiece and, for reproductions of all the illuminations, *The Hours of Etienne Chevalier*, ed. C. Schaefer (London, 1972).

[6] The likeliest candidates are René of Anjou and his son, John, duke of Calabria. The dauphin Louis's absence would rule him out, and the third of the Magi appears to be too old for Charles of France. See Vale, *GBA*, lxxiv (1969), 243.

below. Trumpeters, their instruments hung with blue banners sewn with *fleurs-de-lys*, sound amid the din of the fighting. All too little is known about such enactments at the court of Charles VII. Apart from references to a performance of a 'mystery of St-Charlemagne' before him at Tours in 1451, and the dancing of a Morris in his presence after supper on Shrove Tuesday 1459, documentation of court entertainment is almost entirely lacking.[1] The illumination in the Chevalier Hours is thus a precious source.

The king's costume in this painting is wholly convincing. Thomas Basin noted that he habitually dressed in short green tunics.[2] The accounts of his *argenterie* – which supplied him with clothes – confirm this preference for jackets made up by his tailor from green cloth of Rouen.[3] Red and green vie with each other. Green was the colour of 'new love' and of sensuality. It was 'cheerful and belongs to youth. . . . It signifies beauty, gaiety, passion, joy and endlessness. . . . This colour changes so much through the passage of time that it signifies that passions are changeable.'[4] Sicily Herald's treatise on colours thus suggests reasons for the king's choice. He vied with the *mignons*. His wardrobe was very large – in 1458-9 no less than twenty-seven silken and velvet robes were made for him, as well as fifty woollen robes.[5] Charles VII never shared his son's nonchalant shabbiness in dress. The elegance and richness of his clothes and personal jewellery contrasted starkly with Louis's drab costumes and his battered old hats adorned with pilgrims' badges. It was perhaps one more manifestation of his desire to be as unlike his father as possible. Charles's predilection for green came into its own at the Maying festivities. In April 1459 five green *robes decoppées*, 'similar to those of the king', were made for Charles of France, the duke of Britanny, and the *mignons* Vauvert, Châteaubrun and Rochefort.[6] They were to be worn on the first day of May, with scarlet hats and doublets of black satin of Lucca. The Maying scene in the *Très Riches Heures* of Jean, duke of Berry, had its counterpart at the court of France. Between October 1458 and September 1459 Charles's tailors were busy. They made him a short scarlet robe in which to ride, a grey hat garnished with plumes and silver-gilt ornaments, belts embroidered with the king's device of roses and briars, hose of many

1 Beaucourt, VI, 400; A.N., KK.51, fol. 96ʳ; for the Epiphany rites see K. Young, *The Drama of the Medieval Church* (Oxford, 1963), II, 29–101, 432–3.
2 See above, 22, 89n. 7; Basin, II, 280.
3 See, for examples, A.N., KK.51, fols 9ᵛ, 87ᵛ (1458–9).

4 Sicily Herald, *Le Blason des Couleurs*, ed. H. Cocheris (Paris, 1860), 83–4.
5 Beaucourt, VI, 424; A.N., KK.51, fols 3ʳ–21ʳ.
6 A.N., KK.51, fols 87ᵛ, 88ʳ.

colours, and other clothing in what Beaucourt described as 'incredible profusion'.[1]

The king's clothes at each of the feasts of the court are known. At All Saints' 1458 he wore a green hat, and, suitably, a black hat on All Souls' Day.[2] On the Sunday after Epiphany he wore a short blue robe, and on the morrow of Pentecost he wore a scarlet robe.[3] These were lined with silk or satin. A doublet of grey damask was made for him to 'wear under his robe when it was cold'.[4] The pleated cloth worn over his chest and stomach was provided in large quantities. A short robe of crimson satin was made for him to wear at the wedding of one of the court *damoiselles*, Marguerite Bradefer, in August 1459.[5] Not only was the king fitted out by the *argenterie*, but the princes, such as Charles of Orléans, were also catered for. He had two fine hats – one covered with sable fur – made for him at royal expense.[6] The king gave him a plume made of Florentine gold thread and white silk in October 1458, and both Jean, count of Angoulême, and Pierre de Brézé received gifts of hats.[7] Brézé's was decked out with five plumes in the king's livery colours – a sign of both favour and proprietorship. Even the *grand sénéchal* of Normandy's headgear signified to the people that he was one of the king's men. All the hats given by the king were of green velvet.

The queen was not forgotten among the beneficiaries of his gifts. She received the somewhat unexciting New Year's Day gift of a lump sum in January 1459 with which she was to have jewels made 'at her pleasure'.[8] Both the pampered Charles of France and the king's daughter Madelaine received livery collars. René of Anjou's taste was no doubt met by the gift of a painting on gold of the Annunciation, adorned with 'many fine diamonds and a fine ruby', costing 1,100*l. tournois*.[9] These gifts or *étrennes* were not only made by the king. He himself received a motley assortment of presents in January 1459.[10] These included a roll of parchment on

1 Beaucourt, VI, 424; A.N., KK.51, fols 3ʳ, 18ʳ (6 October 1458: this hat seems very similar to that which the king wore at the *lit-de-justice* at Vendôme; see Plate 10), 75ʳ. There are many references to 'robes à relever' and 'journades' in these accounts. Some of the latter had slashed sleeves and were trimmed with fur.
2 A.N., KK.51, fols 9ʳ, 9ᵛ.
3 Ibid., fols 3ʳ, 9ʳ, 9ᵛ. On 2 January 1459 a short green 'robe decoppée' was made for him to wear 'on the Day of the Kings', and another on 23 April for May Day

(ibid., fol. 9ᵛ).
4 Ibid., fol. 10ʳ (7 May 1459).
5 Ibid., fol. 21ʳ.
6 Ibid., fols 86ʳ–86ᵛ.
7 Ibid., fols 91ʳ–91ᵛ, 92ʳ, 93ʳ.
8 Ibid., fol. 119ʳ. But she had been given a gold clasp set with diamonds, a ruby, and pearls, in the shape of three white roses, as a pendant to a gold collar enamelled with the letters 'E.E' in blue, in January 1452 (B.N., MS. fr. 10371, fol. 5ᵛ).
9 A.N., KK.51, fol. 119ᵛ.
10 Ibid., fols 122ʳ–122ᵛ.

which were rhyming verses in praise of the Virgin, and a letter-missive in rhyme addressed to him. This was the gift of Jean du Chastel, a Benedictine with a taste for versifying. Another useful gift was a pot from which a lily protruded, made entirely of wax – the present of one Pierre le Faucheur. Master Jean Domer, 'chronicler', gave a roll on which there were Latin verses, ominously 'making mention of certain things which have arisen in this kingdom since a certain time'.[1] What these were will never be known.

What is certain, however, is that one index of membership of, and favour at, court was the receipt of *étrennes* and pensions from the king. It has been said of the knights, esquires, gentlemen and clerks of the Yorkist household that 'they wore the king's liveries of cloth or collar; they pocketed his fees and wages and rewards and gifts; they divided their time between his court and their own countries in a seasonal interchange which was not their least important feature'.[2] This might have been written of the court of Charles VII. The evidence for the distribution of pensions is, unlike that for *étrennes*, very fragmentary and scattered. It is often difficult to estimate exactly how much a certain courtier was getting from the extant pension lists. There is evidence that men such as Anthoine de Chabannes's brother, Jacques, counsellor and chamberlain, *grand maître d'hôtel*, was getting an annual pension of 1,200 *livres* plus 600 *livres* 'to maintain his estate' in 1451.[3] The greater magnates, and princes of the blood such as René of Anjou, were receiving pensions of 4,000 and 5,000 *livres*. By 1454 there is evidence of the payment of pensions from the proceeds of the royal *aides* for war.[4] Taxation was, once more, being appropriated for purposes which it was not intended to serve. The continued existence of war taxes, used for distinctly non-military purposes, is perhaps a symptom of the king's ability to take taxes without the intervention of representative assemblies from the 1440s onwards.

It can be calculated from a surviving account that some of these pensions were in fact grants to certain of the magnates of the *aides* levied within their own lordships.[5] Charles of Orléans was drawing a pension of

---

[1] Ibid., fol. 122ᵛ. He was responsible for translating texts relating to the history of France 'from the destruction of Troy onwards', with Master Noël de Fribois. In June 1459 Fribois had presented the king with a copy of his *Abregé des chroniques de France* (ibid., fol. 97ʳ; Beaucourt, VI, 405). It may be this volume which is preserved as B.N. MS.

fr. 6465, which ends, as did Fribois's book, with the reign of Charles VI. See above, 197.
[2] Morgan, op. cit., 4.
[3] B.N. MS. fr. 32511, fol. 141ʳ.
[4] Ibid., fol. 141ʳ. Cf. above, 186.
[5] See B.N. MS. fr. 2886, fols 3ʳ–25ʳ (1 October 1454–30 September 1455).

12,115 *livres* from the *aides* at Orléans, Blois and Châteaudun. Jean, count of Angoulême, got a pension of 6,000 *livres* from the *aides* in Angoumois and the *haut pays* of Limousin. Jean, count of Nevers, got his 3,070 *livres* from the *aides* at Nevers; Charles of Anjou, 12,000 from Maine, Poitou and the receivership of Beaumont; Jean II, duke of Bourbon, 14,400 from the *aides* in Bourbonnais, Forez and Beaujolais. René of Anjou's pension reached 7,300 *livres* in 1454–5, drawn on the *aides* at Angers, Saumur and Loudun.[1] It would be tedious to multiply instances. But sums of this order of magnitude could bolster seigneurial incomes to a substantial extent. The magnates had a vested interest in seeing that Charles VII got at least some of his taxes. It was perhaps one of the more effective means by which the king controlled his nobility. He was evidently paying little heed to Jean Juvenal des Ursins's advice: 'when you cease to pay the said pensions, the lords will be more contented than they are at present; for it's all these jealousies that produce covert hatreds, and each one thinks that he deserves to have more than another . . .'.[2] In fact, the withholding of a pension could have precisely the opposite effect. To reduce a pension, let alone to withdraw it, could be very damaging to a great, or lesser, lord. The cases of Jean V, count of Armagnac, and of Jean II, duke of Alençon, suggest that a pension at court was becoming an indispensable part of a magnate's income. Exclusion from the pension list did not merely mean a loss of prestige and power – it meant a reduction in liquid capital. Liquid capital was an indispensable requirement for the business of 'living nobly' in fifteenth-century France.[3]

If an appearance on the pension list was one measure of favour at court, then the receipt of *étrennes* was another. As dauphin, Charles VII gave New Year's Day gifts to his entourage from January 1418 onwards.[4] These took the form of money payments, ranging from 150 *livres* for the *valets de chambre* to 400 *livres* for the members of his council. The king himself took his own present – in 1452 and 1459 it took the form of a diamond, which, in 1452, was accompanied by 'gold rings and other little things which he has had bought for his pleasure and desire'.[5] A distinction was

[1] B.N. MS. fr. 2886, fols 4ᵛ, 5ʳ, 22ᵛ (Orléans), 7ᵛ, 20ᵛ (Angoulême), 5ᵛ, 23ʳ (Nevers), 8ʳ, 11ᵛ, 12ʳ (Charles of Anjou), 14ʳ, 14ᵛ, 15ʳ (Bourbon), 10ʳ, 10ᵛ, 11ʳ, 12ʳ, 12ᵛ (René of Anjou).
[2] See Beaucourt, IV, 176.
[3] See E. Dravasa, '"Vivre noblement". Recherches sur la dérogeance de noblesse du xivᵉ au xviᵉ siècles', *Revue juridique et*

économique du Sud-Ouest, sér. juridique, xvi (1965), 135–93, xvii (1966), 23–119; and, for lack of it, P. Wolff, 'Une famille . . . les Ysalguier de Toulouse', *Mélanges d'histoire sociale*, i (1942), 35–58.
[4] Beaucourt, I, 412–13.
[5] B.N. MS. fr. 10371, fol. 5ᵛ; A.N., KK.51, fol. 119ʳ.

then made between *grosses* and *menues étrennes*, the former being gifts of money, robes or jewels, the latter gifts of badges or pendants for the livery collars worn by the court.[1] In 1452 badges in the shape of a winged stag were distributed to the courtiers and household officers. Some of them, such as the lords of Clermont, Armagnac, Vendôme, Castres, Tancarville, Villequier, Torcy, Gaucourt, Vauvert and Guillaume Jouvenel des Ursins, got supplementary gifts of cut diamonds.[2] The *damoiselles* of the court were well represented, being fitted out with robes at the king's expense.[3] By January 1459 the king was giving additional gifts of precious stones to be set into the badges given to selected courtiers and officers. Apart from Charles of France, the chancellor, Philip of Savoy, John, lord of Lorraine, Anthoine d'Aubusson, and the lords of Vauvert, Châteaubrun, Rochefort and La Brosse were members of this charmed circle.[4] The major civil servants each received a sum of money – in 1459 these were Jean Bureau, Jean Hardouin, Pierre Bérard and Etienne Chevalier, *trésoriers*, Jean le Boursier, Pierre Doriole, Pierre de Refuge and Jean Hébert, *généraux des finances*, and Mathieu Beauvarlet, receiver-general. The wives of the *mignons* also did well.[5]

That the king appreciated at least one of the presents which he received every New Year's Day is implied in the account which Pierre de Janouillac, acting *argentier* during Jacques Cœur's imprisonment, rendered in 1454. The king had been given a large pearl set into a gold clasp by a merchant of Paris. But it had fallen into the fire while the king was wearing it and was destroyed.[6] The recipients of the king's *étrennes* were no doubt pleased with their gifts. They were *the* courtiers, the favoured few around the person of the sovereign. The accounts for the giving of these presents thus provide precious evidence for the composition of the court at any one time. They were another means by which the king controlled his entourage and his nobility. As long as the pensions and *étrennes* flowed from the court, the drums of war were less likely to be heard. With the honorific offices and the supplementary rewards, they provided prestigious and profitable incentives for men to serve the king. To get to the king's ear was clearly much easier if one was a counsellor and chamberlain, or if one had influence over a counsellor and chamberlain. It is in this light that the alliance which was made between Pierre de Brézé and Gaston IV,

[1] A.N., KK.51, fols 118ᵛ ff.
[2] B.N., MS. fr. 10371, fols 11ʳ–11ᵛ.
[3] A.N. KK.51, fols 12ʳ–121ᵛ; cf. B.N. MS. fr. 10371, fols 7ʳ, 7ᵛ, 8ʳ (1452).
[4] A.N., KK.51, fol. 120ʳ.

[5] Ibid., fols 120ᵛ, 121ʳ. It is worth pointing out that the name of Antoinette de Maignelais does not appear in the accounts for *étrennes*.
[6] B.N. MS. fr. 10371, fol. 36ʳ.

count of Foix, on 18 May 1445 may be viewed.[1] Its purpose, like that of others of its kind, was to keep Foix in the king's favour. Such informal operations lay outside the bureaucratic apparatus of government. Beside the formal hierarchy of power lay an ill-defined area in which the courtiers and their clients operated. The great central offices at Paris – Chancery and *Chambre des Comptes* – played a supporting role in the business of government. With the *Parlement*, they might act as watchdogs. But decisions were made by the king and his council at Montils-lès-Tours, Chinon or Mehun-sur-Yèvre. The court and its inmates formed a sort of impermeable membrane between king and country. It was a pattern of government which did not die with Charles VII.

[1] ABP, E.440.

Conclusion

The face that peers out from the Louvre portrait of Charles VII is not prepossessing.[1] The small, hooded, rodent-like eyes, the long bulbous nose, the thick sensual lips, and the unhealthy colouring exclude the sitter from consideration among the finer types of royal physiognomy. But some of his contemporaries did not consider Nature to have been unduly unkind to this member of a line which was not renowned for its physical beauty. Chastellain thought that his face was 'pallid, but good-looking enough' and Thomas Basin considered him pleasing enough to look at.[2] Neither of these verdicts seems borne out by his portrait. But both writers agreed that he was short, skinny, had poor legs, and shoulders which were too broad. These combined to give him a grotesque appearance, especially when he wore short jackets, as was his wont. Fifteenth-century standards of physical beauty were not those of today. Attempts to read character from the face are, moreover, often doomed to serious error. That Charles was a sensual man, and one who, like Machiavelli, was not able to wield much influence over others, does not need to be supported by the evidence of a portrait. The so-called 'kingly' qualities – military prowess, constancy magnanimity, and so on – were not much in evidence in the case of Charles VII. If he was magnanimous it was because he could not afford to be otherwise. He was never constant, and rarely led his troops in battle. He could be fickle and irresponsible. But he was probably no more irresponsible than other monarchs of his age.

This book has attempted to examine Charles VII as a king and as a man. In a period during which the personal qualities of rulers were not yet irrelevant to the business of government, the king and the man sometimes merge. Chastellain was one of the very few contemporary observers to point this out. The king's three major personal defects – mutability, distrust and envy – could, and did, play some part in determining his political behaviour. The rise and fall of 'favourites', the justified suspicions about the conduct of his entourage, and the jealous resentment of others'

[1] See Plate I. For general remarks about the historiography of Charles VII and the significance of the reign, see Chapter 1 above.
[2] Chastellain, II, 178; Basin, II, 278.

good fortune can be substantiated from the events of a long reign. Charles's envy turned very sour in at least one case. His rancour against Philip the Good of Burgundy – whom he had never met – increased markedly towards the end of his reign. When Chastellain was at his court in December 1454, he claimed that the king had addressed a Burgundian knight with the words: 'St John! Our brother-in-law is much better attended than we are.'[1] His entourage was fit for a king. But Charles had few grounds for complaint on this score. Perhaps he was merely goading his own courtiers, or, more probably, Chastellain's memory was, intentionally, at fault. Philip the Good might derive satisfaction from such a passage in the work of his own court chronicler. Charles's rancour against him, especially after the dauphin Louis had sought refuge at the court of Burgundy, had a decisive impact upon Franco–Burgundian relations. It very nearly led to open war during the last three years of the king's life.

The shadow of his son lies heavily over his reign. He has often paled into insignificance beside the allegedly more intelligent, more resourceful, more engaging Louis XI. I have tried to show how hindsight may distort the perspective in which Louis's behaviour as dauphin during his father's lifetime must be viewed. Neither king nor dauphin could fully control their servants. No fifteenth-century ruler – not even the tyrants of Milan – could ever hope to do so. A fifteenth-century French king might wish to act as a tyrant. But his tyranny could never be an effective one. It has been said that 'from the fifteenth to the eighteenth centuries, the early modern state whose twin pillars were the absolute prince and the bureaucracy operated in western Europe through officials for whom the normal image is one of venality, extortion and large illegitimate profit'.[2] The France of Charles VII – and of Louis XI – was no exception. Royal edicts such as that of April 1454 on the sale of office and absenteeism remained a dead letter.[3] A king, if he was to be served at all, had to connive at many things. Charles VII ruled over an essentially weak régime, in which survival was perhaps the one and only concern. In 1422 his title was fiercely contested by the Lancastrian claimant. By 1461 that title

[1] See Chastellain, III, 15–19.
[2] D. M. Bueno de Mesquita, 'The place of Despotism in Italian Politics', in *Europe in the Late Middle Ages*, ed. Hale, Highfield and Smalley (London, 1965), 323–4. For the ineffectiveness of the 'tyranny' of the Sforzas of Milan in the later fifteenth century, and their inability to keep public order, see Bueno de Mesquita, 'Ludovico Sforza and his Vassals', in *Italian Renaissance Studies*, ed. E. F. Jacob (London, 1960), 184–215.
[3] Ord., XIV, 304–5. The edict also called for the collection and redaction of local judicial usages and customs. This process was still being undertaken in 1539. There was no common law in France until the Civil Code of Napoleon I.

was more or less secure. The efforts of his servants, whose own stake in the survival of the Valois title was not unimportant, had transformed the 'king of Bourges' into the 'very victorious king'. Both titles were misleading. His kingdom at his accession in 1422 comprised much more than the city of Bourges and the *pays* of Berry. His victoriousness at his death in 1461 had not been gained without strains and conflicts which did not die with him. The permanency of his conquests remained in doubt. If he established peace, it was peace at a price. That price was taxation which was heavy, and which got heavier, war or no war. Commynes estimated that Charles raised about 1,800,000 *francs* a year. His son was raising 4,700,000 by his death.[1] The English war had been effectively over for thirty years. The French were among the most heavily taxed people in Renaissance Europe.

But in some respects they were sold a lame horse. The standing army which helped to drive out the English under Charles VII could promote, rather than reduce, disorder in the country. It had to be employed, and it was best employed outside the kingdom of France. The king's subjects, though they paid their taxes, were not protected from violence by the régime. There was often too little, rather than too much, government in fifteenth-century France. But Charles VII's subjects would not have thought of ridding themselves of the monarchy. It would have been an act of sacrilege. The king's servants had again been at work, creating and elaborating upon a public image of the Valois monarchy which was designed to produce a climate in which treason might perish. The treasonable activities of the magnates were exposed and punished. Charles VII subdued the count of Armagnac by force, the duke of Alençon by trial, the duke of Brittany by compromise over the question of homage. His lawyers were anxious to translate the theoretical concepts of sovereignty into hard fact. In the process they served not only the king's interests, but their own. The king might not wish to act as an 'absolute' monarch, but his officers sometimes forced him to do so. They stood to gain—in terms of power, money and status – from more extreme interpretations of the scope of his sovereignty than he himself might have advanced. Charles VII was, again, sometimes the victim of his own servants.

Yet his son was no less exempt from their pressures and demands. Charles and Louis were less dissimilar than has often been claimed. Both were conventionally pious; both were superstitious and constantly consulted astrologers; both were hard-working as kings; both were intelligent. Charles's ability to put his own defects – especially his inconstancy –

[1] Commynes, *Mémoires*, II, 220.

to good use, and to set men to work for him, clearly surpassed that of his indiscreet son. Chastellain alone possessed the acuteness of mind to realise the king's competence in this area. Lesser minds – Thomas Basin and Jean Juvenal des Ursins, hide-bound with clerical prejudice – were unaware of the way in which the king operated. He let his servants serve him, let them entangle themselves in the webs that they spun, then threw them out. He normally spared their lives. Like his son, he could be cruel, he could be capricious, and he could be extremely devious. Unlike him, he dressed, spoke, and tried to behave according to the conventions of fifteenth-century kingship. He did not need to be bellicose or militarily active in order to observe them. The good example of his grandfather, Charles V, was there for him to emulate. Unlike his son, he could hold his tongue to such an extent that many of his servants had no idea of what he was thinking. He could be inscrutable and impenetrable of mind. Unlike his son, he had no evident passion for hunting or animals. He preferred reading and music to the pleasures of the chase. He does not seem to have enjoyed low company. Sometimes he preferred no company at all, alone in his 'retreat'. His fears of the unknown and the unfamiliar meant that his public appearances were few. Illness made them even fewer in the last years of his life. But this did not mean that he was inactive or inaccessible as a king. His fear of the future was perhaps mitigated only by the predictions of those who consulted the stars for him. He was, like most other rulers of his day, very insecure, fearing treason from both within and without. He could have had no close confidants or friends, because he was too distrustful of men's motives. Perhaps the mercurial Pierre de Brézé was a kindred spirit – clever, often over-subtle, a brilliant talker, a wit, and the slipperiest fish in a well-stocked pond. Brézé's cynicism may have commended him to Charles.[1] And it was perhaps to him that he owed Agnès Sorel.

I have tried in this book to describe, analyse and explain Charles VII's behaviour, not to pass judgement upon it. Beaucourt's great biography strove to judge the king. It will never be ousted as a definitive statement of the facts about the king and his reign. All that one can hope to do is to suggest alternative interpretations of those facts. Many of these are highly speculative, others need to be pursued and, perhaps, qualified or rejected. If a concise assessment of the king's achievement is needed, then this book can end as it began – with Chastellain: 'he taxed his kingdom heavily; he

---

[1] For his wit, and his cynicism, see Commynes, I, 21. He spoke to Louis XI just before the battle of Montlhéry in July 1465 'jestingly, as he was wont to talk'.

gave his men a lean time; he restored peace, but few ruins'. Chastellain was not always right. His notion of 'peace' was, perhaps, not ours. The mere absence of the English from France – with the exception of Calais – after 1453 did not bring an immediate end to conflict within the kingdom. Chastellain's judgement of Charles VII was, in any case, somewhat distorted by the need and desire to render his own patron, Philip the Good of Burgundy, in a flattering light. He thus laid too great a stress on the king's reconciliation with Philip at Arras in 1435. That event, it could be argued, had a more decisive effect on the fortunes of England than on those of France.[1] The king's political technique did not change as a result of it. But Chastellain omitted one aspect of Charles VII's character from his analysis. The king was a gambler, not only at the gaming tables of his court, but in his political practice. He may have gambled away some of his subjects' money. But, in politics, he was playing for the very highest stakes – his own survival.

[1] See my article on 'Sir John Fastolf's "report" of 1435: a new interpretation reconsidered', *Nottingham Medieval Studies*, xvii (1973), 78–84.

Table of Events

1403 Charles VII born (22 February).

1407 Louis, duke of Orléans, assassinated by the supporters of John the Fearless, duke of Burgundy (23 November).

1413 Victory of the Armagnac faction over the Burgundians at Paris. John the Fearless leaves the city (23 August). Charles betrothed to Marie of Anjou.

1415 Henry V invades France. Battle of Agincourt (25 October). Death of the dauphin Louis, duke of Guyenne (18 December).

1417 Death of the dauphin Jean, duke of Touraine (5 April). Charles becomes dauphin. Henry V invades Normandy.

1418 Victory of the Burgundian faction over the Armagnacs at Paris. Charles flees to Melun (29 May), then to Bourges. He assumes the title of lieutenant-general of his father against the Burgundians (29 June).

1419 Assassination of John the Fearless, duke of Burgundy, on the bridge at Montereau (10 September). Philip the Good succeeds his father as duke of Burgundy, and allies himself with Henry V against Charles.

1420 Treaty of Troyes (21 May). Henry V marries Charles's sister Catherine and is to become king of France after Charles VI's death. Henry V as Regent of France in the interim.

1421 Charles disinherited by Charles VI (3 January). He is victorious at the battle of Baugé (22 March).

1422 Death of Henry V (31 August). Death of Charles VI (21 October). Charles becomes Charles VII of France.

1423 Birth of the dauphin Louis, later Louis XI (23 July). Charles's army defeated by the English at Cravant (31 July).

1424 Defeat of Charles's forces at Verneuil (17 August).

1425 Arthur de Richemont becomes constable of France in Charles's service (8 March). Fall of Jean Louvet (5 July).

1427 Rise of Georges de la Trémoïlle (July). Jean V, duke of Brittany, allies himself with Henry VI of England (8 September). Richemont banished from Charles's court.

1428 Joan of Arc arrives at Vaucouleurs (May). Siege of Orléans begun by the English (12 October).

1429 Arrival of Joan of Arc at Chinon (23 February). Entry of Joan to Orléans (29 April). Relief of Orléans (8 May). Victory of Joan at Patay (18 June). Coronation of Charles VII at Rheims (17 July).

1430   Joan captured by the Burgundians at Compiègne (23 May).

1431   Opening of the trial of Joan at Rouen (9 January). Execution of Joan
       (30 May). Coronation of Henry VI as king of France at Paris (16 December).

1432   Reconciliation between Charles and Richemont (5 March).

1433   Fall of La Trémoïlle (June). Charles of Anjou in power.

1434   Charles holds his court, and a meeting of the Estates, at Vienne. Negotiations with Burgundy.

1435   Treaty of Arras (20 September). Charles and Philip the Good of Burgundy reconciled.

1436   Entry of Richemont into Paris in Charles's name (13 April). Philip the
       Good lays siege to the English in Calais (9 July), but is forced to retire.

1437   Pontoise recovered by the English (12 February). Siege of Montereau by
       Charles (September–October). Entry of Charles into Paris (12 November).

1438   Assembly of the French clergy at Bourges. Pragmatic Sanction enacted
       (May–July).

1439   Meaux captured by Richemont for Charles (August). Meeting of the
       Estates at Orléans (September). First *ordonnance* on military reforms
       (November).

1440   Outbreak of the Praguerie (February). The revolt is put down by
       Charles (April–July). Charles of Orléans released from captivity in
       England (9 November).

1441   Appearance of the *écorcheurs* in Champagne and Lorraine. Pontoise
       recovered for Charles (19 September).

1442   Demands made by the magnates at Nevers (February–March). Charles's
       expedition to Guyenne (June–October). Fall of Tartas (24 June). Death
       of Yolande of Aragon (14 November).

1443   The English fail to regain Dieppe (August).

1444   Truce between England and France at Tours (20 May). Betrothal of
       Henry VI and Margaret of Anjou (23 May). Expedition of Charles to
       Alsace and Lorraine. Louis, the dauphin, leads an army as his father's
       lieutenant.

1445   Siege of Metz ends with its surrender to Charles (February). Marriage of
       Henry VI and Margaret of Anjou (March). Charles's *ordonnances* on
       military reform issued (9 January and 26 May). Death of Margaret of
       Scotland, wife of the dauphin Louis (16 August). Guillaume Jouvenel des
       Ursins appointed chancellor of France (16 June).

1446   Arrest of Gilles de Bretagne at Charles's instigation (26 June). Alliance
       between Charles and Filippo Maria Visconti of Milan (29 December).
       Birth of Charles of France.

1447   Failure of French intervention at Genoa (January–February). Arrest of
       Guillaume Mariette (October).

1448   Le Mans surrenders to Charles (16 March). Maine handed over to him.
       Extension of the Anglo-French truce until 1 April 1450. Guillaume
       Mariette tried (March). Pierre de Brézé disgraced (April).

1449   Fougères taken for the English by François de Suriennes (24 March).
       Breach of the truce. Charles declares war on the English (31 July).
       French invasion of Normandy, with Breton support. Fall of Coutances
       (12 September), St-Lô (15 September), Carentan (29 September),
       Gavray (11 October), Fougères (5 November), Rouen (10 November),
       Château-Gaillard (23 November), Harfleur (24 November), Bellême
       (December).

1450   First inquiry by Charles into the case of Joan of Arc (15 February).
       Death of Agnès Sorel (9 February). Victory over the English at For-
       migny (15 April). Fall of Vire (April), Avranches (May), St-Sauveur
       and Valognes (May). Surrender of Caen (24 June) and Cherbourg
       (12 August). Recovery of Normandy from the English completed. The
       dauphin Louis marries Charlotte of Savoy (9 March).

1451   First reconquest of Guyenne by Charles. Fall of Blaye (24 May), St-
       Emilion, Bourg, Libourne, Fronsac (5 June), and Bordeaux (30 June).
       Capitulation of Bayonne (20 August). Arrest of Jacques Cœur
       (July).

1452   Inquiry into the case of Joan of Arc by Cardinal Guillaume d'Estouteville
       (May). Revolt of the Bordelais (October). Treaty between Charles and
       Louis of Savoy (27 October).

1453   Second expedition to Guyenne (June–October). Victory of Charles
       over the English and Gascons at Castillon (17 July). Fall of Bordeaux
       (20 October). Condemnation of Jacques Cœur (29 May). Failure of René
       of Anjou's Italian expedition.

1454   *Ordonnance* on the administration of justice enacted at Montils-lès-Tours
       (April).

1455   Execution for treason of members of the Scots guard (August). Charles's
       illness (September). Expedition against Jean V, count of Armagnac.

1456   Arrest of Jean II, duke of Alençon (May). Rehabilitation of Joan of Arc
       (May–July). The dauphin Louis flees to the court of Burgundy (31
       August).

1457   Charles resumes government of the Dauphiné (8 April). His second bout
       of illness (December).

1458   Condemnation of Jean II, duke of Alençon, at Vendôme (10 October).
       Death of Richemont (26 December).

1459   Congress of Mantua.

1460   Recurrence of Charles's illness.

1461   Charles and Philip the Good of Burgundy prepare for war (January–
       March). Defeat of Margaret of Anjou and the Lancastrians at Towton
       (Palm Sunday). Failure of French intervention at Genoa (9 March).

Philip the Good swears an oath of allegiance to the dauphin Louis, as future king of France (4 April). War between France and Burgundy is imminent (June). Charles dies at Mehun-sur-Yèvre (22 July). Buried in St-Denis (8 August).

Note on Coinage

The sums of money mentioned in this book reflect the division between the two types of money which existed side by side in later medieval France. These were *money of account*, which was the measure of value, and *actual coin*, which was the medium of exchange. Thus Charles VII's accounts were kept in the former, actual transactions made in the latter. With a considerable variety of coins in circulation, the need for some yardstick and standard of value was imperative. This was provided by money of account. The two systems were as follows:

I *Money of account*

(a) *Livres tournois*. The most common money of account in fifteenth-century France. The *denier tournois* was its basis. The *sou tournois* was worth 12 *deniers tournois*; the *livre tournois* was worth 20 *sous tournois*. It was thus the French equivalent of the English system of pounds, shillings and pence sterling. I have left it in its French form, rather than translate *livre tournois* as 'pound of Tours'.
(b) *Livres parisis*. Much less common by the fifteenth century. The system comprised the same denominations as the *tournois*. I have again left it in its original form, rather than 'pounds of Paris'. 8 *deniers parisis* = 10 *deniers tournois*.

II *Actual coin*

(a) Gold

Franc d'or	Issued from 1360. Worth 20 *sous tournois*. Wt: 3·88 gm.
Ecu	Issued from 1388–1475 as the *écu à la couronne* or crown. Worth 20 *sous tournois*. Wt in 1388: 3·99 gm. Wt in 1475: 3·496 gm. Its value rose steadily. Worth 22 *sous* 6 *deniers tournois* in *c.* 1400.
Mouton	Issued first by Philip IV in 1311. Wt subject to fluctuations, but about 3·50 gm. So called because it bore a paschal lamb.
Salut	Issued by the English administration of Lancastrian France and Normandy from 1421–49. Wt in 1421–3: 3·885 gm; 1423–49: 3·495 gm. Ousted by the *écu* as a result of the Valois recovery under Charles VII.
Florin	Issued first at Florence in 1252. Wt about 3·50 gm.

(b) Silver

Blanc   Issued from 1364, replacing the *gros tournois*, first issued by St Louis.

The value of all these denominations in terms of money of account was subject
to marked variations as their gold and silver content was increased or decreased
by the mints. For further information on this subject see P. Spufford, 'Coinage
and Currency', in *CEH*, iii (Cambridge, 1963), 576–602; J. Lafaurie, *Les
monnaies des rois de France* (Paris, 1951), 1; P. Spufford, *Monetary problems and
policies in the Burgundian Netherlands, 1433–96* (Leiden, 1970), esp. 13–46.

Glossary

Aide Indirect tax on consumables first levied in 1360. Part of the *extraordinary* revenues of the Crown. Sometimes used to mean all taxes imposed by the Crown.

Ampoule Vessel in which the sacred oil used to anoint the kings of France was kept at the cathedral of Rheims.

Apanage Part of the royal *domaine* granted to a cadet son by the king for his subsistence.

Argentier Officer responsible for the *argenterie* of the king or a great noble. This office was responsible for supplying the royal household with luxury goods, clothing and plate.

Arrêt Formal judgement of the Paris *Parlement*.

Aumônier Officer responsible for the giving of alms to the poor in a royal or seigneurial household.

Bailli Royal officer set over a *bailliage*, entrusted with the administration of justice and the *domaine (ordinary)* revenues of the Crown. By the later Middle Ages he was normally non-resident in his *bailliage*.

Bailliage Area over which the *bailli* held jurisdiction, so called because it had been leased or farmed (*baillé*) to its original holders.

Ban et arrière-ban Feudal levy of all those owing military service to a lord.

Cadet Younger child of a royal, or noble, house.

Chambre aux deniers Office of finances in a seigneurial household, responsible for receipts and disbursements of cash.

Chambre des Comptes Chief office of account for royal finances, established at Paris. Competence ill-defined, but responsible for *ordinary* revenues, whose administration it shared with the *Trésor* (see below).

Chambre des Requêtes Office of the Paris *Parlement* dealing with petitions.

Châtelet Court of first instance at Paris, dealing largely with criminal cases.

Chevaucheur Mounted messenger. Those of the *écurie du roi* carried the king's letters and were recognisable by the box bearing the *fleurs-de-lys* which they carried.

Commis Officer appointed by the king to conduct an inquiry, or attend to any specific item of business on his behalf.

Comté Lordship held by a count.

Damoiselle Unmarried woman, usually young and attendant upon the queen or a female member of the nobility.

Domaine Royal demesne. The property of the Crown, whether gained by inheritance, purchase, feudal right, or conquest.

Echanson Cupbearer. Officer in a royal or seigneurial household.

Echevin Member of a municipal council, often with judicial functions.

Ecorcheur Freelance mercenary, active in the 1430s and 1440s.

Ecurie Stable. Office in a royal or seigneurial household.

Ecuyer d'écurie Esquire of the stable.

Elu Officer set over an *élection*, the area from which *extraordinary* revenues of the Crown were collected in certain parts of France. First mentioned in 1355, primarily responsible for raising the *aides*.

Etrennes Gifts given on New Year's Day.

Fille d'honneur Lady-in-waiting at court.

Fleuron Ornament in the shape of a *fleur-de-lys* set around the open crown worn by the kings of France.

Franc-archer Archer raised by the royal *ordonnance* of 1448 which created infantry to supplement the companies of *ordonnance* (see below). The *francs-archers* were exempt from taxation, and served at the normal rate of roughly one per fifty hearths in every parish. Organised and mobilised by the *bailliage*, they were an ill-disciplined and troublesome force, soon to be reduced and ultimately disbanded in favour of Swiss and other foreign mercenaries in the early sixteenth century.

Gabelle Tax on the compulsory purchase of salt, first introduced in 1341. Part of the Crown's *extraordinary* revenues.

Général des finances One of the four *généraux* set over the *extraordinary* revenues of the Crown, and responsible to the *trésorier* of France. The four units were: Languedoïl, Outre-Seine, Normandy, and Languedoc. Outside these areas, *extraordinary* revenues were administered by royal commissioners specially appointed to do so.

Grenetier Officer in charge of a *grenier*, or salt-granary, where salt was stored in order to ensure a royal monopoly of this vital commodity. Responsible to the *généraux* for the administration of the *gabelle*.

Hanouar Carrier of salt. The Parisian *hanouars* bore the king's coffin and effigy during the funeral procession.

Hôtel-Dieu 'God's House', a charitable foundation for the relief of the sick and the indigent poor.

Huissier Usher, or process-server. An unpopular class. Those of the Paris *Parlement* were identifiable by the maces which they carried.

Lettres de jussion Royal order to the *Parlement* insisting upon immediate registration of a piece of legislation. First used in 1392.

Lit-de-justice Plenary session of the *Parlement*, in which a royal edict was forcibly registered, or a peer of the kingdom tried.

Main-de-justice Staff headed with an ivory hand, borne by the kings of France on ceremonial occasions. The symbol of the king's Justice.

Maître des arbalétriers Master of the crossbowmen. Office in the royal household.

Maître d'hôtel Master of the household. Generally an honorific position by the fifteenth century.

Maître des Requêtes Royal officer, normally a lawyer, responsible for the receipt of petitions to the king. An important member of the royal household in the fifteenth century.

Mignon Male favourite of a king or prince.

Ordonnance Royal edict, registered in its records by the Paris *Parlement*.

Ordonnance, company of Unit of the standing army created in 1445. Each company of this cavalry force consisted of 100 *lances*. Each *lance* comprised 6 men. By 1450, the companies were divided into those of *grande* and *petite ordonnance* – the former being a field army, the latter a garrison force. There were 20 companies, which, if they were ever at full strength, would have given the king about 12,000 mounted troops.

Parlement Supreme court of appeals from the kingdom of France sited in the Palais de Justice on the Ile-de-la-Cité at Paris. Provincial *Parlements* were founded at Poitiers, Toulouse and Grenoble during the reign of Charles VII.

Président Normally used to describe the principal judicial officer of a *Parlement*.

Prévôt Royal officer responsible for local justice in a *bailliage* or *sénéchaussée*, subordinate to the *bailli* or *sénéchal*.

Prévôt des maréchaux Royal officer empowered to try cases of military indiscipline.

Procureur Officer representing the king in the administration of justice or finance.

Receveur-général One of four officers under the four *généraux des finances*, responsible for the receipt of the Crown's *extraordinary* revenues. They were based at Tours, Paris, Rouen and Montpellier.

Receveur-particulier Financial officer at the bottom of the hierarchy entrusted with the collection of *extraordinary* revenues, accountable to the *élu*.

Receveur des aides Financial officer responsible for the receipt of the *aides* in each of the four *généralités*.

Routier Freelance mercenary, originally a product of the demobilisation of soldiery after the Treaty of Brétigny in 1360.

Sénéchal Royal officer set over a *sénéchaussée*, entrusted with the administration of justice and *domaine* revenues. The equivalent of the *bailli*, found generally in Southern France, although there were exceptions to this rule. Non-resident in the fifteenth century.

Taille Major direct tax, levied according to the status of the person or property. Part of the *extraordinary* revenues of the Crown, from which the nobility were exempt.

Trésor des Chartes Office in which documents issued by the king were stored. Part of the Chancery, it was situated in a building adjacent to the Sainte-Chapelle on the Ile-de-la-Cité.

Trésorier One of the four *trésoriers* appointed by the king to administer his *domaine* revenues. Accountable to the *Trésorier de France* at the apex of the financial pyramid. They were the equivalents of the *généraux* in the administration of the *extraordinary* revenues, and were set over the four *trésoriers* of Languedoïl-Guyenne, Outre-Seine and Yonne, Languedoc, and Normandy.

Vicomté Lordship held by a *vicomte*, except in Normandy where it was an administrative and judicial area, roughly equivalent to a *bailliage*.

Manuscript Sources

The list of sources which follows contains only those documents cited in the course of this book.

LONDON, *British Museum*
Additional Charters 3168, 3169, 3549, 3588, 4069, 4074, 4075, 4087–8, 4090, 12417
Cotton MS. Titus E.V

OXFORD, *Bodleian Library*
MS. Gough Gaignières 2

PARIS, *Archives Nationales*
JJ.177–82 (*Trésor des Chartes, Registres*)
K.67, 69 (*Monuments Historiques, Cartes des Rois*)
KK.51, 52 (*Chambre des Comptes: argenterie et hôtel du roi*)

PARIS, *Bibliothèque Nationale*
MSS français 1104, 2679, 2701, 2886, 5022, 5028, 5061, 5738, 5943, 6465, 6750–4, 10371, 15537, 18439–42, 20373, 20417, 20427, 20485, 20487, 20490–1, 20494, 20498, 20855, 23259, 26079, 26083–6, 32511
MSS français, nouvelles acquisitions 1001, 5083–4
MSS latins 1052, 6020
MS. Duchesne 108
MSS Dupuy 38, 76, 761

PAU, *Archives Départementales des Basses-Pyrénées* (now *Pyrénées Atlantiques*)
E.229 (Albret), E.432, 434, 438–40 (Foix)

Select Bibliography

This bibliography makes no pretence of being a comprehensive list of sources for the life and reign of Charles VII. I have included only those works which I have found useful while working on this book.

Primary Works

ARTIÈRES, J. (ed.), *Documents Historiques sur la ville de Millau* (Millau, 1930)

BARCKHAUSEN, H. (ed.), *Archives Municipales de Bordeaux*, v, *Livre des Coutumes* (Bordeaux, 1890)

BASIN, THOMAS, *Histoire de Charles VII*, ed. C. Samaran, 2 vols (Paris, 1933, 1944)

BEAUCOURT, G. DU FRESNE DE (ed.), 'Roles de dépenses du temps de Charles VII (1450–51)', *ABSHF*, cxxiv (1864), 123–53

—— 'Trois documents inédits sur la seconde campagne de Guyenne (1453)', *ABSHF*, cxxiv (1864) 154–9

—— 'Extraits du compte des obsèques de Charles VII', *ABSHF*, cxxiv (1864), 178–98

—— 'Recueil de Pièces pour servir de Preuves à la Chronique de Mathieu d'Escouchy', *Chronique de Mathieu d'Escouchy*, III (*SHF*, Paris, 1864)

BEKYNTON, THOMAS, *Official Correspondence*, ed. G. Williams, 2 vols (Rolls Series, London, 1872)

BLANCHARD, R. (ed.), *Lettres et Mandements de Jean V, duc de Bretagne*, 5 vols (Nantes, 1889–95)

CAGNY, PERCEVAL DE, *Chroniques*, ed. H. Moranvillé (*SHF*, Paris, 1902)

CALMET, DOM A., *Histoire . . . de Lorraine*, III, *Preuves* (Nancy, 1728)

CHARAVAY, E., VAESEN, J., and MANDROT, B. DE (eds), *Lettres de Louis XI, roi de France*, 11 vols (*SHF*, Paris, 1883–1909)

CHARTIER, ALAIN, *Le Curial*, ed. F. Heuckenkamp (Halle, 1899)

CHARTIER, JEAN, *Chronique*, ed. A. Vallet de Viriville, 3 vols (Paris, 1858)

CHASTELLAIN, GEORGES, *Œuvres*, ed. Kervyn de Lettenhove, 7 vols (Brussels, 1863–5)

COMMYNES, PHILIPPE DE, *Mémoires*, ed. J. Calmette and G. Durville, 3 vols (Paris, 1924–64)

DELACHENAL, R. (ed.), *Chroniques des règnes de Jean II et Charles V*, 4 vols (*SHF*, Paris, 1910–20)

DESCHAMPS, EUSTACHE, *Poésies*, ed. G. A. Crapelet (Paris, 1832)

DONCŒUR, P., and LANHERS, Y. (eds), *La minute française des interrogatoires de Jeanne la Pucelle* (Melun, 1956)

—— *La Réhabilitation de Jeanne la Pucelle. L'Enquête ordonnée par Charles VII en 1450 et la Codicile de Guillaume Bouillé* (Paris, 1956)

—— *L'Enquête du Cardinal d'Estouteville en 1452* (Paris, 1958)

—— *La Rédaction Episcopale du Procès de 1455-6* (Paris, 1961)

DOUËT-D'ARCQ, L. (ed.), *Comptes de l'hôtel des rois de France* (*SHF*, Paris, 1865)

ESCOUCHY, MATHIEU D', *Chronique*, ed. Beaucourt, 3 vols (*SHF*, Paris, 1863-4)

FENIN, PIERRE DE, *Mémoires*, ed. L. Dupont (*SHF*, Paris, 1837)

GAGUIN, R., *Chronique*, in *Compendium super Francorum gestis* (Paris, 1511)

GRUEL, GUILLAUME, *Chronique d'Arthur de Richemont*, ed. A. le Vavasseur (*SHF*, Paris, 1890)

GUERIN, P. (ed.), 'Recueil de documents concernant le Poitou contenus dans les registres de la Chancellerie de France', *AHP*, xxii-xxv (1903-6)

KENDALL, P. M., and ILARDI, V. (eds), *Dispatches, with Related Documents, of Milanese Ambassadors in France and Burgundy (1450-83)*, 2 vols (Ohio, 1970, 1971)

LA MARCHE, OLIVIER DE, *Mémoires*, ed. H. Beaune and J. d'Arbaumont, 4 vols (*SHF*, Paris, 1883-8)

LESEUR, GUILLAUME, *Histoire de Gaston IV, comte de Foix*, ed. H. Courteault, 2 vols (*SHF*, Paris, 1893, 1896)

MARTIAL DE PARIS, dit d'Auvergne, *Poésies*, 2 vols (Paris, 1724)

MOLLAT, M. (ed.), *Les Affaires de Jacques Cœur. Journal du Procureur Dauvet*, 2 vols (Paris, 1952-3)

MONSTRELET, ENGUERRAND DE, *Chronique*, ed. L. Douët-d'Arcq, 6 vols (*SHF*, Paris, 1857-62)

MORICE, DOM H., *Mémoires pour servir de Preuves à l'Histoire ecclésiastique et civile de Bretagne*, 3 vols (Paris, 1742-6)

MURATORI, L., *Rerum Italicarum Scriptores*, xx (Milan, 1731)

Ordonnances des roys de France de la troisième race, 22 vols (Paris, 1723-1846)

PHARES, SYMON DE, *Recueil des plus célèbres astrologues*, ed. E. Wickersheimer (Paris, 1929)

PISAN, CHRISTINE DE, *The Fayttes of Armes and of Chyvalrye*, ed. A. T. P. Byles (*EETS*, clxxxix, 1937)

PLANCHER, DOM U., *Histoire générale et particulière de la Bourgogne*, 4 vols (Dijon, 1739-81)

QUICHERAT, J. (ed.), *Procès de condamnation et de réhabilitation de Jeanne d'Arc*, 5 vols (*SHF*, Paris, 1841-9)

Rotuli Parliamentorum, 6 vols (London, 1783-1832)

RYMER, T., *Foedera*, 20 vols (1st edn, London, 1704-35)

SALA, PIERRE, *Hardiesses des grands roys* (Paris, 1516)

SICILY HERALD, *Le Blason des Couleurs*, ed. H. Cocheris (Paris, 1860)

STEVENSON, J., (ed.), *Letters and Papers illustrative of the wars of the English in France during the reign of Henry VI*, 2 vols (Rolls Series, London, 1861–4)

TISSET, P., and LANHERS, Y. (eds), *Procès de condamnation de Jeanne d'Arc*, 3 vols (*SHF*, Paris, 1960, 1970–1)

VENETTE, JEAN DE, *Chronique*, ed. R. A. Newhall (New York, 1953)

Secondary Works

ALLMAND, C. T., 'The Anglo-French negotiations, 1439', *BIHR*, xl (1967), 1–33

ARMSTRONG, C. A. J., 'La politique matrimoniale des ducs de Bourgogne de la maison de Valois', *AB*, xl (1968), 5–58, 89–139

BATAILLE, G., *Le Procès de Gilles de Rais. Les documents* (Paris, 1965)

BEAUCOURT, G. DU FRESNE DE, 'Jeanne d'Arc trahie par Charles VII', *RQH*, lxxi (1867), 1–6

—— *Histoire de Charles VII*, 6 vols (Paris, 1881–91)

—— 'Le Procès de Jacques Cœur', *RQH*, xciv (1890), 433–70

BERNUS, P., 'Essai sur la vie de Pierre de Brézé (vers 1410–65)', *Positions des Thèses de l'Ecole des Chartes* (1906), 7–17

—— 'Le rôle politique de Pierre de Brézé au cours des dix dernières années de Charles VII (1451–61)', *BEC*, lxix (1911), 315–24

—— 'Louis XI et Pierre de Brézé (1440–65)', *Revue de l'Anjou*, new series, lxiii (1911), 241–89, 355–71

BIET, J. E., *Souvenirs du Musée des Monumens Français* (Paris, 1821–6)

BLOCH, M., *Les Rois Thaumaturges* (Paris, 2nd edn, 1961)

BOISSONADE, P., 'Une étape capitale de la mission de Jeanne d'Arc', *RQH*, 3rd series, xvii (1930), 12–67

BONENFANT, P., *Philippe le Bon* (Brussels, 1955)

—— 'Du meurtre de Montereau au traité de Troyes', *Mémoires de l'Académie Royale de Belgique, Classe des Lettres*, 2nd series, iii (1957–8)

BOSSUAT, A., *Perrinet Gressart et François de Suriennes, agents de l'Angleterre* (Paris, 1936)

—— 'L'idée de nation et la jurisprudence du Parlement de Paris au xvᵉ siècle', *RH*, cciv (1950), 54–61

—— 'Le rétablissement de la paix sociale sous le règne de Charles VII', *MA*, lx (1954), 137–62

—— *Le bailliage royal de Montferrand, 1425–1556* (Paris, 1957)

—— 'La Formule "Le Roi est empereur en son royaume". Son emploi au xvᵉ siècle devant le Parlement de Paris', *RHDFE*, 4th series, xxxix (1961), 371–81

—— 'Le Parlement de Paris pendant l'occupation anglaise', *RH*, ccxxix (1963), 19–40

BOUAULT, J., 'Les bailliages du duché de Bourgogne aux xive et xve siècles', *AB*, ii (1930), 7–22

BOUDET, M., 'Charles VII à St-Flour et le prélude de la Praguerie (1437)', *AM*, vi (1894), 301–26.

BOUTRUCHE, R., *La Crise d'une Société* (Paris, 2nd ed., 1963)

—— (ed.), *Histoire de Bordeaux IV: Bordeaux de 1453–1715* (Bordeaux, 1966)

BRACHET, A., *Pathologie Mentale des Rois de France* (Paris, 1903)

BRENET, M., 'Jean de Ockeghem, maître de la chapelle des rois Charles VII et Louis XI', *Mémoires de la Société de l'Histoire de Paris*, xx (1893), 1–32

BURCKHARDT, J., *The Civilisation of the Renaissance in Italy*, 2 vols (New York, 1958)

CAILLET, L., *Etude sur les relations de la commune de Lyon avec Charles VII et Louis XI (1417–83)* (Paris–Lyon, 1909)

CALMETTE, J., *The Golden Age of Burgundy* (London, 1967)

CARTELLIERI, O., 'Philippe le Bon et le roi de France en 1430 et 1431', *AB*, i (1929), 78–83

—— *The Court of Burgundy* (London, 1929)

CAZELLES, R., *La Société Politique et la Crise de la Royauté sous Philippe de Valois* (Paris, 1958)

—— 'Une problème d'evolution et d'intégration: les grands officiers de la couronne de France dans l'administration nouvelle au Moyen Age', *Annali della Fondazione Italiana per la Storia Administrativa*, i (1964), 183–9

CHAMPION, P., *Louis XI*, 2 vols (Paris, 1927).

CHAPLAIS, P., 'La souveraineté du roi de France et le pouvoir législatif en Guyenne au début du xive siècle', *MA*, lxix (1963), 449–69

CHRIMES, S. B., *English Constitutional Ideas in the Fifteenth Century* (Cambridge, 1936)

CONTAMINE, P., *Guerre, Etat et Société à la fin du Moyen Age* (Paris–The Hague, 1972)

COSNEAU, E., *Le connétable de Richemont* (Paris, 1886)

DAVID-DARNAC, M., *Histoire Véridique et Merveilleuse de la Pucelle d'Orléans* (Paris, 1965)

DELACHENAL, R., 'Une clause de la paix d'Arras. Les conseillers bourguignons dans le Parlement de Charles VII', *Bulletin de la Société de l'Histoire de Paris*, xviii (1891), 76–83

DELISLE, L., *Recherches sur la Librairie de Charles V*, 2 vols (Paris, 1907)

DENIAU, J., *La Commune de Lyon et la guerre bourguignonne, 1417–35* (Lyon, 1934)

DEWICK, E. S., *The Coronation Book of Charles V* (London, 1899)

DODU, G., 'Le Roi de Bourges', *RH*, clix (1928), 38–78

DUPONT, A., 'Pour ou contre le roi d'Angleterre ...', *Bulletin de la Société des Antiquaires de Normandie*, liv (1957–8), 160–8

DUPONT-FERRIER, G., *Gallia Regia ...* (Paris, 1942–61)

DURRIEU, P., *Le Boccace de Munich* (Munich, 1909)

FAVIER, J., 'L'histoire administrative et financière du Moyen Age depuis dix ans', *BEC*, cxxvi (1968), 427–503

GARILLOT, J., *Les Etats Généraux de 1439* (Nancy, 1947)

GIESEY, R. E., *The Royal Funerary Ceremony in Renaissance France* (Geneva, 1960)

GILLES, H., *Les Etats de Languedoc* (Toulouse, 1965)

GIRARD, BERNARD DE, sire du Haillan, *De l'estat et succez des affaires de France* (Paris, 1570)

GODEFROY, T., *Le Cérémonial françois* (Paris, 1649)

GRANDEAU, Y., 'Les enfants de Charles VI', *BPH*, ii (1967), 809–49

GUENÉE, B., 'La géographie administrative de la France à la fin du Moyen Age', *MA*, 4th series, lxvii (1961), 293–323

—— *Tribunaux et Gens de Justice dans le bailliage de Senlis à la fin du Moyen Age* (Paris, 1963)

—— 'L'histoire de l'Etat en France à la fin du Moyen Age, vue par les historiens français depuis cent ans', *RH*, ccxxxii (1964), 331–60

—— 'Etat et nation en France au Moyen Age,' *RH*, ccxxxvii (1967), 17–30

—— 'Espace et Etat en France médiévale', *Annales*, xxiii (1968), 744–58

—— and LEHOUX, F., *Les Entrées Royales françaises de 1328 à 1515* (Paris, 1968)

—— *L'Occident aux xive et xve siècles. Les Etats* (Paris, 1971)

HARGREAVES-MAWDSLEY, W. N., *A History of Legal Dress in Europe* (Oxford, 1963)

HAY, D. (ed.), *New Cambridge Modern History* (Cambridge, 1947), I

HUBRECHT, G., 'Juridictions et compétences en Guyenne recouvrée', *Annales de la Faculté de droit de l'Université de Bordeaux, série juridique*, iii (1952), 63–79

ILARDI, V., 'The Italian League, Francesco Sforza and Charles VII (1454–61)', *Studies in the Renaissance*, vi (1959), 129–66

JACOB, E. F. (ed.), *Italian Renaissance Studies* (London, 1960)

—— *Essays in Later Medieval History* (Manchester, 1968)

JARRY, E., *La vie politique de Louis de France, duc d'Orléans, 1372–1407* (Paris, 1889)

—— *Les origines de la domination française à Gènes, 1392–1402* (Paris, 1896)

JOUET, R., *La résistance à l'occupation anglaise en Basse-Normandie (1418–50)* (Caen, 1969)

KANTOROWICZ, E. H., *The King's Two Bodies* (Princeton, 1957)

KENDALL, P. M., *Louis XI* (London, 1971)

KNOWLSON, G. A., *Jean V, duc de Bretagne et l'Angleterre (1399–1442)* (Cambridge–Rennes, 1964)

LAFAURIE, J., *Les monnaies des rois de France*, 2 vols (Paris–Basle, 1951–6)

LA MARCHE, A. LEÇOY DE, *Le Roi René*, 2 vols (Paris, 1875)

LA MARTINIÈRE, J. DE, 'Frère Richard et Jeanne D'Arc à Orléans, mars–juillet 1430', *MA*, xliv (1934), 189–98

LANG, A., *The Maid of France* (London, 1908)

LEA, H. C., *A History of the Inquisition of the Middle Ages*, 3 vols (London, 1888)

LEGUAI, A., *Les ducs de Bourbon pendant la crise monarchique du xvᵉ siècle* (Paris, 1962)

LENOIR, A., *Description historique et chronologique des monumens de sculpture réunis au Musée des Monumens français* (Paris, 1802)

LEROUX, A., *Nouvelles recherches critiques sur les relations politiques de la France avec l'Allemagne de 1378 à 1461* (Paris, 1892)

—— 'Passages de Charles VII et du dauphin . . . à Limoges en 1439', *BEC*, xlvi (1885), 303–14

LEWINSOHN, R., *A History of Sexual Customs* (London, 1958)

LEWIS, P. S., 'The failure of the French medieval Estates', *Past and Present*, xxiii (1964), 3–24

—— 'Decayed and non-feudalism in later medieval France', *BIHR*, xxxvii (1964), 157–84

—— 'Jean Juvenal des Ursins and the common literary attitude towards tyranny in fifteenth-century France', *Medium Aevum*, xxxiv (1965), 103–21

—— *Later Medieval France. The Polity* (London, 1968)

—— (ed.), *The Recovery of France in the Fifteenth Century* (London, 1971)

MCFARLANE, K. B., *Lancastrian Kings and Lollard Knights* (Oxford, 1972)

—— *The Nobility of Later Medieval England* (Oxford, 1972)

MACNALTY, A. D., *Henry VIII: a difficult patient* (London, 1952)

MANDROT, B. DE, 'Etude sur les relations de Charles VII et Louis XI . . . avec les cantons suisses, 1444–83', *Jahrbuch für Schweizerische Geschichte*, v (1880), 59–182; vi (1881), 203–77

MESQUITA, D. M. BUENO DE, 'The place of Despotism in Italian Politics', in *Europe in the Late Middle Ages*, ed. Hale, Highfield and Smalley (London, 1965), 301–31

MIROT, A., 'Charles VII et ses conseillers assassins presumés de Jean Sans Peur', *AB*, xiv (1942), 197–210

MOLLAT, M., 'Une Equipe: les commis de Jacques Cœur', *Hommage à Lucien Fèbvre* (Paris, 1953)

—— 'Jacques Cœur', *Citta Mercanti Dottrine nell' Economia Europea dal iv al xviii secolo*, ed. A. Fanfani (Milan, 1964), 191–206

MONOD, G., 'Nécrologie . . . Gaston du Fresne de Beaucourt', *RH*, lxxx (1902), 328–9

MONTFAUCON, B. DE, *Monumens de la monarchie françoise* (Paris, 1734), III

MORGAN, D. A. L., 'The king's affinity in the Polity of Yorkist England', *TRHS*, 5th series, xxiii (1973), 1–25

MYERS, A. R., *The Household of Edward IV* (Manchester, 1959)

NEUVILLE, DIDIER, 'Le Parlement royal à Poitiers (1418–36)', *RH*, vi (1878), 1–28, 272–314

ODOLANT-DESNOS, P. J., *Mémoires historiques sur la ville d'Alençon*, 2 vols (Alençon, 1787)

OMONT, H. (ed.), *Les Grandes Chroniques de France enluminées par Jean Foucquet* (Paris, 1906)

OURLIAC, P., 'La Pragmatique Sanction et la légation en France du Cardinal d'Estouteville (1451–3)', *Mélanges d'archéologie et d'histoire de l'Ecole française de Rome* (1938), 403–32

PÄCHT, O., 'Jean Fouquet: a Study of his style', *JWCI*, iv (1940–1), 85–102

PERNOUD, R., *Joan of Arc, by herself and her witnesses*, tr. E. Hyams (London, 1964)

PERROY, E., *The Hundred Years War* (London, 1962)

PIPONNIER, F., *Costume et Vie Sociale. La cour d'Anjou, xive–xve siècles* (Paris–The Hague, 1970)

POCQUET DU HAUT-JUSSÉ, B. A., 'Le connétable de Richemont, seigneur bourguignon', *AB*, vii (1935), 309–36; viii (1936), 7–30, 106–38

—— 'Une idée politique de Louis XI: la sujétion éclipse la vassalité', *RH*, ccxxxvi (1961), 383–98

POSTAN, M. M., RICH, E. E., and MILLER, E., *Cambridge Economic History of Europe* (Cambridge, 1963), III

QUICHERAT, J., *Aperçus nouveaux sur l'histoire de Jeanne d'Arc* (Paris, 1850)

—— *Rodrigue de Villandrando, l'un des combattants pour l'indépendance française au xve siècle* (Paris, 1879)

RENOUARD, Y. (ed.), *Histoire de Bordeaux III: Bordeaux sous les rois d'Angleterre* (Bordeaux, 1965)

RING, G., *A Century of French Painting, 1400–1500* (London, 1949)

ROWE, B. J. H., 'John, duke of Bedford and the Norman "Brigands"', *EHR*, xlvii (1932), 583–600

ST-RÉMY, H. DE SURIREY DE, *Jean II de Bourbon* (Paris, 1944)

SAMARAN, C., 'Pour la défense de Jeanne d'Arc', *ABSHF* (1952–3), 50–63

SCARISBRICK, J. J., *Henry VIII* (London, 1968)

SCHAEFER, C. (ed.), *The Hours of Etienne Chevalier* (London, 1972)

SHAW, BERNARD, *St Joan*, ed. A. C. Ward (London, 1964)

SHENNAN, J. H., *The Parlement of Paris* (London, 1968)

SHERMAN, C. R., *The Portraits of Charles V of France* (New York, 1969)

SPONT, A., 'La taille en Languedoc, 1450–1514', *AM*, v (1890), 365–513

SPUFFORD, P., *Monetary problems and policies in the Burgundian Netherlands, 1433–96* (Leiden, 1970)

STEIN, H., *Charles de France, frère de Louis XI* (Paris, 1919)

TESSIER, G., *Diplomatique Royale française* (Paris, 1962)

THIBAULT, M., *La Jeunesse de Louis XI* (Paris, 1907)

THOMAS, A., *Les Etats provinciaux de la France centrale sous Charles VII* (Paris, 1879)

—— 'Le "Signe Royal" et le secret de Jeanne d'Arc', *RH*, ciii (1910), 278–82

—— *Jean de Gerson et l'éducation des dauphins de France* (Paris, 1930)

THORNDIKE, L., *A History of Magic and Experimental Science*, iv (Columbia, 1934)

TUETEY, A., *Les Ecorcheurs sous Charles VII*, 2 vols (Montbéliard, 1874)

VALE, M. G. A., 'Jean Fouquet's portrait of Charles VII of France', *GBA*, lxxi (1968), 243–8

—— 'The livery colours of Charles VII in two works by Fouquet', *GBA*, lxxiv (1969), 243–8

—— 'The last years of English Gascony, 1451–3', *TRHS*, 5th series, xix (1969), 119–38

—— *English Gascony, 1399–1453* (Oxford, 1970)

VALLET DE VIRIVILLE, A., *Nouvelles recherches sur Henri Baude* (Paris, 1855)

—— 'Recherches historiques sur Agnès Sorel', *BEC*, xi (1849), 297–326, 477–99

—— *Histoire de Charles VII et de son époque*, 3 vols (Paris, 1862–5)

VALOIS, N., *Le conseil du roi aux xive, xve et xvie siècles* (Paris, 1888)

—— 'Jeanne d'Arc et la prophétie de Marie Robine', *Mélanges Paul Fabre* (Paris, 1902), 453–67

—— *La Pragmatique Sanction de Bourges sous Charles VII* (Paris, 1906)

—— 'Conseils et prédictions adressés à Charles VII par un certain Jean du Bois', *ABSHF*, xlvi (1909), 206–38

VAUGHAN, R., *Philip the Bold* (London, 1962)

—— *John the Fearless* (London, 1966)

—— *Philip the Good* (London, 1970)

VIALA, A., *Le Parlement de Toulouse et l'administration royale laïque, 1420–1525 environ*, 2 vols (Albi, 1953)

WAYMAN, D. G., 'The Chancellor and Jeanne d'Arc, February–July 1429', *Franciscan Studies*, xvii (1957), 273–305

WILLARD, C. C., 'The MSS of Jean Petit's Justification. Some Burgundian propaganda methods of the early fifteenth century', *Studi Francesi*, xxxviii (1969), 271–80

WIND, E., *Pagan Mysteries in the Renaissance* (London, 1967)

WOLFF, P., 'Une famille . . . les Ysalguier de Toulouse', *Mélanges d'histoire sociale*, i (1942), 35–58

ZELLER, G., *Les Institutions de la France au xvie siècle* (Paris, 1948)

Index